NICHOLAS SHAXSON

Nicholas Shaxson is the author of *Poisoned Wells: The Dirty Politics of African Oil*, and an experienced journalist who has written regularly for the *Financial Times*, *The Economist*, *Vanity Fair*, and many others.

ALSO BY NICHOLAS SHAXSON

Poisoned Wells: The Dirty Politics of African Oil

NICHOLAS SHAXSON

Treasure Islands

Tax Havens and the Men Who Stole the World

VINTAGE

For George, Oscar and Emma

10

Vintage
20 Vauxhall Bridge Road,
London SW1V 2SA

Vintage is part of the Penguin Random House
group of companies whose addresses can be found at
global.penguinrandomhouse.com

 Penguin
Random House
UK

This edition reissued in Vintage in 2016
First published by Vintage in 2012
First published in Great Britain by The Bodley Head in 2011

penguin.co.uk/vintage

A CIP catalogue record for this book
is available from the British Library

ISBN 9780099541721

Printed and bound by Clays Ltd, St Ives Plc

Penguin Random House is committed to a sustainable future
for our business, our readers and our planet. This book is made
from Forest Stewardship Council® certified paper.

Contents

Preface

Offshore after Brexit

Successful revolutions, a famous economist once said, are the kicking in of a rotten door. Since *Treasure Islands* was first published in 2011, the rotten door of offshore has been properly exposed – and the time to kick is now.

It seems the world has come to accept the reality of how far offshore has infiltrated our financial systems and governments. The basic facts of the system were considered pretty revolutionary when *Treasure Islands* first came out, but now they are received wisdom. Even supporters of tax havens don't deny it.

Tax havens and the offshore system are at the heart of the world economy. Their tentacles reach *everywhere*. And the damage they wreak on our tax systems is just a subset of a much bigger set of threats they pose to our democracies and to the world economy: they are the ultimate escape routes for our wealthiest citizens and corporations from a menagerie of laws, rules, financial regulations and democratic accountability. Offshore is globalisation's rotten core.

A string of offshore leaks by whistle-blowers – most importantly, the 'Panama Papers' scandal of 2016, implicating some of the world's most powerful people, have provided fresh, hard evidence to confirm and underline everything that's in this book.

It is now clear that Britain sits, spider-like, at the centre of a vast international web of tax havens, which hoover up trillions of dollars' worth of business and capital from around the globe and funnel it up to the City of London. The British Crown Dependencies and Overseas Territories – Jersey, the Cayman Islands, the British Virgin Islands, and several others – are some of the biggest players in the offshore world. While partly independent of Britain, these islands sport the Queen's head on their postage stamps and banknotes, and Britain ultimately has the power to strike down their tax haven laws if it wishes.

Nobody denies, either, that there is something very peculiar about the City of London Corporation, the ancient and fortress-like body that governs the 'Square Mile' of prime financial real estate in central London and casts a protective, almost invisible political umbrella over an increasingly piratical financial sector. Few deny now that the United States is also a gigantic tax haven, hosting trillions of dollars' worth of the world's wealth – much of it criminal in origin – wreathed in tight, made-in-America secrecy. Send your money to the US and, if you play your cards carefully, you can hide it from your own tax authorities and your criminal justice system.

Nobody has come close to overturning the steadily expanding body of research and analysis that demonstrates the sheer scale of harm wreaked on the world by these elitist, crime-infested fortresses for the rich. And despite endless denials and deflection from the tax havens, people are starting to take seriously my argument that tax havens and the City of London financial sector were a central ingredient in the global financial crisis – and will be in the next one. These places are serving as silent battering rams of financial deregulation, amok in the world economy.

And yet despite this exposure new havens pop up all the time, like poisonous mushrooms. You probably heard that Panama is a crooked tax haven – but did you know about Dubai? Or Mauritius? Latvia? New Zealand?

Or *Kenya?* In June 2016, just a few weeks before writing this, the Kenyan government proposed new legislation, drafted with the help of the City of London Corporation, promising to create a new off-shore financial centre in Nairobi. This new legislation would mean that anyone who divulges confidential information faces jail terms of up to three years. This is designed to create classic offshore *omertà*, fit for hiding and protecting endless crimes and abuses. Kenyan anti-corruption campaigner John Githongo warned that the tax haven they have in mind risks being like 'a financial crime aircraft carrier, self-contained and able to cause considerable damage'. Those words could describe the whole offshore system.

The shape-shifting offshore monster is growing, as countries vie with each other to attract the world's hot money with the latest and most devious new secrecy facility, say: or the next wheeze to facilitate offshore hedge fund shenanigans. To stay in the game other havens, urged by teams of skilled offshore accountants, lawyers and bankers, then enact something nastier still, just to keep up with the latest 'advance', and new players are steadily entering the race. And this is a race to the bottom, whose only winners are our increasingly unaccountable elites and their wealth management teams.

As offshore metastasises, expands and pushes constantly into new nooks and crannies in the world economy, researchers, journalists and other sleuths are entering the field: prodding and measuring, questioning and describing. The results are steadily solidifying, and amounting to a frightening body of work. But keeping up with the evolving incarnations of offshore isn't easy.

I'm writing this a couple of weeks after the latest jolt to the system, Britain's Brexit vote.

A plausible post-Brexit scenario sees a mischievous Britain, unmoored from Europe's moderating influences, reinvigorating its already dominant offshore establishment and pitching itself into a new sprint to become ever more haven-ish. If Brexit deprives the City of London of its privileged access to huge European markets, the anti-tax, anti-regulation fantasists will urge Britain to race faster to the bottom to attract the world's hot money, and to emulate places like Panama, the British Virgin Islands, or mucky little Luxembourg. These countries' core business model is to turn ever more of a blind eye to the criminal or unhealthy origins of the money that's handled through their territories, and in Britain's case to indulge the world's banks and shadow banks who want to use London as an ever more unregulated offshore playground to engage in profitable risk-taking and crookery – at everyone else's expense. If you think the City of London is corrupt today, wait and see what the Brexit-boosted lobbyists and fantasists have in mind.

Within hours of the Brexit vote, these fantasists were already coming out of the woodwork. The Swiss Bankers' Association suggested a so-called 'F4 Alliance' of financial centres, with Switzerland and the UK joining the fast-rising tax havens of Hong Kong and Singapore to present a strong and united bloc to push for the interests of offshore finance. Chris Cummings, the Chief Executive of the lobbying body TheCityUK, an influential outgrowth of the City of London Corporation, began calling for steps to reinforce the 'competitiveness' of the UK in financial services. That c-word is often code for an ideology that says we must constantly shower the biggest players with tax cuts, deregulation and other goodies, for fear they'll all run away to Geneva, Dublin or Hong Kong.

Meanwhile, outgoing UK Chancellor George Osborne, in an apparently panicky reaction to the Brexit vote, said he'd cut corporate taxes to just 15 per cent – a brutal slashing from the 26 per cent that prevailed when *Treasure Islands* was first published, and a move that would be devastating for public finances. Days later, officials in the Netherlands promised to follow suit, in a tit-for-tat. Others will no doubt join in.

The Brexit vote was, in the end, about globalisation. The hottest issue was immigration, which is, as Professor John van Reenen of the London School of Economics points out, 'globalisation made flesh'. But behind the vote we can also discern a powerful role played by tax havens, the dark twisted souls of financial globalisation.

For one thing, the Brexit vote was a once-in-a-lifetime opportunity for exasperated people to kick Britain's rotten establishment in the teeth. The discovery that David Cameron had once had a stash in a family fund in the tax haven of Panama was just the most pointed recent example of a system-wide problem.

On the other hand, and more importantly, the offshore system has been engineering a gigantic and ever-rising transfer of wealth from ordinary taxpayers to our offshore-diving corporations and wealthy individuals, in multiple ways. This has worsened economic and political inequality in Britain, heightened the popular rage – and as a result, hastened Brexit.

The offshore system boils down to two words: 'escape' and 'elsewhere'. You take your money elsewhere to escape whatever rules and laws you don't like. Tax havens are a financial technology to create these escape routes. So this book isn't, as some have suggested, merely about 'tax avoidance', or even really about tax. It's about a far bigger geopolitical phenomenon, of which tax is just one of many moving parts.

But there is a new hope abroad, which wasn't the case when *Treasure Islands* was first published.

Something in the *Zeitgeist* has changed. I've been watching closely, and I see the cultural and social acceptability of this stuff being transformed. Ordinary people and world leaders are now talking seriously about tackling tax havens, in way I could hardly have imagined five years ago. Efforts to reform the system, though messy and disappointing so far, contain some real substance for the first time.

In this Trumpy, Brexity world, the old certainties of left and right are broken, and the pieces are still up in the air. A new system hasn't coalesced yet. It is a time of rapid change, pregnant with possibilities. If we can harness the anger so many people feel about the system now, this is an opportunity for positive change that may not come around again for a very long time.

I'm far from the only one working in this area. This book rests on decades of work by a few offshore dissident pioneers, mostly now associated with the Tax Justice Network. Together we've created a completely new story about financial globalisation: a new lens through which to understand the world.

Treasure Islands is a furious book. It could hardly be otherwise: offshore is corrupting our world economy and our societies and cultures. But the anger embedded in the pages to come doesn't lie in the adjectives. In the words of David Marchant, an offshore fraud investigator who's seen it all, there's no need to embellish the stories. Because the facts are just so amazing.

Berlin, July 2016

Prologue

How colonialism left through the front door, and came back in through a side window

One night in September 1997 I returned home to my flat in north London to find that a man with a French accent had left a message on my answering machine. Mr Autogue, as he called himself, had heard from an editor at the *Financial Times* that I was to visit the former French colony of Gabon on Africa's western coastline, and he said he wanted to help me during my visit. He left a number in Paris. Curious as hell, I rang back the next morning.

This was supposed to be a routine journalist's trip to a small African country: I wasn't expecting to find too much to write about in this sparsely populated, oil-rich ex-colony, but the fact that English-speaking journalists almost never ventured there meant I would have the place all to myself. When I arrived I discovered that Mr Autogue had flown out to the capital Libreville with an assistant on first-class Air France tickets and had booked the most expensive hotel for a week – and their sole project, he cheerfully admitted, was to help me.

I had spent years watching, living in and writing about the countries along the curve of Atlantic coastline ranging from Nigeria in the north, through Gabon and down to Angola in the south. This region supplies almost a sixth of US oil imports[1] and about the same share of China's, and beneath the veneer of great wealth lies terrible poverty, inequality and conflict. Journalists are supposed to start on the trail of a great story somewhere dramatic and dangerous; unexpectedly I found my story here, in a series of polite if unsettling meetings in Libreville. Lunch with the Finance Minister? No problem. Monsieur Autogue arranged it with a phone call. I drank a cocktail in a hotel lobby with the powerful half-Chinese foreign minister Jean Ping, who later became president of the UN General Assembly. He gave me as much of his time as I needed for my interview and asked graciously about my family. Later, the oil minister clapped me on the shoulder and jokingly offered me an oilfield – then withdrew the proposal, saying, 'No, these things are only for *les grands* – the people who matter.'

Never more than two hundred yards from abject African poverty on the streets of Libreville, I spent a week wandering about in a bubble. The estimable Mr Autogue opened for me a zone of air-conditioned splendour: I was ushered to the front of queues to see powerful people, and they were always delighted to see me. This parallel, charmed world, underpinned by the unspoken threat of force against anyone inside or outside the bubble who might disrupt it, is easy to miss, but Mr Autogue's attempts to keep my diary full made me determined to find out what it was he might be wanting to hide. In fact, I had stumbled into what later became more widely known through a scandal in Paris as the Elf Affair.

The Elf Affair began from tiny beginnings in 1994, when the US-based Fairchild Corporation began a commercial dispute with a French industrialist. The dispute triggered a stock exchange inquiry in France, and an investigating magistrate, Eva Joly, got involved. Unlike more adversarial Anglo-Saxon legal systems, where the prosecution jousts with the defence to produce a resolution, the investigating magistrate in France is more like an impartial detective inserted between the two sides. He or she is supposed to scrutinise the matter until the truth is uncovered. Every time the Norwegian-born Joly investigated something, new leads would emerge – and her probes just kept going deeper. Before too long she received death threats: a miniature coffin was sent to her in the post, and on one raid she found a fully loaded Smith & Wesson revolver pointed at the entrance. But she persisted, more magistrates became involved, and as the extraordinary revelations accumulated, they began to discern the outlines of a gigantic system of corruption that connected Elf Aquitaine, the French political and intelligence establishments and Gabon's corrupt ruler, Omar Bongo.

Bongo's story is a miniature of French decolonisation. Countries formally gained independence, but the old masters found ways to stay in control behind the scenes. Gabon became independent in 1960, just as it was starting to emerge as a promising new African oil frontier, and France paid it particular attention. The right president was needed: an authentic African leader who would be charismatic, strong, cunning and, when it mattered, utterly pro-French. Omar Bongo was the perfect candidate. He was from a tiny minority ethnic group and had no natural domestic support base, so he had to rely on France to protect him. In 1967, aged just thirty-two, Bongo became the world's youngest president, and France placed several hundred paratroopers in a barracks in Libreville, connected to one of his palaces by underground tunnels. This deterrent against coups proved so effective that by the time Bongo died in 2009 he was the world's longest-serving leader. A local journalist summed the situation up for me: 'The French went out of the front door,' he said, 'and came back in through a side window.'

In exchange for France's backing, Bongo gave French companies almost exclusive access to his country's minerals on highly preferential terms. He would also become the African linchpin of a vast, spooky web of global corruption secretly connecting the oil industries of former French African colonies with mainstream politics in metropolitan France, via Switzerland, Luxembourg and other tax havens. Parts of Gabon's oil industry, Joly discovered, had been serving as a giant slush fund, making hundreds of millions of dollars available for the use of French elites. The system developed gradually, but by the 1970s it was already serving as a secret financing mechanism for the main French right-wing party, the RPR.[2] When a socialist, François Mitterrand, became French president in 1981, he sought to break into this Franco-African offshore cash machine, installing Loïk le Floch-Prigent as the head of Elf to do the job. But Mitterand's man was wise enough not to cut out the RPR. 'Le Floch knew that if he cut the financing networks to the RPR and the secret services it would be war,' wrote Valérie Lecasble and Airy Routier in an authoritative book on the subject.[3] 'It was explained that instead, the leaders of the RPR – Jacques Chirac and Charles Pasqua – did not mind the socialists taking part of the cake, if it were enlarged.'

This was not only a question of party political finance; France's biggest corporations were also able to make use of this west African oil pot as a source of money that enabled them to pay bribes from Venezuela to Germany to Jersey to Taiwan, while ensuring that the money trails did not lead to them. Elf's dirty money also greased the wheels of French political and commercial diplomacy around the globe. One man told me how he had once carried a suitcase of money provided by Omar Bongo to pay off a top rebel separatist in the Angolan enclave of Cabinda, where Elf had a lucrative contract. President Bongo, one of the smartest political operators of his generation, tapped into French Freemasonry networks and African secret societies alike and became one of the most important power brokers in France. He was the key to French leaders' ability to bind *les grands* – opinion formers and politicians from across Africa and beyond – into France's post-colonial foreign policy. As the Elf system became more baroque, complex and layered, it branched out into international corruption so grand that le Floch-Prigent described France's intelligence services, which also dipped freely into the slush fund, as 'a great brothel, where nobody knows any more who is doing what'.[4]

This immensely powerful system helped France punch above its weight in global economic and political affairs, and flourished in the gaps between jurisdictions. It flourished offshore.

My trip to Gabon in late 1997 came at an exquisitely sensitive time. On 7 November, less than a week after I left Libreville, Christine Deviers-Joncour, a former lingerie model, was sentenced to jail in Paris, still protecting the secrets of her lover Roland Dumas, President Mitterrand's foreign minister. Deviers-Joncour was jailed for suspected fraud after investigating magistrates discovered that Elf Aquitaine had paid her more than six million dollars to help 'persuade' Dumas, a haughty prince of the Paris political scene, to do certain things – notably to reverse his public opposition to the sale of Thomson missile boats to Taiwan. On an Elf credit card she had bought him gifts, including a pair of handmade ankle boots from a Paris shop so exclusive that its owner offered to wash customers' shoes once a year in champagne.

Nobody thanked Deviers-Joncour for her discretion, and five and a half months in jail gave her time to reflect on this. 'A flower, a single flower, even sent to me anonymously would have been enough,' she later explained.[5] 'I would have known it came from Roland.' The following year, casting aside her silence, she published a book, *The Whore of the Republic*, which became a best-seller in France.

So when I arrived in Gabon at that especially tricky moment, the Elf network must have wondered why an English journalist was nosing around in Libreville. Was I actually a journalist? No wonder Mr Autogue took such an interest in me. I recently tried to locate him, to ask him about our week together. His old phone numbers no longer work; several Africa experts in Paris hadn't heard of him; Internet searches couldn't find him or the company he claimed to represent; and the only person with that name in the French phone book has – a surprised-sounding wife in a Dordogne village informed me – never been to Gabon.

Following the scandal, French politicians declared the Elf system dead and buried, and Elf Aquitaine has been privatised and entirely transformed since then: it is now part of the Total group. But Elf was not the only player in the corrupt Franco-African system. One might ask why the first foreign leader President Nicolas Sarkozy of France telephoned after he came to power in 2007 was not the president of Germany, the United States or the European Commission, but Omar Bongo; or why those French troops remain in place in Gabon today, still connected by tunnels to the presidential palace now inhabited by Bongo's son, President Ali Bongo. The Elf system may be dead, but something else has probably replaced it. In January 2008 the French aid minister, Jean-Marie Bockel, complained that the 'rupture' with a corrupt past 'is taking its time to arrive'. He was summarily sacked.[6]

The Elf system was part of, and a metaphor for, the offshore world. Gabon is not on any published lists of tax havens, though it did provide secret, corrupt facilities for non-resident elites, a classic tax haven feature. Like the offshore system, it was a kind of open secret. Some well-connected French people knew all about it, and many outsiders knew something important was happening, but they largely ignored it, almost nobody could see the whole thing in overview. Yet it was a truly gargantuan octopus of corruption, affecting ordinary people in both Africa and France in the most profound, if mostly invisible, ways.

Everything was connected through tax havens. The paper trails, as the magistrates were discovering during my Libreville trip, typically passed through Gabon, Switzerland, Liechtenstein, Jersey and else-where. Eva Joly admitted that even she only ever saw fragments of the whole picture. 'Endless leads were lost in the shifting sands of the tax havens. The personal accounts of monarchs, elected presidents-for-life and dictators were being protected from the curiosity of the magistrates. I realised I was no longer confronted with a marginal thing but with a system,' she said, speaking about both French politics and the offshore world. 'I do not see this as a terrible, multi-faceted criminality which is besieging our [onshore] fortresses. I see a respectable, established system of power that has accepted grand corruption as a natural part of its daily business.'

Long before my first visit to Libreville, I had noticed how money was pouring out of Africa, but the secrecy surrounding the offshore world made it impossible to trace the connections. Financial institutions and lawyers would surface in particular stories, then slip back into an offshore murk of commercial confidentiality and professional discretion. Every time a scandal broke, these players' crucial roles escaped serious scrutiny. Africa's problems, the story went, had something to do with its culture and its rulers, or the oil companies, or the legacy of colonialism. The providers of offshore secrecy were clearly a central part of all the dramas, but the racket was very hard to penetrate, and nobody seemed very interested either.

It was only in 2005 that the threads properly started to come together for me. I was sitting with David Spencer, a New York attorney previously with Citicorp, talking about transparency in the public finances of west African oil-producing nations. Spencer was getting worked up about matters that were not at all on my agenda: accounting rules, tax exemptions on interest income and transfer pricing. I was wondering when he was going to start talking about west African corruption when I finally made the connection. The United States, by offering tax incentives and secrecy to lure money from overseas, had been turning itself into a tax haven.

The US government needs foreign funds to flow in, and it attracts them by offering tax-free treatment and secrecy. This, Spencer explained, had become central to the US government's global strategy. Tides of financial capital flow around the world in response to small changes in these kinds of incentives. Not only did almost nobody understand this, Spencer said, but almost nobody *wanted* to know. Once he gave a speech at a major United Nations event outlining some of these basic principles, and afterwards a top US negotiator told him that shedding light on this subject made him 'a traitor to your country'.

In the Harvard Club I began to see how the terrible human cost of poverty and inequality in Africa connected with the apparently impersonal world of accounting regulations and tax exemptions. Africa's supposedly natural or inevitable disasters all had one thing in common: the movement of money out of Africa into Europe and the United States, assisted by tax havens and a pinstriped army of respectable bankers, lawyers and accountants. But nobody wanted to look beyond Africa at the system that made this possible.

The very term 'capital flight', if you think about it, puts the onus on the country losing the money – it's another way of blaming the victim. But each flight of capital out of Africa must have a corresponding inflow somewhere else. Who was researching the inflows? The offshore system wasn't just an exotic sideshow in the stories I was covering. Offshore *was* the story. It binds together Libreville and Paris, Luanda and Moscow, Cyprus and London, Wall Street, Mexico City and the Cayman Islands, Washington and Riyadh. Offshore connects the criminal underworld with the financial elite, the diplomatic and intelligence establishments with multinational companies. Offshore drives conflict, shapes our perceptions, creates financial instability and delivers staggering rewards to *les grands*, to the people who matter. Offshore is how the world of power now works. This is what I want to show you in what follows.

Most of what follows was published in 2012. This new edition has a long update at the end, with a chapter looking at the Panama Papers. That rolling scandal helps me explore how the offshore world has changed in the past five years. It reveals how a determined pushback against tax havens is now underway – but such is the scale and scope of the offshore system that the battle has only just begun.

1

Welcome to Nowhere
An introduction to offshore

The offshore world is all around us. More than half of world trade passes, at least on paper, through tax havens.[1] Over half of all banking assets and a third of foreign direct investment by multinational corporations, are routed offshore.[2] Some 85 per cent of international banking and bond issuance takes place in the so-called Euromarket, a stateless offshore zone that we shall soon explore.[3] The IMF estimated in 2010 that the balance sheets of small island financial centres alone added up to $18 trillion – a sum equivalent to about a third of the world's GDP. And that, it said, was probably an underestimate.[4] The US Government Accountability Office (GAO) reported in 2008 that 83 of the USA's biggest 100 corporations had subsidiaries in tax havens. The following year research by the Tax Justice Network, using a broader definition of offshore, discovered that ninety-nine of Europe's hundred largest companies used offshore subsidiaries. In each country, the largest user by far was a bank.

Nobody agrees what a tax haven is. In truth, the term is a bit of a misnomer, for these places don't just offer an escape from tax; they also provide secrecy, an escape from financial regulation, and a chance to shrug off laws and rules of other jurisdictions, the countries where most of the world lives. In this book, I will offer a loose definition of a tax haven, as a 'place that seeks to attract business by offering politically stable facilities to help people or entities get around the rules, laws and regulations of jurisdictions elsewhere'.[5] The whole point is to offer escape routes from the duties that come with living in and obtaining benefits from society – tax, responsible financial regulation, criminal laws, inheritance rules and so on. This is their core line of business. It is what they *do*.

My definition is a broad one, and I have chosen it for two main reasons. First, to challenge the common idea that it is acceptable for a place to get rich by undermining the laws of other places. My second aim is to offer a lens through which to view the history of the modern world. This definition will help me show that the offshore system is not just a colourful outgrowth of the global economy, but instead lies right at its centre.

Several features help us spot tax havens.

First, as my colleagues have found through painstaking research, all these places offer secrecy, in various forms, combined with varying degrees of refusal to cooperate with other jurisdictions in exchanging information. The term 'secrecy jurisdiction' emerged in the US in the late 1990s, and in this book I will use that term interchangeably with 'tax haven', sometimes depending on which aspect I want to stress.

Another common marker for tax havens is very low or zero taxes, of course. They attract money by letting people escape tax, legally or illegally.

Secrecy jurisdictions also routinely ring-fence their own economies from the facilities they offer, to protect themselves from their own offshore tricks. Offshore is fundamentally about being an *elsewhere* zone of escape – and offshore services are provided for non-residents. So a tax haven might, say, offer a zero tax rate to non-residents who park their money there, but tax its own residents fully. This ring-fencing between residents and non-residents is a tacit admission that what they do can be harmful.

Another way to spot a secrecy jurisdiction is to look for whether its financial services industry is very large compared to the size of the local economy. The IMF used this tool in 2007 to finger Britain, correctly, as an offshore jurisdiction.[6]

Another, more light-hearted telltale sign of a tax haven is that its spokespeople periodically claim, 'we are not a tax haven', and strenuously work to discredit critics who, they claim, are using 'outdated media stereotypes' that do not correspond to 'objective reality'.

But the most important feature of a secrecy jurisdiction – and it is a defining one – is that local politics is captured by financial services interests (or sometimes criminals, and sometimes both), and meaningful opposition to the offshore business model has been eliminated. This is why I include 'politically stable' in my definition: there is little or no risk that democratic politics will intervene and interrupt the business of making (or taking) money. This political capture produces one of the great offshore paradoxes: these zones of ultra-freedom are often highly repressive places, intolerant of criticism.

Insulated from domestic challenges and alternative viewpoints, these places have come to be steeped in a pervasive inverted morality, where turning a blind eye to crime and corruption has become accepted as best business practice, and alerting the forces of law and order to wrongdoing has become the punishable offence. Rugged individualism has morphed into a disgregard, even a contempt, for democracy and for societies at large.

'Taxes are for the little people,' the New York millionairess Leona Hemsley once famously said. She was right, though she wasn't big enough to escape prison herself. The media baron Rupert Murdoch is different. His News Corporation, which owns Fox News, MySpace, the *Sun* newspaper and any number of other media outlets, is a master of offshore gymnastics, using all legal means available. Neil Chenoweth, a reporter who probed its accounts and found that its profits, declared in Australian dollars, were A\$364,364,000 in 1987, A\$464,464,000 in 1988, A\$496,496,000 in 1989 and A\$282,282,000 in 1990.[7] The obvious pattern in these numbers cannot be a coincidence. As the reporter John Lanchester wrote in the *London Review of Books*, 'That little grace note in the sums is accountant-speak for "Fuck you." Faced with this level of financial wizardry, all the ordinary taxpayer can do is cry "Bravo l'artiste!"'

The French have a quaint term for a tax haven: *paradis fiscal* – fiscal paradise, like the similar *paraíso fiscal* in Spanish. The players in the secrecy jurisdictions love this language: the word 'paradise' (some say this comes from mistranslating 'haven' as 'heaven') contrasts with what they like to paint as oppressive, high-tax onshore hellholes, from which tax havens are welcome escapes. They certainly are escapes – only not for ordinary folk. Offshore is a project of weathy and powerful elites to help them take the benefits from society without paying for them.

Imagine you are in your local supermarket and you see well-dressed individuals zipping through a 'priority' checkout behind a red velvet rope. There is also a large item, 'extra expenses', on your checkout bill, which subsidises *their* purchases. Sorry, says the supermarket manager, but we have no choice. If you did not pay half their bill, they would shop elsewhere. Now pay up.

Offshore business is, at heart, about artificially manipulating paper trails of money across borders. To get an idea of how artificial it can be, consider the banana.

Each bunch takes two routes into your fruit bowl. The first route involves a Honduran worker employed by a multinational who picks the bananas, which are packaged and shipped to Britain. The multinational sells the fruit to a big supermarket chain, which sells it to you.

The second route – the accountants' paper trail – is more round-about. When a Honduran banana is sold in Britain, where are the final profits generated, from a tax point of view? In Honduras? In the British supermarket? In the multinational's US head office? How much do management expertise, the brand name, or insurance contribute to profits and costs? Nobody can say for sure. So the accountants can, more or less, make it up. They might, for example, advise the banana company to run its purchasing network from the Cayman Islands and run its financial services out of Luxembourg. The multinational might locate the company brand in Ireland; its shipping arm in the Isle of Man; 'management expertise' in Jersey and its insurance subsidiary in Bermuda.

Say the Luxembourg financing subsidiary now lends money to the Honduras subsidiary and charges interest at $20 million per year. The Honduran subsidiary deducts this sum from its local profits, cutting or wiping them out (and its tax bill). The Luxembourg's subsidiary's $20 million in extra income, however, is only taxed at Luxembourg's ultra-low tax haven rate. With a wave of an accountant's wand, a hefty tax bill has disappeared, and capital has shifted offshore.

Big Banana has done a common offshore trick known as *transfer pricing*, or *transfer mispricing*. US Senator Carl Levin calls transfer pricing 'the corporate equivalent of the secret offshore accounts of individual tax dodgers'. By artificially adjusting the price for the internal transfer, multinationals can shift *profits* into a low-tax haven and *costs* into high-tax countries where they can be deducted against tax. In this banana example, tax revenue has been drained out of a poor country and into a rich one. And poor countries with under-paid tax officials always lose out to multinationals' aggressive, highly paid accountants.

Who is to say that the $20 million loan from the Luxembourg subsidiary was conducted at the real market rate? It is often hard to tell. Sometimes the prices for these transfers are adjusted so aggressively that they lose all sense of reality: a kilogram of toilet paper from China has been sold for $4,121, a litre of apple juice has been sold out of Israel at $2,052; ballpoint pens have left Trinidad valued at $8,500 each. Most examples are far less blatant, but the cumulative total of these shenanigans is vast. About two-thirds of global cross-border world trade happens inside multinational corporations. Developing countries lose an estimated $160 billion each year just to corporate trade mispricing of this kind. That much spent on health-care, Christian Aid reckons, could save the lives of 1,000 under-five children per day.[8]

Worldly readers may still shrug and tell themselves that this is just part of the ugly flip side of living in a rich nation. If they do, in their reluctantly cynical way, they are suckers – for they suffer as well. The tax bill is not only cut in Honduras, but in Britain and the United States too. The *Guardian* found that in 2006 the world's three biggest banana companies, Del Monte, Dole and Chiquita, did nearly $750 million worth of business in Britain but paid just $235,000 in tax between them:[9] less than a top-rank footballer's earnings.[10] An annual report of a real banana company listed in New York notes 'The company currently does not generate US federal taxable income. The company's taxable earnings are substantially from foreign operations being taxed in jurisdictions at a net effective rate lower than the US statutory rate.' Rough translation: we don't currently pay US taxes because we do transfer pricing, via tax havens.

Multinationals generally find it hard to use offshore to cut their taxes to *zero* since governments take countermeasures, but it is a battle they are losing. A study by Britain's National Audit Office in 2007 found that a third of the country's biggest 700 businesses had paid *no tax at all* in the UK in the previous financial boom year.[11] When the *Economist* investigated in 1999 it reckoned that Rupert Murdoch's sprawling News Corporation paid a tax rate of just 6 per cent.[12] This ability to engage in transfer mispricing is one of the most important reasons why multinationals *are* multinationals, and why they usually grow faster than smaller competitors. Anyone concerned about the power of global multinationals should pay attention.

Tax havens claim that they make global markets more 'efficient'. But this system I am describing is profoundly inefficient. Nobody has produced a better or cheaper banana here. What has happened instead is a transfer of wealth. These untargeted government subsidies for multinationals affect their real productivity in the same way that untargeted subsidies generally do: they reduce it. Focusing energies on tax avoidance takes the pressure off capitalists to do what they do best: create better and cheaper goods and services. And that is by no means all. When, for example, the Caymans hatches up a new and ingenious offshore loophole, the United States will take countermeasures, and the Caymans will create new loopholes to get around those. The battle continues, and America's tax code gets ever more complex. This, in turn, creates new opportunities for the wealthy and their cunning advisers to find pathways through the expanding legal thickets. Huge industries grow up to service the avoidance industry: a gigantic inefficiency in the world economy.

Then consider the secrecy. A fundamental building block of modern economic theory is transparency: markets work best when two sides to a contract have access to equal information. *Treasure Islands* explores a system which works *directly and aggressively* against transparency. Offshore secrecy shifts control of the information – and the power that flows from information – decisively towards the insiders. They get the cream and shift the costs onto the rest of society. David Ricardo's theory of comparative advantage elegantly describes principles that lead different jurisdictions to specialise in certain things: fine wines from France, cheap manufactures from China, and computers from the US. But when we find that the British Virgin Islands, with fewer than 25,000 inhabitants, hosts over 800,000 companies, Ricardo's theory loses its traction. Companies and capital migrate not to where they are most productive, but to where they can get the best tax break. There is nothing *efficient* about any of this.

And it is not just your bananas, of course. Much of the food in your house, your furniture and clothes will have taken a similarly twisted route into your home. The water in your tap may have taken a ghostly offshore route; your television and its components doubtless took a similarly weird paper pathway – as did many of the programmes it shows. The offshore world envelops us.

The world contains about sixty secrecy jurisdictions, divided roughly into four groups. First are the European havens. Second, comes a British zone centred on the City of London, which spans the world and is loosely shaped around Britain's former empire. Third is a zone of influence focused on the United States. A fourth category holds a few unclassified oddities, like Somalia and Uruguay, which have not been greatly successful and which I won't explore here.

The European havens got going properly during the First World War, as governments raised taxes sharply, to pay for war costs. Switzerland's famous secrecy law, making violation of banking confidentiality a criminal offence for the first time, was enacted in 1934, though Geneva bankers had sheltered the secret money of European elites since at least the eighteenth century. Little-known Luxembourg, specialising since 1929 in certain kinds of offshore corporations,[13] is among the world's biggest tax havens today. In March 2010 South Korean intelligence officials indicated that North Korea's 'Dear Leader' Kim Jong-Il had stashed some four billion dollars in Europe – from selling nuclear technology and drugs, insurance fraud, counterfeiting and projects using forced labour. Picturesque little Luxembourg, they said, is a favoured destination for this money.[14]

The Netherlands is another major European tax haven. About $18 trillion flowed through Dutch offshore entities in 2008 – equivalent to 20 times Dutch GDP.[15] The Irish musician Bono, while browbeating western taxpayers to boost aid to Africa, shifted his band's financial empire to the Netherlands in 2006, to cut its tax bill. Austria and Belgium are also important European havens of banking secrecy, though Belgium softened its laws in 2009. A couple of European micro-state havens are active players – Liechtenstein and Monaco are the most notable ones – with occasional cameo roles from odd places like Andorra or the Portuguese island of Madeira, recently implicated in a bribery scandal involving major US oil companies in Nigeria.

*   *   *

The second offshore group, accounting for about half the world's secrecy jurisdictions, is the most important. It is a layered hub-and-spoke array of tax havens centred on the City of London. As we shall see,[16] it is no coincidence that London, once the capital of the greatest empire the world has known, is the centre of the most important part of the global offshore system.

The City's offshore network has three main layers. Two inner rings – Britain's Crown Dependencies of Jersey, Guernsey and the Isle of Man; and its Overseas Territories, such as the Cayman Islands – are substantially controlled by Britain, and combine futuristic offshore finance with medieval politics. The outer ring is a more diverse array of havens, like Hong Kong, which are outside Britain's direct control but nevertheless have strong historical and current links to the country and the City of London. One authoritative account estimates that this British grouping overall accounts for well over a third of all international bank assets; add the City of London and the total is almost a half.[17]

This network of offshore satellites does several things. First, it gives the City a truly global reach. The British havens scattered all around the world's time zones attract and catch mobile international capital flowing to and from nearby jurisdictions, just as a spider's web catches passing insects. Much of the money attracted to these places, and the business of handling that money, is then funnelled through to London. Second, this British spider's web lets the City get involved in business that might be forbidden in Britain, providing sufficient distance to allow financiers in London plausible deniability of wrongdoing. The old City of London adage 'Jersey or jail' means that if you want to do dirty business but don't want to get caught, you just step out into the spider's web and do it there. The outer rings of this spider's web are often less hygienic than the inner ones. John Christensen, formerly a Jersey financial sector professional, remembers the Overseas Territory of Gibraltar being a Jersey favourite. 'We in Jersey regarded Gibraltar as totally subprime,' he said. 'This was where you put the real monkey business.' Later, a Caymanian character who introduced himself to me only as 'The Devil' will help illustrate just how dirty this business can be. So this spider's web is, in part, a laundering network. By the time the money gets to London, often via intermediary jurisdictions, it has been washed clean. The web even serves as a storage mechanism. If all those offshore assets flowed directly to London and stayed there, the inflows would play havoc with Britain's exchange rate.[18]

It is worth examining each ring of the spider's web very briefly.

The three Crown Dependencies in the inner ring are substantially controlled and supported by Britain but have enough independence to allow Britain to say: 'There is nothing we can do' when other countries complain of abuses run out of these havens. They channel very large amounts of finance up to the City of London: just in the second quarter of 2009 the UK received net financing of US$332.5 billion just from its three Crown Dependencies.[19] Jersey Finance promotional literature makes the point plainly. 'Jersey,' it says, 'represents an extension of the City of London.'[20]

The Bailiwick of Guernsey near Jersey includes other sub-havens such as the island of Sark, once infamous for the 'Sark Lark'. City of London company directors would sail in, eat lunch, pretend to have a directors' meeting to tick the British regulators' boxes, then return, inebriated, to London. There is also Alderney, a playground for online, offshore gambling, and Brecqhou, an eighty-seven-acre island housing the luxury offshore castle hideaway of the Barclay brothers, owners of Britain's *Telegraph* newspaper. The authoritative US publication *TaxAnalysts* estimated conservatively in 2007 that the Crown Dependencies hosted about US$1 trillion of potentially tax-evading assets.[21] At an annual rate of return of 7 per cent and a top income tax rate of 40 per cent, the tax evaded on those assets alone could be almost $30 billion per year – three times Britain's aid budget. This is just for those three havens – and income tax evasion is just one of several forms of offshore tax and financial losses.

The fourteen Overseas Territories, the next ring in the spider's web, are the last surviving outposts of Britain's formal empire. With just a quarter of a million inhabitants between them they include some of the world's top secrecy jurisdictions: the Cayman Islands, Bermuda, the British Virgin Islands, the Turks and Caicos islands and Gibraltar.[22]

Just like the Crown Dependencies, the Overseas Territories have close but ambiguous political relationships with Britain. In the Caymans the most powerful person is the governor, appointed by Her Majesty the Queen. He (never a she, so far) presides over a cabinet of local

Caymanians, who are elected locally but who have quite limited real power. The governor handles defence, internal security and foreign relations; he appoints the police commissioner, the complaints commissioner, the auditor general, the attorney general, the judiciary and other top officials. The final appeal court is the Privy Council in London. MI6, Britain's Secret Intelligence Service, is highly active here[23] – as are the CIA and other intelligence agencies. It is the world's fifth largest financial centre, hosting 80,000 registered companies, over three-quarters of the world's hedge funds, and $1.9 trillion on deposit – four times as much as in New York City banks. And, at the time of writing, one cinema.

As an indication of how murky things are here, the Cayman Islands reported to the IMF $2.2 trillion in equity liabilities (deposits and other obligations) in 2008. These figures should be matched by a roughly equal sum of assets – but the Caymans reported only $750 billion in portfolio assets. This enormous discrepancy simply goes unexplained.

Britain's understated but controlling role is the bedrock that reassures flighty global capital and underpins the Overseas Territories' offshore sectors. The gesture towards local representation keeps Caymanians happy and, as with the Crown Dependencies, affords Britain the chance to say 'it is not our business to interfere' when something unpleasant breaks the surface. Periodically, the charade is exposed. In August 2009 Britain imposed direct rule in the Turks and Caicos islands after corruption there spun out of control.[24] Britain plays down these episodes as much as possible, to distract from its control.

The third, outer ring of the British spider's web includes Hong Kong, Singapore, the Bahamas, Dubai and Ireland, which are fully independent though deeply connected to the City of London.[25] Many other smaller ones exist, like Vanuatu in the South Pacific whose small offshore centre was created by the British government in 1971, nine years before it got its independence. New havens continue to emerge. In February 2006 Ghana said it would enact offshore legislation, with help from Britain's Barclays Bank. The thought of a new secrecy jurisdiction situated among a swathe of legendarily corrupt African oil producing nations – and just as Ghana takes its own first steps as a big oil producer – is horrible to contemplate.

I am struck by some similarities between Britain's post-colonial offshore network and what I encountered in oil-rich Gabon, the epicentre of France's own quasi-offshore system. Gabon fits no conventional definition of offshore but it is, like the British spider's web, a relic – or even a rebirth – of an old empire, still used by today's elites to do things that would not be allowed at home. The Elf system, with its subterranean bargains between African rulers and French politicians, helped France retain a great degree of control over its former colonies after independence. Britain's spider's web is different. Most of its former colonies in Africa, India and elsewhere really are independent. What Britain has done instead is to retain a large degree of control over and involvement with the vast flows of wealth in and out of these places, under the table. Illicit capital flight from Africa, for example, flows mostly into the modern British spider's web, to be managed by interests controlled from London. 'It has taken me a long time to understand,' said Eva Joly, 'that the expansion in the use of these jurisdictions [tax havens] has a link to decolonisation. It is a modern form of colonialism.'

The United States anchors the third offshore pole. Here, tax havenry has always been more contested than in Britain, where the City of London has neutered domestic opposition to its global offshore strategy. US officials have tried to crack down on offshore tax abuse at least since 1961, when President Kennedy asked Congress for legislation to drive these tax havens 'out of existence'.[26] Barack Obama's co-sponsorship of the Stop Tax Haven Abuse Act in 2008 before he came to power, and its subsequent evisceration by offshore lobbyists, is merely a recent skirmish in an old war.

Over time, the United States government has shifted from being an outright opponent of tax havenry towards adopting a half-hearted 'if you can't beat 'em, join 'em' attitude. From the 1960s American financiers flocked offshore to escape domestic rules and taxes – first to the offshore Euromarket in London, then into the British spider's web and beyond. This offshore option helped Wall Street get around strong US financial regulations, progressively regain its powers and its influence over the US political system, and then, mostly from the 1980s, turn the US itself into what is now, by some measures, the world's single most important tax haven in its own right.[27]

The US-based offshore system operates on three tiers too. At the federal level, the US dangles a range of tax exemptions, secrecy provisions and laws designed to attract foreigners' money in true offshore style. US banks may, for instance, legally accept proceeds from a range of crimes, such as handling stolen property – as long as the crimes are committed overseas. Special arrangements are made with banks to make sure they do not reveal the identities of foreigners parking their money in the US. The second offshore tier involves individual US states, where a range of offshore lures are on offer. Florida, for example, is where Latin American elites do their banking. The US generally does not share banking information with those countries, so a lot of this is tax-evading and other criminal money, protected by US secrecy. Florida banks also have a long history of secretly harbouring Mob and drugs money, often in complex partnerships with the nearby British Caribbean havens. Smaller states like Wyoming, Delaware and Nevada offer very low-cost and very strong forms of almost unregulated corporate secrecy that has attracted large amounts of illicit money, and even terrorist finance, from around the globe.

The USA's third offshore rung is a small overseas satellite network. The American Virgin Islands, a US 'Insular Area', has a 'half-in, half-out' constitutional relationship with the US, a bit like Britain's offshore satellites, and is a minor haven. Another is the Marshall Islands, a former Japanese colony under American control after 1947, now under a Compact of Free Association with the US. The Marshall Islands are primarily a 'flag of convenience' which, the *Economist* recently noted, 'is much prized among shipowners for its light regulatory touch'. The Marshall Islands registry was set up in 1986 with USAID help by Fred M. Zeder II, a golfing buddy of George H.W. Bush who later ran the US Overseas Private Investment Corporation (OPIC). Now run by a private American corporation out of offices in Virginia near Washington Dulles Airport, this is the flag of convenience for, among others, the *Deepwater Horizon*, the BP-operated oil rig that caused environmental chaos off the US Gulf Coast in 2010.[28] A small, opaque tax haven grew alongside the shipping registry. When Khadija Sharife, a South African journalist, posed as a shipping client pretending to be worried about disclosure, she was told that that forming a Marshall Islands company could be done in a day for an initial filing fee of $650, plus annual maintenance fee of $450, and

If the authorities . . . come to our Registry and Jurisdiction and ask us to disclose more information, regarding shareholders, directors of the company etc . . . we are not privy to that information anyway, since all the business organization and conduct of the entity is performed by the entity's lawyers and directors directly. Unless the name of directors and shareholders are filed in the Marshall Islands and become a public record (which is NOT mandatory), we are not in a position to disclose that.[29]

Similarly, Liberia was set up in 1948 as a 'flag of convenience' by Edward Stettinius Jr., a former US secretary of state, and its maritime code was 'read, amended, and approved by officials of Standard Oil', according to historian Rodney Carlisle. Its sovereign shipping registry is now run by another private corporation in Virginia, based about five miles from the Marshall Islands registry.[30] Liberia tried setting up offshore finance too, but nobody would trust black African governments with their money, and the plan flopped. Sovereignty is, literally, available for sale or rent in such places.

The biggest US-influenced haven is Panama. It began registering foreign ships in 1919 to help Standard Oil escape American taxes and regulations. Offshore finance followed in 1927, when Wall Street interests helped Panama introduce lax company incorporation laws, which let anyone start tax-free, anonymous corporations, with few questions asked. 'The country is filled with dishonest lawyers, dishonest bankers, dishonest company formation agents and dishonest companies,' one US Customs official noted. 'The Free Trade Zone is the black hole through which Panama has become one of the filthiest money laundering sinks in the world.'[31]

This strange and little-known US-centred pattern, echoing the somewhat colonial role of the secrecy jurisdictions in the British zone, is a pointer to the fact that offshore finance has quietly been at the heart of Neoconservative schemes to project US power around the globe for years. Few people have noticed.

It should be clear by now that the offshore world is not a bunch of independent states exercising their sovereign rights to set their laws and tax systems as they see fit. It is a set of networks of influence controlled by the world's major powers, notably Britain and the United States. Each network is deeply interconnected with the others. Wealthy

US individuals and corporations use the British spider's web extensively: of Enron's 881 offshore subsidiaries before it went bust, 692 were in the Cayman Islands, 119 in the Turks and Caicos, 43 in Mauritius and 8 in Bermuda: all in the British spider's web. In December 2008 the US Government Accountability Office (GAO) reported that Citigroup had 427 subsidiaries in tax havens, including 91 in Luxembourg and 90 in the Cayman Islands; News Corporation, the owner of Fox News, had 152 – including 62 in the British Virgin Islands, 33 in Cayman, and 21 in Hong Kong.[32]

The world's most important tax havens are not exotic palm-fringed islands, as many people suppose, but some of the world's most powerful countries. Marshall Langer, a prominent supporter of secrecy jurisdictions, neatly outlines the gulf between perceptions and the reality. 'It does not surprise anyone when I tell them that the most important tax haven in the world is an island,' he said. 'They are surprised, however, when I tell them that the name of the island is Manhattan. Moreover, the second most-important tax haven in the world is located on an island. It is a city called London in the United Kingdom.'

One Australian academic, Jason Sharman, decided to check how easy it was to set up secrecy structures, using only the Internet and those seedy offshore advertisements that infest the back pages of business publications and airline magazines. In his report published in 2009, he records making 45 bids for secret front companies. He found 17 companies that agreed to set up secrecy structures without even checking his identity. Only four were in the 'classic' havens like Cayman or Jersey, while the other 13 were in OECD countries: seven in Britain and four in the US.

This is the English-speaking version of Swiss bank secrecy. Most were not selling bank secrecy, where discreet men in plush offices promised to take their clients' names to the grave. 'This is a more insidious form of secrecy, in which authorities and bankers do not bother to ask for names,' the Economist noted of Sharman's study. 'For shady clients, this is a far better proposition: what their bankers do not know, they can never be forced to reveal. And their method is disarmingly simple. Instead of opening bank accounts in their own names, fraudsters and money launderers form anonymous companies, with which they can then open bank accounts and move assets.'

*   *   *

The governments of wealthy OECD nations have recently been quite successful in persuading their publics that they have conducted a major crackdown on secrecy jurisdictions. 'The old model of relying on secrecy is gone', said Jeffrey Owens, head of tax at the OECD. 'This is a new world, with better transparency and better cooperation.'³³ Many people believed him. French president Sarkozy went further: 'Tax havens and bank secrecy are finished.'³⁴

Yet OECD member states, notably Britain, the United States and several big European havens, are guardians of the offshore system. It continues to process vast tides of illicit money – yet an OECD blacklist of tax havens has been empty since May 2009. This is not a blacklist, but a whitewash – and to the very, very limited extent that rich countries have taken steps to address the problem, low-income countries are being left on the sidelines as usual.³⁵ When the fox says it has done an excellent job of beefing up the security of the henhouse, we should be very cautious indeed.

The offshore world is an endlessly shifting ecosystem. Each jurisdiction offers one or more offshore specialities and attracts particular kinds of financial capital; each has developed its own particular infrastructure of skilled lawyers, accountants, bankers and corporate officers to cater for their needs.

Many offshore businesses are almost unknown. You may well have heard of the Big Four accounting firms KPMG, Deloitte, Ernst & Young and Pricewaterhouse Coopers. But have you heard of the Offshore Magic Circle? It includes multi-jurisdictional law firms such as Appleby, Carey Olsen, Conyers, Maples and Calder, Mourant du Feu & Jeune, and Ozannes and Walkers.³⁶ These are respectable players among a much larger regiment of smartly dressed accountants, lawyers and banks forming a private global infrastructure which, in league with captured legislatures in the secrecy jurisdictions, makes the whole system work.

Offshore services range from the legal to the illegal. In terms of tax, the illegal stuff is called tax *evasion*, while tax *avoidance* is technically legal but, by definition, it also involves getting around the intent of elected legislatures. This is a slippery topic: between evasion and avoidance a vast grey area exists and it often takes lengthy court cases to find out which side of the law a multinational corporation's tax shelter lies. Former British Chancellor Denis Healey, neatly defining the dividing line, explained that 'the difference between tax avoidance and tax evasion is the thickness of a prison wall.'

Secrecy jurisdictions also routinely convert what is technically *legal*, but abusive, into what is seen as *legitimate*. But of course what is legal is not necessarily what is right: slavery and apartheid were both legal in their day.

On the illegal side, there is tax-evading private banking or asset management; sham trusts; corporate secrecy, illegal reinvoicing, and more, often hidden behind soothing bromides like 'tax optimisation' or 'asset protection' or 'an efficient corporate structure'. Typically, junior offshore employees are shielded from understanding the tax evasion and other illegal services, because they can only see a part of what is happening. 'Once you become part of senior management and gain international experience,' a former senior offshore accountant explains, 'then you are part of the inner circle and things become much clearer. You are part of the plot. You know what the real products and services are, and why they are so expensive.' As the old offshore joke goes: 'Those who know don't talk. And those who talk don't know'.

On the legal side, one important matter concerns something known as double taxation. Say a US multinational invests in a manufacturing plant in Brazil and earns income there. If both Brazil and the United States taxed the same income, without giving credits for the other country's taxes, the multinational would get taxed twice on the same income. Tax havens do help companies eliminate this double taxation, though they are not necessary: double taxation can be ironed out with appropriate treaties and tax credits. The problem, when tax havens eliminate double taxation, is that they allow something else to happen: double *non*-taxation. The corporation doesn't only avoid being taxed twice on the same income. It avoids being taxed at all.

Each jurisdiction tolerates different levels of dirt. Terrorists or Colombian drug smugglers probably use Panama rather than Jersey – though Jersey's trust companies probably still contain some of their money, and the island remains a gigantic sink for nefarious activity and illicit loot. Bermuda is a magnet for offshore insurance and reinsurance, frequently for the purpose of avoiding or evading tax; the Caymans are favoured locations for hedge funds which use it to escape tax, legally or illegally, and to get around financial regulations. In securitisation, Wall Street has long favoured locating its Special Purpose Vehicles in the Caymans and Delaware; in Europe the preferred locations are Jersey, Ireland, Luxembourg and the City of London. All are major secrecy jurisdictions.

Inside this ecosystem, each jurisdiction struggles constantly to stay abreast of the others. When one degrades its taxes or financial regulations or hatches a new secrecy facility to attract hot money from elsewhere, others then degrade theirs, to stay in the race. Meanwhile, financiers threaten politicians in the US and other large economies with the offshore club – 'don't tax or regulate us too heavily or we'll go offshore', they cry – and the onshore politicians quail and relax their own laws and regulations. As this has happened, supposedly onshore jurisdicitons have increasingly taken on the characteristics of offshore, and in the large economies tax burdens are being shifted away from mobile capital and corporations, onto the shoulders of ordinary folk. US corporations paid about two-fifths of all US income taxes in the 1950s; that share has now fallen to a fifth.[37] The top 0.1 per cent of US taxpayers saw their effective tax rate fall from 60 per cent in 1960 to 33 per cent in 2007, as their income soared. Had the top thousandth paid the 1960 rate, the Federal Government would have received over $281 billion more in 2007.[38] When the billionaire Warren Buffett surveyed his office he found that he was paying the lowest tax rate among his office staff, including his receptionist. Overall, taxes have not generally declined. What has happened instead is that the rich have been paying less, and everyone else has had to take up the slack.

The roles of Ronald Reagan, Margaret Thatcher and Milton Friedman in these huge shifts and in the broader globalisation project are well known. But very little attention has been paid to the secrecy jurisdictions – the silent warriors of globalisation that have been forcing nation states rich and poor to compete through them, and in the process cutting swathes through their tax and regulatory systems and regulations whether they like it or not.

Tax havens often target other large economies, usually nearby. Switzerland's wealth managers focus most on tax-evading rich Germans, French and Italians – Switzerland's immediate neighbours and its three main language groups. Monaco caters especially to French elites: wealthy French and Spaniards use Andorra, sandwiched between their two countries. Rich Australians often use Pacific havens like Vanuatu. Malta, another former British outpost in the Mediterranean, handles illicit money out of North Africa; US corporations and wealthy individuals prefer Panama and the Caribbean havens, wealthy Chinese use Hong Kong, Singapore and Macau. Money does not always flow through obvious geographical routes, however. Russian dirty money favours Cyprus, Gibraltar and Nauru, all with strong historical British links, as stepping stones into the global financial system, where it can be legitimised before entering the mainstream global financial system in London and elsewhere. Much foreign investment into China goes via the British Virgin Islands.

Some jurisdictions specialise in being conduit havens: way stations offering services that transform the identity or character of assets in specific ways, en route to somewhere else. The Netherlands is a big conduit haven. Mauritius, off the African coast in the Indian Ocean, is a new and fast-growing conduit haven that is the source of over 40 per cent of foreign investment into India. It also specialises in channeling Chinese investments into Africa's mineral sectors.

Offshore financial structures typically involve a trick sometimes known as laddering – a practice also expressed by the French word *saucissonage*, meaning to slice something into pieces like a sausage. When a structure is sliced between several jurisdictions, each provides a new legal or accounting 'wrapper' around the assets, which are usually located elsewhere. A Caymanian lawyer in the 1970s explained how his clients would worry about Fidel Castro's Cuba next door, and would insist on special clauses to compensate them if Castro invaded. 'I have to explain that Castro wouldn't find any [money] in the safe,' he said. 'They're all really held in New York or London.'

Laddering deepens the secrecy, and the complexity. A Mexican drug dealer may have twenty million dollars, say, in a Panama bank account. The account is not in his name but is instead under a trust set up in the Bahamas. The trustees may live in Guernsey, and the trust beneficiary could be a Wyoming corporation. Even if you can find the names of that company's directors, and even get photocopies of their passports – that gets you no closer: these directors will be professional nominees, who direct hundreds of similar companies. They are linked to the next rung of the ladder through a company lawyer, who is prevented by attorney–client privilege from giving out any details. Even if you break through *that* barrier you find that the corporation is held by a Turks and Caicos trust with a flee clause: the moment an enquiry is detected, the structure flits to another secrecy jurisdiction. Even if a jurisdiction cooperates with an inquiry, it can drag its feet for months or years. 'Even when they cooperate to eliminate the fraud,' said Robert Morgenthau (until recently the Manhattan District Attorney) of the Caymans, 'it takes so long that when the door is finally closed, the horse has been stolen and the barn has been burned down.' At the time of writing, Hong Kong is preparing legislation to allow incorporation and registration of new companies within minutes.

In 2010 Luxembourg's authorities pleaded laddering as an excuse for potentially harbouring North Korean money. 'The problem is that they do not have "North Korea" written all over them,' a spokesman said. 'They try to hide and they try to erase as many links as possible.'[39] That is, after all, the point. Magistrates in France only ever saw a limited part of the Elf system because of this *saucissonage*. 'The magistrates are like sheriffs in the spaghetti westerns who watch the bandits celebrate on the other side of the Rio Grande,' wrote the magistrate Eva Joly, furious about how tax havens stonewalled her probes into the Elf System. 'They taunt us – and there is nothing we can do.'

Even if you can see parts of the structure, the laddering stops you seeing it all – and if you can't see the whole, you cannot understand it. The activity doesn't happen *in* any jurisdiction – it happens *between* jurisdictions. 'Elsewhere' becomes 'nowhere': a world without rules.

I already mentioned some ballpark numbers suggesting how big the offshore system has become: half of all banking assets, a third of foreign investment and more. But there have been very few attempts to quantify the damage that this system causes. This is partly because it is so hard to measure, let alone detect, secret, illicit things.

Recently, however, think tanks and non-governmental groups have sought to assess the scale of the problem. In 2005, the Tax Justice Network estimated that wealthy individuals hold perhaps $11.5 *trillion* worth of wealth offshore. That is about a quarter of all global wealth, and equivalent to the entire gross national product of the United States. That much money in dollar bills, placed end to end, would stretch 2,300 times to the moon and back. The estimated $250 billion in taxes lost on just the income that money earns each year is two to three times the size of the entire global aid budget to tackle poverty in developing countries. But that just represents tax lost on money wealthy *individuals* hold offshore. Add to that all the corporate trade mispricing, and you start to get a handle on the size of illicit financial flows across borders.

The most comprehensive study of illicit cross-border financial flows comes from Raymond Baker's Global Financial Integrity (GFI) programme at the Center for International Policy in Washington. Developing countries, GFI estimated in January 2011, lost $1.2 trillion in illicit financial flows in 2008 – losses that have grown at 18 per cent per year.[40] Compare this to the $100 billion in total annual foreign aid, and it is easy to see why Baker concluded that 'for every dollar that we have been generously handing out across the top of the table, we in the West have been taking back some $10 of illicit money under the table. There is no way to make this formula work for anyone, poor or rich.' Remember that, the next time some bright economist wonders why aid to Africa is not working.

In an earlier study in 2005, subsequently endorsed by the World Bank,[41] Baker broke down his figures from illicit financial flows into three categories. Criminal money – from drug smuggling, counterfeit goods, racketeering and so on – amounted to $330 –$550 billion, or a third of the total. Corrupt money – local bribes remitted abroad or bribes paid abroad – added $30–50 billion, or three per cent. The third component, making up two-thirds, was cross-border commercial transactions. Another profoundly important point emerges out of this. The drugs smugglers, terrorists and other criminals use *exactly* the same offshore mechanisms and subterfuges – shell banks, trusts, dummy corporations – that corporations use.

We will never beat the terrorists or the heroin traffickers unless we confront the whole system – and that means tackling the tax evasion and avoidance and financial regulation and the whole paraphernalia of offshore. It is hardly surprising, in this light, that Baker estimates that the US success rate in catching criminal money was 0.1 per cent – meaning a 99.9 per cent failure rate. 'Laundered proceeds of drug trafficking, racketeering, corruption, and terrorism tag along with other forms of dirty money to which the United

States and Europe lend a welcoming hand,' said Baker. 'These are two rails on the same tracks through the international financial system.' You cannot tackle one without tackling them all.

And that, remember, is just the illegal stuff. The legal offshore tax avoidance by individuals and corporations, which further gouges honest hardworking folk – adds hundreds of billions of dollars more to these figures.

Almost no official estimates of the damage exist. The Brussels-based non-governmental organisation Eurodad has a book called *Global Development Finance: Illicit flows Report 2009* which seeks to lay out, over a hundred pages, every comprehensive official estimate of global illicit international financial flows.[42]

Every page is blank.

Eurodad's aim is to underscore a vital point: the offshore world is the biggest force for shifting wealth and power from poor to rich in history, yet its effects have been almost invisible. As the French sociologist Pierre Bordieu remarked, 'The most successful ideological effects are those which have no need for words, and ask no more than complicitous silence.'

Language itself encourages the blindness. In September 2009, the G20 group of countries pledged in a communiqué to 'clamp down on illicit outflows'. Now consider the word 'outflows'. Like the term 'capital flight', it points the finger at the *victim* countries like Congo – which, this language subtly insists, must be the focus of the clean-up. But each outflow must have a corresponding inflow somewhere else. How different that pledge would have looked if they had promised to tackle 'illicit *inflows*'.

On the subject of developing countries, here is something else to think about.

When a tax haven creates an innovative new way for wealthy individuals or corporations to escape taxes, high-income countries tend to take countermeasures, patching up their own tax or regulatory systems as best they can to defend against the new abuses. Yet developing countries, blind and inexperienced to the ever-deepening offshore complexity, are defenceless. They will slip further behind and their elites will have ever more opportunities for abuse, rotting local politics. Meanwhile the high-income countries, more secure behind their sophisticated defences against offshore abuse, are less concerned. The message from Switzerland? 'Not our problem. Fix it yourselves.'

Yet all this is not only a problem for low-income countries. It harms the big wealthy nations too – even those that have turned themselves into tax havens.

Aside from having created a gigantic global hothouse for crime, the global offshore system was one of the central factors that helped generate the latest financial and economic crisis since 2007. I will explore this in more detail later, but here is a short summary. First, they provided financial corporations with what the accountant Richard Murphy calls a 'get out of regulation free' card. This escape route from financial regulation helped financial firms grow explosively, achieving 'too-big-to-fail' status and gaining the power to capture the political establishments in Washington and London. Second, as the secrecy jurisdictions degraded their own financial regulations they acted as berserkers in the financial system, forcing onshore jurisdictions to 'compete' with them in a beggar-thy-neighbour race to towards ever laxer regulation. Third, huge illicit cross-border financial flows, much of it unmeasured by conventional national statistics, have created massive net flows into deficit countries like the US and Britain, adding to the more visible global macroeconomic imbalances that under-pinned the crisis. Fourth, offshore incentives encouraged companies to borrow far too much and helped them hide their borrowings. Fifth, as companies fragmented their financial affairs around the world's tax havens for reasons of tax, regulation or secrecy, this created impene-trable complexity which, mixed with offshore secrecy, foxed regula-tors and fed the mutual mistrust between market players that worsened the financial and banking crisis.

Trust is a central ingredient in any healthy economic system – and there is nothing like the offshore system to erode trust. It is no coincidence that so many of the great houses of financial trickery like Enron, or the empire of the fraudster Bernie Madoff, or Long Term Capital Management, or Lehman Brothers, or AIG, were so thoroughly entrenched offshore. When nobody can find out what a company's true financial position is until after the money has evapor-ated, bamboozling abounds. And in helping our richest citizens continue to escape tax and financial regulation, the tax havens undermine our efforts both to pay for the cost of the mess and to clean it up.

Offshore did not exactly cause the financial crisis. It created the enabling environment. Jack Blum, an offshore expert, explains:

Trying to understand the role of offshore secrecy and regulatory havens in the crisis is like the problem a doctor has treating a metabolic disease with multiple symptoms. You can treat several symptoms and still not cure the disease. Diabetes, for instance, causes high cholesterol, high blood pressure and all sorts of other problems. There are plenty of discrete aspects of the meltdown to talk about and many possible treatments for symptoms, but offshore is at the heart of this metabolic disorder. Its roots reach back decades, in bankers' attempts to escape regulation and taxation and make banking a highly profitable growth business that mimics the industrial economy.[43]

This is not a book about the recent financial crisis. It is about something older and deeper. It is the great untold story about big finance and the supremely powerful weapon it has deployed in its battle to capture political power around the world.

Finally, a word about culture and attitudes. Europe's biggest conduit for criminal money from the former Soviet Union is probably Cyprus, a 'way station for international scoundrels' as one offshore promoter puts it. Yet in December 2007 the accountancy giant KPMG judged Cyprus the best of all the European jurisdictions in its ranking of how 'attractive' their corporate tax regimes are.[44]

Something is clearly wrong here.

Tax is the missing element in the corporate social responsibility debate. Modern company directors do, it is true, face a dilemma. To whom are they answerable – to shareholders only or to a wider set of stakeholders? There are no useful guidelines.[45] Many treat tax as a cost to be minimised in order to boost short-term shareholder value. Ethical directors see tax not as a cost of production but as a distribution of profits to stakeholders, ranking on the profit and loss account alongside dividends. It is a distribution to society which pays for the roads, educated workforces and other parts of the enabling environment in which corporations make their profits.

The corporate world has lost its way, and nowhere is this more true than with the big accountancy firms. The Australian actor Paul Hogan, who has been investigated by Australian tax authorities for his own tax affairs and denies any impropriety, described the situation quite clearly. 'I haven't done my own tax for thirty years,' he said. 'They talk about me going to jail. Erm, excuse me: there's about four law firms and about five accounting firms – some of the biggest ones in the world – that'd have to go to jail before you get to me.'[46] On this point, Hogan is right – or at least he should be. These firms, responding to their clients' wishes to cut their tax bills, have become steeped in an inverted morality that holds tax, democracy and society to be bad; and tax havens, tax avoidance and secrecy to be good. Serial tax avoiders are made knights of the realm; journalists seeking guidance in this complex terrain routinely turn to these very same offshore cheer-leaders for their opinions. Bit by bit, offshore's corrupted morality becomes accepted into our societies.

Offshore finance is, in important respects, similar to more trad-itionally recognised forms of corruption, like bribery. Some argue that bribery is 'efficient' because it helps people get around bureaucratic obstacles, and get things done. Bribery *is* efficient in that very narrow sense. But consider whether a *system* plagued by bribery is efficient, and the answer is the exact opposite: it is highly inefficient. Similarly, secrecy jurisdictions argue that they promote 'efficiency' by helping people and corporations get around certain obstacles. But those obstacles are tax, regulation and transparency, whatever their partic-ular failings – all put in place for good reason. What looks 'efficient' for an individual or corporation looks inefficient when you look at the system as a whole. By allowing the cream of society to escape, tax havens undermine the rules, systems and institutions that promote the public good, and they undermine our faith in those rules. They are corrupting international finance.

The fight against the offshore system will differ from all that has gone before it. Like the battle against corruption, this struggle does not fit neatly into the old political categories of left and right. It will not involve rejecting cross-border trade, or seeking solace in purely local solutions. This fight needs an international perspective, to build new forms of international cooperation. It provides a rubric for tax-paying citizens in rich countries and poor to fight for a common cause. Wherever you live, whoever you are or what you think – this affects you.

Millions of people around the world have for years had a queasy feeling that something is rotten in the global economy, though many have struggled to work out what the problem is. This book will reveal the original source of the trouble.

2

Technically Abroad

Taxing the Vestey brothers: squeezing rice pudding

In the winter of 1934, the Argentine coastguard detained a British-owned ship, the *Norman Star*, as it was about to sail for London. The raid had been triggered by an anonymous tip-off, and it was part of an investigation into a cartel of foreign meat packers suspected of manipulating prices and shipping profits illegally overseas.

This was the era of the Great Depression, and ordinary Argentineans were furious. Their farms were mostly in the hands of a few wealthy landowners, and it was especially galling to see foreign meat packers making large profits while paying local workers a pittance. Not only that, but British and American meat packers had organised themselves so that while the prices they paid ranchers for their beef plummeted, profits on their investments actually rose. How much profit were these foreigners really making? Nobody could be sure, but London's influence was undoubtedly immense. 'Without saying so in as many words, which would be tactless,' the British ambassador had noted in 1929, 'Argentina must be regarded as an essential part of the British empire.' However, the power of the USA was growing. 'The United States under Hoover means to dominate this continent by hook or by crook,' the ambassador noted. 'It is British interests that chiefly stand in the way. These are to be bought out or kicked out.'[1] Argentineans hated their country being the battleground of foreign powers. 'Argentina cannot be described as an English dominion,' said Lisandro de la Torre, the fire-breathing Argentinean senator who was leading the investigation, 'because England never imposed such humiliating conditions on its colonies.'[2]

De la Torre was especially pleased, therefore, with what the coast-guard found in the ship's hold, buried beneath a reeking load of guano fertiliser: over twenty crates labelled CORNED BEEF and bearing the seal of Argentina's Ministry of Agriculture. What they held was not corned beef, but documents. Exposed to public view for the first time were the financial details of William and Edmund Vestey, founders of the world's biggest meat retailers, members of Britain's richest family and among the biggest individual tax avoiders in history.

Brothers William and Edmund Vestey were pioneers of the global corporation. They started out in 1897 by shipping meat trimmings from Chicago to their native Liverpool, where they had built cold-storage facilities that gave them an edge over their competitors. They branched out into poultry farming in Russia and China in the first decade of the twentieth century, and began processing and shipping vast quantities of super-cheap eggs to Europe. They set up more cold stores and retail outlets in Britain, and then in France, Russia, the United States and South Africa. Moving into shipping in 1911, they expanded into ranches and meat packing in Argentina from 1913, then, at the outbreak of war, began buying up more farmland and plant in Venezuela, Australia and Brazil.[3] Theirs was one of the first truly inte-grated multinational corporations, and the brothers soon learned to live by two business rules above all: first never reveal what you are up to, and second never let other people do something for you if you can do it yourself. 'We're not doing business with them,' a competitor once said. 'They're in everybody's business and they want everybody's business.'

The secret of their success was that they were at heart monop-olists. They gave their companies different names to disguise their ownership, and bought up rivals. If a rival resisted them, they would use their extraordinary market power – derived from owning the whole supply chain from the grass, via the cows, the slaughter houses, the freezers, the ships, to the distribution and retail outlets – to undercut and drive them out of business. 'Vestey has got control – or almost complete control – of the meat market,' the Duke of Atholl wrote in a letter to the British prime minister in 1932. 'He holds the British market. This combine, being only sellers, crashed prices in the Argentine to the producers, and cattle are being produced at a dead loss, and large numbers of producers, who are many of them quite

small people, will go to the wall. Vestey does not produce, but purchases
. . . he scoops a great deal of money out of the Argentine.'

The beef export industry was the economic basis of the political
power of the Argentine elite. Philip Knightley, in his book *The Rise
and Fall of the House of Vestey*, described the brothers' huge political
and economic impact on the country. 'It can be argued that in Argentina
the Vesteys' crippling effect on the Argentine labour movement and
early economic development led almost directly to the formation of
militant labour organisations that pushed Peron into power, the subsequent dictatorship of the generals, the terrorism, the Falklands War
and the country's economic disasters.'[4]

It was not only the Argentines who suffered, however. The brothers
showed the same controlling behaviour at the sales end in Britain too.
'He brings meat in his own ships to Smithfield, where he again controls
the price,' the Duke of Atholl continued. 'This crashes the price for
his competitors on the wholesale market, and he purchases the meat
at this crashed price . . . He charges high prices to the retailer in places
like Brighton, where there is no competition, but he is prepared to
cut his price in the London market if anybody should show his nose.

'If you mention his name near a meat market, people look over
their shoulders.'

The key to their success was squeeze at the producer end, squeeze
at the consumer end and push all the profits into the middle. It was
a philosophy that they would also later deploy, with astonishing success,
against tax administrations around the world, making them pioneers
of today's global tax-avoidance industry.

William and Edmund both dressed in dark, sober suits and hats,
and perhaps the biggest visible extravagance for each of them was a
watch and chain. They had no interests beyond business: they did not
smoke, drink or play cards, and despite their fabulous wealth lived in
modest houses and ate cheaply. On honeymoon in Ceylon, William
heard of a fire at a company packing plant in Brazil. He packed his
new wife off home on the next steamer and left to sort out the mess.
Frugal and puritan, they refused to trade in alcohol and would even
inspect their employees' fingers for tobacco stains. One manager
remembered quietly agreeing to pay a foreman ten shillings a week,
without telling London. Almost immediately, Edmund was on the
phone telling him to cut the amount.

They lived by the maxim that it is not what you earn that makes you rich, but what you can keep. It was not their income that they lived on, or even the interest on their income, it was the interest on the interest that kept them going. 'I never spend any of my profits,' William once said. 'I save every farthing. I live on what I earned twenty years ago.' And the Vestey family fortune has endured over the decades: although the family lost a lot of money in the 1990s, it remains among Britain's wealthiest. Peers of the realm, masters of foxhounds, personal friends of the Prince of Wales, and that sort of thing, the extended Vestey family still enjoys so much inherited money that some members only discover they are heirs when presented unexpectedly, on their eighteenth birthday, with large cheques. One distant heir, when she was suddenly presented with a quarter of a million pounds in the 1990s, said, 'I can't handle it,' and turned it down.

Theirs was not an especially easy entry into the British establishment, however. For centuries British elite interests could be divided roughly between three economic classes: first, the landed aristocracy with centuries of tradition and wealth behind it; second, the financial services sector and the City of London, especially after the seventeenth century; and third, the manufacturers. Essentially an alliance of the landed aristocracy and the City financiers ran Britain's service economy. 'Out of this union of land and service wealth,' wrote the historians P. J. Cain and A. G. Hopkins in their landmark study of British imperialism, 'the new gentlemanly capitalist class was born.' It was a class that often looked down their noses – and still do – at grubby manufacturers who had to get their hands dirty to make money. The meat-packing Vesteys carried the taint of manufacturing and, perhaps even worse, they were from Liverpool, not London, so they did not fit into the clubs of the dominant classes. Yet in reality these pioneers of the multinational corporation, combining traditional manufacturing with equally important supply-chain and financial-service operations, straddled the categories.

As their business grew increasingly multinational, it became ever harder for anyone to even guess what they were up to. 'The juggling acts El Inglés [the Vestey company] performed with the packing houses were enough to give the best aviator a dizzy spell,' an Argentinian businessman wrote. 'It is not surprising that the company tax inspector had a difficult job to unravel it all when El Inglés, in the end, was left with just one packing house.' So when Senator de la Torre's investigation stumbled across the documents on the *Norman Star*, he had achieved quite a coup. Not only had the Vesteys been involved in tax frauds and tricks, de la Torre alleged, but top members of the Argentinean government were colluding in, and even profiting from, their subterfuges. A dirty political brawl broke out. Insults, counter-insults and furious denials ricocheted around the Argentine political landscape, and culminated in an assassination attempt on de la Torre, in which an aide died after taking a bullet intended for him.[5]

In those early days, governments were groping in the dark to understand, and to tax, emerging multinational corporations. (They still are.) Before the First World War, Britain did not tax British-based companies on profits they made overseas – only if they repatriated these profits. This suited the Vesteys just fine: most of their profits, they could argue, were made overseas. But when war broke out, Britain, like many other countries, needed to raise a lot of money fast. Income taxes rose startlingly – the standard rate rose from just 6 per cent at the beginning of the war in 1914, to 30 per cent in 1919, the year after the war ended. But in 1914 Britain did something else too, which was especially pertinent to the Vesteys: it also started to tax British companies on all their income worldwide, whether or not it was brought home.

The Vesteys, of course, were furious. First, they tried a lobbying operation in London, which, in the new wartime environment, was doomed to fail. Taxes on business profits never *stop* you from earning the profits, Britain's tax authorities noted drily, they only kick in once there *are* profits. Still, William and Edmund were having none of it. In November 1915, as 50,000 British soldiers died at the Battle of Loos, the Vestey brothers moved overseas to cut their tax bill. Their first stop after leaving was Chicago, where they clearly weren't the first wealthy Britons to arrive. 'What's the matter with you people?' a friendly American tax lawyer asked. 'You are the third Englishman I've had in here this week in the same business.' From there they moved to Argentina, where they paid no income tax at all, and even then they fought to cut the residual company taxes they still had to pay in Britain. As the Great War progressed, however, the brothers increasingly wished they could return home, where they would be closer to their empire's real profit centre. So they hatched up a scheme: to let them return to Britain and *still* escape the tax net. And they did it with a two-stage plan.

First, they returned in February 1919, taking legal precautions to ensure they continued to be treated as visitors, not taxable residents, and began lobbying. They wrote an impassioned plea to the prime minister, dressing it up with appeals to patriotism and claims of how they would contribute to local employment, arguments that multinational corporations still routinely try today. They also complained bitterly about how unfair it was that a big competitor, the American Beef Trust, faced lower taxes. The prime minister referred them to a royal commission, which set about interviewing the Vesteys. William's testimony, which has been cited in academic papers ever since, posed the old question of double taxation that I referred to in the introduction, which goes to the core of a problem right at the heart of global capitalism. If you are going to avoid double taxation in a business spread across several countries, which country gets to tax which bit of the company? This is no simple matter. 'In a business of this nature you cannot say how much is made in one country and how much is made in another,' William said. 'You kill an animal and the product of that animal is sold in fifty different countries. You cannot say how much is made in England and how much abroad.'

William had put his finger on the central problem. By their nature multinationals are integrated global businesses, but tax is national. Multinationals are made up of many subsidiaries and affiliated companies in different countries, and untangling which country gets to tax which part of their profits is fearsomely complicated.

Britain was the first country to introduce a general income tax and apply it to the worldwide profits of any person resident in the UK. In the case of companies, judges decided that they should be treated as resident where the company's most important decisions were taken, at meetings of their boards of directors. This suited Britain, since thousands of firms with activities all over the world were financed through the City of London, and their boards were normally there. Germany, by contrast, placed more emphasis on the 'seat of management' – that is, where the company's actual operations were managed – a subtly different definition.[6] The United States was different again: it based its test on citizenship. US citizens and corporations formed under United States laws were taxed on their income from all sources worldwide. These differences produced further complications in the international tax arena.

Tax systems sometimes clashed. A 'source' country hosting investment from a multinational based in another country would want to tax its local investment income, but the 'residence' country – the multinational's home – would also want to tax that same income. Initially this double taxation was not such a problem: only a few states taxed business income, and rates were low. But ahead of the First World War countries began to increase taxes to pay for military spending and new social security schemes. Double taxation became a hot issue, and businesses began to complain. An International Chamber of Commerce was set up in 1920, with tax squarely on its agenda from the outset.[7]

Discussions began under the League of Nations in the 1920s to establish some common rules and principles, but progress was slow. Capital-rich nations like Britain that hosted a lot of multinationals investing overseas wanted rules that gave most taxing rights to residence countries, while source countries hosting a lot of inward investment – often poorer states – wanted to be able to tax those investors' income locally. The original League of Nations treaty in 1928 gave substantial taxing rights to source countries, which included many low-income nations, but after the Second World War, the OECD model giving more rights to the richer residence countries became more dominant. But the multinationals stayed a few jumps ahead of tax collectors in the rich world too.

As the Vesteys used their muscle to squeeze competitors at both the producer and consumer ends, they and other multinationals also began to squeeze the tax authorities, by deploying teams of lawyers and accountants to drive the profits away from the producer and the consumer countries and into the low-tax middle. If you own the ranches, the cattle, the freezers, the docks, the ships, the insurers, the wholesalers and the retailers, then you can, by adjusting the prices one subsidiary charges another for goods, take your profit at the most convenient place down the line. 'And the most convenient stage,' noted Knightley, 'is naturally where you will pay the least taxation, preferably where you will pay none at all.' It was exactly the same transfer pricing principle used by the banana companies that I described in the last chapter.

'By siphoning these profits, often through a chain of intermediaries, to a holding company in a tax haven, instead of sending them back to the parent company, they could avoid being taxed anywhere,' explained Professor Sol Picciotto, a leading expert in international tax. They often did this through chains of intermediaries, so that the profits pooled in the low-tax places, while the costs migrated to where taxes were highest. The multinationals had turned a system designed to avoid double taxation into one of double *non*-taxation. This gave them plenty of cheap capital for reinvestment, helping them expand faster than their smaller, less international competitors.

The United Nations, the successor organisation to the League of Nations, produced a draft model tax treaty in 1980 that was supposed to shift the balance back in favour of source taxation and developing countries. The OECD intervened aggressively to stop this, not only by ensuring that its own model treaty favouring rich countries remained the preferred standard, but also by lobbying fiercely to weaken the United Nations' own model. The rich countries' model has achieved a position of near-total dominance today. Not only is there double non-taxation, but plenty of tax that would in a fairer world be paid in poor countries is paid in rich countries instead. Elites in the poor countries don't mind the poverty around them so much, because tax havens let them keep their loot offshore and tax free, letting their poorer compatriots and foreign donors pay the bills.

William Vestey's testimony to the Royal Commission in 1920 reveals a man accustomed to getting his way. 'If I kill a beast in the Argentine and sell the product of that beast in Spain, this country can get no tax on that business,' he said. 'You may do what you like, but you cannot have it.'[8] He threatened to take his business, and thousands of jobs with him, if he did not get what he wanted. The Commissioners, stung by the Vesteys' lack of patriotism towards a country that had just been through a major war, hit back. 'Are you not to pay anything for the advantage of living here?' one asked. William Vestey refused to answer. 'With respect,' the commissioner continued, 'I should like to have an answer. It is one that has agitated me a good deal since the witness has been in the chair.'

Britain was simply not going to give the Vestey brothers what they wanted. And yet they still hankered to return. 'I was born in the good old town of Liverpool,' William said, 'and I want to die in this country.' So, having failed in their lobbying, they hatched up something more devious, something that helps us get a much better glimpse of the slippery world of offshore. They set up a trust. This was the second stage of their plan.

In the popular imagination, the best way to achieve secrecy in your financial affairs is to shift your money to Switzerland or Liechtenstein, say, cloaked under strong bank secrecy laws. Now, bank secrecy is not to be sniffed at, but what most people do not realise is that trusts are, in a sense, the Anglo-Saxon equivalent. Not only that, but trusts potentially create forms of secrecy that are more difficult to penetrate than the straightforward reticence of the Swiss variety.

The concept of trusts emerged in the Middle Ages, when knights leaving for the crusades would leave their possessions in the hands of trusted stewards, who would look after them while they were away on behalf of the knights' wives and children. It was a three-way arrangement binding together the owners of the properties (the knights), with the beneficiaries (their families) via an intermediary (the stewards, or trustees). Over the centuries, a body of law grew up to formalise these three-way arrangements, and now you can enforce these things in the courts.

Trusts are silent, powerful mechanisms, and it is usually impossible to find any evidence of them at all on public record. They are secrets between lawyers and their clients. What a trust does, at heart, is manipulate the ownership of an asset. You might think ownership is a simple thing: you have, say, a million dollars in the bank; you own it, and you can spend it any time. But ownership can be unbundled into separate strands. This happens, if you think about it, when you buy a house with a mortgage: the bank has some ownership rights over your house, and you have other rights. Variants of the trust exist, such as the *Anstalt*, the foundation (*Stiftungs*) and the *Treuhand*, which are more common in continental Europe, and which also separate out the different aspects of ownership.

A trust unbundles ownership into different parts, very carefully. When a trust is set up the original owner of an asset in theory gives it away to a trust. At this point, the trustee becomes the legal owner of the asset – though they are not free to spend or consume it, for they must legally obey the terms of the trust deed, the set of instructions that tells them exactly how to share out the benefits to the beneficiaries. Under trust law, the trustee has no choice but to obey these instructions, and apart from fees they may not receive any benefits from the asset. A rich man with two children might put a million dollars into a bank account owned by a trust, and then appoint a lawyer as the trustee, instructing him that when each is twenty-one they should receive half the money. Even if the wealthy man dies long before the money is paid out, the trust will survive and the trustee is bound in law to pay out the money as he is told. It is very hard indeed to break a trust.

Trusts can be perfectly legitimate. But they can be, and very often are, used for more nefarious purposes, like criminal tax evasion. This raises a question which puzzles a lot of people. If you must give the asset away to avoid your tax bill, is that not an excessive price to pay? The answer is not straightforward.

In part, this is a cultural issue. The British upper classes feel comfortable separating themselves from their money and leaving it to be managed by trusted strangers. Centuries of gentlemanly capitalism have taught them that they can rely on trusted servants and professional retainers, and their sense of entitlement doesn't rest on something as trivial as legal ownership. Their education prepares them to recognise those who will respect their claims and whom they can therefore trust.

Trusts make two main things happen. First, they create a solid legal barrier that separates the different components of ownership. Second, this legal barrier can become an unbreakable information barrier. Trusts can shroud assets in cast-iron secrecy. Imagine the assets in a trust are shares in a company. The company may register the trustee – the legal owner – but it will not register the beneficiaries – the people who will be getting and enjoying the money – anywhere. If you have a million dollars in a trust in Jersey and the tax inspectors come after you, it will be hard for them to even start their enquiries as trust instruments in Jersey are not registered in any official or public register. If, though, the tax inspectors get lucky and find out the identity of a trustee, this is likely to be a Jersey lawyer who does this for a living, and who may be the trustee for many thousands of trusts. The lawyer may be the only person in the world who knows you are the beneficiary, and they are bound by professional confidentiality not to reveal this fact. The tax inspector has hit a stone wall.

You can make this secrecy deeper still, by layering one secrecy structure on another. The asset held in the Jersey trust may be a million dollars sitting in a bank in Panama, itself protected by strong bank secrecy. Even if the tax inspectors used torture they could never get the Jersey lawyer to reveal the beneficiary because they wouldn't necessarily know it: they merely send the cheques to another lawyer somewhere else, who also isn't the beneficiary.* And you can keep on going: you can layer a trust in Jersey on another trust in the Cayman Islands, then perch that on top of a secretive company structure in Delaware. If Interpol comes looking they must go through difficult, slow and costly court procedures, in country after country, to trace the money. Even then, some places allow flee clauses – the asset will automatically hop elsewhere at the first whiff of an investigation.

The trust arrangement that the Vesteys set up in December 1921 – which was signed in the Paris offices of the British lawyers Hall & Stirling – was fairly simple compared to the great offshore embroideries that are so common today. Yet, even so, it took Britain's Inland Revenue eight years to discover it even existed. In the meantime, while the Vesteys' Paris trust ticked over quietly, a new scandal erupted.

In June 1922, seven years after leaving the country to escape British wartime taxes, it emerged that William Vestey had bought himself a peerage. There was nothing particularly unusual about this. Plenty of people who had made fortunes in the Great War desperately craved the respectability of a peerage to mask the taint of profiteering, and Prime Minister Lloyd George was only too happy to oblige, selling off official honours willy-nilly, causing outrage up and down the land. 'Gentlemen received titles,' one member of parliament spluttered in 1919, 'whom no decent man would allow in his home.

When William became Lord Vestey, outrage was widespread. 'The feeling of most people,' Lord Strachie said in parliament, 'would be that this was not the sort of man who ought to be rewarded for

---

* The Jersey authorities say that trustees are required to know the identity of all beneficiaries. Contacts indicate that Jersey and other offshore jurisdictions do not adequately police these laws, and trustees often do not in fact know the beneficiaries.

evading taxation and thereby throwing a heavier burden of taxation upon those who have to pay taxes.'[9] Strachie invited Lord Vestey to assure parliament that he had not paid for his peerage.

Vestey, of course, did no such thing, and he did not endear himself to anyone when he stated, 'I am technically abroad at present . . . the present position of affairs suits me admirably. I am abroad. I pay nothing.'

Even King George V was moved to write. 'I do appeal most strongly for the establishment of some efficient and trustworthy procedure,' he wrote in his quaint, royal prose, 'to protect the Crown and the Government from the possibility of similar painful if not humiliating incidents, the recurrence of which must inevitably constitute an evil, dangerous to the social and political well-being of the state.' The scandal rumbled on, but in the end nothing was done, and the Vesteys returned home to Britain as they had wished, their secret Paris trust keeping the tax authorities at bay.

Residents of modern Britain might be struck by the resemblance between this episode and a scandal involving Lord Ashcroft, the deputy chairman of Britain's Conservative Party and a wealthy Belize-based businessman, who admitted in March 2010 that he was not resident in the United Kingdom for tax purposes, but instead was a so-called non-domiciled taxpayer, a category that exempts wealthy people from paying British taxes on their earnings outside Britain. EASY PEERAGES FOR MPS STINK. NOW THE REEK IS INTOLERABLE, read one headline in the *Guardian* in March 2010, in the wake of the scandal. 'At the rate Ashcroft is going,' one parliamentarian remarked, 'he will be a member of the royal family by Christmas.'[10]

The Vesteys had returned to Britain and escaped tax, but even after the British tax authorities found the Paris trust, through patient detective work, they still could not get the Vesteys to pay tax on it. For secrecy is not the only subterfuge that trusts provide. Trusts also let people pretend they have given away their money – meaning that they cannot be taxed on it – while in reality keeping control of it. The US Internal Revenue Service sums it up quite simply: 'Although these schemes give the appearance of separating responsibility and control from the benefits of ownership, as would be the case with legitimate trusts, the taxpayer in fact controls them.'[11] And the preamble to the Vestey's Paris trust deed hints at exactly that pretence. 'In consideration of the natural love and affection of the settlors [the Vesteys] for

the beneficiaries,' it began, 'and for divers other good causes and considerations . . .' The money, it was saying, had really been given away
to their dear beneficiaries, their wives and children. But what the
Vesteys actually did was this. First, they leased most of their overseas
empire to Union Cold Storage Ltd, a company based in Britain. In
any normal arrangement, Union would have simply paid rent to the
Vestey brothers, but instead Union paid the rent to two lawyers and
a company director in Paris whom the Vesteys trusted. So far, so
normal. But the trustees were then given very wide powers of investment, to be carried out under the direction of certain 'authorised
persons'. And who were those persons? Why, the Vestey brothers! So
the trustees, under the Vesteys' direction, lent large sums to another
company in Britain, which the Vesteys also controlled, and used as
their own personal piggy bank.[12]

Tax authorities, it is true, are constantly seeking ways to counter
new avoidance strategies, and regularly enact laws and regulations to
defend the tax base. Wealthy tax avoiders then put in place more
complex strategies to get around the new rules. This becomes an
ever-evolving game of cat and mouse, whose effect is to make the tax
system steadily more complex. Secrecy jurisdictions constantly – and
often very rapidly – tailor their laws to let the wealthy perfect their
deceits and to stay one step ahead of the tax collectors. Over the years,
offshore trust subterfuges have proliferated and grown more sophisticated. Many offshore jurisdictions allow things called revocable trusts
– trusts that can be revoked and the money returned to the original
owner. If the owner can do that, then they have not really separated
themself from the asset. Until it is revoked, though, it looks as if the
asset has been passed on, and the authorities cannot tax it.

There are endless variations. A trust might have a 'trust protector',
who has some kind of influence over the trustees and is acting on
behalf of the person who pretended to give the money away. A Cayman
Islands 'star trust' lets the original owner make the trust's investment
decisions – and the trustee is not obliged to ensure the investments
are in the interests of other beneficiaries. Or you might use a Jersey
'sham trust', where you can replace the trustees with more pliable
ones later, and change their instructions at will. And so it goes on.
There are offshore lawyers who sit in their offices all day, doing little
more than dreaming up deviant new flavours of trusts.

Trusts are not only about tax, either. As we shall see, many of the structured investment vehicles that helped trigger the latest economic crisis were set up as offshore trusts. Most people would be surprised, even shocked, to find out how central they are to global finance: there are up to $400 billion of assets tied up in trusts from the tiny tax haven of Jersey alone – and several *trillion* dollars' worth worldwide, shrouded in deep secrecy.

In choosing the trust mechanism to protect their vast wealth, the Vesteys had picked a powerful weapon indeed. And when Senator de la Torre found those crates of Vestey documents buried under the guano on the *Norman Star* in 1934, he was probably unaware just how crafty his adversaries were. Soon after the raid, further incriminating Vestey documents turned up in Uruguay, and the senator achieved another coup when he got the British Foreign Office, whose diplomats were deeply uneasy with the Vesteys' unpleasant business practices, to agree to turn Argentina's quest into a multi-country joint committee of investigation.

'William immediately saw the danger,' wrote Knightley. 'Such a committee would want to inspect the Vestey books in London, and there was no telling what such a probe might uncover.' So the Vesteys went on the offensive. When their manager in Argentina died of a heart attack, William Vestey wrote to the committee and accused Senator de la Torre of murdering him. Argentina's government responded furiously, calling Vestey's letter 'an unprecedented piece of insolence'. The Foreign Office agreed that William's letter was offensive, but said there was not much they could do about it. And things went downhill from there.

The committee worked for two years, while the Vesteys pulled strings in London to emasculate it, and despite sixty meetings and a report filled with detail about the Argentine meat trade, it never got to see the Vestey books in London. Philip Knightley described what happened next: 'Senator de la Torre, the man who had come nearer than anyone else to penetrating the secrecy of the Vestey empire, shot himself on January 5, 1939, leaving a suicide note which expressed his disappointment at the general behaviour of mankind.'

Even so, Britain's Inland Revenue had already started marshalling its forces for the next assault on the Vestey trusts, with the Finance Act of 1938, which they hoped would enable them to tax overseas trusts. And they continued their assault in 1942, at the height of the

Second World War. William had died two years earlier, fighting the taxman to his last breath and leaving only £261,000 in Britain and railing against 'unjust death duties'. The trust, alive and well, just kept paying out to the family. The new British law determined that someone was taxable if they had 'power to enjoy' the income – a term which seemed to cover the Vestey family. To start with, the Inland Revenue seemed to be winning, but they failed to secure the original documents for the Paris trust, whose last known whereabouts, according to the family, was in a box in Bordeaux, shortly before the Germans overran it. Nevertheless the tax authorities kept making progress, knocking down appeal after appeal. At the final hurdle, however, the tide turned. Before the law lords, the Vesteys argued that they did not have *individual* rights to control the income, but *joint* rights. With that, as Britain's young men gave their lives once again, in the Second World War, the Vesteys wriggled free again.

And the game went on for decades more. The Inland Revenue did make some small gains in subsequent attacks, but all the time the Vesteys were refining their defences, and slipping most of their wealth through the tax net. 'Trying to come to grips with the Vesteys over tax,' one tax officer said, 'is like trying to squeeze a rice pudding.' In 1980, shortly after one such assault by the Inland Revenue, an investigation by the *Sunday Times,* then one of the world's most respected newspapers, revealed that in 1978 the Vesteys' Dewhurst chain of butchers in Britain had paid just £10 tax on a profit of more than £2.3 million – a tax rate of 0.0004 per cent. 'Here is an immensely wealthy dynasty which for more than sixty years has paid trivial sums in tax,' the newspaper wrote. 'All that time its members have enjoyed the considerable pleasures of being rich in England without contributing anything near their fair share to the defences which kept those pleasures in being – against foreign enemies in wartime, against disorder and disease in times of peace.'

It is unpleasant to note that the large majority of readers' comments in response to the article supported the Vesteys. 'Good luck to them,' remarked Lord Thorneycroft, a grandee of Britain's Conservative Party. And Edmund Vestey, the grandson of the original Edmund, put the icing on this particular cake. 'Let's face it, nobody pays more tax than they have to. We're all tax dodgers, aren't we?'[13]

The Paris trust loophole was closed in 1991, but opportunities for legal tax avoidance for Britain's wealthy remain abundant.[14] When the Queen finally started paying income tax in 1993 after a public outcry, the latest Lord Vestey smiled and said, 'Well, that makes me the last one.'

As we shall soon see, this was not the case. He was very far from alone.

3

The Profitable Shield of Neutrality

Switzerland, Europe's ancient secrecy jurisdiction

At ten past four on 26 October 1932 a Paris police squad raided an elegant house on the Champs-Élysées housing the discreet Paris offices of Switzerland's Basler Handelsbank.[1] The police soon discovered that their information, from a whistle-blower high up in the bank who had supplied a list of 1,300 tax-evading customers, was solid. In the reception area police found a handful of people with over 200,000 francs in cash between them. As their investigation branched out, the list of suspects grew to 2,000 people, including some of the wealthiest and loftiest names in France.

Two weeks after the raid, in a tempestuous debate in parliament, Fabien Albertin, a socialist deputy who had obtained the list of the bank's clients, responded to deputies' demands for 'Names! Names!' by offering a political striptease of tantalising snippets. Two bishops were on the list, he revealed; there were a dozen generals, the army's comptroller-general, three senators, some former ministers, along with leading industrialists including the Peugeot family, the right-wing owner of *Le Figaro*, and the owner of its rival, *Le Matin*. Five more Swiss banks were involved. He estimated that France was losing four billion francs annually, a truly vast amount in those days.[2] A communist in parliament contrasted the lenient treatment of rich tax avoiders with that of a small tradesman who had been imprisoned for three years for defrauding French social security.

In the 1920s, while the Vesteys were setting up their own tax gymnastics, Swiss bankers were advertising their 'utmost discretion' so brazenly that the Swiss foreign minister, wary of retaliation, urged them to tone down their message. European governments were bothered not only about losing tax revenues, but also by the flight of German capital to Switzerland, undermining payment of the reparations from the First World War imposed on Germany by the Versailles Treaty. The Swiss Federal Council in 1924 said it had 'decided strictly to reject . . . any measure combating this evasion'.[3]

But this new scandal was different. Amid the Great Depression, France was preparing a vicious austerity budget, and the public mood was poisonous. All thirty-eight examining magistrates in Paris were assigned to the prosecution of those on the list, and the French finance minister promised to attack tax evasion 'by all the means available to a government'.[4] Switzerland rejected every French request for collaboration. 'It would in no way be in our interest to grant French agents judicial cooperation,' a confidential official document noted,[5] 'which might have very unfavourable repercussions on the substantial business accruing to our banks from foreign deposits.' But when the French jailed two officials from the Basler Handelsbank for not cooperating, Switzerland and its bankers acted.

First, a flurry of articles appeared in the Swiss media, focusing heavily on the French police's strong-arm tactics, ignoring the problem of tax evasion amid austerity and painting Switzerland as the victim of large, bullying foreign governments. This was an OFFENSIVE AGAINST SWITZERLAND and a 'veritable hate campaign,' local newspapers proclaimed. It was an almost exact pre-echo of the headlines that fill Swiss newspapers today after US authorities caught UBS staff in flagrante helping rich Americans avoid their taxes.

What happened next is important. A pervasive story now exists that Switzerland put bank secrecy into place to protect German Jewish money from the Nazis. This myth dates back to a bulletin[6] in 1966 from the Schweizerische Kreditanstalt (today's Credit Suisse), and Swiss bankers have wielded it to great effect ever since. American officials negotiating a new tax treaty with Switzerland at that time lodged an official complaint after being frequently lectured about the supposed origins of bank secrecy as a protection for Jewish money. A Swiss Federal Council report in March 1970 officially endorsed the story[7] and this was backed up in 1977 by a lurid book[8] by a former Geneva newspaper editor outlining a fabulous story of Gestapo agents infiltrating Switzerland to worm out Jewish bank details. The problem with the story is that it is not true. Amid the Great Depression, Swiss farmers' and workers' movements began in 1931 to clamour for more control over the banks. Bankers feared state inspection of their hitherto closely controlled financial domain would risk secrets leaking out, and they pressed fiercely for a new law, to make it a crime to violate Swiss bank secrecy. By August 1931, the highly influential right-wing daily *Neue Zürcher Zeitung* was attacking government oversight of the banks, and in February 1932 a top banker sent the government draft legislation with a clause making it a crime to violate bank secrecy. It was the French scandal that October, however, which really spurred the government into action. A new banking law was prepared and an official draft was ready by February 1933, just eighteen days after Hitler came to power and long before he had consolidated his grip on the German state or even gained control of all of Germany's intelligence services. The Swiss law finally adopted in 1934 for the first time made it a criminal offence punishable by fines and prison to violate bank secrecy, and was almost unchanged from the original draft.[9] In Germany the death penalty for having foreign accounts undeclared to the Third Reich only appeared in 1936. Even the Swiss Bankers' Association has no records of the supposed activities of Gestapo agents coming to Switzerland to squirrel out information about Jewish money.

Even though the story about Swiss bank secrecy having its origins in concern for the welfare of German Jews is a myth, it is widely seen as fact. It 'has provided the beleaguered Swiss with a rallying point,' wrote the financial author Nicholas Faith, 'a flag of morality which they could wrap securely round themselves when they were accused of harbouring criminals of every nationality and description.' The story was wheeled out several times after the US government in 2008 began investigating the activities of the Swiss bank UBS in helping wealthy American clients evade US taxes. 'Their secrecy laws date back to 1934,' the *Financial Times* noted in 2009, 'when they were enacted partly to protect German Jews and trade unionists from the Nazis.'

Secrecy has very old, very deep roots in Swiss history. 'Switzerland is probably the oldest and strongest of the tax havens,' explained Sébastien Guex, professor of contemporary history at the University of Lausanne.[10] 'Cayman and the Bahamas are outgrowths of London –

they have no real autonomy. Switzerland is not just a strongbox for rich Americans; it became a tax haven on the basis of a powerful secular tradition dating back seven centuries involving the strategies of thirty or forty families. If you are one of them, then you count in the world. This has a weight that is independent of finance.'

Switzerland's big founding myth – equivalent, perhaps, to America's Boston Tea Party – is the thirteenth-century story of William Tell, who schoolchildren know as the man who had to shoot an apple off his son's head after insulting an imperial tax collector. The tale of the hardy mountain bowman who obeyed no authority beyond his narrow valley community encapsulates an important truth about Switzerland's self-image as a land of plucky Alpine resistance to tyranny, and fits closely with the very Swiss notion of *Sonderfall* – that Switzerland has a rather special, rather superior place in the world.[11]

Over the centuries the Swiss organised themselves into extended, self-reliant mountain valley communities, making it impossible for foreign armies to control, and Switzerland emerged as a land of loosely linked self-reliant units riven by deep fissures. The country is divided roughtly into four linguistic blocs: a German majority focused on Zürich and living in the centre and east; a French-speaking minority based around Geneva in the west, relatively fewer Italian speakers clustered near Lugano in the south; and a smattering of mostly rural Romansh-speakers in the eastern valleys. Overlapping the divisions are rifts between cantons and communities, between Protestants and Catholics, and even between ideologies.

The Swiss dealt with these divisions in two ways. The first was neutrality in foreign conflicts. Taking sides in a war between France and Germany, for example, could pit French-speaking Swiss against their German-speaking compatriots, and lead to civil war. Swiss traditions of neutrality date back centuries, and were formally recognised in Europe in the Vienna Congress of 1815. The other way Switzerland managed its internal fractures was to create an extremely decentralised political system of intricate complexity and direct democracy, giving local units great powers. Frequent referendums keep Switzerland's constitution in a constant state of evolution, one step ahead of popular unrest. The Swiss 'believe there will always be a political compromise or bit of constitutional machinery which will get around a given difficulty', explained the historian Jonathan Steinberg. Switzerland is 'an ancient historic entity that happened to escape the centralisation of the modern era. It is a bit of the Holy Roman Empire which survived the rise and fall of the centralised modern state.'[12]

In this extremely decentralised set-up the national government gets only about a third of the total taxes: the rest is divided roughly equally between the twenty-six cantons and the 2,750-odd municipalities. This structure in turn creates another offshore dynamic: competition between cantons to undercut each other on tax rates, leading to ever lower taxes, which today, along with the secrecy, attract some of the world's biggest corporations. The pretty lakeside canton of Zug, for example, very discreetly hosts 27,000 corporations – about one for every four inhabitants. These include giant commodity firms such as Glencore and Xstrata and the company building the pipeline for much of Europe's gas supplies from Russia; it became the bolt-hole for the fugitive financier Marc Rich, controversially pardoned by President Clinton in 2001; and it hosts celebrities like the German former tennis star Boris Becker. The giant multinationals dwarf the cantons in economic clout, giving them great power to influence local legislators. 'It is such a small canton, you have access to the authorities,'[13] explained Priska Roesli, a senior official from Tyco Electronics Ltd in nearby Schaffhausen canton, where the firm negotiated its own special tax rate after relocating from Bermuda.

Yet something else here reassures the financial capitalists too. Swiss politics is based on what they call *Concordance*: this means, in essence, negotiated agreement between factions. Switzerland's ruling Federal Council is made up of seven members who represent different parties but must always support the collective will over and above the interests of their own party. So the cut and thrust of opposition-based democracy, which makes for colourful politics elsewhere, is curiously muted here: politicians are not really allowed to disagree very much. So although the socialist party has long opposed bank secrecy its leaders in the the Federal Council must follow the official line – to support it. In public, party leaders resort to circumlocutions: a kind of 'Yes, well, but . . .' and this weakens opposition. Concordance, it is true, has been upset in recent years with the rise of the noisy right wing anti-immigrant Schweizerische Volkspartei (SVP). But the SVP aggressively supports bank secrecy.

Financial capitalists can trust the Swiss not to rock the boat. Even better, Switzerland's political design creates another level of reassuring solidity. Having grown out of free peasant or urban associations, Swiss communities 'are in a curious sense bottom-heavy, rather like those dolls which spring up no matter how often the child pushes them over', Steinberg explained. 'The weight is at the base. The communities have a deep equilibrium, to which, as the point of rest, the social and political order tends to return.' There is also relatively little tradition of working-class agitation. Switzerland's mountainous terrain fractured the country's economic structure, so the textile industry, for instance, fanned out along the mountain streams that powered the mills, meaning that it was made up of small, specialised units. Workers were scattered, and it was hard for a self-conscious and militant working class to emerge.[14] This, and the system's ability to neutralise potential conflict, helps explain why Swiss society tolerates one of the most unequal wealth distributions among developed nations. There will be no popular revolution here any time soon. Which is just how the world's financiers like it.

Swiss financial secrecy has existed for centuries. Catholic French kings valued Geneva bankers' discretion highly – it would have been disastrous for it to be known they were borrowing from heretical Protestants. In 1713 the great council of the Geneva canton, then an independent city-state, ruled that bankers were 'prohibited from divulging this information to anyone other than the client concerned, except with the expressed agreement of the City Council'. But it was in the nineteenth century, as Swiss elites began to dream of empire, that secret Swiss banking really began to flower.

Between 1860 and 1870 a number of smaller states south of Switzerland coalesced into a unified Italy, and something similar happened to the north when Germany unified in 1871. European states were also scrambling for overseas empires. Britain's rapid imperial expansion was followed by France, Germany, Belgium, the Netherlands and Italy. But Switzerland had no access to the sea, so its own empire was out of the question. Plans were floated by the Swiss industrial and banking elites to order the army to force a corridor to the sea, or to negotiate a path to the port of Genoa via treaty; there was even a plan to buy Madagascar from France.

'So you are the Swiss bourgeoisie, and you have this problem,' Guex explained.

Most of the bourgeoisies competing with the Swiss – especially Germany [and France] – suddenly have vast armies, and the big powers are carving up the world in a colonial and imperialist race. Switzerland is surrounded by big powers with colonial empires, with access to primary materials, naval power, commerce, and so on. But where is Switzerland? What do the Swiss do? This is an ancient and proud bourgeoisie, and they cannot have an empire.

A radically different path, already half-formed, began to solidify, anchored in Swiss neutrality. If you are neutral in a foreign war, you can make a lot of money. You can still do business with all the belligerents – and also profit as a trusted, unthreatening intermediary. 'If a German wants to do business in France or vice versa,' Guex said, 'they come through Switzerland, which can provide the camouflage and hidden companies to complete the transactions. They can protect their goods, and they love the tranquillity too: the capitalist can bring his wife and children and they won't be killed.' Not only that, but as warring countries plunge into economic chaos, capital flows naturally to peaceful neutrals, whose currencies remain strong and even strengthen as foreign money floods in.

The Swiss had already found that trade and living standards were never as good as they had been during the Thirty Years War of 1618–48, one of the most destructive in Europe's history. That, the historian Jonathan Steinberg said, was when 'the Swiss began to associate neutrality with profit, virtue and good sense'.[15] By the eighteenth century bankers from the area that is modern Switzerland were highly active across Europe. His Imperial Majesty in Vienna, the kings of France and England, the little German kinglets and the French municipalities – all were in debt to Swiss bankers. 'From the Bank of England to the East India Company,' wrote the Swiss historian Jules Landsmann, 'there was practically no instrument of collective capital investment in which the authorities of the Swiss Cantons were not involved.'[16]

Profits multiplied again in the Franco-Prussian war of 1870–1.[17] 'This is what the Swiss bourgeoisie are thinking,' Guex continued. 'That's our future – we will play on the contradictions between the European powers – and, protected by the shield of our neutrality, our arm will be industry and finance.' The First World War was more profitable still, and the Swiss elites began to dream of becoming one of the great world centres of financial capital. And something else was happening: European nations were ramping up taxes to pay for their wars. France, for example, adopted an income tax only in 1914, and by 1925 the top marginal rate was 90 per cent.[18] As taxes rose, wealthy citizens looked to escape – and pretty, neutral Switzerland was the obvious choice. Yet the First World War, of course, was not nearly as profitable as what happened after Adolf Hitler came to power.

On a bright day in October 1996, a small, withered woman named Estelle Sapir testified before a US Senate committee investigating Swiss banks and the Holocaust. She had last seen her father through barbed wire in southern France shortly before he went to die in a Polish concentration camp, but before he died he had carefully explained where his assets were. After the war she visited several banks in Britain and France, where they traced the accounts and emptied them for her, without any kerfuffle. She then explained what happened when she went to Switzerland with a Credit Suisse deposit slip from 1938, which she had found among her father's papers.

'I saw a young man come out behind,' she explained, 'and the first thing he asked me, "Show me the death certificate for your father." And I answer him, "How can I have a death certificate? I have to go find Himmler, Hitler, Eichmann and Mengele." And I start to cry. I run out from the bank, into the street. The same day, I go back to the bank, but could not compose myself. Never went back to Switzerland. Never went back to Switzerland. Never.' Credit Suisse offices around the world turned her away on twenty visits between 1946 and 1957.

For many Swiss, the Second World War was a time of resistance and heroism that underlined Swiss exceptionalism. Trapped between Mussolini's fascist Italy to the south and Hitler's Germany to the North, plucky little Switzerland stood free and alone. On 25 July 1940 General Guisan assembled the Swiss officer corps and pledged to defend the nation. He ordered a strategic redeployment: the army would no longer defend the frontiers but would instead withdraw to the massive chain of the Alps. Hitler's armies might capture Zürich, Geneva or Lucerne in the lowlands, but they would have a terrible time extracting Switzerland's finest from their fortified positions in their own impregnable mountains. Switzerland, Guisan was saying, would fight to the end. This was the Swiss army's finest hour. But behind this story lies a less noble tale. The first part is about Swiss banks. But there is something else, less well known, that emerges too.

Switzerland had long had a constitutional obligation to shelter political refugees. Yet in April 1933, just weeks after Hitler came to power, Switzerland passed a new law effectively denying Jewish refugees automatic asylum, on the grounds that they were not political but racial refugees. 'We must protect ourselves with all our strength, and, where necessary, without mercy against the immigration of foreign Jews, especially those from the east,' said Heinrich Rothmund, head of police in Switzerland's Justice and Police Ministry. To make discrimination easier at the border posts, Rothmund even persuaded the Gestapo in 1938 to stamp Jews' passports with J.[19] This, it has to be said, was the response of Swiss leaders, not the people. Many Swiss welcomed and protected immigrant Jews, and protested loudly about brutal treatment. According to many accounts, most of the population was anti-Nazi.[20]

When war broke out in 1939 Switzerland intensified its restrictions, forcibly expelling many Jews who had crossed ravines and mountains to flee the Nazis. Local Jews had to pay and care for any new Jewish arrivals. 'Refugees are subjected to a rigorous interrogation before being allowed to benefit from the right to refuge on the soil of the Confederation,' one Swiss paper remarked. 'Capital benefits the right to asylum without any enquiry.'[21] Neutrality, Swiss officials explained, meant only military neutrality. Economic neutrality was, as the Swiss president put it, an 'unknown legal concept'. In 1942 Switzerland effectively closed its borders to Jews.[22] The ones who got in legally, according to Tom Bower in his book *Blood Money: the Swiss, the Nazis, and the Looted Billions*, 'were the fortunate few who had co-operated in allowing the Swiss to profit from their misery'. One Jewish German businessman, for example, sold his shoe factory in Berlin to a Swiss firm for one mark plus a guaranteed entry visa to Switzerland.

Even early in the war, senior German individuals and corporations were amassing wealth in Switzerland to plan for a possible German defeat, in order eventually to establish a new Fourth Reich.[23] Germany's Economy Ministry opened a special foreign exchange control division in September 1939, with Switzerland as its hub, to disguise German property abroad. Leading German industrial corporations, including arms makers and IG Farben, the chemical giant which manufactured poison gas used in Nazi death camps, hired Swiss trustees and managers to organise secret legal frameworks of ownership.[24] Swiss agents for Hermann Göring, Joseph Goebbels, Joachim von Ribbentrop and Hitler himself helped store a mass of valuables, gold and art works looted from galleries and private collections across Europe. A US State Department briefing based on captured German documents outlines schemes familiar to the modern offshore expert: false invoicing, dummy corporations, 'cloaks', deferred payments on false contracts, and more. A senior Berne banker told a British diplomat in 1941 that 'every leading member of the governing groups in all Axis countries has funds in Switzerland'.[25] Hitler never invaded, partly because Switzerland was an 'indigestible lump', as one top Nazi official described it,[26] but also partly because Switzerland and tiny neighbouring Liechtenstein were, as one Berne lawyer called them, his two 'safes'.[27]

Just as tax havens in the modern era have welcomed waves of corrupt money from developing nations, Switzerland, it seems, was directly and actively complicit in Adolf Hitler's corrupt system of political patronage in Germany. In 1941 Nazi Germany's gold and foreign exchange reserves ran out, and the Swiss government stepped in with a loan of 850 million Swiss francs, and Swiss manufacturers supplied weapons and instruments. As a Swiss independent commission of experts report concluded in 2001–2, 'Switzerland helped to bankroll the German war effort.' Swiss chemical industries, mechanical engineering, watchmaking and precision instruments, it added, experienced 'a real boom'.[28]

Allied ambassadors to Switzerland who protested were lectured by Swiss officials 'aggrieved' by 'unreasonable' Allied demands to limit trade with Germany. The Swiss demanded the right to trade with Japan too.[29] According to the US consul in Basel, Switzerland's bankers had become 'pro-Fascist financial operators'. When Swiss Red Cross officials received direct and incontrovertible evidence of genocide in autumn 1942 and considered an appeal against it, the government ordered their silence.[30] When British Foreign Secretary Anthony Eden called in the Swiss ambassador to Britain that year to protest at negotiations for a new Swiss–German trade pact, it gradually dawned on him that the ambassador simply did not comprehend that Nazism was an evil to be destroyed.[31] That October, Switzerland granted Germany another major credit to buy arms. By December, the conservative

Neuer Zürcher Zeitung was writing, 'The Jewish Question has become a Jewish slaughter.'

After the 1944 Normandy landings Allied intelligence agents noted a dramatic increase in loot flowing into Switzerland, along with fast-rising gold reserves in the other officially neutral countries of Spain, Turkey, and Sweden. They also noted extra traffic from Spain to Latin America, presumably laden with Nazi treasure. The Allies launched a programme code-named Safehaven to hunt down German property and press neutral countries to reject Nazi loot. Countries were urged to 'take immediate measures' not to receive, store, transfer or conceal illicit wealth.[32]

In September 1944, as the Allies swept through France towards the Swiss border, the Swiss Bankers' Association promised to stop collaborating with the Germans – but only via self-regulation, not with outside monitoring. Britain seemed satisfied, but the Americans were not. The Swiss bankers held firm, and the US stepped up the pressure, but Britain was lukewarm. Tracking Nazi loot certainly was not easy: William Sullivan, British commercial secretary in Berne, reported after months of investigative effort 'the impenetrability of the racket'.[33] However, Britain's stance was even less than lukewarm. 'For Switzerland,' wrote E. H. Bliss, a British official in the Ministry of Economic Warfare, 'cloaking by the Germans is neither illegal nor wrong.' Neutral countries, he argued, were not obliged to surrender German assets unless it could be proven that they were stolen. 'We believe that the neutrals can use the German money to offset their own claims against Germany.'[34] The Americans were stunned.

US Treasury Secretary Henry Morgenthau found he faced resistance from within the US State Department to his efforts to track down Nazi loot hidden by the Swiss. 'Morgenthau suspected,' wrote Tom Bower in his book *Blood Money*, 'that London's influence should not be underestimated.'[35] US and British intelligence agents bickered over the Johann Wehrli Bank, which the Allies knew was a conduit for transferring Nazi assets to Latin America. Britain resisted American efforts to blacklist the bank, which the Americans believed was being protected by Captain Max Binney, Wehrli's son-in-law and the honorary British consul in Lugano.[36] Prime Minister Winston Churchill, in a speech in December 1944, praised Switzerland with 'the greatest right to distinction' as 'a democratic state, standing for freedom in self-defence among her mountains, and in thought, in spite of race, largely on our side'.[37] This may have been true for most Swiss, but absolutely not for their leaders or bankers.

By February 1945 Allied victory seemed inevitable and Switzerland made new concessions, promising to freeze German property and return Nazi loot assets to its original owners. Allied lawyers soon spotted hedges, evasions and loopholes against a background of only gradual enforcement. One Allied lawyer described it as 'more a warning to Germans to hide their wealth and escape future controls'. As the pressure mounted, Switzerland posed Britain a question. Changing Swiss laws and opening banks to a search for heirless assets might mean authorising an investigation of British accounts in Swiss banks. That suggestion, notes Bower, 'was greeted in the British Treasury as "explosive stuff" requiring "great wariness"'. A senior British official warned that interfering in Swiss banking secrets would 'have the effect that British banks will be compelled to reveal the ownership of numbered accounts in certain cases'. Eddie Playfair, a senior UK Treasury official, said Britain should 'go slow on this . . . we don't want to be forced to reveal British banking secrets'. Dingle Foot, a British lawyer, was told in an urgent telegram from London, 'You are not (repeat not) doing anything which would lead to requests for disclosure of information by British banks.'[38]

On 8 March the Swiss signed a wide-ranging agreement with the Allies to stop dealing with the Nazis and to freeze their accounts. But Switzerland was still playing both sides. Three weeks later Swiss officials signed a secret agreement with German officials, to accept three more tons of looted gold, some from melted-down dental fillings and wedding rings from Jews and Gypsies in concentration camps.[39]

After Germany surrendered in May 1945, a long and complex tale unfolded involving American anger, Swiss deceit and stonewalling, and British soft-pedalling. Some in Britain defended indulging the Swiss bankers, arguing that this had kept Switzerland sweet during the conflict. Yet Britain's position did not budge *after* the war. Britain's diplomats, whom James Mann, a senior US Treasury official, called the 'Weak Sisters', continued to undermine threats of sanctions. Mann believed that Britain was seeking Swiss loans – and he was right. A week before negotiations were due to start between Switzerland and the western Allies in Washington, the first one arrived: the Swiss ambassador in London said the loan was for 'ensuring the indulgence of the English government . . . in view of negotiations with the Allies'. France got an even bigger loan, which another Swiss official admitted was made 'to avoid upsetting the French' during the negotiations.

Switzerland never had to hand over the identities of its non-German foreign banking clients, and the procedure for identifying German assets in Switzerland was carried out by a semi-public Swiss office, which delegated much of its work to the banks.[40] A first self-audit by the Swiss Bankers' Association found just 482,000 francs' worth of heirless assets from Nazi victims. In another audit in 1956, under new pressure from Jewish organisations, banks reported 86 accounts valued at 862,000 francs. In the 1990s pressure mounted from American Jews, and another self-audit in 1995 identified 775 foreign accounts worth 38.7 million francs. But the pressure kept mounting. In May 1996 an intrusive independent investigation under former US Federal Reserve chairman Paul Volcker was accepted, and the Swiss parliament agreed to conduct its own investigation. By this time a series of class-action suits were also under way in American courts. The Volcker Commission found another 53,886 accounts with a possible Holocaust connection,[41] and in August 1998 Swiss banks agreed to pay out $1.25 billion to settle the class-action suits. British banking secrets were never revealed. Credit Suisse settled with Estelle Sapir for half a million dollars, after finally discovering her father's account.

Switzerland remains one the world's biggests repositories for dirty money. In 2009 it hosted about $2.1 trillion in offshore accounts owned by non-residents, about half from Europe – this had been $3.1 trillion in 2007 before the global financial crisis.[42] Swiss financial analysts Helvea in 2009 estimated that about 80 per cent of the European money was not declared to the owners' tax authorities;[43] for Italians and for Greeks, that figure rose to 99 per cent.[44]

Rudolf Strahm, a Swiss parliamentarian and leading opponent of bank secrecy, makes an important point for foreign governments trying to stem tax evasion via Switzerland. Because of the offshore centre's strong and venerable roots in Swiss society, politics and history, domestic pressure to restrict secrecy has never succeeded. Foreign pressure aimed directly at the Swiss government has routinely failed too. The successful foreign interventions have been directed against Swiss banks, which have in turn forced changes through domestically. The latest example of this is Switzerland's agreement in 2010 to share information on over 4,000 of UBS's American account holders, after the US government threatened the bank with dire consequences. 'It is no use pressuring the Swiss government,' Strahm said. 'To get change, you must pressure a bank.'[45]

Yet recent claims that these changes have, as *Time* magazine put it in 2010, 'blown the lid off bank secrecy',[46] hide the fact that Switzerland has given up relatively little. The US agreement is ground-breaking, but deals to exchange information with other countries are only applicable under risibly inadequate standards of transparency, which I will explore later. And these changes, modest though they are, have only benefited the citizens of a handful of wealthy countries. Developing nations have been left out of these agreements – as usual.

4

The Opposite of Offshore
John Maynard Keynes and the struggle against financial capital

It was in a strangely defensive tone that Robert Skidelsky, the best-known biographer of John Maynard Keynes, prefaced the American edition of volume three of his biography of the great British economist. He took issue with an accusation by Bradford DeLong, a well-known American economist, that he (Skidelsky) had fallen under the influence of 'a strange and sinister sect of British imperial conservatives'.[1] Skidelsky argued that for Britain the Second World War had been in fact two wars: one pitting Britain under Winston Churchill against Nazi Germany; the other, behind the facade of the western alliance, pitting the British empire, led by John Maynard Keynes, against the United States. America's main war aim after the defeat of the Axis powers, he argued, was to destroy the British empire. 'Churchill fought to preserve Britain and its empire against Nazi Germany; Keynes fought to preserve Britain as a Great Power against the United States. The war against Germany was won; but in its effort to win it, Britain spent its resources so heavily that it was destined to lose both its empire and its Great Power status.'[2]

The arguments are complex, not least because Keynes' main US 1944 Bretton Woods conference negotiating partner, Harry Dexter White, was almost certainly passing information to the Soviet Union. But Skidelsky's account leaves no doubt that the two countries were quietly locked in a titanic struggle for financial dominance. It was only long after the war that the two economic competitors would eventually work out an arrangement. It happened, as I shall explain in the next chapter, through the construction of the modern offshore system.

This chapter explores what came before it: an international system that Keynes helped design, involving close cooperation between nation states and tight control over flows of capital between them. This system was, in a sense, the very opposite of today's fragmented laissez-faire offshore system. And for all its problems, it was a tremendous, resounding success.

Keynes was as complex a character as any that have taken to the world stage. He crammed the lives of twenty people into one. The ageing Alfred Marshall, arguably the leading economist of his generation, once declared after reading a pamphlet by the young economist, 'Verily, we old men will have to hang ourselves, if young people can cut their way so straight and with such apparent ease through such great difficulties.' Keynes first properly made his reputation in 1919 with his world-changing pamphlet *The Economic Consequences of the Peace*. It argued that the vast reparations being heaped on Germany after the First World War would ruin it, and Europe with it, with terrible results. 'The peace is outrageous and impossible,' Keynes wrote, 'and can bring nothing but misfortune behind it.' He was right: the mess laid the foundation for the rise of Adolf Hitler and the Second World War.

Later Keynes began speculating in the famously treacherous terrain of international currencies and commodities, applying himself to this task for just half an hour a day while still in bed.[3] Disdaining the kind of corrupt insider information that was helping drive the 1920s Wall Street boom, and armed with an encyclopedic knowledge of finance and world affairs and of all the neuroses and financial prejudices of those whom he dealt with, he dived instead into company balance sheets and statistics. Of the latter discipline, he wrote, 'nothing except copulation is so enthralling'.[4] It made him a fortune, though he nearly went bust in the process – something that taught him hard lessons about the irrationality of markets.

Years later, while writing his *General Theory of Employment, Interest and Money*, arguably the most famous economics textbook of the last century, Keynes was also building a theatre in Cambridge with his own money, drawing graphs of receipts from the theatre restaurant, collecting tickets when the clerk failed to materialise and, improbably, turning the whole thing into a huge artistic and commercial success.

He married a Russian ballerina and was a respected art critic, a towering civil servant and diplomat, a hyperactive editor of economic journals and a journalist whose articles could make currencies swoon. He wrote a book on mathematical probability that the polymath and philosopher Bertrand Russell said was 'impossible to praise too highly', adding that Keynes' intellect was 'the sharpest and clearest that I have ever known'. Russell felt that when he argued with Keynes he 'took his life into his hands'. His thoughts are profoundly relevant today: sixty-three years after Keynes' death the Nobel prize-winning economist Paul Krugman concluded, in a preliminary post-mortem of the new global economic crisis, 'Keynesian economics remains the best framework we have for making sense of recessions and depressions.' He was, famously, the economist 'who never dipped his headlights' and who noted, late in life, that his only regret was not to have drunk more champagne.

Many biographers, perhaps seeking to bolster Keynes' personal and professional legacy, have airbrushed over aspects of his life they felt society would consider unsavoury. In a raucous letter to his close friend Lytton Strachey Keynes once said he wanted to 'manage a railway or organise a Trust, or at least swindle the investing public'. One biographer, Sir Roy Harrod, replaced 'swindle the investing public' with an ellipsis. Keynes was by no means a swindler, though he was full of mischief, and Strachey delighted Keynes with his unerring ability to shock people out of their Victorian pieties. The two indulged in what Skidelsky called 'a common taste for blasphemy and attractive young men', though Keynes did feel hamstrung by what he himself called his own 'repulsive appearance'. In an era when homosexuality was savagely repressed – even long after Keynes' death gay men were being sentenced to chemical castration – he was perhaps fortunate in belonging for much of his life to the welcoming cultural milieu of Cambridge, where as Keynes said, 'Even the womanisers pretend to be sods, lest they shouldn't be thought respectable.'[5]

Keynes had elitist ways too. He was a core member of the haughty Bloomsbury Group, whose members – at least until the First World War made life difficult – saw themselves as being at the leading edge of British art, philosophy and culture, and engaged in a 'revolt against the Victorians', as one member put it. Although a maverick on an atheist, pacifist sexual merry-go-round, Keynes was also very much a man of the British establishment, at various points a director of the Bank of England, bursar of King's College, Cambridge and a governor of Eton College.

It is ironic, as Robert Heilbroner notes, that while Keynes belonged to Britain's elite, sharing many of its arrogant and sometimes anti-democratic prejudices, it was he who offered – in his *General Theory*, which emerged in the aftermath of the Great Depression of the 1930s – the great hope of alleviating poverty and unemployment for the common man. His recipe, when private-sector investment collapsed, was to bring government temporarily into the equation to fill the gap. It would seem logical, Heilbroner notes, 'that the man who would seek to solve this paradox of not enough production existing side by side with men fruitlessly seeking work would be a Left-Winger, an economist with strong sympathies for the proletariat, an angry man. Nothing could be further from the truth.'

Since his death, his critics have repeatedly sought to associate his ideas with socialism or communism. When the first Keynesian intro-ductory textbook was published in 1947, a right-wing campaign in the United States got many universities to cancel their orders, and one conservative ideologist, William F. Buckley, attacked those who adopted the book for propounding 'evil ideas'. Most recently, oppo-nents of Barack Obama have claimed that his Keynesian attempts to resuscitate the US economy through deficit-financed public works constitute a Soviet-style takeover of the free enterprise system. But Keynes was never the socialist of the conservative imagination. He loathed Marx and Engels; he saw government intervention as a tempor-ary fix and believed passionately in markets and trade as the best routes to prosperity. 'I am in favour,' he wrote, 'of retaining as much private judgment and initiative and enterprise as possible.' He wanted to save capitalism, not bury it.

Most critics of Keynes don't realise that they themselves have come to embrace a great many of his assumptions, even as they purport to be scandalised by his ideas and his lifestyle. Indeed, the American economy has been committed to vast taxpayer supplements to private investment since the late 1940s. As the economist Paul Krugman put it in 2005, echoing the words of Richard Nixon in 1965, 'We are all Keynesians now.'

*   *   *

For much of the nineteenth century free traders had held sway: it was self-evident, many people thought, that free trade delivered prosperity *and* brought peace, by increasing economic entanglements between nations and creating interdependencies that made it harder to wage war. It was a bit like an argument memorably made in the 1990s by Thomas Friedman, who said that no two countries with a McDonald's – that symbol of free trade and the 'Washington Consensus' – had ever fought a war with each other. (That ended in March 1999, when NATO forces bombed Belgrade.) Keynes was a firm believer – for a while. 'I was brought up, like most Englishmen, to respect free trade,' he wrote in the *Yale Review* in 1933, 'almost as a part of the moral law. I regarded ordinary departures from it as being at the same time an imbecility and an outrage.'[6]

When two parties trade goods with each other it is more or less a meeting of equals. But Keynes understood that finance is different. With finance, the lender and the borrower are in a hierarchy. James Carville, Bill Clinton's adviser, famously articulated this when he said that if reincarnated he wanted to come back as the bond market, because then 'you can intimidate everybody'. Industrial capitalists are subservient to financial capitalists, and their interests often conflict. Financiers, for instance, like high interest rates, from which they can derive considerable income; but industrialists want low interest rates, to curb their costs. Keynes agreed, but added a perspective. Financial entanglements between nations do not necessarily safeguard international peace. In 1933, an era of soup kitchens, suicidal brokers and massive, system-wide unemployment, his views were transformed. 'It is easier, in the light of experience and foresight, to argue quite the contrary.' 'Let goods be homespun whenever it is reasonably and conveniently possible,' he wrote. 'Above all, let finance be primarily national.'

The Great Depression that had started in 1929 was the culmination of a long period of deregulation and economic freedom and a great bull market built on an orgy of debt and mind-bending economic inequality. In the late throes of the boom the richest 24,000 Americans, for example, received 630 times as much income on average as the poorest six million families,[7] and the top 1 per cent of people received nearly a quarter of all the income – a proportion slightly greater than the inequalities at the onset of the global crisis in 2007. 'We have involved ourselves in a colossal muddle,' Keynes wrote, 'having blundered in the control of a delicate machine, the working of which we do not understand.' The similarities with our current situation can hardly be missed.

In those days there was no coherent, interconnected offshore system to speak of. What existed instead were a few foreign jurisdictions that wealthy elites used to hide their wealth and income from their tax authorities. Rich Europeans looked primarily to Switzerland, while wealthy Britons tended to use strategies focused on the nearby Channel Islands and the Isle of Man. A letter in 1937 from Henry Morgenthau, then US Treasury secretary, offers a flavour of what wealthy Americans were doing.[8] 'Dear Mr President,' it begins. 'This preliminary report discloses conditions so serious that immediate action is called for.' American tax evaders had set up foreign personal holding corporations in places where 'taxes are low and corporation laws lax' – he singled out the Bahamas, Panama and Newfoundland, Britain's oldest colony. 'The stock-holders have resorted to all manner of devices to prevent the acquisition of information regarding their companies. The companies are frequently organized through foreign lawyers, with dummy incorporators and dummy directors, so that the names of the real parties in interest do not appear.'

Although extremely rudimentary by modern standards, the schemes Morgenthau outlined would be familiar to followers of today's offshore shenanigans. 'The ordinary salaried man and the small merchant does not resort to these or similar devices. Legalized avoidance or evasion by the so-called leaders of the business community . . . throws an additional burden upon other members of the community who are less able to bear it, and who are already cheerfully bearing their fair share.'

Despite the differences between then and now, Keynes still offered penetrating insights that help us understand the offshore system. They are also eerily prescient in the light of the recent global economic crisis.

Investment in factories, training, research, wages and so on – the things that make society richer – are one thing. Financial investments and capital are quite another. It is often assumed that when one company buys another, some kind of capital investment is taking place. Most of the time, though, these purchases may have nothing to do with new real investment at all. When a company or government sells bonds or shares, investors hand over money in exchange for pieces of paper that give the holder title to a future stream of income. When bonds or shares are *first* issued, savings are mobilised, funds are raised, and they flow into productive investment. This is generally healthy. Next, however, a secondary market appears, where these shares and bonds are traded. These trades do not directly contribute to productive investment; they merely shuffle ownership. Well over 95 per cent of purchases in global markets today consist of this kind of secondary activity, rather than in real investment.

And Keynes explained what happens when you start to separate real business operations from their owners – the holders of these pieces of paper – and especially when this happens across borders. 'When the same principle is applied internationally,' Keynes, continued, 'it is, in times of stress, intolerable – I am irresponsible towards what I own, and those who operate what I own are irresponsible towards me.' There may be some theoretical calculation showing that shuffling pieces of paper around the world according to market supply and demand is efficient, Keynes said. 'But experience is accumulating that remoteness between ownership and operation is an evil in the relations among men, likely or certain in the long run to set up strains and enmities which will bring to nought the financial calculation.'

His words are more apt than ever in a world where credit derivatives and other financial engineering have caused economic chaos, by placing ingenious but impenetrable barriers between investors and the assets they own. Vast mortgage and credit-card debts have been packaged into great clouds of financial candyfloss, then repackaged and resold down chains of investors across the world, each more distant than the last from the coal faces of real people and businesses. Shuffling ownership of bits of paper ought, in theory, to help capital flow to those projects that offer the highest risk-weighted returns. Good projects should get financed. A little speculative trading in these markets improves information and smooths prices. But when the volume of this dealing is a hundred times bigger than the underlying volume of trade, the result has proved to be a catastrophe.

The offshore system, applying a sort of super-lubricant to the flow of capital around the world in the name of efficiency, dramatically widens this chasm inside capitalism. As we have discovered since 2007, the system was wildly inefficient. Consider the wealth destroyed and the costs heaped on the shoulders of taxpayers. And that is not to mention the other generators of remoteness and artificiality that lurk offshore: secrecy and the complexity that offshore generates as corporations distribute their financial affairs around the world's tax havens. Tax havens then deepen the remoteness still further, by shielding investors against other nations' laws and regulations.

Offshore prevents effective oversight of financial markets, makes crises more likely and enables rich insiders to shift all the risks and the costs of bailouts onto the working majority and away from the investing minority. The efficiency that boosters of the offshore system claim for themselves is bogus. Capital no longer flows to where it gets the best return, but to where it can secure the best tax subsidies, the deepest secrecy, and to where it can best evade the laws, rules and regulations it does not like. None of these attractions has anything to do with allocating capital more efficiently. Keynes was quite right.

With this in mind, we can now turn to one of Keynes' greatest feats: the construction of a new world order after the Second World War, the antithesis of the offshore system.

When the Second World War came Keynes was sent to Washington to negotiate with the Americans. He came to realise he had a job on his hands: most Americans were rather more hostile to Britain than he had supposed. Roosevelt, notes Skidelsky, hated the British empire, mistrusted England's aristocracy, and 'suspected the Foreign Office of pro-fascist tendencies'.[9] After the collapse of the credit bubble in the 1920s and the Great Depression that followed, Americans had fairly effectively chained and muzzled Wall Street, and many regarded the more lightly regulated City of London – the true epicentre of the hated British empire – with deep suspicion. Britain was discriminating against American goods in international trade, and Roosevelt's Republican opponents were horrified at the prospect of entanglement in another foreign war. Why help Britain again, many asked, after Britain had snared America into entering the First World War, then refused to pay its war debts *and* hung onto its empire? After the British army was forced into a humiliating retreat from Dunkirk in 1940, some in Wahington were also reluctant to back what looked like a lost cause.

Although global economic heft had already shifted decisively across the Atlantic from London to New York, Britain still held India by force, along with much of Africa and the Middle East, and it refused to be pushed around. Keynes' combative and too-clever-by-half style fitted American stereotypes of the British as super-wily imperial puppeteers, ready to bamboozle them at the first chance. When Keynes first met US Treasury secretary Henry Morgenthau, no lover of technicalities, he spoke for an hour, in great detail. Morgenthau 'did not understand one word', a Washington insider later wrote to a friend, until someone 'wrote it all down in words of one syllable and read it out to Henry, who understood it perfectly'.[10] Harry Hopkins, one of Roosevelt's advisers, called Keynes 'one of those fellows that just knows all the answers'.

Keynes' problem was this: America wanted Britain to fight fascism, and it gave huge military aid under its Lend-Lease Act of March 1941. But at the same time Americans wanted to dethrone Britain and its empire once and for all. As Keynes wrote later, the US administration took every possible precaution to see that the British were 'as near as possible bankrupt before any assistance was given'. Britain's chief aim, by contrast, was 'the retention by us of enough assets to leave us capable of independent action'.[11]

It was a gruelling war for Keynes, and a decidedly unequal contest. 'Why do you persecute us like this?' he once asked his American counterparts.[12] He was seriously ill, diagnosed with septic tonsils and a 'large heart and aorta', and he was representing an empire on its knees. 'When Keynes disagreed with [his American counterpart Harry Dexter] White,' the American economist Brad DeLong wrote, 'he usually lost the point because of the greater power of the United States. And in almost every case it seems to me that Keynes was probably right.'[13]

What Keynes was negotiating in Washington was the construction of a new cooperative international monetary order to govern relations between the countries of the world. It drew upon the experience of the rampant international capitalism that had preceded and created the Great Depression, as private and central bankers, led by Wall Street and the City of London, had sought to restore the laissez-faire pre-1914 financial order in which they had been so prominent, an order that had involved freely floating currencies, balanced government budgets and free flows of capital around the world – a little like the modern global financial system.

The Great Depression had destroyed their dream and thoroughly discredited the liberal financial order. 'The decadent international but individualistic capitalism,' Keynes wrote, 'is not a success. It is not intelligent, it is not beautiful, it is not just, it is not virtuous – and it doesn't deliver the goods. In short, we dislike it, and we are beginning to despise it.' At the Bretton Woods Conference in 1944, the culmination of a global negotiating marathon which would shape the international financial architecture for decades, Morgenthau said that the aim must be 'to drive the usurious money-lenders from the temple of international finance'.[14]

The conference involved a multitude of nations but was something of an American stitch-up: the US Treasury stage-managed the drafting committees and the conference to produce the result the Americans wanted. Commission chairmen would, as Harry Dexter White put it, 'prevent a vote' on anything they didn't want voted on, and would 'arrange the discussion' to stop inconvenient topics from being aired.[15] Negotiators from other nations largely sat on the sidelines. It was hard to see what the international 'monkey house' of delegations would *do*, Keynes archly commented. 'Acute alcohol poisoning would set in before the end.'

Keynes was not able to form the new World Bank, and especially the International Monetary Fund, in the image he hoped for. He had hoped that the IMF would become a de-politicised institution, overseeing mechanisms by which global financing imbalances would resolve themselves automatically, removing politics – and raw American power – from the equation as far as possible. He didn't want the institutions sited in Washington either, for the same reasons. But his efforts came to nothing, and when these matters were decided at a subsequent meeting in 1946, Keynes said acidly that he hoped 'there is no malicious fairy, no Carabosse, whom he has overlooked and forgotten to ask to the party'. Fred Vinson, a top US negotiator who was probably the target of that remark, was heard to say, 'I don't mind being called malicious – but I do mind being called a fairy.'[16]

The outcome would have been still worse for Britain, however, without Keynes' astonishing powers. 'This is the most extraordinary creature I have ever listened to,' one obviously spellbound Canadian official said after watching Keynes speak. 'Does he belong to our species? There is something mythic and fabulous about him. I sense in him something massive and sphinx-like, and yet also a hint of wings.'[17] When a sick Keynes shuffled tiredly into the grand banquet at the end of the Bretton Woods conference, the hundreds of assembled guests stood up and waited, in deep silence, until he had taken his seat.

Many people today see the IMF and World Bank – children of the Bretton Woods conference – as the handmaidens of globalisation, unfettered trade and capital flows, and the instrument of Wall Street bankers. This was not the original idea. Keynes set out to build a completely different system – almost the exact antithesis of today's world of free capital flows wired-through offshore centres. Keynes wanted a world of open trade, but he believed that the free movement of goods would only be possible if finance remained tightly regulated by government. If not, surges of flighty capital would generate recurrent crises that would hamper growth, disrupt and discredit trade, possibly driving fragile European economies into the arms of the communists. As he had noticed, there is a basic tension between democracy, on the one hand, and free capital movements, on the other. In a world of free capital flows, if you try to lower interest rates to boost struggling local industries, say, capital will drain overseas in search of higher returns. Investors hold veto power over national governments and the real lives of millions of people are determined by what the Indian economist Prabhat Patnaik has called 'a bunch of speculators'. Demand management by governments is replaced by uncontrolled bubbles and busts. Freedom for financial capital means less freedom for countries to set their own economic policies: from this particular kind of freedom, a form of bondage emerges.

Keynes' answer was simple and powerful: control the flow of capital across borders. Capital controls had first emerged in the First World War. Governments had sought to stop capital fleeing their countries in order to be able to tax capital income and keep interest rates low, so as to finance their war efforts. Controls evaporated after the war then returned partially during the Great Depression, and finally swept the world after the Second World War and the Bretton Woods arrangements. They slowly became leaky, and then were progressively dismantled around the world from about the 1970s. The United States got rid of its most important controls in 1974.

Capital controls can be hard to imagine for those who have not experienced them. Professor Sol Picciotto once showed me his old passport, which has a section headed 'Foreign Exchange Facilities – Private Travel'. It is covered with official stamps and signatures. To get foreign exchange for overseas trips, you needed official permission. Companies had to get permission too to shift money across borders. It is a system that seems almost unthinkable today. What capital controls did was to loosen the link between domestic and foreign economic policies, providing governments with room to pursue other objectives like the maintenance of full employment. Instead of having limits put on democracy by the whims of flighty speculators and financiers, Keynes' answer was limit the international mobility of capital.

Geoff Tily, author of a book on Keynes, believes the main reason he supported capital controls was his belief that interest rates should be set and held low. This would place Keynes firmly on the side of the industrialist (for whom interest payments are a cost) against the financier (for whom interest payments are income).[18] As Keynes put it, 'Control of capital movements should be a permanent feature of the post-war system.' Finance should be the society's servant, not its master. The Bretton Woods plan, for all its faults, did just that.

This helps us to see how very far we have now travelled from the system created by Keynes and White. Dismantling capital contols is one thing, but we have now taken a full step again beyond that, into a world where capital is not only free to flow across borders, but is actively and artificially encouraged to move, lured by any number of offshore attractions: secrecy, evasion of prudential banking regulations, zero taxes and so on. A pin-striped infrastructure of lawyers, accountants and bankers has emerged, all with a vested interest in accelerating the flows and deepening the perverse incentives. Keynes would be horrified.

There is something else relevant here which is rather less well known.

Mainstream economics today embraces a simple theory that goes something like this. Poor countries lack capital and foreign investment can fill the gap, so it makes sense to free up capital, to let it flow into these capital-starved countries. This seems like a very good idea on the face of it, but what mainstream theory has failed seriously to address is that if you free up capital, money might not necessarily flow in; it might, instead, flow *out*. Keynes was well aware of this problem. 'Advisable domestic policies might often be easier to compass, if the phenomenon known as "the flight of capital" could be ruled out,' he said. Chillingly prescient words, for capital flight in his day was as nothing when compared to the mind-bending amounts that flood across borders today.

Even in the post-war world of tight capital controls, there was leakage. Multinational companies needed permission to move investment capital overseas but had much more freedom when moving money for current purposes – for financing trade and other day-to-day business. Of course, you could easily disguise a capital payment as a current one. But Keynes and Harry Dexter White had an answer. 'What is often forgotten,' the Canadian scholar Eric Helleiner notes, 'is that Keynes and White addressed this with a further proposal. They argued that controls on capital would be more effective if the countries receiving that flight assisted in their enforcement.'[19] In the earliest drafts of the Bretton Woods agreements, both Keynes and White required the governments of countries receiving flight capital to share information with the victims of flight. Without the lure of secrecy, far less capital would flee. In short, they wanted transparency in international finance. Enter the American bankers and their lobbyists.

US banks had profited hugely from handling European flight capital in the 1930s and – fearing that transparency would hurt New York's allure – they gutted the proposals. While early drafts of the IMF's articles of association 'required' cooperation on capital flight, the final version saw that word replaced with 'permitted'. And through that one-word gateway drove a great, silent procession of coaches and horses across the Atlantic, laden with treasure from a shattered Europe.

The capital flight that ensued was as bad as Keynes and White had feared. A US government analysis in June 1947, while admitting that it saw only part of the picture, found that Europeans held $4.3 billion in private assets, an enormous amount in those days and far bigger than America's jumbo post-war loan to Britain that year. American bankers were thrilled. And a new economic crisis exploded

in Europe. America filled the hole with aid: the giant Marshall Plan
of 1948. It is widely believed that the plan worked by offsetting
European countries' yawning deficits. But its real importance, Eric
Helleiner argues, was 'simply to compensate for the US failure to
institute controls on inflows of hot money from Europe'. Even in
1953 the authoritative *New York Times* correspondent Michael Hoffman
noted that American post-war aid was less than the money flowing
in the other direction.[20]

Henry Cabot Lodge, a Republican senator, noticed the stink. 'There
is a small, bloated, selfish class of people whose assets have been spread
all over the place,' he said. 'People of moderate means in this country
are being taxed to support a foreign aid program which the well-to-
do people abroad are not helping to support.'[21] His words would be
painfully familiar today to citizens of Argentina, Mexico, Indonesia,
Russia and so many other nations who have watched powerlessly while
local elites mount raids on their countries' wealth and collude with
Western financiers and businessmen to hide it offshore and avoid
paying tax on their income. The Marshall Plan set an ominous precedent – American taxpayers would foot the bill for policies that delighted
Wall Street and its clients. What was presented as enlightened self-
interest was substantially a racket, in the precise sense of a fraud,
facilitated by public ignorance. As we shall soon see, the rackets have
multiplied ever since.

When Keynes died in April 1946, less than a year after the Nazis
surrendered in Europe, the accolades poured in. 'He has given his
life for his country, as surely as if he had fallen on the field of battle,'
said Lionel Robbins, one of his most potent ideological adversaries.
Friedrich Hayek, Robbins' former pupil, who was just then fathering
a new free-market ideology to dethrone Keynesianism, called him
'the one really great man I ever knew'. Though Keynes had failed
in many ways, many things he advocated were in place, not least
the widespread use of capital controls, in pursuit of states' freedoms
to choose their own domestic economic policies. And events seem
to have proved him right – or at least not wrong. The first two years
after the war marked a brief period when US financial interests
dominated policymaking, and the restrictive international order was
in abeyance. It was a disaster, leading to a new economic crisis in

1947. This discredited the bankers, and the following year things became more restrictive.[22]

The quarter-century that followed from around 1949, in which Keynes' ideas were widely implemented, is now known as the golden age of capitalism, an era of widespread, fast-rising and relatively untroubled prosperity. It was memorably summarised by British Prime Minister Harold Macmillan, who noted in 1957 that 'most of our people have never had it so good'. From 1950 to 1973 annual growth rates amid widespread capital controls (and extremely high tax rates) averaged 4.0 per cent in America and 4.6 in Europe. It was not just rich countries that enjoyed steady, rapid growth: as the Cambridge economist Ha-Joon Chang notes, the per capita income of developing countries grew by a full 3.0 per cent per year in the 1960s and 1970s, amid widespread capital controls – far faster than the rate since then.[23] In the 1980s, as capital controls were progressively relaxed around the world and as tax rates fell and the offshore system really began to flower, growth rates fell sharply. 'Financial globalisation has not generated increased investment or higher growth in emerging markets,' top-ranking economists Arvind Subramanian and Dani Rodrik explained in 2008. 'Countries that have grown most rapidly have been those that rely least on capital inflows.'[24]

Average growth is one thing, but to get an idea of how well most people are doing, you need to look at inequality too. In the offshore era, from the mid-1970s onwards, inequality has exploded in country after country. According to the US Federal Bureau of Labor Statistics, the average American non-supervisory worker actually earned a lower hourly wage in 2006, adjusted for inflation, than in 1970. Meanwhile, the pay of American CEOs rose from under thirty times the average worker's wage to almost 300 times. This is not just a story about growth and inequality either. Another study found that between 1940 and 1971, roughly the time of the golden age, developing countries suffered *no* banking crises and only sixteen currency crises; but in the quarter-century after 1973 there were seventeen banking crises and fifty-seven currency crises – not to mention a cavalcade of other economic disasters. Longer-dated historical research bears this out too: a major new study in 2009 by the economists Carmen Reinhardt and Kenneth Rogoff, looking back over 800 years of economic history, concluded that, as their reviewer Martin

Wolf put it, 'financial liberalisation and financial crises go together like a horse and carriage'.[25]

We must be cautious about inferring too much from these facts. Other reasons exist for the high growth rates during the golden age, not least post-war rebuilding stimulated by massive government demand and productivity improvements during the war. The 1970s oil shock surely goes some of the way towards explaining the subsequent slide into crisis and stagnation.

However, less drastic, but still powerful, conclusions do emerge. The golden age shows that it is quite possible for countries, and the world economy, to grow quickly and steadily while under the influence of widespread and even bureaucratic curbs on the flow of capital. China today – which carefully and bureaucratically restricts inward and outward investment and other flows of capital – is growing rapidly.[26] Clearly such controls, unfashionable for so many years, ought to be a policy option. In fact, mainstream thinking on this is, at last, shifting a little. In February 2010 the IMF issued a paper[27] arguing that capital controls are sometimes 'justified as part of the policy toolkit' for an economy seeking to deal with surging inflows. Most of the time countries can, as Keynes believed, get by with their own domestic credit systems and localised capital markets, without exposing themselves to killer waves of global offshore finance. The basis for Keynes' fears – the waves of hot money that constrained national governments – are even more important today than they were in his day.

What has happened since the 1970s is not simply a return to free movement of capital, but financial liberalisation on steroids: the offshore system that tore financial controls apart from the 1970s onwards has served both as an accelerator for flighty financial capital, and also as a distorting field, bending capital flows so that they end up not where they necessarily find the most productive investment, but where they can find the greatest secrecy, the most lax regulations and freedom from the rules of civilised society. It seems sensible to take our foot off the accelerator.

In the years after Keynes' death, even as his ideas became orthodoxy among policymakers, a resurgent liberalism sought to destroy their credibility. By 1980, the Chicago economist Robert Lucas could write that they were so ridiculous that 'at research seminars, people don't take Keynesian theorizing seriously anymore; the audience starts to whisper and giggle to one another'. The assault on Keynes in academia was one thing, and is well known. Parallel with this was something that emerged first in the City of London, and was then embraced by Wall Street. Ideology mixed liberally with cash would create the conditions for the creation of a new world of offshore.

5

Eurodollar: The Bigger Bang

The Eurodollar markets, the banks and the great escape

As the Bretton Woods system got properly under way in the 1950s, the US economy was growing nicely and citizens across the country were buying refrigerators and televisions for the first time. Wall Street was tied down with any number of regulations, many of them dating from the period after the Great Depression. Democratically elected politicians had tamed the bankers, and Wall Street began to search around for escape routes from the tight domestic constraints. They found their way out in London.

Some time in the mid-1950s, a new strain of offshore activity was noticed in the City of London. Nobody quite agrees when the unusual activity started, but it was probably first spotted in June 1955 by staffers at the the Bank of England, who noticed some odd trades going on at the Midland Bank, now part of the globe-trotting HSBC.[1] At the time Keynes' ideas were reigning supreme in the markets, based on his recognition that setting global finance free would tether nations in different forms of bondage. Exchange rates were mostly fixed, banks were not supposed to trade in foreign currencies unless it was for the purpose of financing specific trades for their clients and not allowed to take deposits in foreign currencies, and governments were tightly controlling how fast financial capital could flow in and out of their economies.

The Midland Bank was contravening exchange controls by taking US dollar deposits that were not related to its commercial transactions. What is more, the Midland was offering interest rates on dollar deposits that were substantially higher than those permitted by US regulations.

A Bank of England official called in Midland's chief foreign manager for a chat. Afterwards, he noted that the Midland official 'appreciates that a warning light has been shown'.[2] In those days regulation typically consisted of being invited to the Bank of England for tea, where an eyebrow would be raised in your direction if you were out of line. Luckily for the Midland, Britain was struggling to shore up its shaky foreign exchange reserves and the Bank of England was reluctant to snuff out a new area of international business. 'We would be wise, I believe, not to press the Midland any further,' it concluded.[3]

The City of London was the epitome of the British old boys' network, bound by elaborate rules and rituals. Discount brokers wore top hats, and every evening, during the rush hour, a platoon of guardsmen would march through the City in scarlet tunics and bearskins. 'A banker could show his disapproval of sharp practice by crossing the road,' wrote Anthony Sampson in the 2005 edition of his *Who Runs Britain?* 'Behind all the conventions lay the assumption of a club based on common values and integrity. It was a club which could easily work against the interests of the public or outside shareholders, through insider trading and secret deals; and it was based on cartels which could exclude competitors and newcomers. But it was also quite effective.'[4] A firm handshake was often enough to secure a man's credit. 'A great deal of business,' remarked Jo Grimond, the leader of the Liberal Party, 'is done without all the paraphernalia of memoranda, conferences, contracts, and so forth.'[5]

In fact, members of this informal club had already found pathways around exchange controls. 'Nobody but small fry,' remarked one top official, 'takes any notice of exchange controls now.' At the more roguish end of the City, bankers were up to some of their old tricks, more or less tolerated by the Bank of England. One favourite was bond washing: a high-taxpayer would sell a bond just before it was due to pay a coupon, then buy it back afterwards at a lower price, creating a tax-free capital gain. The momentary owner who received the coupon would be someone else, typically offshore, who through one wheeze or another could avoid the tax on it. Bond washing was, a Bank of England official noted drily, 'common talk in all the bars in Switzerland'.[6] A Bank of England director, caught cabling a co-conspirator in Hong Kong to 'anticipate tighter money' just ahead of a swingeing rise in official interest rates, caused hilarity when, pressed by a commission of inquiry to explain what was said and when, pleaded, 'It is difficult for me to remember the exact timing of conversation on a grouse moor.'[7]

Yet despite these occasional thrills, the City of London was deep in slumber. 'By Thursday afternoon at four,' an American banker remembered,[8] 'one of the senior partners would come across to the juniors and say, "Why are we all still here? It's almost the weekend."' Oliver Franks, a chairman of Lloyds Bank, compared it to driving a powerful car at twenty miles per hour. 'The banks were anaesthetised,' Franks said. 'It was a kind of dream life.'

It is hard now to imagine those days, an era when bankers fumed impotently at politicians' mighty powers. Those few years after the Second World War were the only time in several hundred years when politicians had any kind of control over the banking sector. Before the bankers slammed the political shutters down, the politicians had sneaked in the National Health Service, which, for all its faults, has been one of the country's most popular institutions ever since. A letter of the late 1940s captures the mood. Lord Harlech, a member of the Midland Bank board, was responding to a speech by the left-wing president of the Board of Trade, Sir Stafford Cripps.

I decline to receive in future copies of his or his typical colleague that swine Dalton's speeches. In the interests of their political and personal ambition & venom against the interests of the Empire, commerce, industry & all fair play, these two enemies of all we stand for at the Midland Bank are the two worst elements in this bloody government and I seek your protection against such missives.[9]

Hugh Dalton was Britain's Labour chancellor of the exchequer in a government that had just nationalised the Bank of England, and plenty more besides. Dalton loved to quote Keynes' dictum that low interest rates would lead to 'euthanasia of the *rentier*' – with *rentier* defined as a 'functionless investor' who does not roll up his sleeves and grow a real business but instead merely watches while his existing capital grows through someone else's toil. This is a notion I am wearily familiar with, having spent years watching oil-rich African dictators and their retinues grow super-rich from valuable minerals that can be almost effortlessly removed from the ground.

Keynes' saying underlines the generic and profound tensions that have always existed between financial and *rentier* capitalism on the one hand, and industry on the other. As I have noted, high interest rates can be very profitable for bankers – among other things, they help suck in foreign money chasing higher returns – but they mean expensive borrowing and currency appreciation for real productive businesses, making their goods more expensive relative to their foreign competitors'. So when Dalton declared that he 'must be on the side of the active producer, as against the passive *rentier*,' he set himself squarely against the bankers.

While all this was happening, another radical challenge to Keynes was being incubated in Switzerland, then the world's pre-eminent tax haven. In April 1947 Albert Hunold, a senior Credit Suisse official,[10] brought together thirty-six scholars at the pretty Swiss resort of Mont Pèlerin near Geneva to plan for a revival of liberalism (in modern parlance, neoliberalism) under the guidance of Friedrich Hayek, an Austrian liberal economist who had published a best-selling polemic against socialism and big government entitled *The Road to Serfdom*. The Mont Pèlerin Society that emerged from that meeting would become the foundation of the global intellectual fightback against Keynes.[11] 'We must raise and train an army of fighters for freedom,' Hayek said, 'to work out, in continuous effort, a philosophy of freedom.' One of the attendees was the American economist Milton Friedman, whose subsequent work inspired Margaret Thatcher and Ronald Reagan. It was, Richard Cockett wrote in his book *Thinking the Unthinkable*, 'a remarkable gathering, from which much of the intellectual revival of economic liberalism would flow'. From the start the Mont Pelerin Society was funded by the three biggest Swiss banks and two largest insurance companies, not to mention the Swiss central bank.[12]

'Imagine you are Albert Hunold; you are Hayek,' explained Sébastien Guex of the University of Lausanne in Switzerland, close to Mont Pèlerin.

You are confronted with a world that is desolated; the Nazis are gone. During the war the British and American bourgeoisies mobilised lots of poor people and workers, who shed their blood on the battlefields of Europe, and they need to be given something in return. Attlee and Roosevelt are in power;

France is in a semi-revolutionary state; in Italy the Communist Party has two million members. You will not want to go to Franco's Spain. You will not go to Belgium, the Netherlands or Portugal. You will regroup where? Costa Rica?

'You want good air links, good hotels and a bourgeoisie that is sympathetic to you. I know of only one country – Switzerland. It remained liberal throughout the 1930s, and through the war. Switzerland has a big newspaper – the *Neue Zürcher Zeitung*, which represents your ideas. Switzerland has no workers' movement that will put you on the defensive, no integrated movement that will put a spanner in the wheels.

From the start, the Mont Pelerin Society had strong links to the City of London, via Sir Alfred Suenson-Taylor, later Lord Grantchester, chairman of a major insurance company in the City of London and brother of a British Conservative member of parliament. Suenson-Taylor not only provided a welcome link to a network of wealthy anti-government City financiers, but he also helped unlock Bank of England funds to support British delegations to the Mont Pelerin Society meetings.[13] To actively support an overtly anti-government movement is a curious role for a central bank, but that was not the only peculiar thing about it.

The Bank of England had been set up 250 years earlier as a club of wealthy City of London banks, and it was only in 1946, during Keynesianism's brief dominance after the horrors of war and the Great Depression, that the politicians had the political strength to nationalise it. Even after nationalisation, however, the politicians could not control it. The government could not dismiss the bank's governor, and the Bank still kept its internal operations shrouded in secrecy. To this day the bank has continued to draw top officials directly from private financial services companies in the City of London, in a constantly revolving door. A British Treasury paper in 1956 concluded that nationalisation did not represent 'any fundamental change or break' with the past. Keynes had called the Bank of England 'a private institution practically independent of any form of legal control',[14] and after nationalisation, it seems, not much changed.

The Bank of England has also remained a powerful lobbyist within the British state, a sort of praetorian guard protecting the City of

London and its libertarian world view – and by extension the global offshore system. As academic writer Gary Burn puts it, the bank has been 'the single most powerful repository for liberal thought in Britain'.[15] Burn was almost right: there is one like-minded institution that has been even more powerful – the Corporation of London, which we shall meet later.

By 1955, as Midland executed its unusual dollar trades, it was becoming increasingly evident that Britain's formal empire was crumbling. India had secured independence in 1947; communist guerrillas were attacking British colonialists in Malaya; Egypt had broken free; civil war was breaking out in Sudan; and Ghana was preparing for independence. In July 1956, just over a year after the Bank of England had started noticing Midland's activities, Egyptian president Gamal Abdel Nasser nationalised the Suez Canal. The remnants of the imperial establishment in London were horrified, and not just because Britain was the largest holder of shares in the Suez Canal Company. Nasser had challenged the position of the British and the French throughout the Middle East and in the wider world. Britain and France, trying to adjust to their less magisterial post-war roles in world affairs but still driven by imperial-era motivations and arrogance, joined Israel in a three-sided invasion.

It was a colossal mistake. The United States was determined not to permit European imperialism to drive the Arab world into an alliance with the Soviet Union, and refused to help in the face of a dramatic run on the pound, which cost Britain $450 million in reserves just between 20 October and 8 December.[16] Britain was almost bankrupt and had no choice but to retreat. The country had not been so badly humiliated since the fall of Singapore. 'It marked, with brutal clarity, the end of Britain as a world power,' said David Kynaston, historian of the City of London. Months later, Kwame Nkrumah rolled up the Union Jack in Ghana and bid farewell to the British – and the whole termite-infested British imperial edifice began to collapse.

By 1965, an empire that had ruled over 700 million foreigners at the end of the Second World War had shrunk to a population of just five million. This is well known; but there is a financial side to this story which almost nobody knows about, for out of the dust and fire of Suez something new emerged in London, which would eventually grow to replace the old empire, and raise the City of London to even greater financial glories.

At the time of Suez, London's role as a financial centre was based primarily on the empire-based currency zone, whose member countries banked in London and used the pound as their own currency or pegged their currencies to it. Inside the zone, trade and capital could flow quite freely, and strenuous efforts were taken to control reserves leaking out. It was, as Keynes' biographer Robert Skidelsky put it, 'a mutual benefit society in a chaotic world'.

Even as late as 1957, the pound sterling still financed about 40 per cent of world trade, and the Bank of England wanted it to stay that way.[17] 'UK policy,' said George Bolton, a top bank official, 'remains firmly directed towards the maintenance and the growth of the use of sterling as an international currency.'[18] Yet with the empire crumbling and sterling – then fixed against the US dollar at $2.80 = £1.00 – starting to totter, this role was in great peril. 'We have inherited an old family business which used to be very profitable and sound,' Britain's prime minister remarked at the end of 1956. 'The liabilities are four times the assets . . . I do not know who will now buy the Sterling Area banking system.'[19] It was almost too much for the whiskery old gentlemen capitalists in London to bear, but it was at that moment that something really new began to emerge.

Britain's chancellor wanted to stop capital draining away by curbing banks' overseas lending. Yet the Bank of England, hating to see London bankers' business squeezed, had quite another idea for rebalancing Britain's tottering imbalances: ramp up interest rates, so as to attract new money to London and to squash consumption and demand for imports – and if that tipped Britain into recession, well, so be it. It was a classic example of the perennial conflict between financial capital, on the one hand, and democratically elected politicians and other economic sectors, on the other. Prime Minister Harold Macmillan found to his surprise that there was nothing at all in the 1946 act of nationalisation that allowed him to force the Bank of England to change course, so he threatened to change the law to give him that control and to issue direct orders to the banks. It was probably at this moment that he learned who really held the reins of economic power.

Lord Cobbold, governor of the Bank of England, in a stormy speech asserted that he, and only he, had the power to direct the banks.[20]

Not only that, but he threatened to bankrupt the government if they tried anything. Eventually, Macmillan gave in. 'Sterling was saved without any inconvenience to the City,' wrote Gary Burn. 'The Bank had won its battle with the Treasury.'[21] Yet Macmillan did win one concession. The government could apply curbs on lending in pounds sterling by the London merchant banks, for whom this international trade was a lifeblood. The move was a death blow for them, or at least so it seemed, but in fact all that happened was that they shifted their international lending away from sterling and into dollars. And the Bank of England did it not to try stop this new business. It decided not to regulate it either. It simply deemed the transactions not to take place in the UK for regulatory purposes. And, since this trading did in reality happen inside British sovereign space, no other authority from elsewhere was allowed to regulate it either. The private bankers had found an escape route from the close confinement imposed on them after the Second World War.

In those crisis-ridden days the Bank of England was heavily influenced by the flamboyant and bull-headed George Bolton. In his own way, the historian David Kynaston said, Bolton was 'one of the intellectual godfathers of the new right'.[22] Bolton had started out as a City foreign exchange dealer in 1917 and soon – like many in that line of work – developed a visceral hatred of regulation. Admirers and detractors have called him 'a champion of global free enterprise', a 'merchant adventurer'[23] and 'a little mad'. Bolton worked his way up and in 1948 moved to the Bank of England, two years after it was nationalised and two years after Henry Morgenthau had declared his intention to 'move the financial centre of the world from London and Wall Street, to the US Treasury'. A former currency trader in an era of currency controls, Bolton's move to the bank seemed odd, at least on the face of it. 'I was smuggled through the wicket gate after dark,' he said, 'to discuss foreign exchange – in those days a highly suspicious subject.'

A slightly plump, jovial-looking fellow who wore thick horn-rimmed glasses, Bolton became very influential, very fast, and he fought hard for what he believed in. 'There was nothing ambiguous or half-hearted about the attitudes he took,' said legendary merchant banker Siegmund Warburg. 'I have always had to respect his personal and strongly emotional involvements in the statements he makes, and the moral fervour with which he propounds his opinions. He is an idealist through and through, serving single-mindedly the aims in which he believes,' Warburg continued approvingly. 'His influence always favoured individual endeavours as distinct from the more anonymous powers of the state machinery.'

Not only was Bolton eager to help private interests skip around annoying regulations, he was also deeply enamoured of Britain's imperial magnificence. 'If we could throw away the stranglehold of the economists' demand management,' he once remarked, and 'extinguish the disease of socialism, we could become a proud people once more.'[24]

As head of the Bank of England's foreign exchange department, Bolton was in the perfect position to midwife the new unregulated dollar market in London. The bank could easily have decided to regulate this market. In deciding not to and in preventing other nations from trying to do so, it can only be concluded that the Bank of England actively created it; and indeed it was, Bolton said, the result of 'a conscious effort by a number of us to create a money market from the bits and pieces that were floating about'. This was the birth of what Ronen Palan, professor of international economy at Birmingham University, calls 'a regulatory vacuum, which is called the Euromarket, or the offshore financial market'. A British bank, say, would keep two sets of books – one for its onshore operations, where at least one party to the transaction was British, and one for its offshore operations, where neither was British. In other words, as Palan put it, 'the Euromarket might be considered as essentially no more than a bookkeeping device.'[25]

The terms 'Eurodollar' and 'Euromarkets' are actually misnomers. The markets have nothing really to do with today's euro currency, nor do they trade only in American dollars; all the world's main currencies are traded like this today. It was at this point that the modern offshore system really began. And, as is usual with so much that happens in the offshore system, almost nobody noticed.

Straight away, political events started to feed this new market in London. The Soviet Union in those days did not want to hold too many dollars in New York, where they risked being confiscated if the Cold War turned nastier. But they did not want to invest in sterling either, the risky money of a collapsing empire. They saw their chance in this new market: they could hold dollars in London. So, starting with a deposit of a few hundred thousand by the Moscow Narodny bank in 1957, they began to pile in. Karl Marx would have raised his prodigious eyebrows at the irony of an avowedly Marxist nation nurturing the most unfettered capitalist system in history.

Modern histories of London's growth as a financial centre typically point to the Big Bang of 1986 – the sudden deregulation of London's markets driven by Prime Minister Margaret Thatcher – as the moment when London really took off. The Big Bang was important to be sure, but Tim Congdon, perhaps one of the City of London's sharpest and most experienced spokesmen, spotted the real story. 'The Big Bang,' he wrote in the *Spectator* magazine 'is a sideshow to, indeed almost a by-product of, a much Bigger Bang which has transformed international finance over the last 25 years. The Bigger Bang is – on all the relevant criteria – a multiple of the size of the Big Bang.'[26]

'An extraordinary situation has arisen,' he continued, 'where the Euromarket, which has no physical embodiment in an exchange building or even a widely recognised set of rules and regulations, is the largest source of capital in the world.'[27] Gary Burn put it in a different light. The market's emergence, he said, was 'the first shot in the neo-liberal counter-revolution against the social market and the Keynesian welfare state'.

The London loophole, in effect a new banking technology, was the invisible financial counterpart of the Mont Pelerin Society's ideological insurgency. While the ideology provided the enabling environment, it was this new London market and its subsequent spin-offs that ultimately forced through the liberalisation of the world economy, whether the world's citizens liked it or not. The modern offshore system did not start its explosive growth on scandal-tainted and palm-fringed islands in the Caribbean, or in the Alpine foothills of Zürich. It all began in London, as Britain's formal empire gave way to something more subtle. P. J. Cain and A. G. Hopkins, leading historians of British imperialism, summarised the transition. 'As the good ship Sterling sank, the City was able to scramble aboard a much more seaworthy young vessel, the Eurodollar,' they wrote. 'As the imperial basis of its strength disappeared, the City survived by transforming itself into an "offshore island" servicing the business created by the industrial and commercial growth of much more dynamic partners.'

In fact, the formal empire did not quite disappear; fourteen small island states decided not to seek independence, becoming British Overseas Territories, with the Queen as their head of state. Exactly half of them – Anguilla, Bermuda, the British Virgin Islands, the Cayman Islands, Gibraltar, Montserrat and the Turks and Caicos islands, are secrecy jurisdictions, actively supported and managed from Britain and intimately linked with the City of London.

From these beginnings, the London offshore market exploded. By the end of 1959, about $200 million was on deposit; by the end of 1960 this had reached a billion – still small in comparison with the $70-odd billion size of Britain's gross domestic product. But it kept going: it hit three billion in 1961, by which time it was spreading to Zürich, to the Caribbean and beyond, as jurisdiction after jurisdiction got in on the game. Before, countries had been relatively well insulated against financial calamities that happened elsewhere, but the Euromarket connected up the world's financial sectors and economies. A shock rise in interest rates in one place would, as if transmitted by electricity, almost instantly affect anywhere else plugged into the system. And, as it grew and grew, tides of hot money once again began to surge back and forth across the globe.

Britain's politicians grew concerned about the sheer political muscle of the Bank of England, and its libertarian leanings. The bank put them firmly in their place. 'Exchange control is an infringement of the rights of the citizen,' Lord Cromer, the Bank of England's governor, said in 1963. 'I therefore regard it ethically as wrong.' Cromer was the archetypal Bank of England man, steeped in empire. An Eton-educated godson of King George V whose maternal grandfather was the first British viceroy of Egypt at the turn of the century and whose grandfather on his father's side had been the viceroy of India and a governor general of Canada, his prime goal was to restore the City of London to its former imperial glory. 'There is no doubt,' the *Banker* magazine wrote, 'that the restoration of London's international role is a cause close to Lord Cromer's heart.'[28]

American bankers soon realised that if this strange new market in London was free of US political control, then it was free of US banking laws too. One such regulation was the famous Glass-Steagall

Act of 1933, which prevented ordinary banks owning certain types of more dangerous financial companies, and which was considered so useful that it survived until it was repealed in 1999 under President Clinton and his treasury secretary, the former Goldman Sachs banker Robert Rubin. This banking genius might have heeded the words of G. K. Chesterton: 'Before you take down a fence, you might want to know why the previous owner put it up.' Yet long before this happened, American banks were already avoiding Glass-Steagall. They did it by coming to London.

George Bolton clearly saw the potential: by February 1957 he had left his post at the Bank of England and joined the Bank of London and South America, now part of Lloyds Bank. Within a month, BOLSA had $3 million in Eurodollar deposits; in three years it had $247 million – a whole lot of money in those days – and rising. Soon BOLSA was the biggest player in the market. Almost as soon as Bolton joined, it opened a joint venture in the Bahamas, a reassuringly British haven where the Bank of England had a seat on the currency board. BOLSA then expanded into the Cayman Islands, Antigua and beyond, hoovering up dollar deposits from North and South America and spiriting them silently to the unregulated London offshore market.

As the 1960s wore on, the US deficit ballooned. America was overspending overseas in relation to its earnings, and an army of dollars left the United States for service in the Euromarket.

This offshore London market received another fillip in 1963, with the birth of Eurobonds. These new-fangled instruments were unregulated, offshore bearer bonds – which are just what the name suggests: whoever bears the pieces of paper in their hands, owns them. They are a bit like ultra-valuable dollar bills: no records are kept of who owns them, and so they are perfect for tax evasion. Bearer bonds are the kind of thing that feature in villain-infested Hollywood movies like *Beverley Hills Cop* and *Die Hard*, and are considered so pernicious that many countries have since outlawed them. A Bank of England memo from 1963 crystallised the cynicism. 'However much we dislike hot money, we cannot be international bankers and refuse to accept money.'[29] All kinds of new Eurobond wheezes were cooked up. A London-based bank issued Eurobonds in Schiphol Airport in Amsterdam, to dodge British stamp duty; the bond coupons were routinely cashed in Luxembourg to avoid British income taxes.[30]

This global deregulatory impulse fitted rather well with the rebellious cultural politics of the 1960s and London's flowering as a mould-breaking centre of world fashion. Ideas about outsiders and rebellion against authority percolated into the fabric of society, and James Bond's forays offshore, to Switzerland in *Goldfinger* in 1964, and to Nassau in *Thunderball* in 1965, injected a subversive frisson into the image of tax havens. Radio Caroline ('the world's most famous offshore radio station') started broadcasting from a ship in the English Channel outside the reach of Britain's radio licensing regulations, giving a new and popular twist to the word 'offshore'.

The Euromarket kept booming. By 1970 it was measured at $46 billion, and by 1975 it was reckoned to have grown to exceed the size of the entire world's foreign exchange reserves. As the oil shocks hit in the 1970s, this market was the route through which the oil-rich states' surpluses were routed to deficit-plagued consumer countries. As the Euromarket bonfire raged ever higher, capital began its assault on the citadels of power and the democratic nation state. Alexander Sachs, a renowned economist, was not exaggerating when he called this 'a new banking order . . . transforming the rubric of accounting'.[31] Gary Burn, one of very few academics to have studied the market in depth, went even further, describing Eurodollars as 'a new form of money, and a market in which to trade it'.

And the market just kept snowballing: $500 billion in 1980, then a net $2.6 trillion eight years later.[32] By 1997, nearly 90 per cent of all international loans were made through this market. It is now so all-enveloping that the Bank for International Settlements, which oversees global financial flows, has given up trying to measure its size; it simply bundles everything together into wider foreign exchange markets.

Every now and then a government has tried to tax this market, or regulate it – and has failed each time. 'The Eurodollar is a pesky, elusive creature,' wrote the economist Jane Sneddon Little in 1975. 'In attempting to tame the market, central bankers have been in the untenable position of chasing an elephant with butterfly nets. Although individual authorities have from time to time rapped his knee or tangled his trunk, generally the animal has been able to dash through the gaps . . . they pose problems never before encountered by central bankers.'[33] It is all the more remarkable then that what Gary Burn calls 'this most momentous financial innovation since the banknote' is still largely unresearched.'[34] It is the same old offshore problem: nobody was paying attention.

A quick numerical exercise shows why the unregulated offshore Euromarket, and offshore finance more generally, can be unusually profitable, far beyond the potential for avoiding tax. Governments require banks to hold reserves against the deposits they take. Let's imagine a French bank, under official reserve requirements, must hold 10 per cent of the value of its deposits in cash. The going rate is 5 per cent annually for loans, and 4 per cent for depositors. Now for every $100 deposit, the bank may only lend $90 at 5 per cent, earning it $4.50. The bank must then pay the depositor 4 per cent, leaving it 50 cents. Subtract the bank's operating costs of, let's say 40 cents, and it has made 10 cents profit on its hundred bucks. Now imagine, instead, a bank in the London offshore Euromarket. In this market there are no reserve requirements. Now the bank can lend all of its $100 at 5 per cent, earning $5. Subtract $4 to pay interest to the depositor, and subtract the 40 cents operating costs, and the profit now is 60 cents – a staggering six times the onshore profits.

This is a caricature of a more complex reality of course, but the basic principle works. And note that nobody has made a better or a cheaper widget, and banking has not suddenly become more efficient. All that has happened is that regulations have been avoided, and bankers have multiplied their profits six-fold.

On the face of it, this seems like a cost-free benefit for everyone as, in a competitive market, the bankers will pass some of their extra profits on to borrowers and depositors. But the bank's offshore customers will almost always be the world's wealthier citizens and corporations. Free money for bankers and the representatives of the world's wealthy at the expense of everyone else is a basic leitmotif of the offshore system. We will find it again and again. And that is not the only problem. Governments make banks hold capital and reserves for a very good reason: to protect against financial panics. It may seem like free money in good times, but as the investor Warren Buffett memorably put it, 'It is only when the tide goes out that you realise who has been swimming naked.' As the world has been rediscovering since 2007, it is ordinary taxpayers not gambling financiers who ultimately pick up the bill. But there is another offshore secret here too. It hinges on why banks are required to hold reserves against deposits in the first place.

Imagine you put $100 cash into your onshore bank, with a 10 per cent reserve requirement, meaning that the bank may lend out only $90 of that to someone else. That person now has $90 to spend. By a roundabout route, that $90 will end up in another bank account. That next bank may then lend 90 per cent of *that* out – meaning that $81 more will end up being lent. And the process just goes on. This is a well-known principle – fractional reserve banking – and if you follow the calculations tirelessly through you will find that with a 10 per cent reserve requirement, your $100 balloons out into $1,000 spread across the economy.

It is hard to believe that money can be simply conjured out of thin air like this, but this is one of the most important things banks *do*. 'Money creation is a bizarre thing to ponder,' said the economist J. K. Galbraith. 'The process by which money is created is so simple that the mind is repelled.' This is the central mystery of banking: a bank can 'expand its balance sheet' by extending credit to others. In the banking world, money can be created merely by the act of lending it – it is money as debt.

Money creation by banks is not a bad thing in itself, but the question is: how much borrowing is safe? Regulators try to control liquidity – to make sure that the amount of money sloshing around in the system does not grow out of control – by enforcing reserve and capital requirements. But now imagine a situation in the unregulated London-based Euromarkets, where a bank isn't required to hold any reserves. The first $100 deposit will let the bank lend out the full $100, which turns into another $100 deposit, leading to another $100 loan, and so on endlessly.

That is the simple theory, but of course it never happened quite like that. If it had, we might have drowned in hyperinflation long ago. No, there is only so much demand for credit at any time, and if credit grows in the offshore market it will, up to a point, contract elsewhere to compensate. Not only that, but offshore Eurodollars will eventually leak back onshore, where they will slow down again under normal reserve requirements. And to be fair, prudent bankers often hold back reserves even when they are not forced to.

There has been huge controversy for decades about how much the Euromarket has really contributed to expanding the amount of money sloshing around in the world, boosting risk and building an unsustainable pyramid of increasingly wobbly debt. Since the one institution that could have measured this market – the Bank for International Settlements – has stopped measuring it, it is hard to come to any solid conclusions about how it has, for example, contributed to the latest financial crisis and the explosion of debt globally. Yet some things seem fairly clear. If you create an enormous arena for generating unregulated new credit, these markets will expand to displace better-controlled banking operations, and demand will rise to meet potential supply. Credit will start expanding into places where it wasn't previously able to, and often to where it really shouldn't be. As Sidney Wells and Alan Winters wrote in their book *International Economics*, the Eurobanks 'have almost certainly found customers who could not borrow on national systems'. Euromarkets, in other words, made it possible for credit quality to deteriorate out of sight of the regulators.

Trawling through the archives from the 1960s and 1970s, I am astonished how regulators around the world, struggling to get to grips with this strange new offshore phenomenon, were fretting about exactly the kinds of trouble that brought the world economy to its knees in the recent economic crisis starting in 2007. 'One concern,' a senior British civil servant wrote in a 'top secret' memo I dug up from 1968, 'is the effect of the practice of "rolling over" short-term debt to provide, in effect, long-term finance.' This is just what destroyed the British bank Northern Rock in 2007. An article in the *Banker* magazine around the same time asked, 'Is the growth of this market a welcome tonic, or a slow poison to the international financial system in general? Is it ensuring that the adjustment process will again take the form of a collapse of the international financial system? Is Britain's part in the development of the market once again ensuring that we shall be in the front line of such a collapse?' The answer is now in.

What would Keynes have made of all this? One might think that his furiously pro-British stance and his resolute, though not uncritical, defence of the British imperial project would have welcomed it. As he wrote in 1941, as he negotiated for US help, 'America must not be allowed to pick out the eyes of the British empire.'[35] Not only that, but he also fought strongly, at times, to help the City of London retain its global primacy. But at every turn Keynes fought for an international order based on cooperation between nations, not competition. London, he hoped, could hold on to its position primarily by being at the centre of a cooperative sterling currency bloc, and he despised the idea of degrading regulations simply as a way of getting one over on one's neighbours. He would have viewed the explosion in beggar-my-neighbour offshore finance from the 1970s, not to mention the massive capital flight it fostered, with horror.

The 1960s may have been an exciting time to be in London, but American regulators weren't quite so happy. In 1960 the Federal Reserve Bank of New York, believing that the Euromarket was already making 'the pursuit of an independent monetary policy in any one country far more difficult',[36] sent a team to London to investigate. It is ironic that the growth in influence of the ideas of Milton Friedman, who argued that governments should focus on money supply as the lever to use to manage their economies, was taking place just as this market, which Friedman supported, started to make this lever ineffective.

Bank of England staff offered the Americans a great number of cups of tea but did next to nothing to address their concerns, even after the Americans said the Euromarket posed 'a danger to stability'. Periodic statements from the Bank of England merely confirmed American fears: 'lending by authorised banks is not controlled, as regards amount, nature or tenor,' said one; 'reliance is placed on the commercial prudence of the lenders.' James Robertston, vice chair of the Federal Reserve, put his finger on one source of worry: the emerging Euromarket centres in havens like the Caymans and Bahamas, linked to Britain and regulated by the Bank of England. 'My primary objection is that they aren't branches in any sense of the word. They are simply desk drawers in somebody else's desk. Why make banks go through a sham proceeding to obtain certain privileges?'

On 18 July 1963 President Kennedy tried to stem American currency outflows by taxing the interest on foreign securities, supposedly removing any incentive to lend in the more profitable overseas markets. It had the opposite effect: a stampede for the unregulated London offshore market, free of tax and regulations. 'This is a day you will remember,' said Henry Alexander of Morgan Guaranty bank, when the new regulations came into force. 'It will change the face of American banking and force all the business to London.'[37]

US policymakers grew increasingly worried about financial stability. By 1963, by which time American banks were already the biggest player in this market, the US Treasury had concluded that the market had aggravated a 'world payments disequilibrium'[38] and suggested to American bankers that they 'ask themselves whether they are serving the national interest by participating in this sort of activity'.[39] Once again, the Americans conveyed their fears to the Bank of England, and the US comptroller of the currency was sent to London to inspect American banks. The Bank of England's response was, effectively, that the Americans could go and screw themselves. 'It doesn't matter to me whether Citibank is evading American regulations in London,' one top bank official said. 'I wouldn't particularly want to know.'[40]

In 1967 Robert Roosa, the clever and energetic US under-secretary for the Treasury, added that the market had hugely amplified destabilising capital flows 'in magnitudes much larger than anything experienced in the past, massive movements'. The response from London was always the same: either 'Mind your own business,' or 'This is nothing to worry about.' As Lord Cromer told the Federal Reserve Bank of New York in 1963, responding to Roosa's concerns about tax evasion, 'I think it is unlikely that the volume of this type of operation will grow to any very great extent.' Cromer's chutzpah is even more extraordinary in light of the fact that British officials were nervous too. 'While the members were not unhappy,' notes a Bank of England memo in 1960, 'I did get the impression some of them were rather keeping their fingers crossed.'[41]

A bizarre Alice-in-Wonderland logic lay behind the Bank of England's decision not to regulate these markets – the kind of logic that permeates the offshore system. If there was a run on a regulated bank in London, the Bank of England, by virtue of being its regulator, would feel some obligation to come in and pick up the pieces. In other words, regulation, as a bank memo put it, 'would mean admission of responsibility'. Better then, the logic went, not to regulate them![42]

So why did the United States let its banks dive head first into this unregulated London market, knowing that they were undermining American financial controls?

For one thing, most people saw the Euromarket as a weird, slightly unclean, temporary anomaly, something that would disappear soon enough. In 1962 *Time* magazine concluded that 'the Eurodollar, most experts agree, will gradually disappear if US interest rates rise to European levels, or the US payments deficit ends'.[43] Many American bankers also saw Eurodollars as a kind of funny money, best left to Europeans. 'Eurodollars, indeed!' an American banker in London told *Time*. 'It's hot money – and I prefer to call it by that name.' And it *was* hot money. The Euromarket had become a kind of anti-Keynes global transmission belt making short-term capital movements more sensitive, rippling interest-rate changes instantly around the globe and allowing enough money to pool together in one place to allow large speculative attacks against currencies that flighty speculators decided were vulnerable.[44]

There was something else keeping American policymakers at bay. Powerful American banking interests wanted to keep this offshore playground as quiet as possible. When Hendrik Houthakker, a junior member of the US Council of Economic Advisors, tried to bring the Euromarket to the attention of the US president, he was slapped down with 'No, we don't want to draw attention to it.'[45] As one frustrated academic explained, bankers 'deliberately avoided discussing it'.[46]

Meanwhile, the Bank of England remained the enemy of regulation. In 1973 some German bankers went to see a Bank of England official, to ask what permissions they needed to become an authorised bank in London. 'The official looked at us,' one banker remembered, 'and he said, "A bank is a bank if I consider it to be one."' And that, pretty much, was it – apart from what the historian David Kynaston calls the 'occasional, indispensable afternoon ceremony'. As a Belgian banker explained, regulation involved having 'to go around and have a cup of tea at the Bank of England from time to time, and explain what you are doing'.[47]

Even in 1975, years after people started raising concerns, a US congressional committee report expressed amazement at how this new market had stayed so far beneath the political radar. These concerns would be echoed a generation later by the Bank for International Settlements in June 2008, as financial panic spread around the globe. 'How could a huge shadow banking system emerge,' it asked forlornly, 'without provoking clear statements of official concern?' It turns out, as we shall see, that the offshore Euromarkets are to a large degree the enabling environment for this shadow banking system: the deep and unregulated financial sea populated by all the big, dangerous sharks of the latest economic crisis – the bizarre structured investment vehicles, conduits and their like that recently caused so much grief.

It was not only American politicians who failed to see through this carefully constructed veil of secrecy and obfuscation. Bank of England letters reveal in bold colours the central role it played in keeping the rise of offshore off the political agenda. 'The Bank have on a number of occasions in the past strongly resisted the Treasury's attempts to obtain fuller information,' states a memo from 1959. 'The Deputy Governor refused to allow details of the authorised bank's positions to be divulged to HM Treasury.'[48] As Gary Burn put it, the Bank of England 'guarded its control over the British banking system from other state institutions, especially the Treasury, only then to delegate much of this authority, in turn, via "representative associations", to the City's banks.'

Who in Britain questioned this kind of arrangement seriously and got a proper hearing? In a debate in parliament in 1959, a former Bank of England director baldly stated that there could be no conflict of interest between the bank's public and private roles, because there was 'an identity of interest between such directors and the national interest'.[49]

Back to the question of why the United States, despite periodic expressions of concern in official circles, ultimately collude with Britain in letting its banks do business offshore? The answer to this question gets us closer to where real power lies in the world. And herein lies another curious tale.

Today the US dollar is the world's main reserve currency. While less privileged nations are periodically constrained by shortages of foreign exchange, the USA can borrow in its own currency – it can print money to acquire real resources, and live beyond its means for a long time. 'If I had an agreement with my tailor that whatever money I pay him returns to me the very same day as a loan,' French presidential adviser Jacques Rueff once famously commented, 'I would have no objection at all to ordering more suits from him.'

And that changes everything. It gives US presidents what one angry

French finance minister, Valéry Giscard d'Éstaing, called America's 'exorbitant privilege' – in effect, a gigantic free ride for the United States. As France's *Le Monde* newspaper put it, 'The market makes the American position in monetary negotiations very much stronger than it ought to be. Americans are maintained in a state of security which is unhealthy and prejudicial to serious reform of international financial payments.'[50] This ability to pay foreign debts in its own currency – which it can print – helped America fight and pay for the Vietnam war; more recently it helped President George W. Bush cut taxes and rack up huge deficits. And when the time comes one day to pay for the mess, you can shift a lot of the burden of adjustment onto other states.

Countries use dollars for their reserves because dollar markets are large and liquid, and the dollar is trusted to be relatively stable. Oil is priced in dollars. People trade in dollars. When I was the Reuters correspondent in war-ravaged Angola in the mid-1990s, the raucous street money changers in downtown Luanda plumped up their ample brassieres not with European currencies, Francs, or renminbi – but with US dollars. Today two-thirds of the world's official foreign exchange reserve are held in dollars. Dollars make the world go round, and if you have the licence to print the stuff, you are made.

'Every historian knows,' Keynes' biographer Robert Skidelsky wrote in 2009, 'that a hegemonic currency is part of an imperial system of political relations.'[51]

And the Euromarkets, this huge new, unregulated and highly profitable dollar arena, whose liquidity was growing explosively, were perfect to support this imperial role for the U.S. currency. As Douglas Dillon, US under-secretary of state for economic affairs, enthused, the Euromarkets provided 'quite a good way of convincing foreigners to keep their deposits in dollars'.[52] Eurodollars helped America cement its exorbitant privilege, finance its deficits, fight foreign wars and throw its weight around. American bankers didn't want to go through months of kerfuffle convincing Congress to change the laws at home. Far easier, instead, to skip over to London.

'With the creation of the Euromarket,' wrote Eric Helleiner, 'bankers in both countries stumbled on a solution to the problem of how to reconstruct the London–New York financial axis that had been prominent in the 1920s.'[53] Even more strikingly, the project to restore the City of London to its former imperial glory, Gary Burn noted, 'was pursued unhesitantly and unstintingly, without, it seems, any prior or subsequent debate by the Prime Minister, the Treasury, by Cabinet, Government or Parliament.

'Central to the success of this project was the Bank of England, which after 1945 set about re-establishing the hegemony of international financial capital.' And all the time Britain's offshore satellites, Jersey, Cayman, and their like, had their own special parts to play in this great financial game.

As Ronen Palan described it, the Euromarkets rippled outwards, driven from the centre in London along 'a clear geographical path, beginning from those islands nearest to the UK mainland, namely the Channel Islands, soon followed by the British-held Caribbean jurisdictions, then Asia and lastly British-held Pacific atolls.' The process, Palan reckons, took about ten years. So, from the 1960s, these island semi-colonies and other assorted satellites of London came into their own as offshore Euromarket booking centres: secretive and semifictional way stations on a path through accountants' workbooks, hidey-holes where the world's wealthiest individuals and corporations, especially banks, could park their money, tax free and in secrecy, and where they could grow faster than their regulated onshore counterparts.

The book-keeping exercises might involve one or two people sitting behind a desk on a palm-fringed island, while the heavy lifting work – the real business of hammering together big banking syndicates, making the accounting cogs mesh properly and ensuring that the paperwork was legally watertight – would be done in London. This umbilical, two-way relation between London and its overseas satellites has remained a defining feature of the entire offshore system ever since.

Each place offers its own special range of services. Cayman might decide to change its laws to provide a platform for one special kind of zero-tax gymnastics. The Bahamas then lowers its own standards to keep up with its nimble neighbour. Luxembourg and Jersey join in. And so on. The dynamic that this competition creates has an unforgiving internal logic: you must keep deregulating and then deregulate some more to stay one step ahead and to stop the money draining away. There is no other possible path and only one outcome: ever laxer regulation.

A new market had emerged, ushering in the rebirth of London as the world's largest financial centre, and supported by a cat's cradle of connections to former colonies and other assorted imperial oddities. Even as Eden's dreams of defeating Arab nationalism collapsed in ignominy at Suez, the financial establishment in London was piecing together the means by which London would restore its position as the capital of a world ruled in the interests of an elite of investors. At the moment of its apparent destruction, the British empire began to rise from the dead.

6

Construction of a Spider's Web

How Britain built a new overseas empire

The Euromarkets were not the fruit of an original master plan but instead grew under their own internal logic, rapidly becoming an unstoppable force in the global economy. But from the 1960s they also grew hand in hand with a second, more deliberately constructed counterpart: a London-centred web of half-British territories scattered around the world that would catch financial business from nearby jurisdictions by offering lightly taxed, lightly regulated and secretive bolt holes for money. Criminal and other money could be handled by the City of London, yet far enough from London to minimise any stink. The new, high-octane offshore system developed its own private infrastructure and vision and even a sense of shared mission and peculiar, quasi-aristocratic codes of behaviour.

The British Crown Dependencies of Jersey, Guernsey and the Isle of Man would form the inner ring of the spider's web and would focus mostly on Europe, while the Caribbean members of its fourteen Overseas Territories, the last outposts of the formal empire, would focus mostly on the Americas. A scattering of other territories elsewhere would expand the network's global reach: British-controlled Hong Kong, as a gateway to China and the sub-region; and some ex-colonial oddities in the Pacific, the Middle East and elsewhere.

The more that countries around the world deregulated and opened their economies, the more business would fly around in the vicinity of each offshore node, and the more would come into the reaches of the web. Not only that, but each offshore centre would put competitive pressure on the tax, legal and regulatory systems of the jurisdictions nearby – forcing the pace of their financial liberalisation whether they liked it or not. Financial institutions from London, Wall Street, Amsterdam, Frankfurt and Paris, would spread into these territories at high speed. An offshore explosion which began with the rise of the Euromarkets in London in the mid-1950s would spread first to the Crown Depencencies near the British mainland, then to the British-held Caribbean jurisdictions, then to Asia, and finally to British-held Pacific atolls. Here is how this strange episode unfolded: an episode that almost nobody has studied – until now.

In the Caribbean, the modern offshore system traces its origins back to the time when organised crime took an interest in the US tax code. When Al Capone was convicted of tax evasion in 1931, his associate Meyer Lansky became fascinated with developing schemes to get Mob money out of the US in order to bring it back, dry-cleaned. A slick Mafia operator – almost certainly the inspiration for the figure of Hyman Roth in the film *The Godfather* – Lansky would beat every criminal charge against him until the day he died in 1983. He once boasted that the Mob activities he was associated with were 'bigger than US Steel'.

Lansky began with Swiss banking in 1932, where he perfected the loan-back technique.[1] First he moved money out of the US in suitcases, diamonds, airline tickets, cashiers' cheques, untraceable bearer shares or whatever. He would put the money in secret Swiss accounts, perhaps via a Liechtenstein *Anstalt* (an anonymous company with a single secret shareholder) for extra secrecy. The Swiss bank would then loan the money back to a mobster in the United States and the money returned home, clean. The recipient could also deduct the loan interest repayments from his taxable business income in the US.

By 1937 Lansky had started casino operations in Cuba, outside the reach of the US tax authorities, and he and his friends built up gambling, racetrack and drugs businesses there. It was, effectively, an offshore money-laundering centre for the Mob: an 'anti-Disneyland' as the author Jeffrey Robinson put it; 'and the most decadent spot on the planet'. Lansky's links with Cuba's right-wing leadership helped stoke the violent anger that eventually brought Fidel Castro to power in 1959.

Lansky then moved to Miami and plotted to find his next Cuba, small enough and corrupt enough to be able to buy the political leadership, and close enough to the United States for the gamblers to come and go at will. 'The tyrant would have to be so firmly in place that the political environment would remain stable no matter what,' Robinson explained. 'The Mob's money would have to be spread so thick and wide that, if some other tyrant seized power, he'd need them to maintain his own stability.'[2]

The Bahamas, the old staging post for British gun-running to the southern US slave states of the Confederacy, was perfect. Lansky set about making this British colony, now dominated by an oligarchy of corrupt white merchants known as the Bay Street Boys,[3] the top secrecy jurisdiction for North and South American dirty money. A quaint memo from a Mr W. G. Hulland of the Colonial Office to a Bank of England official in 1961, just as Lansky began major operations there, illustrates the uneasy nature of this encounter between the British upper classes and American organised crime: 'We feel that this [lack of provision of an effective regulatory system] might be a grave omission, since it is notorious that this particular territory, in common with Bermuda, attracts all sorts of financial wizards, some of whose activities we can well believe should be controlled in the public interest.'

London did nothing. Two years later, a memo[4] from M. H. Parsons, a colonial administrator, to Sir Dennis Rickett, KCMG, CB, warned that the Bahamas' white racist finance minister Stafford Sands,[5] who had recently taken a $1.8 million bribe from Lansky's associates,[6] wanted to make it a criminal offence to break bank secrecy. Sands had told Parsons that there were $1 billion or more of dirty money to be tapped by reinforcing bank secrecy, and he was prepared to anger the US to get it. This proposed new legislation 'will surely bring protests by the US Government to Her Majesty's Government', Parsons wrote. 'We would look pretty feeble if we had to say that we could do nothing to influence the course of offensive legislation in a territory for which we still have outward responsibility . . . I admit the point is a ticklish one.'

London seems to have given the go-ahead, and Lansky built his empire.

Yet many locals were unhappy. In 1965 Lynden Pindling, a populist

Bahamas politician, threw the ceremonial speaker's mace out of a parliament window to a primed crowd in a dramatic power-to-the-people gesture. He was elected prime minister in 1967 on a platform that included hostility to gambling, corruption and the Bay Street Boys' Mob connections.[7] Few realised that Lansky was backing Pindling too.[8] The casinos, and the Mob-infested offshore industry, continued to boom.

But when Pindling led the Bahamas to full independence in 1973, offshore players fled in droves. Milton Grundy, an influential Caribbean offshore lawyer, put his finger on the problem: 'It wasn't that Pindling said or did anything to damage the banks; it was just that he was black.'[9]

Yet as it happened there was a reassuringly British place just next door, where the locals were far more friendly: the Cayman Islands. Money began to pour in.

The Cambridge-educated Milton Grundy, now the author of several respected books on offshore finance, remembers first arriving in the Caymans. Cows wandered through the town centre, there was one bank, one paved road and no telephone system. The *Cayman Financial Review* claims that mosquitoes would swarm densely enough in those days to suffocate cows. In 1967 the Caymans published its first trust law, which Grundy drafted, and which a British Inland Revenue official subsequently said 'blatantly seeks to frustrate our own law for dealing with our own taxpayers'. Within just a few months Grand Cayman was connected to the international phone network and the airport was expanded to take jet aircraft.

Some have argued that Britain set up the offshore networks simply out of a short-sighted desire to find a way for its overseas territories to pay their way in the world. After the Second World War, an exhausted Britain found that its empire, once a source of great profits, was becoming more expensive and difficult to run, as locals began to agitate for independence. But the evidence points to a different, more troubling explanation for Britain's decision to turn its semi-colonies into secrecy jurisdictions.[10] The archives tell a consistent story about how the tax havens grew: private sector operators working in a zone of extreme freedom began to call the shots, with little opposition from Britain and its inexperienced emissaries.

*   *   *

A British government team in the Cayman Islands in 1969 noted a 'frightening absence of certain types of expertise', adding that 'the civil service still reflects in structure and staffing the out-moded pattern of a bygone age'. It continued: 'The flood of private sector activities, progressively drowning basic government functions, has placed an unsupportable burden on senior staff.' Flocks of developers were arriving

usually backed by glossy lay-outs and declaimed by a team of business-men supported by consultants of all sorts. On the other side of the table – the Administrator and his civil servants. No business expertise, no consultants, no economists, no statisticians, no specialists in any of the fields. Gentlemen vs. Players –with the Gentlemen unskilled in the game and unversed in its rules. It is hardly surprising that the professionals are winning, hands down.

In the archives, two schools of opinion emerge within the British civil service. On one side sits the Treasury, and especially its tax collectors in the Inland Revenue who virulently opposed tax havenry and found the Cayman Islands especially obnoxious. The US authorities were clearly highly vexed too, and the British Foreign Office broadly opposed havenry, though its position was more nuanced. On the other side sits the Bank of England, the most vociferous cheerleader for the new arrangements, and its far less influential supporter, the British Overseas Development Ministry.[11] Battle lines were drawn; the exchanges become vigorous and even acrimonious.

The Inland Revenue was especially alarmed, while their mandarin bosses in the Treasury showed some, but rather less, concern. They put together a working party, whose report in 1971 said Britain should, in effect, stop encouraging tax havenry in its overseas territories, which in the case of the Caymans had become, as one internal memo in London put it, 'quite uncivilised'. A confidential Foreign Office memorandum from 1973 expressed the concern. 'The Cayman Islands set up as a tax haven in 1967 and passed appropriate legislation which went considerably beyond what the UK Treasury was prepared to wear,' it said. The bill quietly passed after an unnamed desk officer failed to submit the legislation to London for consent. This 'administrative error', the memorandum continued, drove a wedge into the Treasury's carefully constructed defences against abuse of tax havenry.

Britain later patched the holes in its own tax code as best it could, the memorandum noted – leaving the elites of Latin America, the United States and the rest of the world free to use the Caymans' offshore facilities. Despite this warning, nothing was done.

Yet the Caymans became a tax haven through more than an 'administrative error'. A letter marked SECRET from the Bank of England dated 11 April 1969 gives a better sense of the forces driving the changes in the Caribbean.

We need to be quite sure that the possible proliferation of trust companies, banks, etc., which in most cases would be no more than brass plates manipulating assets outside the Islands, does not get out of hand. There is of course no objection to their providing bolt holes for non-residents but we need to be sure that in so doing opportunities are not created for the transfer of UK capital to the non-Sterling Area outside UK rules.

Once again: no objection to the looting of other countries – so long as Britain was protected.

The Sterling Area was a zone of mostly British colonies and dominions whose member countries either had the pound sterling as their own currency or pegged their currency to it. Payment was free across the zone, but flows of capital outside the Sterling Area were tightly controlled. The Bank of England's main concern at this time was that the new Caribbean centres were weak points: sources of financial leakage outside the Sterling Area. So in 1972 Britain shrank the area to Britain, Ireland and the Crown Dependencies, excluding the new havens. The Cayman Islands acquired the Cayman dollar as its new currency, which has been pegged at 1.20 US dollars to one Cayman dollar since 1974.

The year the Sterling Area shrank, the British officials working against tax havens disappeared from the archive files. Their replacements seemed unaware of the 1971 report and only discovered it in 1977, sitting on the shelf, unimplemented. Again they express concerns – and again nothing is done. The episode looks like an institutional groundhog day inside the civil service. Reports are written, memos are drafted – but nothing changes. History repeats itself within and between the departments, all in less than ten years.[12] And, each time, the Bank of England fought the tax haven corner.

While all this happened, the representative of the Overseas Development Ministry clearly supported the Bank of England's line. He seemed concerned almost exclusively with the well-being of 10,000 Cayman Islanders – apparently blinkered to the terrible impact this business may have had on the several hundred million victims of capital flight in nearby Latin America. Whatever the ministry's motivations – hopeless myopia or a cynical attempt to privilege its turf at the expense of the rest of the developing world – it stoutly defended the emerging offshore system.

Something else emerged from the archives, which helps us understand more about Britain's role in supporting offshore finance.

'This is no tropical paradise,' said Kenneth Crook, the newly arrived British Governor of the Cayman Islands. 'I could enlarge, in terms of a magnificent but mosquito-ridden beach; of a fairly new but rather ill-designed and sadly-neglected house; of a pleasant but very untidy little town; of swamp clearance schemes which generate smells strong enough to kill a horse; of an office which will one day ere long collapse in a shower of termite-ridden dust.'

He was running a place with just 10,000 inhabitants: a large, partly English village. As a reminder then, as today, the Governor was appointed by the Queen on the British government's advice, and is the most powerful person on the island. He (and it has always been a he) presides over a cabinet – which is where local Caymanians come in, after a fashion. They do have elections in Cayman, with revved-up political rallies and all the fun of the fair – but the governor remains responsible for defence, internal security and foreign relations; he appoints the police commissioner, the complaints commissioner, auditor general, attorney general (AG), the judiciary and a number of other senior public officials. The final appeal court is the Privy Council in London. Caymanian Dollar notes carry the British Queen's head and the national anthem is *God Save the Queen*.

This is certainly an odd appointment for a Diplomatic Service Officer. How many of my colleagues, like myself, contemplating the inanities of some Head of State, have said to themselves, 'If only the fool would do so and so, how easy it would be.' But have they really thought how it feels to be the fool in question? . . . I might invite my colleagues to try running a Parliament in the best Westminster tradition, in which one Member leaves, and as a result throws the entire Finance Committee into confusion for want of a quorum, because he has to drive the school bus – which he owns. Sir, I hope I may be forgiven if underlying this despatch so far is a note of perhaps unbecoming levity.[13]

But on politics, and the strange relationship between Britain and its little quasi-colony, his tone hardens. 'Caymanians don't want independence,' Crook wrote. 'They don't want internal self-government either – they are very unwilling to trust each other with effective power . . . they quite well understand that the British connection gives them a status which they would otherwise not command. Hence they are delighted to have a Governor around; apart from anything else he's very handy for taking unpopular decisions.' He then put his finger on the subtleties of the relationship: giving Britain effective control, while pretending not to be in control.

They realise that if the Governor is seen to have effective power then the others appear to be essentially cyphers. The elected politicians among them find this bad for their image. What they want is to make the Constitution look as if it obliges the Governor to do what they want, even though they know it doesn't. I think we are in the world of semantics here. The more Caymanians we can put in positions of power, the better; they will act as lightning conductors for political dissent.[14]

Nothing of substance seems to have changed, as a senior Caymanian politician, who asked not to be quoted, explained to me in 2009. 'The UK wants to have a significant degree of control,' he said, 'but at the same time it does not want to be seen to have that control. Like any boss, it wants influence without responsibility; they can turn around when things go wrong and say "it's all your fault" – but in the meantime they are pulling all the strings. The Governor can bring an agent of the Crown to come here and do whatever they want,' he said. 'The hand has always been behind the scenes, in the shadows: it has not shown its face.' Keeping the reality hidden from Caymanians is, he said, part of political leadership, like having children. 'It is not necessary to tell them all the burdens and challenges you face. Eighty per cent of the masses who turn up at our meetings believe they have control.'

The gesture towards elected representation plus all the money keeps the locals happy, so they do not rock the boat. And Caymanians solidly support the link with Britain today. Roy Bodden, a former minister and author of a history of the Cayman Islands, remembers the Falklands War between Britain and Argentina in 1982, when influential Caymanians, not content with having helped Argentinian generals and their wealthy friends loot their country, launched a 'Mother Needs Your Help' fund. Collection tins were rattled in the street, and a million dollars raised, he said, then simply handed over to Britain for the war effort.[15]

This attitude of the locals towards Britain reassures investors, but the political bedrock underpinning the world's fifth biggest financial centre is Britain's role. If Caymanians gained full control, most of the money would flee.

While these changes were happening in the Caribbean, something similar was under way far closer to the City of London, in the Crown Dependencies. A constituent's letter forwarded and endorsed by Tony Benn, a British member of parliament, to Chancellor Denis Healey, about a tax conference in Jersey, gives a flavour:

I am somewhat surprised to see a Mr Gent from the Bank of England giving advice on how to avoid paying tax. I wonder if this is really part of the Bank of England's duties? Mr Gent suggests that the Bank of England will not be prepared to pass on information required by the Inland Revenue! Does the UK Treasury have no control over the Bank of England? Surely Bank employees should not be working against Government Policy? And just what sort of arrangements and deals are made at these events 'behind the scenes'? It really is just a bit too sordid to be true.[16]

Jersey, the most important of the Crown Dependencies, had been profiting from offshore business for a long time before that. In the eighteenth century it was already a kind of offshore centre when wealthy merchants from other countries used it to avoid English customs duties and engage in other nefarious activities. After the Napoleonic Wars, demobilised British army officers came to escape British income taxes on their pensions, and it also then became a refuge and hothouse for European radicals many of whom fled first to England to escape persecution, then were shuffled off to this strange quasi-English halfway house, partly to provide the plausible deniability that enabled Queen Victoria to avoid embarrassment in front of her various cousins in France, Belgium, Russia, Hungary and beyond. British officials returning from the colonies also began to settle here, and Jersey bankers used their colonial connections to find new business back in the colonies or further afield. First it was mostly British colonials working in Africa, the Middle East and the Far East, who wanted to to keep their assets safe but close to the UK. Then as the colonies became independent, people either moved to Jersey, or stayed in the ex-colonies but kept their assets outside, worried about political instability or inheritance taxes. 'If you were living in the Middle East and wanted to invest in London property,' explains Colin Powell, a former chairman of the Jersey Financial Services Commission, 'you wouldn't do it in your own name – there would be inheritance taxes when you died – but you would invest through a Jersey company.'

As in the Caribbean, offshore banking blossomed here from the 1960s, when merchant banks like Hambros and Hill Samuel (now part of Lloyds TSB) opened for deposits. Foreign travel was getting easier and more and more British expatriates opened accounts in Jersey, where the banks were reliable and comfortingly British, but where bank interest was untaxed and secret. Many did not declare their income to their countries of residence, often poverty-racked African nations, knowing they would not be caught.

Martyn Scriven, secretary to the Jersey Bankers' Association, described how Jersey's network grew.[17] He had run Barclays Bank in Birmingham in the English Midlands, mostly lending to manufacturers, before moving to Jersey to head Barclays' local operations there. 'I came here and I jumped over to the other side of the balance sheet – from lending to deposit gathering,' he said. 'We had, here in Barclays, probably 100,000 British expatriates – they were working on oil rigs, in hospitals, and so on.' Smaller packets – up to £25,000, say – were saved in the clearing banks, while bigger packets went into the more secretive trust companies.

'The biggest business developer is client recommendation,' said

Scriven. 'The client will say, "I'm happy, and I'd like to introduce you to my friend" – and you build it up like that. You get some seriously interesting people . . . someone who goes abroad as a rigger twenty years ago for Shell may now be in charge of the company's west Africa operations.'

It seems reasonable to imagine how a client recommendation might, one day, deliver Nigeria's oil minister, say, or a top Indian businessman, or a South African casino operator. The network grows, mostly following old colonial links – and is channelled to London. 'We gather deposits from wealthy folk all around the world, and the bulk of those deposits are sent to London,' Scriven continued. 'The banks consolidate their balances every day, and surplus funds won't sit here – they either go to another bank or on and through to the City. If I have money to spare, I pass it to the father. Great dollops of money go into London from here.'

As in the Caymans, Jersey has carefully protected the ambiguous relationship with Britain. Jersey's most senior public sector officials are appointed in London; its laws are all approved by the Privy Council in London, and Britain handles Jersey's foreign relations and defence, and his Excellency the Lieutenant Governor represents the Queen. London almost never protests. 'I can't see why they'd ever turn around and say "Don't do that!",' said Powell.[18]

And, as in the Caymans, Britain goes to great lengths to hide its control.

When Britain began its long negotiations to enter the European Community from the 1960s, it worked hard to help Jersey stay outside the structures of the Treaty of Rome. Sir Geoffrey Rippon, Britain's chief negotiator ahead of its accession in 1973 (and a member of the extreme right-wing Monday Club group) said on a visit to Jersey in 1971: 'Your fiscal autonomy has been guaranteed – I say that deliberately and slowly. There is no doubt whatever about that and I can say quite categorically that there will be no question of your having to apply . . . any part of Community policy on taxation.'[19] Jersey remains outside the European Union, though it cherry-picks the European laws it likes, plus some of those advocated by periodic British commissions of enquiry, and casts the rest aside.

John Christensen, Jersey's Economic Adviser from 1987 to 1998, remembers that when Britain got embarrassed about something

Jersey was doing, a kind of theatre would begin where Jersey would have to change, but without being seen to have been *forced* to do so.

He would travel to London once or twice a month for discussions with the British government, noting that 'it is all done in winks and nods – an idea is floated, "would this be accepted by UK government?" London would say "no don't do that," or give it the green light. It was an incredibly subtle process, dealing with them; they (the British civil servants) would say "this is all a bit of a bother but the EU is putting pressure on us and we don't want to put ourselves in a position where we are required to make you do this." The unspoken understanding was that forcing Jersey to do something would reveal that Britain has the power. We all knew it: these are highly intelligent people and these things don't need to be said.

'Keeping Britain's power hidden allows them in international forums to say "Jersey is politically autonomous: there is not a lot we can do."'

He remembers new international money-laundering regulations coming in in the 1980s, forcing big banks to shed particularly unsavoury clients. The solution was to hive them off to tiny trust and company businesses in Jersey – which would still bank with the same big banks but now distanced far enough to provide plausible deniability. A raft of small trust company administration businesses popped up, with such low ethical standards that London began to apply pressure for Jersey to clean this area up. Christensen was acting secretary of a working party given this task. 'The aim was to find a figleaf: an appearance of action. That was evident to me,' he said. 'It illustrated this very hand-in-glove relationship between Jersey and London.'

Jersey even *feels* very British. Its capital St Helier looks like any British seaside town: teenagers in the latest British fashions hang around outside chip shops, and Body Shops, Dixons and Marks & Spencers line its High Street, all taking British or Jersey pounds as payment. Yet this extreme Britishness masks an alien political system, semi-autonomous from Britain's, with no political parties and a government utterly captured by the financial services industry – as we shall see later.

Wealthy tax exiles to Jersey, Christensen remembers, were always extremely interested in the relationship with Britain. As with the Cayman Islands, the relationship with the mother country reassures the wealthy and the financial services industry that Britain will step in if needs be, to protect the tax haven from external attacks. Their money is safe in Jersey.

As all this happened, something similar was occurring in Asia. Hong Kong – which the US economist Milton Friedman called the world's greatest experiment in laissez-faire capitalism – was to be the new Asian offshore jewel, attracting wealth as a tax haven gateway to China and the wider region. Britain kept the guiding hand, but gave the financiers free rein. The colony's financial secretary Sir John Cowperthwaite, installed in 1961, was known to have such stridently anti-government views that he curtailed the publication of official statistics – which would, he said, attract too much interest from civil servants.

When China introduced its 'Open Door' policy of market reforms and export opening in 1978, Hong Kong grew rapidly. 'The British had set it up as an "anything goes, no-regulation" world,' remembers the veteran US crime-fighter Jack Blum. 'Corporations doing business in China set up Hong Kong companies with secret shareholdings,' Blum continued. 'Today Hong Kong is where most of the corruption in China is accomplished.'

When Britain handed it over to China in 1997 China preserved this offshore centre as a 'special administrative zone', and Hong Kong's Basic Law states that it shall 'enjoy a high degree of autonomy' from China in all matters except foreign relations and defence. The resemblance with the ambiguous Britain–Jersey link, or the Britain–Cayman arrangement, is no coincidence. Chinese elites want their own offshore centre, complete with political control and judicial separation. When the G20 countries sought to approve a tax haven blacklist at a summit meeting in April 2009, Chinese premier Hu Jintao fought intransigently with Barack Obama to get Hong Kong and Macau, another notorious Asian offshore hub, excluded. He got them relegated to a footnote.

Despite Chinese control, City of London interests remain closely engaged, not least through Britain's largest bank HSBC – the Hong Kong & Shanghai Banking Corporation. Known affectionately by the colonials as the 'Honkers and Shankers,' HSBC moved its CEO from London to Hong Kong in March 2010 to reflect its shifting focus.

Although Hong Kong is growing fast, it is still a fairly small player in the offshore world: its $149 billion in non-resident deposits in 2007 were just one-eleventh as big as the Cayman Islands' $1.7 trillion. Hong Kong will be a lesser player for years, though perhaps one day it could become a financial tool in Chinese imperial strategies.

Singapore set up its financial centre in 1968, while it was still part of the British Sterling currency zone.[20] 'Singapore's success came mainly from being the money-laundering centre for corrupt Indonesian businessmen and government officials,' Andy Xie, Morgan Stanley's star Asia economist, wrote in an internal email in 2006. 'To sustain its economy, Singapore is building casinos to attract corruption money from China.'[21]

Something else turned up in the archives from that era. Dated 23 February 1969, it is a cutting from the *Sunday Times* of a piece written by its financial editor Charles Raw. While it is not unusual to find newspaper clippings in the British government historical archives, the presence of this particular one – closing the file, and with no attendant commentary – is intriguing. Might it have been left as a marker for historians? Something that couldn't be stated explicitly? The name of the clipping is at least suggestive: WHY NOT TURN THE CITY INTO A TAX HAVEN?

Raw's article, written during the great boom phase of the offshore Eurodollar market in London, is a piece of unashamed cheerleading for the City. It derides a 'notorious' section of the UK tax code giving tax collectors powers to curb offshore leakage, and says London should let non-residents buy tax-free funds. 'Most of the authorities' energies over the past few years have been devoted to stopping money going out,' Raw wrote. 'But perhaps it would be more rewarding to pay greater attention to money coming in.' The article begins by praising a Geneva-based mutual fund group called Investors Overseas Services (IOS), which Raw says 'has done wonders for the US balance of payments by pumping the world's savings into US shares'. It touts a new Bermuda-based fund that would 'like to do the same for the UK balance of payments'.

IOS was no ordinary company. Raw went on to write a book about it whose title, *Do You Sincerely Want to be Rich?* was the line IOS salesmen used around Europe as they hoovered up retail investments. Bernie Cornfeld, who founded and built IOS, called it 'people's capitalism', and he made IOS into the largest foreign institutional investors on the US stock exchange. His board of directors included a former governor of California, Pat Brown, and FDR's son James Roosevelt, and many of his advisers came from the Bank of England.[22] Cornfeld bought castles in France, sailed a forty-two-foot yacht and drove a Lancia Flaminia convertible. He dated the *Dallas* soap opera star Victoria Principal and the Hollywood madam Heidi Fleiss, and his company bought banks in the Bahamas, Luxembourg and Switzerland. 'I had mansions all over the world, I threw extravagant parties,' Cornfeld said. 'And I lived with ten or twelve girls at a time.'

He originally left the United States 'looking for a less competitive market' as one obituary put it. As ever, the offshore system proved a welcoming playground for those who find normal market competition in well-regulated home markets too much trouble. IOS's fragmented national identity – it was incorporated in Panama and headquartered in Switzerland – was the key to its success. The US tax authorities considered it a European company and it was so fragmented that nobody could find out what it was all about: a quintessentially offshore company. When the authorities in France became suspicious of it, Cornfeld moved to Switzerland – where he teamed up with the same secretive bank in Geneva that the mobster Meyer Lansky was using as the depository for the skim from his casinos.

Cornfeld started taking money from US military personnel stationed in Germany, then began looking further afield: first targeting the estimated 2.5 million US expatriates around the world; then the British networks – traders in Hong Kong and settlers in Kenya; then French rubber planters in Laos and Vietnam, Belgian miners in Congo, the Lebanese in west Africa, the overseas Chinese, and so on. When he bought his first aircraft, a joke went around inside IOS that he was starting up 'capital flight airlines'. Its couriers, according to Tom Naylor's book *Hot Money*, spirited huge sums out of developing countries. 'As civil war raged in Nigeria and international relief for the traumatised civilian population rolled in,' Naylor wrote, 'IOS was on the scene to help: the international aid funds often wound up in the safe in Geneva.' Even bigger sums were being bled from Latin America.

This, remember, is the company that was being held up as a model for turning the City of London into a tax haven. Worse, by the time Raw's article emerged, IOS was *already* enmeshed in high-profile scandals, including illegal operations discovered in a Brazilian police raid in 1966 and a high-profile *Life* magazine exposé of a joint IOS-Lansky courier operation in 1967. What was Raw thinking?

Tom Naylor notes another curiosity about illegal offshore money. Banks take in deposits (which are liabilities of the bank) and make loans (which are its assets), but they also hold buffers of capital, which is what investors put in. If loans go bad, this capital serves as a kind of shock absorber: it is the investor capital, not the deposits, that takes the hit – though if more and more loans go bad and the capital gets exhausted, then the bank runs into real trouble, as happened in the latest financial crisis. Prudent bankers will restrict their loans up to a multiple (ten times, say) of the capital buffer. Capital is more valuable to bankers than deposits: the more capital you have, the more you may multiply your balance sheet.

This helps us understand why banks like secret offshore deposits so much. Investigators who probed IOS said it operated under an assumption that 10–20 per cent of its deposits were effectively permanent capital – because the owners could not withdraw it, either because it was too risky for them to do so, or because they were dead. No wonder Swiss bankers were so reluctant to hand over the deposits of Jews who died in Hitler's concentration camps: the US Volcker commission probing the assets of dead Jews in the Second World War found an internal memorandum from a large Swiss commercial bank that creaming off money from dead people's accounts was the 'usual way . . . to accumulate reserves'.[23] Not only that, but offshore bank deposits in secrecy jurisdictions are yet more profitable because depositors willingly accept below-market interest rates, in exchange for secrecy. It is hardly a surprise that banks became so very interested in offshore private banking.

By 1970 Cornfeld's IOS was tottering. Its Swiss employees started complaining that Cornfeld owed them money. More importantly, an insider accountant, quietly picking through IOS's international labyrinth, realised that it was a house of cards. It collapsed and fell into the hands of Robert Vesco, a businessman one partner called 'a sonofabitch who hurt, denigrated or corrupted everyone he had contact with'. Another associate said Vesco 'could talk you right out of your socks, or blast you out of them, or you would find somebody else owned your socks'. Though Vesco had supported Lynden Pindling, US pressure forced him out of the Bahamas in 1973 after he was found to have secretly donated $200,000 to Richard Nixon's Committee to Re-Elect the President (Creep) part-financing the Watergate burglary.

The archives from the 1960s and 1970s paint a clear picture of British interests, led by the Bank of England, pushing for the expansion of this new offshore web, though more research is needed on exactly when and how this thinking coalesced into the spider's web strategy. While civil servants argued over what was to be done, locals were simply getting on and building their new private domains, almost entirely free of interference from London.

One of the very earliest offshore practitioners was Casey Gill, an ethnic Indian lawyer and author of a book about the Cayman Islands' offshore attractions, who arrived early enough to see it grow from a slow, sleepy fishing village.[24]

Tax experts and accountants would fly in from around the world to give seminars. 'They would come and say "these are the loopholes in our system."' And Caymans legislation would be designed accordingly. Local practitioners would also note what other offshore jurisdictions were up to, and adopt the local laws to stay ahead. 'Someone would say, "we are competing with Liechtenstein." Or in those days the Bahamas was still trying to come through. Panama was there; and Switzerland.' The Caymans got to work targeting the gaps. 'There was also the Red Threat: the Russians. Investors were seeing shadows and ghosts everywhere. We had Castro clauses: if any government tries to expropriate assets, it would turn out they were simultaneously domiciled somewhere else.'

Plenty of business came from poor countries of Latin America, William Walker, a veteran of the Cayman financial sector, told a visiting journalist in 1982. Most of the 1,400 registered companies whose names festooned the walls outside his office, Walker said, 'don't require too much work – just signing occasional documents and perhaps holding two meetings a year. We funnel a lot of money from Central and South America ... Most of the money coming out of Latin

America, of course, is in breach of their governments' exchange control regulations.'

Gill was a founder member of a body called the Private Sector Consultative Committee, an association representing every branch of the burgeoning financial sector: trust practitioners, accountants, bankers, lawyers and so on. Any government legislation that impacted on Cayman's role as a tax haven would go through the PSCC.

The government has a legal draftsman. We would meet them. He would go and prepare a draft and circulate it back to us. We would come back with suggestions. It would be redrafted and circulated to the PSCC. It would get the OK, then the government would pass it into law. The governor would send it to the FCO (Foreign and Commonwealth Office) – and they would say 'no problem.' Usually business would say, 'This is what we want,' and the FCO would let you do what you want to do.

I asked Gill if Britain ever said no or raised objections to the new legislation. 'No. Not ever. Never.' He qualified that a little: there had been a case 'eight or nine years ago' when London delayed some legislation a little. But his basic point was clear. While the Gentlemen in London buzzed around like irritated bluebottles, the wizards of global finance – not to mention half the world's criminals – were forging their own private Caribbean domains, all under Britain's benevolent, protective gaze – and almost entirely free from outside interference.

And so the offshore industry grew. Rich, sophisticated countries patched up their tax and regulatory systems as best they could, leaving developing nations ever more exposed to the drains. And so poverty was entrenched ever more deeply, around the world.

Just as the Bank of England had officially tolerated but quietly encouraged the growth of the offshore Eurodollar market from 1955, so Britain adopted a policy of official tolerance and quiet encouragement towards its new secret empire.

In 1976 the Caymans' offshore industry got a new and unexpected fillip. It started when Anthony Field, the managing director of Castle Bank & Trust (Cayman) Ltd, was served with a subpoena on arriving at Miami airport, on suspicion that his bank was facilitating tax evasion by American citizens. The US authorities wanted him to testify before a grand jury, but he refused. In response, the Cayman

Islands drafted the infamous Confidential Relationships (Preservation) Law, which makes it a crime punishable by prison to reveal financial or banking arrangements in Cayman. You can go to jail not only for revealing information, but just for *asking* for it.[25] It was a giant, fist-pumping Fuck You aimed squarely at American law enforcement – and became a cornerstone of Cayman's success. Cayman offshore practitioners remember cash literally flying in on private aircraft. Chris Johnson, an accountant, remembered in an interview in 2009 how people would arrive with large amounts of money in suitcases and get a police escort to the bank if they requested it. Britain did nothing. In one banking audit his company raised an objection – which the government simply ignored. 'That, coupled with the leather-clad hot-panted secretarial staff strutting through the deep-pile carpets in high heels – might also have been construed as a red flag,' he said. The bank failed two years later. And the fiascos, he added wearily, just kept coming.

By the early 1980s the Caribbean was the world's main offshore drugs turntable, as Colombian Medellin cartel kingpin Carlos Lehder smuggled industrial quantities of cocaine from Norman's Cay in the Bahamas, which he had set up as the ultimate male libertarian fantasy. Carlos Toro, a former Lehder pilot, remembers being picked up by naked women at the airport. 'It was Sodom and Gomorrah,' he said. 'Drugs, sex, no police . . . you made the rules.'[26] Lehder's goons played hide and seek with the US Coast Guard across Biscayne bay, landing planes on US interstate highways and leaving bodies strewn across Florida. As cocaine flooded into America, money flew back out in shrink-wrapped bills loaded on wooden pallets and the Cayman Islands would then return it to the Federal Reserve. This business was, at least, saving Britain tens of thousands in foreign aid. How, the Fed wanted to know, could this tiny island selling trinkets to cruise ships send them such a torrent of money? Finally, they put their foot down, and began to plug some of the worst leaks.

Today the era of suitcases of drug money flooding into Cayman is pretty much over. Jack Blum explained what happened next. 'They would say "We don't do that now." Each time they were exposed, they would clean up the thing that was exposed. They'd say things like "We're in financial deals now; we're in insurance." You go back to

Cayman today, and all the guys are in pin-striped suits.' The crimes have continued, but in different guises. In March 2001 the US Senate Permanent Subcommittee on Investigations took testimony from an American owner of a Cayman Island offshore bank who estimated that 100 per cent of his clients were engaged in tax evasion and 95 per cent were US citizens.

'One problem we have in trying to recover the assets,' said Chris Johnson, 'is that we don't even know who the directors are.' Cayman's infamous confidentiality law, which Johnson thinks should be shredded, shrouds everything in deep secrecy.[27]

As a liquidator, I am following the money. If I want to negotiate with a director I have no way, no clue. If I go and ask someone, 'Are you sitting on half a million dollars of my money?' that's breaking the law, and the penalty is jail. It is preposterous that these directors, some of whom sit on the boards of more than a hundred companies – one sits on over 450 boards of directors – are charging fees of up to £20,000 a company.

Company law statutes in the Cayman Islands come from English law as far back as 1862 – with certain democratic provisions removed – one of which means that frequently the directors of hedge funds or mutual funds are indemnified from litigation. 'So you can't be sued for negligence. Suppose I'm liquidating a fund and $200 million is gone. Why shouldn't I be able to sue them? The directors are steering the ship, but when it sinks they can't be sued.'

The companies that provide directors, other sources indicate, do not owe a duty of care to the company or its creditors to ensure that the directors they provide perform their functions properly.[28] No wonder directors and companies – not to mention fraudsters – love the Cayman Islands. And no wonder so many Cayman vehicles have come to so much grief in the latest financial crisis.

Dig beneath the Cayman Islands' sunny spin, and you will find incentives to mischief everywhere. 'Client privacy,' a government website notes, 'is protected by the fact that the Registrar of Companies can only release the name and type of company, its date of registration, the address of the registered office and the company's status.'[29] You cannot find a list of directors of companies in Cayman, or even a charter that describes what a company is about, without going through a court battle. Trusts do not have to be registered – and there lies another very large and murky tale.

The form and the context has changed, for sure, but at root Cayman still does what it always did: find clever new ways to undermine the rules and laws of other nation states.

7

The Fall of America

How America learned to stop worrying and love offshore business

Early in 1966 a young economist working at the New York head-quarters of Chase Manhattan Bank was in a company elevator when a former State Department operative handed him a memo. It isn't clear if Chase management knew of the memo – it came from Washington, not from Chase – but the young economist, Michael Hudson, was staggered by its contents. Hudson had got into banking by chance: after studying economics at New York University in 1960 he took a job in real estate banking and later, when an opening came up at Chase to look at balance of payments issues, he was the only applicant. Now a respected if controversial American economic commentator, Hudson said his time at Chase – during which, incidentally, he fired a 'nasty little twit' called Alan Greenspan – taught him most of what he ever learned about international economics.

Chase was the oil companies' preferred bank, and it had asked Hudson to study the balance of payments of the petroleum industry, in order to show that the oil companies were 'good for America' and help them lobby for special perks from the government. Hudson had been asked to find out where the oil companies made their profits. At the producing end? At the refineries? In the gas stations? David Rockefeller, Chase's president, arranged for Hudson to meet Jack Bennett, treasurer of Standard Oil of New Jersey, now part of the ExxonMobil empire. Bennett gave him his answer. 'The profits are made right here in my office,' the oil man said. 'Wherever I decide.'

He was talking about transfer pricing, the practice I explained earlier, in which banana companies trail their accounts around the world's tax havens in order to shift paper profits into low-tax countries and costs into high-tax countries. Bennett showed Hudson exactly how large vertically integrated multinationals could shift profits around the globe, apparently without breaking the law. The company would sell its crude oil cheap to a shipping affiliate registered in zero-tax Panama or Liberia, which in turn sold it on at nearly retail price to its refineries and marketing outlets. In the high-tax countries where the oil is produced and consumed, the subsidiaries buy at a high price and sell cheap, so they are unprofitable. But in the middle, in zero-tax Panama or Liberia, the subsidiaries buy cheap and sell dear, making vast profits. But these havens levy no tax on those profits. To this day, accounting standards effectively hide this kind of trickery, letting companies shovel results from different countries into a single category (often called simply 'international') which cannot be unpicked to work out who takes what profit where. 'Only the immense political power of these extractive sectors,' said Hudson, 'could have induced their governments to remain so passive in the face of the fiscal drain.'

In the 1960s this kind of offshore leakage was relatively restrained when compared to today. Capital flows were strongly regulated, taxes were high, and the Euromarkets were growing fast but still small. The golden age of capitalism was in full swing: American households, and particularly the poorest, were seeing tremendous improvements in wealth and welfare; Germans were basking in their *Wirtschaftswunder*; France was in the midst of its *Trente Glorieuses*; Italy was installing the springboard for its *Il Sorpasso* moment twenty years later, when its GDP outgrew Britain's; and Japan was unleashing its own economic miracle. In large swathes of the developing world infant mortality was falling, economies were growing, unemployment was tumbling and hungry children were finding meat regularly on their dinner tables.

Although change was coming, and Britain was nurturing the Euromarket in London and starting to set up its post-imperial spider's web, the United States still contained major and powerful opponents of the offshore system. After the Great Depression, Wall Street, diluted in a large and diversified industrial economy, had relatively little political clout to veto progressive New Deal-style legislation. By contrast, the City of London's position at the centre of the globe-spanning British empire gave it the domestic political heft to sabotage any British version of the New Deal. Not only had British finance not been so directly implicated in the excesses of the 1920s, London was perfectly placed to provide American banks with an escape route from regulation at home. They could rebuild their powers offshore. The brief memo passed to Hudson in the elevator suggested, however, that some Americans were hoping to transform the US approach to the offshore world.

'Like Switzerland, flight money probably flows to the US from every country in the world,' the memo began. Then the complaints started. 'US-based and US-controlled entities are badly penalized in competing for flight money with the Swiss or other foreign flight money centers.' One reason America lagged behind in the quest for dirty money, it argued, was the 'demonstrated ability of the US Treasury, Justice Department, CIA and FBI to subpoena client records, attach client accounts and force testimony from US officers of US-controlled entities, with proper US court back-up.' There were also American taxes, plus risks associated with the Cold War and a view among 'sophisticated' foreigners that American money managers were 'naive and inexperienced in manipulation of foreign funds'.[1] It also criticised investment and brokerage restraints 'which limit the flexibility and secrecy of investment activity.'

The message was unequivocal. America ought to turn itself into a tax haven. 'They were saying, "We want to replace Switzerland. All this money will come here if we make this the criminal centre of the world. This is how we fund Vietnam,"' Hudson said. 'We wanted foreign criminal money, which was patriotic, but not the American criminal money.' The staffer in the elevator suggested to Hudson that he might find out how much foreign illicit money the United States might be able to get.

By 2005 US banks were free to receive the proceeds from a long list of crimes committed outside the country, including alien smuggling, racketeering, peonage and slavery.[2] Profiting from crime is legal, so long as the crime itself happens offshore. A few of these loopholes have now been closed, and the US has laws that address *some* of the others, though often only in tangential, incomplete ways. But it remains true that a US bank can knowingly receive the proceds of a wide range of foreign crimes, such as handling stolen property generated offshore. The United States is wide open for dirty money, just as Hudson's memo anticipated.

Even before Hudson stepped into that elevator, the US had some tax haven characteristics. From 1921, the United States has let foreigners deposit money with American banks and receive interest tax-free, as long as the deposit isn't connected with a US business.[3] And Wall Street had ensured that America wasn't going to tell foreign governments about their citizens' holdings, despite the best efforts of John Maynard Keynes and Harry Dexter White to combat capital flight with financial transparency. When President John F. Kennedy launched his Alliance for Progress with Latin America in 1961 – 'a vast cooperative effort, unparalleled in magnitude and nobility of purpose', as he put it – he said he hoped to coax Latin Americans into repatriating all the money they had stashed in American banks, and reinvest it at home. Latin Americans pointed out that this would not happen unless America amended its tax laws and ended secret banking. Substantial pockets of secretly held foreign wealth already existed, not just on Wall Street, but elsewhere too – in Texas, but also most especially in the Southern District of Florida.

Just as Latin Americans used the USA as a home for tax evasion, immigrant communities in the US, and especially first-generation Americans, are major tax evaders. 'For various cultural reasons they didn't trust anyone – so they put it offshore,' said Mike Flowers, a former US Senate staffer. As well as the Latin Americans, there are large concentrations of Iranians and Russians in California, 'New Asians' on the West Coast and Jewish communities in various locations. 'They tend to come clean after they have kids and have been here a while,' he continued. 'They get settled and then they think, "Oh my God, I have all this offshore money and what do I do now? If I get caught, I'm screwed."'

In an article entitled MIAMI, THE CAPITAL OF LATIN AMERICA, *Time* magazine hinted at its in-between quasi-offshore status: Miami was 'Latin America's Wall Street . . . a hemispheric crossroads for trade, travel and communications in the 21st century – a sort of Hong Kong of the Americas'.[4] From the 1950s and 1960s Florida became a pivot for the French Connection heroin route, for Kuomintang drugs flowing into the US via Hong Kong, which Lansky laundered through Florida real estate, for Latin American flight money, and for Colombian drug money, often routed via the Bahamas, Panama and the Netherlands Antilles.[5]

Jack Blum, then a Senate investigator, remembers sitting on his veranda in Miami and hearing the gunfire. 'This place was nuts,' he said. 'The stories in the *Miami Herald* were so fantastic, you'd say, "Why hasn't any national editor picked up on this?"' The reason, he found, was that they simply didn't believe them. Blum tells of a small aircraft coming in from Colombia via the Bahamas being chased by US helicopters. The pilot tried to escape by hiding just under a commercial jetliner, then swerving out just before landing. He then put the plane on autopilot and threw out the cocaine. 'The first bag goes through the roof of a house – and nobody complains. The second whacks the steeple off the South Miami Baptist Church. The third bag falls into a community swimming pool and soaks the audience – a meeting of Crime Stoppers. The plane went down in the Everglades – the last bags probably got dragged off by alligators. He got busted.'

By the 1980s, 40 per cent of the money on deposit in Miami banks was reckoned to originate overseas, particularly in Latin America. After 1976, the Florida region became the only one of the Federal Reserve's regions to show persistent (and huge) cash surpluses.[6] 'Half the property in Miami is owned by offshore shell companies, and the largest yachts on the Intracoastal waterway are registered offshore,' said Blum. 'Miami is the facility of choice for Latin ex-heads of state, generals and former friends of the CIA.'

Washington did not push hard on transparency: it might frighten foreign capital owners, leading to large net outflows, and worsening an already bad balance-of-payments situation. Kennedy first tried to curb these outflows in July 1963 with the Interest Equalisation Tax, a levy of up to 15 per cent on income Americans received from foreign securities. The aim was to stop them exporting capital to buy foreign bonds.[7] Instead, businesses flocked to the offshore Euromarkets to finance their activities. In one year, between 1962 and 1963, London-based borrowing tripled. America continued to bleed capital, and in 1965 President Johnson introduced limited controls on outward capital flows.[8] 'This was the first time in US history there were rules to stop capital flowing out,' said Jack Blum. 'And the corporate community went ape shit.'

In the face of all the lobbying that ensued, a compromise was quietly accepted. Corporations could legally keep their money offshore, and it would mostly remain untaxed unless they repatriated it.

This is a concept called *deferred* tax – and it is a crucial element of the offshore system. Corporations hold their profits offshore, indefinitely, and only when they bring it back home to pay out as dividends to shareholders does it get taxed. Deferred taxes – taxes that a corporation should (in a fair world) pay this year but choose to delay – are described by Richard Murphy of Tax Research UK as 'a tax-free loan from the government, with no repayment date.' This sharply reduces multinationals' cost of capital – a very big deal, especially when this is accumulated over many years – and this in turn gives them a huge competitive advantage against smaller, locally based firms.[9] US corporations alone were believed to hold a trillion dollars' worth of untaxed foreign profits offshore in 2009.

Sometimes, corporations can bring this offshore money back through loopholes or amnesties: in 2004 George W. Bush's administration offered his corporate friends a chance to repatriate profits and pay just five per cent tax rate instead of the normal 35 per cent. Over $360 billion whooshed back to the US, much of which went into share buybacks, boosting executive bonuses. 'There is no evidence,' said the non-profit research organisation Citizens for Tax Justice, 'that the amnesty added a single job to the US economy.'

President Kennedy had put in place legislation to crack down hard on deferred tax – so this new compromise, relaxing the provisions, was a tremendous political boost for the offshore system, just as US banks were discovering the wonders of offshore. 'Suddenly,' Blum explained, 'every major corporation uses an offshore account.' Companies focused especially on London, centre of the new Eurodollar market, but also on Panama, then ruled by a right-wing strongman who venerated Adolf Hitler, and on the Bahamas, where Meyer Lansky had the politicians in his pocket. In America, Lansky had close links to the Mob lawyer Sidney Korshak, a true American Mafia kingmaker who in turn helped the careers of several Hollywood actors, including Ronald Reagan. Some large US corporations even opened their own offshore banks.

The interests of big-time criminals, the intelligence services, wealthy Americans and US corporations converged ever more closely offshore. The system was working two transformations simultaneously: it was helping criminal enterprises imitate legitimate businesses, and encouraging legitimate businesses to behave more like criminal enterprises.

'The trouble is,' Blum said, 'you can't separate the channels for paying people off from the other purposes.' Although it was tax, not criminality, that most interested the industrial corporations (and lax financial regulation that interested the banks), the big American crime families were especially pleased with the political umbrella that the corporations and spies had hoisted over their offshore playgrounds. And the secrecy, in turn, provided the managers of large corporations with fabulous new opportunities for bribery, insider trading and fraud. A new crime-friendly environment was being created for American capitalism. The scale of this criminality can hardly be guessed at. But secrecy makes criminality possible. And in competitive markets whatever is possible becomes necessary.

As this offshore expansion accelerated, the erosion of America from the inside gathered pace.

The oil crises of the 1970s led to high inflation: this, plus the legacy of Vietnam-era deficits, sent the dollar spiralling downwards. In August 1979 President Carter appointed Paul Volcker, a renowned hard-money man, to head the Federal Reserve Board and reassure the markets. Carter cut spending, and Volcker tightened monetary policy savagely. But Volcker had a problem. Monetarist theories of tackling economic problems by focusing on the money supply were coming into vogue just as the Euromarkets, lacking regulation and official checks on banks' abilities to create money out of thin air, were starting to disrupt the Fed's efforts to control that very money supply.[10] Volcker called for a new cooperative international framework through the Bank for International Settlements in Switzerland, to get other countries to clamp down on uncontrolled money creation in the offshore system. But New York bankers, in alliance with the Bank of England and the Swiss National Bank, killed the initiative.[11]

The bankers of Manhattan now began to wield the offshore system as a weapon to attack the New Deal regulations that had so effectively clipped their wings at home. In the words of Professor Ronen Palan, a leading academic authority on the offshore system, 'The New York banking fraternity, led by Chase Manhattan, used the real or imagined threat posed by the Euromarket and the Caribbean tax havens – which the same banks had of course helped establish as large financial centres in the first place – to achieve their aim of more liberal financial laws.'[12] If you can't beat the offshore markets, the lobbyists argued, then join them. In June 1981, less than six months after Ronald Reagan got into the White House, America approved a new offshore possibility, the International Banking Facility. The US was a step closer to what Hudson's memo had been driving at.

IBFs, as they are known, are a kind of offshore Euromarkets-lite: they let American bankers do at home what they could previously do only in places like London, Zürich or Nassau – lend to foreigners, free from reserve requirements and from city and state taxes. The bankers would sit in the same Manhattan offices as before, but simply open up a new set of books and operate as if they were a branch in Nassau. Before IBFs came in, a Citibank trader had planted a cardboard sign saying NASSAU on a desk in a Citibank trading room in New York, and recorded trades at that desk, booking them offshore and out of sight of the regulators. After someone in Switzerland discovered the ploy, the traders continued as before, but ensured that a clerk copied them into a second set of books in the Bahamas.[13] Once the IBFs were in place, the banks could dispense with the subterfuge entirely and book them openly in New York. The United States had moved closer to the British offshore model.

Bankers in New York signed up with gusto, followed by Florida, California, Illinois and Texas. In three years almost 500 offshore IBFs popped up inside the US, draining money out of the offshore markets in the Caribbean and elsewhere.[14] It was a get-out-of-regulation-free card for Wall Street, and another hole in the American fortress. Not only that, but as the author Tom Naylor put it, 'The US hoped to use the IBFs as a bludgeon to force other countries to relax restrictions on the entry of US banks into their domestic financial markets.'

Japan followed the US lead in 1986 by creating its own offshore market, modelled on the IBFs. This happened just at the start of a massive credit boom, followed by what was at the time the biggest asset market crash in history. That roller coaster had many causes, but was partly powered by the $400 billion that whooshed into Tokyo within twenty-four months and showed local bankers what liberalised finance was all about.[15] This was also the year of the fateful Big Bang of deregulation in the City of London, which provided Wall Street with major new escape routes from financial regulation.

As offshore finance moved onshore, it became ever harder to tell the two apart. And this, crucially, fed a giant blind spot, which persists to this day. Nearly every analyst took the blurring between onshore and offshore as a signal to stop trying to measure or analyse secrecy jurisdictions, or just to focus on a few smaller, more colourful island havens. Palan, in his book *The Offshore World,* explains what was really happening. 'Far from signalling the decline of offshore,' he wrote, the process 'must be interpreted as the embedding of offshore in the global political economy'.[16]

John Christensen remembers noticing this blind spot in 1986. He had been working as a development economist in Malaysia, where he had been investigating some strange local structures known as deposit-taking cooperatives, unregulated quasi-banks which had been taking huge volumes of deposits from Malaysian widows and orphans, and channelling the money offshore.

He had got curious in July 1985 when one of these cooperatives offered him a king prawn luncheon at a sumptuous office penthouse in Kuala Lumpur, washed down with Guinness and Courvoisier. As the lunch wore on the atmosphere grew more relaxed, and it became apparent that the chief financial officer, a leading light in the Malaysian Chinese Association, wanted to steer the conversation towards Christensen's childhood roots over 6,500 miles away in the Crown Dependency of Jersey. The CFO was most interested in talking about its status as a major and growing tax haven. He wanted to know if it was safe to invest.

Christensen resolved to research their cooperatives. 'The whole thing was a massive scam,' he said. The Malaysian Central Bank wouldn't regulate them and nobody else would touch them. Their international offshore dimension made it impossible for anyone locally – whether curious depositors or government regulators – to find out what was really happening: how profits were being shifted to insiders and risks being heaped onto the shoulders of ordinary Malaysian depositors or taxpayers. After detailed research, he got an article published in the *Business Times* in December 1985 and left the country. It caused a huge scandal. Within months, the central bank had suspended twenty-four cooperatives amid a massive run by depositors.

Yet it was what happened afterwards that he found truly odd. He went to Britain, where he spent a couple of months combing libraries and seeing all the economists and capital markets experts he could find to try and understand where the money went and how the offshore system worked. Nobody knew anything. 'I don't think anyone had understood how malevolent this thing has become,' he said. 'There was no useful information anywhere.'

As the Vietnam War heated up, US deficits, later worsened by the great Reagan tax cuts of 1981, posed a quandary. American companies needed to borrow money by issuing bonds, but if they borrowed it all at home, they would compete for funds with the US government, pushing up interest rates and crimping economic growth. So it would be best if they could borrow from overseas. But there was a hitch – the tax system. A French investor, say, who wanted to buy some bonds, faced a simple choice: either invest in American bonds, and pay a 30 per cent withholding tax on the bond income, or hop on the 'coupon bus' to Luxembourg and buy Eurobonds, whose income was tax-free. Many investors saw this as no choice at all and shunned American bonds. So American policymakers had a problem. The US wasn't a tax haven, they reasoned, and they didn't want to help tax cheats unnecessarily. They wanted American companies to borrow overseas, but they wanted to keep the 30 per cent tax too. How to square this circle?

At first, they settled for a compromise. American corporations could cook up a Dutch Sandwich – set up an offshore finance subsidiary in the Netherlands Antilles, use it to issue tax-free Eurobonds and send the proceeds up to the American parent. The US could argue that it did not have to tax this income from the Antilles under the rules of a tax treaty that the islands had with the US. The US Internal Revenue Service (IRS) could easily have decided that the Dutch Sandwich was a sham, and taxed the income, but it chose to look the other way. 'These were Eurobonds, bearer bonds, which were virtually impossible to tax,' explained Michael J. McIntyre, a top US expert on international tax, one of very few people in America to oppose this at the time. 'You British people were quite happy about [the tax-free, secretive Eurobond markets]. And we wanted in. We wanted to attract the hot money too.'

David Rosenbloom, who was in charge of these matters at the US Treasury from 1978 to 1980, also remembers how questionable these officially tolerated offshore antics were. 'People were very nervous.

Those companies wanted access to the Eurodollar market, and they really wanted security,' he said. 'The Antilles structures were kind of phoney – these were paper entities; they weren't doing anything real. They existed in some *notaire*'s desk drawer down in Curaçao.'[17]

The Carter administration decided to commission a major survey of secrecy jurisdictions, the first really serious challenge to the havens in world history. The Gordon Report, as it was called, condemned tax havenry as a situation that 'attracts criminals and is abusive to other countries' and called on America to lead the world in a crackdown. Published a week before Ronald Reagan was inaugurated in 1981, it was buried almost immediately.

Even before Carter left office, the US told the Netherlands Antilles it wanted to renegotiate the treaty. 'A whole bunch of rulings came down that scared the Bejesus out of everybody,' said Rosenbloom. 'These were the days when people were actually afraid of our tax authorities.' Yet there was a hitch: having tacitly encouraged the Antilles loophole, the US was not in a great position to object. 'From the point of view of US tax policy these things were utterly objectionable, but the US government had its hands completely dirty,' Rosenbloom continued. 'The government was in a bad position to start getting all self-righteous about this. The Antilles could have gotten a decent treaty that would have let them carry on doing business in some form. I was prepared to compromise. I didn't think we had the gumption to do this.' Yet the Netherlands Antilles overplayed their hand. 'They were holding out,' Rosenbloom said. 'They thought they could push the United States around in treaty negotiations. They wanted more of this and more of that, and this benefit and that benefit . . . they just held tough on all sorts of positions that we couldn't accept.'

American corporations grew skittish, and out of the commotion a new approach was hatched: from 1984, the United States would bypass the Antilles irritant entirely and waive the 30 per cent witholding tax under a new loophole.[18] American companies would no longer set up fictional entities in Curaçao, but simply issue their bonds at home. Foreign investors would pay no tax on their bond income.

The loophole was supposed to be available to foreign investors only, but unscrupulous wealthy Americans, of course, got around that simply by covering themselves in a cloak of offshore secrecy, and *pretending* to be foreigners. 'The Wall Street types were as happy as clams,' said McIntyre. 'The rules were designed to facilitate tax evasion. It was a very hot business: people in high places liked it and fostered it. They didn't think it was an ethical issue . . . Nobody seemed to object, except my brother Bob and I.'[19]

It was a classic tax haven gambit: plug the deficits by exempting foreigners from tax, and watch as the world's hot money rolls in. It was just as Hudson's memo had anticipated.

The effects were immense. Having set up international banking facilities in 1981, America now had a thriving home-grown offshore bond market. 'Suddenly,' noted *Time* magazine, 'America has become the largest and possibly the most alluring tax haven in the world.' From then on, a drip-drip of new laws and statutes nibbled away at America's onshore defences.

In the late 1990s Bill Clinton's Treasury secretary and former Goldman Sachs co-chairman Robert Rubin deepened the offshore corrosion with a devious new piece of legislation: the Qualified Intermediary (QI) programme. The US authorities wanted to find out about American accounts at foreign financial institutions, yet it could not simply request *all* the information – about both foreigners and US citizens – then simply sift out the American tax cheats and ignore the foreigners. If it did receive information about foreigners, the United States would be obliged under its tax treaties to tell foreign governments about their citizens' US investments. These citizens would then take their money out of the US and park it somewhere else, where it would remain secret, and US deficits would widen.

The answer was to outsource the screening to foreign banks, who would tell the Americans only about US citizens and not pass on any information about foreigners. If the US did not have the information, it would have nothing to exchange with foreign jurisdictions, and it wouldn't be breaking its treaties. 'The rules were designed to make it difficult for the US government to learn who the tax cheats were,' McIntyre explained.[20] 'This evasion was intended to benefit American borrowers by allowing them to borrow from tax cheats at a reduced interest rate.'[21]

This is another classic offshore ruse. A tax haven sets up worthy treaties that require them to exchange information with foreign jurisdictions, then they set up the structures to make sure that they never have the information to exchange in the first place. They keep their secrecy, but – by pointing to their treaties – they can claim that they are a transparent and cooperative jurisdiction. As New York attorney David Spencer put it, the result of QI is that 'the IRS does not have information to exchange with foreign governments, and does not have access to such information. This, of course, is a sophisticated form of bank secrecy.'

Not only that, but banks simply lied to the US authorities about what they were doing. Under cover of the QI programme, members of the Swiss aristocracy trawled the America's Cup and Boston Symphony Orchestra concerts for wealthy Americans to set them up with tax evasion schemes, even smuggling out diamonds in toothpaste tubes. Then they would tick the box to confirm they were respecting American banking laws. David Rosenbloom encapsulated the cynicism. 'The programme was not aimed at identifying Americans,' he said. 'The programme was aimed at protecting the identity of foreigners while allowing them to invest in the US.' This narrow focus meant that only clumsy or poorly advised American tax evaders would ever be caught.

A veteran official Washington investigator who asked to remain anonymous, described how one American lawyer responded to the Qualified Intermediary programme. 'This guy has a wonderful practice teaching people how to game the system,' he said. 'The first thing he does is put together a power point to the banks in central European secrecy jurisdictions, on how to get around the reporting obligations. That sonofabitch yelled at me down the phone,' he continued. 'This is such an abuse of part of our legal culture. They fought [the US government] every step of the way.'

The Clinton administration, to be fair, issued proposed regulations near the end of its second term that would have provided OECD countries with information about their citizens' US bank deposits. American banks, especially those with major deposits in Florida and Texas, lobbied hard, and George W. Bush's administration dropped them.[22]

The United States sells financial secrecy not just at a federal level but at state level too. Delaware is the biggest state provider of offshore corporate secrecy, but Nevada and Wyoming are the most opaque: until 2007 they allowed bearer shares, a vehicle of choice for mobsters and drugs smugglers, and they are particularly lax on allowing company directors and other officers to be nominees, hiding the identities of the real owners. Nevada does not share tax or incorporation information with the federal government, and does not require a corporation to report where it does business. The IRS has no way of knowing whether a Nevada corporation has filed a federal tax return. Arkansas, Oklahoma and Oregon are also routinely used for fraud by eastern Europeans and Russians, and Texas and Florida are havens for illicit Latin American wealth.

In the 1990s the US government provided millions in aid to help the former Soviet Union countries improve security at their nuclear power plants. Much of it went missing. When the US Department of Justice went looking for it, they finally tracked it down to anonymous shell companies in Pennsylvania and Delaware. Most cases involving financial market manipulations that the FBI has studied involved US shell companies from these states. The notorious 'merchant of death', Viktor Bout, the inspiration for the character played by Nicolas Cage in the film *Lord of War*, ran much of his global business running arms to the Taliban and many murderous organisations around the globe through businesses in Texas, Delaware and Florida.[23] 'US shell companies are attractive vehicles for those seeking to launder money, evade taxes, finance terrorism or conduct other illicit activity anonymously,' said Republican Senator Norm Coleman, then chairman of the US Senate Permanent Subcommittee on Investigations. 'Competition among states to attract company filing revenue and franchise taxes has, in some instances, resulted in a race to the bottom.'[24]

A *New York Times* article from 1986 describes the antics of one Delaware official who flew to Taiwan, Hong Kong, China, Indonesia, Singapore and the Philippines, clutching a pamphlet boasting that Delaware could 'protect you from politics'.[25] The official was, the article noted, 'looking forward to a rich harvest of Hong Kong flight capital' after the British pull-out in 1997. 'You don't have to tell us the details of your business; you don't have to list who's on your board or who's holding office; and you don't have to use your name and address – just use your Delaware agent's.' For an extra fifty dollars, you could get this in twenty-four hours. Today, an 'aged shelf company' will help you pretend you have been trading for years when in fact you've just started up. 'It's an effective means to create a perception of business

stability,' one registered agent advertises. 'Most people won't ask . . .
there's nothing wrong with immediate gratification, as long as it's
affordable!' Behind the secrecy, nobody can discover the deception.
All this, and more, is yours for $299.

A limited liability corporation (LLC) might offer certified copies of
the passports of that company's directors. That looks reassuring, but
even with genuine passport copies you are no closer to knowing who
really owns the company or its assets. These directors are probably
professional nominees who work for hundreds of such corporations.
Typically a nominee director will route all queries via a company
attorney who has contact with the real people – and when crime
fighters come looking, the attorney will hide behind attorney–client
privilege and claim they cannot reveal the information. 'That's a secrecy
jurisdiction right there, in his office,' one irate US government investigator told me. 'The lawyers are worse than the bankers. And there
are the securities firms, and accountants. They are all involved.' LLCs
sit between the assets and the owner, screening out the information.
US states cream off a few hundred dollars in fees, and crimes around
the world go unpunished.

A Wyoming-based website boasts, 'Wyoming Corporations and
LLCs have a tax haven within the United States with no income taxation, anonymous ownership and bearer shares . . . Shelf Corporations
and LLCs: Anonymous entity where YOUR NAME IS ON NOTHING!
These companies already exist and are complete with Articles, Federal
Tax ID numbers and registered agents . . . You may have these complete
companies by TOMORROW MORNING!' Yours for sixty-nine dollars,
plus modest state filing fees.[26]

These places are selling a cheap and very strong form of secrecy.[27]
In Switzerland information is typically held there but secrecy laws mean
locals may not disclose it. States like Wyoming have no such prohibitions on breaking secrecy; the trick is simply to ensure no information is available in the first place. All company records may be kept
outside the state – in North Korea, for instance – so even if the authorities wanted to find out what your company was about, they couldn't.
Stock can be transferred instantly and privately, without filing a
public notice. United States corporate laws do not even comply with
the transparency requirements of the rather toothless Financial Action
Task Force, which requires countries to be able to identify beneficial

owners. When congressional staffers and others have tried to change this, they have met ferocious lobbying from the states concerned, and from the American Bar Association.

'When other countries ask us for company owners, we have to stand red-faced and empty-handed,' said Senator Carl Levin. 'The United States has been a leading advocate for transparency and openness. We have criticised offshore tax havens for their secrecy and lack of transparency. We have pressed them to change their ways. But look what is going on in our own backyard. America should never be the mattress that corrupt foreign officials use to hide their money.'[28]

Secrecy is just one of several lures that individual US states offer to tempt financial capital from elsewhere. Tax is another, though a fairly minor one. Certain types of corporation shield residents from state income tax, asset tax, sales tax, stock transfer tax or inheritance tax, and corporations in the US push trademarks, patents and other nebulous things into low-tax US states in a transfer pricing game to cut taxes. WorldCom, for instance, shifted nearly $20 billion tied to 'management foresight' to a Delaware company before it collapsed in 2002. Tax is never the individual states' killer weapon though; corporations paying no state taxes nevertheless are liable for US federal taxes.

Two other lures have turned certain US states into corporate havens. One involves usury; I will explore this in a later chapter. The other involves corporate governance, which in the US is largely regulated by state, not federal, laws. In both of these, Delaware plays a starring role. What ties all these different strands together – tax, secrecy, usury specialities and corporate governance – is the political establishment of this tiny state, where everyone knows everyone else, and Democrats and Republicans seem to share the conviction that local laws must be shaped to satisfy corporate desires in order to attract business for the state – and the rest of the world can take care of itself. Only a definition of 'offshore' which covers how locals prioritise their own interests explicitly at the expense of others enables us to capture all these categories and to understand what is going on.

A brief stroll through Delaware helps bring this historical section of the book up to the present day.

The second smallest state in the USA, Delaware is the home to many of the world's biggest corporations. Conventional definitions of tax havens – those that focus on tax – fail to include Delaware in the offshore system, but something important is clearly happening here. Over half of US publicly traded companies and nearly two-thirds of the Fortune 500 are incorporated here, while the little state hosted over 90 per cent of all initial public offerings in the US in 2007. These corporations don't have their headquarters there; they are just incorporated there, meaning they follow Delaware's laws on how companies may organise themselves internally.

Delawareans derive a warm patriotic glow from living in the *First State*, the first of the 13 colonies to ratify the US Constitution. But patriotism may not be the right emotion: at the constitutional convention, Delaware's delegation fought aggressively for each state to get the right to send two senators to Congress – thus putting tiny Delaware on a par with mighty New York, and giving Delawareans vastly disproportionate representation. A Delaware delegate threatened that if they didn't get their way, 'the small ones would find some foreign ally of more honor and good faith, who will take them by the hand and do them justice'.[29]

In 1899 the Delaware state government, under pressure from the influential du Pont family, who wanted to incorporate their vast chemical operations,[30] adopted a new permissive business regulation called the General Corporation Law, which reflected the laissez-faire spirit of an age of growing corporate power. In Delaware, the message went, company managers gain huge leeway to do what they want at the expense of other stakeholders. Delaware has made it especially hard for shareholders and other stakeholders to get redress. An article in the *American Law Review* that year called Delaware 'a little community of truck-farmers and clam-diggers . . . determined to get her little, tiny, sweet, round, baby hand into the grab-bag of sweet things before it is too late'.

Corporations were once explicitly regarded as vehicles to serve the public good. Delaware, however, cast that notion aside and adopted what one official Delaware account calls 'a decidedly freewheeling, private enterprise mode' in which corporations and individuals pursue their own goals, and government is kept out of the way under the assumption that the public good will advance automatically. It was a subtle but fundamental shift in attitude to the corporate form. Other states followed suit. 'Even as the starter's gun went off,' Delaware's chancery court's official history puts it, 'Delaware was already being accused of leading a "race to the bottom".'

Just before the First World War, Woodrow Wilson, governor of neighbouring New Jersey, changed his state's laws to check rampant corporate abuses, passing antitrust measures and making managements more accountable to shareholders and other stakeholders. Company managers fled across the Delaware River to Wilmington, and by 1929 40 per cent of Delaware's income came from corporate fees and taxes, and it had the lead in incorporations in the US, a lead it never lost.

Back in the twentieth century, in 1974 William Cary, a former chairman of the US Securities and Exchange Commission, wrote in a landmark article in the *Yale Law Journal* that Delaware law had 'watered down the rights of shareholders vis-à-vis management to a thin gruel. They have a direct interest in permitting suits to be brought in Delaware. Necessary high standards of conduct cannot be maintained by courts shackled to public policy based upon the production of revenue, pride in being "number one," and the creation of a "favorable climate" for new incorporations.'

When the mergers and acquisitions craze swept corporate boardrooms in the 1980s, managers came to Delaware to prepare 'poison pills' and other corporate defences to protect their positions. More recently, when outraged shareholders in Walt Disney discovered that its former president Michael Ovitz was getting a $130 million severance package after a lacklustre performance, Delaware courts overruled the shareholders, saying they had no right to interfere in board compensation policies.[31] Many corporate scandals wash up here. It is surely no coincidence that Lord Black, the newspaper tycoon who looted his company and declared his refusal to 're-enact the French Revolutionary renunciation of the rights of the nobility', incorporated in Delaware.

Delaware's approach is summed up in its chancery court's so-called business judgement rule – under which courts should not second-guess corporate managers, provided they did not blatantly violate some major rule of conduct and their decisions are approved by a 'neutral' decision-making body. Whatever one thinks of this approach, Delaware has taken it to extreme lengths, granting corporate bosses extraordinary freedoms from bothersome stockholders, judicial review and even public opinion. Bernard Black, a professor of law at Columbia

University, wrote in 1998, 'Shareholders haven't been able to stop managers, and their allies on the Delaware Supreme Court and in state legislatures, from chilling hostile takeovers through poison pills, anti-takeover statutes, and judicial decisions that let managers "treat shareholders like morons" who are incapable of understanding a firm's true value.'[32]

In 2003 Delaware passed legislation expanding its chancery court's jurisdiction, and the official synopsis said the aim was to 'keep Delaware ahead of the curve in meeting the evolving needs of businesses, thus strengthening the ability of the state to convince such businesses to incorporate and locate operations'.[33] J. Robert Brown, a professor of corporate law at Denver University and a leading critic of Delaware, said, 'Delaware courts have all but eliminated meaningful limits on self-interested transactions.'

A Reuters story in May 2010 provided a fascinating insight into one of the roles that Delaware's incorporation business has played in the latest financial crisis.[34] The story examines the 'dean of CDOs', a retired University of Delaware finance professor who is the sole independent director on the Delaware-based corporations behind more than 200 mostly sub-prime-backed collateralised debt obligations (CDOs), complex financial structures that were instrumental in triggering the latest financial crisis, including ones underwritten by Goldman Sachs and Morgan Stanley. Independent directors are supposed to bring unbiased opinions to company boards and ought to be what one expert terms 'the cornerstone of good corporate governance'.[35] Janet Tavakoli, a Chicago-based structured finance consultant, said these independent directors 'are basically there just as a rubber stamp'. Just as nominee directors help reinforce secrecy, so this practice of providing toothless directors for securitisation deals is offshore business.[36] Richard Murphy of Tax Research UK neatly captures the artificiality of these arrangements: 'Offshore is used to repackage what happens elsewhere. It is used to change the form, but not the substance, of a transaction.'

A famous totem of this artificiality is Ugland House in the Cayman Islands, which Barack Obama once criticised for housing over 12,000 corporations.[37] 'That's either the biggest building,' he said, 'or the biggest tax scam on record.' But Anthony Travers, chairman of the Cayman Islands' Financial Services Authority, shot back that Obama would be better advised to focus his attention in Delaware. 'An office at 1209 North Orange Street, Wilmington, houses the grand total of 217,000 companies.'

The world's biggest building (in this sense), as it happens, is the office of the Corporation Trust, a subsidiary of the Dutch firm Wolters Kluwer. It is a yellowish brick low-rise with a modest maroon awning, the kind you'd expect to find on the front of a pizza restaurant. It sits between an unsightly six-storey car park across Orange Street and a scruffy little parking lot behind it. This is, legally speaking, the corporate home of Ford, General Motors, Coca-Cola, Kentucky Fried Chicken, Intel Corp., Google Inc., Hewlett Packard, Texas Instruments and many more global corporate giants, including a large number of the specialised trusts and special purpose entities (SPEs) behind so many of the toxic CDOs (most of which originate in the Cayman Islands). These SPEs and giant corporations are not here for secrecy but for the corporate governance. The Corporation Trust will, as part of their service, also help your company serve and receive notices, subpoenas, summonses and suchlike. Delaware's state website lists 110 registered agents – which, by the way, are not regulated.[38] In 2008 Delaware hosted 882,000 active business entities.[39]

Before visiting the building, I called repeatedly to request an interview. Each time I was promised a call back, which never came, until I eventually caught a new receptionist who put me through to the office manager, Cory Bueller. Evidently flustered, she agreed to see me. I turned up ten minutes ahead of time, and was buzzed into a reception room, about four yards by four, with an ageing scuffed grey-patterned carpet, two potted plants and light-coloured walls dotted with grease smears. Behind a glass window sat the receptionist, an unshaven man in a baseball jacket, who was replaced soon after I arrived by an attractive well-dressed young woman in a vivid red coat, who smiled brightly and promised that Bueller would be out shortly.

Bueller came through, in faded jeans, white sneakers, a white T-shirt and a grey cardigan, and said sheepishly that she couldn't give me that interview after all. I asked if I could have a quick nose around. That would not be possible, she said, wringing her hands. I pressed again. 'Just a quick peek?' A flush of colour came to Bueller's cheeks and she declined again. Bueller would not give me her own card but instead passed me a piece of headed paper with a phone number for Wolters Kluwer's New York press office.

Back outside, I could see long rows of work cubicles through one window. It looked very similar to what I had been able to see of the ground floor of Cayman's Ugland House. This was clearly secretarial work. Bueller had confessed under my questioning that about eighty people worked there, and none were lawyers. It reminded me of what John Christensen had told me earlier about his work in Jersey as a company and trust administrator. 'These are fantastic job titles, but this was clerical work,' he said. 'They could charge colossal fees for a company and trust administrator but not for a clerk.'

To be fair to Delaware, there are healthier reasons for incorporating here. Its chancery court has become – because of Delaware's success in attracting out-of-towners – a specialist in corporate law, with unrivalled experience and expertise.[40] And its location halfway between New York and Washington gives Wilmington a geographical edge too. Who wants to fly to Alaska to litigate?

As late as the early 1990s mainstream development theorists trying to work out why some countries were failing, or why poverty was so widespread, all but ignored the issue of corruption. Berlin-based Transparency International (TI), founded in 1993, put corruption on the map, launching its famous Corruption Perceptions Index (CPI) two years later. The *Financial Times* nominated 1995 as the International Year of Corruption, and the World Bank, which had previously been so polite towards developing country elites that it all but banished the C-word from its policy documents, followed TI's lead in 1996 when its president, James Wolfensohn, accepted in a landmark speech that the bank needed to deal with 'the cancer of corruption'. The OECD's Anti-Bribery Convention came into force only in 1999, and the UN's Convention Against Corruption only solidified in 2003. In many OECD countries bribery was even tax-deductible until just a few years ago. Even so late, the shift was very good news. But now consider this.

Transparency International's corruption ranking is invaluable to investors trying to assess 'country risk', but Nigerians already know that their country is among the world's most corrupt. They want to know where almost $500 billion in oil money has gone. The CPI gives no clues. After the brutal Nigerian president Sani Abacha died in 1998, poisoned while in the company of Indian prostitutes, it was revealed that he had skimmed off billions of dollars of oil money. Two countries in particular soaked up his embezzled wealth – Britain and Switzerland. Nigerian Finance Minister Ngozi Okonjo-Iweala revealed the problems in an interview with journalist Paul Vallely of the *Independent* in May 2006:

Ngozi: The Swiss have now returned $500 million of stolen resources. Switzerland has set the example.
Vallely: What about the British?
Ngozi: (*Gives a long throaty chuckle.*) Now heaven help me. It's very hard to condemn the British. On debt relief the UK has set the example.
Vallely: So why are the British dragging their feet on the repatriation of stolen resources?
Ngozi: It's been more difficult with the British. Our president has raised it many times with Prime Minister Blair. Eventually he returned $3 million. We understand there are other monies but while all the discussion was going on those monies left the country and went somewhere else.[41]

Transparency International's ranking suggests that Britain and Switzerland – not to mention the United States – are among the world's 'cleanest' jurisdictions. In fact, about half the top twenty in the index are major secrecy jurisdictions, while the nations of Africa – the victims of the gargantuan illicit flows – are ranked 'dirtiest'.[42]

In November 2009 the Tax Justice Network published a new index based on two years of work by a dedicated team. The Financial Secrecy Index ranked countries according to how important they are in providing financial secrecy in global finance. It did this by looking at a range of key secrecy indicators and structures to see how secretive a jurisdiction was, then weighting each according to the scale of cross-border financial services activity that it hosts. Nothing like this had ever been done before, and newspapers and television stations around the globe published the results, with some of the countries traditionally seen as cleanest being ranked as among the world's least transparent.

In fifth place in the Financial Secrecy Index was the United Kingdom. Although it has by far the most important historical role in the emergence of offshore and is the centre of the British offshore spider's web, its domestic secrecy structures are relatively transparent. Third and fourth most important were, respectively, Switzerland and the Cayman Islands. Luxembourg, a gigantic but hardly noticed haven of financial secrecy, came second. And which country was ranked – by a mile – the world's most important secrecy jurisdiction?

Step forward, the United States of America.

8

The Deep Drains
of Development
How tax havens harm
poor countries

By the early 1980s the main elements of the modern offshore system were in place, and growing explosively. An older cluster of European havens, nurtured by European aristocracies and led by Switzerland, was now being outpaced by a network of more flexible, aggressive havens in the former outposts of the British empire, which were themselves linked intimately to the City of London. A state within the British state, the City had been transformed from an gentlemen's club operating the financial machinery of empire, steeped in elaborate rituals and governed by unspoken rules about what 'isn't done', into a brasher deregulated global financial centre dominated by American banks and linked intimately to the new British spider's web. A less complex yet still enormously important offshore zone of influence had also grown up, centred on the United States and also constructed by American banks. The stateless Euromarkets linked all these zones with each other and with the onshore economies, helping to free banks from reserve requirements and other restraints on their behaviour.

While the old European havens were mostly about secret wealth management and tax evasion, the new British and American zones were increasingly about escaping financial regulation – though with plenty of tax evasion and criminal activity thrown in. Players in each zone were warmly welcomed into the other, in true laissez-faire style, and as the offshore system became more interconnected it grew stronger, as states competed with each other on lax financial regulation, tax and secrecy strengthening the offshore dynamic.

The Bretton Woods system of international cooperation and tight control over financial flows had collapsed in the 1970s, and the golden age of capitalism that had followed the Second World War had ended. The world had entered a phase of much slower growth, punctuated by regular financial and economic crises, especially in developing countries.

As all this happened, and the offshore system grew and metasta-sised around the world, a new and increasingly powerful army of lawyers, accountants and bankers emerged to make the whole system work. Offshore, in partnership with changing ideologies, was driving the processes of deregulation and financial globalisation. In particular, the London-based Euromarket, then the wider offshore world, provided the platform for US banks to escape tight domestic constraints and grow explosively again, setting the stage for the political capture of Washington by the financial services industry, and the emergence of too-big-to-fail banking giants, fed by the implicit subsidies of taxpayer guarantees and the explicit subsidies of offshore tax avoid-ance. The emergence of the US as an offshore jurisdiction in its own right attracted vast financial flows into the country boosting bankers' power even further. The old alliance between Wall Street and the City of London, which had collapsed after the Great Depression and the Second World War, had been resurrected.

Many people supposed that by eliminating double taxation and creating nearly frictionless conduits for capital, the offshore system was promoting global economic efficiency. In reality the system was rarely adding value, but instead redistributing wealth upwards and risks down-wards, and creating a new global hothouse for crime. US crime-fighting lawyer John Moscow summarised the problem. 'Money is power, and we are transferring this power to corporate bank accounts run by people who are in the purest sense of the word unaccountable and therefore irresponsible.'[1]

Secrecy jurisdictions had penetrated the public consciousness a little, but still only as dubious oddities on the exotic fringes of civilisa-tion. Under cover of this misunderstanding, often artfully encouraged by those who wanted to conceal the true nature of the new financial revolution, the offshore system would operate in ways that would become increasingly significant as the twentieth century drew to a close. What was actually happening was nothing less than a head-on assault on New Deal principles in the US, on the foundations of social democracy in Europe, and on democracy, accountability and development in vulnerable low-income countries across the world.

Take any significant economic event or process in the last few decades, and offshore is almost certainly behind the headline, and probably central to the story.

Poverty in Africa cannot be understood without understanding the role of offshore. The world's worst war for years has been the civil conflict in the Democratic Republic of Congo, which is tied in with the wholesale looting of its mineral resources via tax havens. Large-scale corruption and the wholesale subversion of governments by criminalised interests across the developing world? Offshore is central to the story every time. Nearly every effort to generate large flows of capital to developing countries since the 1980s has ended in crisis because of offshore. Towering inequalities in Europe, the US and low-income countries cannot be understood properly without exploring the role of secrecy jurisdictions. The systematic looting of the former Soviet Union and the merging of that nuclear-armed country's intelligence apparatus with organised crime is a story that substantially unfolded in London and its offshore satellites. The political strength of Saddam Hussein had important offshore underpinnings, as does the power of North Korea's Kim Jong-Il today. Prime Minister Silvio Berlusconi's strange hold over Italian politics is in great part an offshore story. The Elf Affair, which kept powerful French elites out of reach of French democracy, had secrecy jurisdictions at its heart. Promoters of frauds such as 'pump and dump' schemes to hype up stocks then dump them on an unsuspecting public *always* hide behind offshore entities. The death of a Russian oligarch's lawyer in a mysterious helicopter crash? Arms smuggling to terrorist organisations? The growth of Mafia empires? Offshore. The narcotics industry alone generates some $500 billion in annual sales worldwide,[2] twice the value of Saudi Arabia's oil exports.[3] The profits made by those at the top of the trade find their way into the banking system, the asset markets and the political process through offshore facilities. You can only fit about $1 million into a briefcase. Without offshore, the illegal drugs trade would be a cottage industry.

Financial deregulation and globalisation? Offshore is at the heart of the matter, as we shall see. The rise of private equity and hedge funds?

Offshore. Enron? Parmalat? Long Term Capital Management? Lehman Brothers? AIG? Offshore. Multinational corporations could never have grown so vast and powerful without tax havens. Goldman Sachs is very, very much a creature of offshore. And every significant financial catastrophe in the world since the 1970s, including the latest global economic crisis, is very much an offshore story. The decline of manufacturing industries in many advanced countries has many causes, but offshore is a big part of the tale. Tax havens have been central to the growth of debt in our economies since the 1970s. The growth of complex monopolies in certain markets, or insider trading rings, or gigantic frauds, almost always involve secrecy jurisdictions as major or central elements.

This is not to say that all of these problems don't have other explanations too; they always do. Tax havens are never the only story, because offshore exists only in relation to elsewhere. That is why it is called offshore. Without understanding offshore, we will never properly understand the history of the modern world. The time has come to make a start on filling this gap in our knowledge – to appreciate how offshore has bent the world's economy into its present shape, transforming societies and political systems in its image.

I will begin with a rare episode where offshore's role *is* widely acknowledged: the case of the Bank of Credit and Commerce International (BCCI), arguably the most offshore bank in history. The story is well known, but one or two crucial features are less widely appreciated. The BCCI case broke after Jack Blum, a lawyer and investigator working for US Senator John Kerry's Foreign Relations Committee, began picking up signs of wrongdoing in 1988.

A rumpled easy-going lawyer, Blum was described in the *New York Times* as 'a man aflame over the world's injustice and more than a little impatient with those who fail to do something about it . . . a tenacious, moralistic crusader who produces charges of high-level corruption like a grinding wheel throws off sparks'.[4] He was born in 1941 in the Bronx and founded a crusading newspaper near Poughkeepsie, New York, before studying law and going into government to chase villains. As a congressional staffer in the 1970s he helped break open a global bribery scandal involving the aerospace firm Lockheed Martin; he investigated attempts by ITT to destabilise the government of Salvador Allende in Chile; he helped uncover Bernie Cornfeld's fraudulent offshore empire IOS; and he examined the involvement of Nicaraguan US-backed Contra rebels in drug trafficking.

Like most people, Blum initially saw secrecy jurisdictions mainly as centres for drug-smugglers and other assorted lowlifes. But on a visit to the Cayman Islands in 1974 for the US Senate Foreign Relations Committee he remembers seeing a line of well-dressed men waiting to use the phone in his hotel lobby. He learned that they were US lawyers and accountants arranging to meet Cayman bankers to set up accounts and trusts for tax-evading US clients. American bankers were referring US customers to their Canadian colleagues, and the Canadians were returning the favour. Over time, Blum noticed more sophisticated tricks and realised that this was far bigger than almost anyone imagined. 'I began to see that drugs were only a fraction of the thing,' Blum said. 'Then there was the criminal money. Then the tax evasion money. And then I realised – Oh my God it's all about off the books, off the balance sheet. Offshore, there are no rules about how the books are kept. I refer to offshore as a kitchen, where corporate books are cooked.'

When contacts started fingering BCCI in the late 1980s, Blum already knew it had a bad smell. He had worked previously in private practice, where he remembers his team meeting the staff of Mellon Bank in Pittsburgh, and telling them about BCCI. 'The entire senior international staff at Mellon just about threw up on the table,' Blum said. They would not, under any circumstances, accept letters of credit from BCCI.[5]

The bank was set up in 1972 by an Indian-born banker, Agha Hassan Abedi, who got backing for his venture from members of the Saudi royal family and from Sheikh Zayed Bin Sultan Al-Nahayan, the ruler of Abu Dhabi. BCCI grew super-fast under a simple business model: create the appearance of a reputable business, make powerful friends, then agree to do anything, anywhere, on behalf of anyone, for any reason. BCCI loaded politicians with bribes and served some of the twentieth century's greatest villains: Saddam Hussein, terrorist leader Abu Nidal, the Colombian Medellín drug cartel and Asian heroin warlord Khun Sa. It got involved in trafficking nuclear materials via sales of Chinese Silkworm missiles to Saudi Arabia and in peddling

North Korean Scud-B missiles to Syria. Its branches in the Caribbean and Panama serviced the Latin American drug trade; its divisions in the United Arab Emirates, then enjoying an oil boom and an offshore banking bonanza, serviced the heroin trades in Pakistan, Iran and Afghanistan; and it used Hong Kong to cater to drug traffickers in Laos, Thailand and Burma.

BCCI also penetrated the US banking system, getting around the concerns of American regulators by using offshore secrecy structures to make its ownership invisible. It paid off Washington insiders and built up a solid partnership with the CIA. This gave it fearsome political cover and made Blum's investigations extraordinarily difficult from the outset.

'There was an army of people working in Washington on all sides trying to say this was a wonderful bank,' Blum said. Friends in law enforcement warned him that his life was in danger, but he pressed on. He took his case to Manhattan District Attorney Robert Morgenthau, who shared Blum's outrage and put a team together to take BCCI down. Fighting against what must have seemed like half the political insiders in Washington, Morgenthau shut it down in 1991 and charged BCCI and its founders with perpetrating 'the largest bank fraud in world financial history'.

The most interesting thing about BCCI was its offshore structure. Abedi split his bank between jurisdictions, registering holding companies in Luxembourg and in the Caymans so that no regulator could see the whole thing. Different auditors were used for different parts of the bank too.[6] Yet Abedi also wanted the credibility of being in a world-famous financial centre that was nevertheless lax enough to ask few questions. That meant only one place, the City of London. In 1972 BCCI set up its headquarters in luxury offices in Leadenhall Street, in the heart of the City, and began making generous contributions to Britain's Conservative Party.[7]

A rule of thumb in the sector was that banks should lend no more than 10 per cent of their equity capital to a single borrower, but BCCI was making loans to some clients worth *three times* its capital, or thirty times the accepted ratio. In 1977 the Bank of England tightened the rules. To get around this, Abedi dumped shaky loans in the Cayman Islands, where, as a BCCI official noted at the time, there was 'obviously more flexibility in record-keeping' and which bank officials called 'the dustbin'.[8] Neither the British regulators, nor those in Luxembourg or the Caymans, assumed responsibility.

BCCI also constructed an audacious but simple offshore trick, manufacturing equity capital – the foundation and safety buffer of any bank – out of thin air. The Luxembourg bank would lend money to a BCCI stockholder – one of Abedi's friends – who would then invest this money in the Caymans bank, building up its capital there. The Caymans bank lent money to a stockholder, who would use it to create capital in the Luxembourg bank. From just $2.5 million in equity capital at the beginning, BCCI reached nearly $850 million by 1990, with the help of this offshore bootstrap.[9] Abedi also wrote off his friends' debts, but kept expanding through a so-called Ponzi scheme: milking the staff pension fund and taking in more deposits simply to pay its outgoings. Many of its 80,000 depositors were relatively poor people from the developing world who had no idea that this apparently London-based bank, backed by wealthy Arab sheikhs, was a fiction built on a fiction.

When Morgenthau tried to probe the bank, the Cayman Islands authorities refused to co-operate. 'We subpoenaed BCCI Overseas. They told us, "Sorry: the laws of Cayman don't permit us to do this,"' he said, expressing particular irritation with the attorney-general, a 'crotchety British guy'. 'We tried again. Finally, they said we had to go through the [US–Cayman tax information exchange] treaty. We went through the treaty. Then they said, "The treaty doesn't include local district attorneys: go through the Justice Department. We can't show this to you." The Justice Department wasn't overly cooperative either.'[10] Morgenthau and his deputy John Moscow went to the Bank of England. 'We had no cooperation from the Bank of England,' Morgenthau said. 'we tried to get financial records out of London; they didn't provide us with anything.' With the help of Senator John Kerry, Morgenthau threatened to raise a public storm if the Bank of England did not act. Only then, finally, did the bank agree to shut BCCI down.

In the British parliament, the scandal caused uproar. The Bank of England, forced onto the defensive, claimed it had left BCCI running until 1991 because there had been no 'solid evidence' of fraud until then. It isn't clear what evidence the bank needed. Indictments in the US implicating BCCI in fraud dated back two and a half years; one stated that money laundering was part of its 'corporate strategy'.[11] Price Waterhouse had issued a qualified audit report on a BCCI subsidiary in 1989, and in 1990 BCCI employees had written to the Treasury, the Bank of England and British ministers to warn of fraud inside the bank. That same year Britain's intelligence services had told the Bank of England that Abu Nidal controlled forty-two BCCI accounts in London; the Bank for International Settlements in Basel had expressed concern; and Price Waterhouse had discovered the so-called Naqvi files, revealing widespread fraud, fictitious companies, unrecorded deposits, manufactured loans, and evidence of stealing from depositors, and passed their findings to the Bank of England. There was still no action, even though BCCI headquarters were only a few minutes' stroll from the Bank of England.

'It is difficult to see,' wrote Michael Gillard in Britain's *Observer* newspaper, 'how the required high ethical standards [for BCCI to be allowed to operate in Britain] fit with BCCI pleading guilty to conspiring with its own officials and two representative of Colombia's Medellín drug cartel to commit tax fraud and launder the proceeds of cocaine sales.' However, Robin Leigh-Pemberton, Bank of England governor, neatly encapsulated London's see-no-evil offshore ethic. The present system of supervision, he said, 'has served the community well . . . If we closed down a bank every time we found an instance of fraud, we would have rather fewer banks than we do at the moment.'[12] That statement should have been evidence enough that the City of London was already the world's premier offshore centre. The full Price Waterhouse report on BCCI remains confidential today, on the grounds that it would disturb Britain's 'international partners'. This is a clear admission that London is a tax haven.[13]

Ever since BCCI Morgenthau has struggled to wake people up to offshore crimes, personally pressing four US Treasury secretaries to pay more attention, but with little result. 'I remember giving a speech a couple of years ago to talk about offshore banks. It put everyone to sleep,' Morgenthau said. 'Start talking about offshore money and their eyes glaze over.'[14]

Just as the BCCI scandal calmed down another offshore tale was emerging in the oil-rich African state of Angola, where I was the Reuters correspondent. Jonas Savimbi's UNITA rebels had surrounded major towns, pouring in mortar fire and trying to starve them into submission. In the city of Kuito desperate defenders were eating dogs, cats and rats to survive, and bloodied patients were crawling from hospital beds to join armed raiding parties, who would sneak out to search fields, often mined, for cassava and other crops, sometimes having to fight their way back into town with what they had dug up. The United Nations was calling it the world's worst war, and the government was under an international arms embargo, so in 1992 it turned to secretive French Elf networks – related to the ones I would later encounter in Gabon – to help secure arms supplies. A wealthy Russian-born Jew named Arkady Gaydamak put together $800 million-odd in financing to help Angola procure weapons from a Slovak company – repaid in Angolan oil money, via Geneva, to get around the embargo. French magistrates probing oil-for-arms deals subsequently heard from a participant that the arrangements were 'a gigantic fraud . . . a vast cash pump, generating a 65 per cent margin on the biggest arms contracts'.[15] The financing trails, of course, involved many tax havens.

I tracked Gaydamak down in Moscow in September 2005, where he was the subject of an international arrest warrant for his so-called Angolagate deals.[16] He was eager to set the record straight and to discuss his efforts to – as he put it – bring peace to Africa and the Middle East (just then he was embarking on what would be an ill-fated foray into Israeli politics).[17] Gaydamak left the Soviet Union as a twenty-year old in 1972, moving first to Israel, then to France, where he built up a translation business, mostly servicing Soviet trade delegations. 'Translator means go-between,' he explained. 'If you are active in electronics, your position in the business world is usually with people in electronics. If you are a banker, you have relationships with bankers . . . but when you are a translator – a go-between – you know everybody.'

In those early post-Soviet days Angola's leaders still looked to Russia as their big-power patron, but they had lost their way in a fast-changing Moscow. 'I began to be an intermediary,' he explained. 'Russia was changing so quickly; everything was new. You should know where to go, how to go, how to organise. I was the so-called organiser of everything.' Gaydamak became Angola's trusted man in Moscow. He knew that the big money lay in the elsewhere zone between jurisdictions, and in this context he gave me what must be one of the most offshore quotes of all time.

In the so-called market economies, with all the regulations, the taxation, the legislation about working conditions, there is no way to make money. It is only in countries like Russia, during the period of redistribution of wealth – and it is not yet finished – when you can get a result. So that is Russian money. Russian money is clean money, explainable money. How can you make $50 million in France today? How? Explain to me!

Some have compared the vast upward redistribution of wealth in Russia after the fall of the Soviet Union to the era of the robber barons in the United States in the nineteenth century. But there is a crucial difference. The Americans didn't have a huge offshore network in which to hide their money. In spite of their many abuses, the barons concentrated on domestic investment. While they fleeced unwary investors and subverted the political process, they also built the country's industrial prosperity. They left America stronger, and in time the state was able to rein in their worst excesses. But in late-twentieth-century Angola and Russia the money simply disappeared offshore for ever. African governments have grown weaker and more dependent on aid from the very states that are strengthening the offshore system. It was Africa's curse that its countries gained independence at precisely the same time as purpose-built offshore warehouses for loot properly started to emerge. For many of these countries, independence really meant independence for their elites from bothersome rules. The colonial powers left, but quietly left the mechanisms for exploitation in place.

After the Cold War, Angola was in debt to Russia for about $6 billion, and in 1996 Gaydamak inserted himself into a deal to restructure the debt. The liability was shaved down to $1.5 billion and sliced into thirty-one promissory notes which Angola would pay back in oil via a private company called Abalone set up by Gaydamak and his business partner Pierre Falcone, with a UBS account in Geneva. UBS was uncomfortable about the arrangements. 'Any possible mention of one of the representatives of one or other of the parties,' an internal UBS memo said, 'in a newspaper article, even if a posteriori this is judged to be unfounded or indeed libellous, would not prevent, in the first instance, a Swiss or particularly Genevan judge taking an interest in the people mentioned.'[18] But the deal went ahead.

Unfortunately for Gaydamak, a Swiss judge intervened in February 2001, after Angola had paid off just over half the promissory notes. The judge had found vast mysterious flows of money from Abalone, including over $60 million to accounts in Gaydamak's name, tens of millions more to accounts in the names of senior Angolan officials, and almost $50 million to a former Yeltsin oligarch.[19] But most of it had gone to an array of accounts in Switzerland, Luxembourg, Israel, Germany, the Netherlands and Cyprus. Little or none of it seemed to have flowed to Russia's treasury. Gaydamak claimed that the Russian treasury got paid indirectly, via these mysterious accounts, and added that this was a 'classic trading operation, extremely favourable to us'.[20]

Because of offshore secrecy, it is impossible to tell whether what Gaydamak said is even partly true. What is certain is that Angola's leaders, in partnership with Russian interests and private offshore intermediaries, cooked up a curious deal, routed offshore, with vast profits for some insiders and absolutely no accountability to the people of Angola or Russia. African insiders had thus used offshore to enrich themselves not from Angola's assets, but from its debts. The Swiss judge was later promoted, and his replacement unblocked the notes in October 2003, arguing that neither Angola nor Russia had complained about the deal, and accepting the argument that the accounts held by the Angolan dignitaries amounted to 'strategic funds, placed abroad in a time of war'.

I could have chosen any number of murky African offshore episodes to explore; Gaymadak's deals are only a tiny fraction of what the offshore system has drained from Africa. Two recent studies point to the scale of the problem.

In March 2010 Global Financial Integrity (GFI) in Washington authored a study on illicit financial flows out of Africa.[21] Between 1970 and 2008, it concluded, 'Total illicit financial outflows from Africa, conservatively estimated, were approximately $854 billion. Total illicit outflows may be as high as $1.8 trillion.' Of that overall conservative figure, it estimated Angola lost $4.68 billion between 1993 (when Gaydamak's main Angolagate deals started) and 2002, the year after his Abalone debt dealings ended.[22] My personal belief, based on years of investigating Angola's economy and its leadership, is that the GFI estimate – equivalent to just over 9 per cent of its $51 billion in oil and diamond exports during that time – simply *has* to be a gross underestimate of the looting.[23] Many billions have disappeared offshore through opaque oil-backed loans channelled outside normal state budgets, many of them routed through two special trusts operating out of London.[24]

GFI's shocking estimates complement the figures I mentioned earlier about the global scale of illicit financial flows. Developing countries lost up to a *trillion* dollars in illicit financial outflows just in 2006 – that is, ten dollars out for every dollar of foreign aid flowing in.[25]

Another study emerged in April 2008 from the University of Massachussetts, Amherst, using different methodologies to examine capital flight from forty African countries from 1970 to 2004.[26] Its conclusions are similarly striking: 'Real capital flight over the 35-year period amounted to about $420 billion (in 2004 dollars) for the 40 countries as a whole. Including imputed interest earnings, the accumulated stock of capital flight was about $607 billion as of end-2004.' Yet at the same time, the total external debt of these countries was 'only' $227 billion. So, the authors note, Africa is a net creditor to the rest of the world, with its net external assets vastly exceeding its debts. Yet there is a crucial difference between the assets and the liabilities: 'The subcontinent's private external assets belong to a narrow, relatively wealthy stratum of its population, while public external debts are borne by the people through their governments.'

Having watched people die before my eyes in Angola; having seen an otherwise pretty six-year-old Angolan girl who, without access to basic medicine, was losing a fight with an infection that had rotted a hole in her cheek the size of a golf ball, I am personally acquainted with some of the ways Africa's people 'bear' their public debts, in the forms of poverty, war, a hopeless lack of real opportunities, and the regular physical and economic violence perpetrated against them by corrupt and predatory elites. Raymond Baker, director of GFI, was quite right to call the emergence of the offshore system 'the ugliest chapter in global economic affairs since slavery'.[27]

In February 2003 Phil Gramm, a former Republican US senator for Texas who became vice chairman of the Swiss investment bank UBS Warburg, wrote to US Treasury Secretary John Snow, arguing against a plan to increase international financial transparency. 'This proposal will limit economic freedom,' he wrote, 'and reduce the pressure that potential capital flight imposes on high-taxing countries worldwide.'[28] Illicit flows are good, Gramm was effectively saying, because they discipline the victims. Anyone who understands that there is a difference between wealthy rulers – the beneficiaries of illicit flows – and ordinary citizens – the victims – can see through Gramm's position. Yet for many Western economists, such thinking has become almost an article of faith founded on ageless blame-the-victim accusations that losers are stupid, corrupt, or just didn't flagellate themselves hard enough.

'The conventional roots of the global development crisis is an economist's fairy tale,' said Jim Henry, a former chief economist for McKinsey's, who is almost alone in having investigated this since the 1980s. 'It leaves out all the blood and guts of what really happened.' Henry's shocking 2003 book *Blood Bankers* explores a number of grotesque episodes in low-income countries where offshore banking led to crisis after crisis. First, bankers lent these countries far more than they could productively absorb, then they taught local elites how to plunder the wealth, conceal it, launder it and sneak it offshore. Then the IMF helped bankers pressure these countries to service their debts under threat of financial strangulation. Capital markets were deliberately opened up to foreign capital 'whether or not there were adequate security laws, bank regulations or tax enforcers in place'.

Henry tracked down an American banker from MHT Bank who had taken part in a 'friendly private audit' of the Philippines Central Bank in 1983. 'I sat in a hot, little room at the Central Bank, added up what the Central Bank showed it had received from us on its books, and compared it with our disbursements,' the banker said.[29]

And nearly $5 billion was just not there! I mean, it just had not come into the country. It had been disbursed by us, but it was completely missing from the Central Bank's books. It turned out that most of these loans had been disbursed to account numbers assigned to Philippine offshore banking units or other private companies. Apparently, the Central Bank gave MHT the account numbers, and we never questioned whether they were Central Bank accounts – we just wired the loans to them. And then they disappeared offshore.

Philippines officials clearly realised what he was up to. The following morning the banker was sent a big breakfast in his hotel room, courtesy of the management, but only had time to grab a bite of toast before heading to the airport. By the time he reached Tokyo he was sick, and on the flight home he went into convulsions. He spent three days in a Vancouver hospital recovering from what the doctors said was 'an unknown toxin'. He subsequently told the New York Federal Reserve and a friend at the National Security Council everything he had discovered. 'But apparently they just kept it to themselves. So the Philippines is still servicing all those Central Bank loans.' Henry later went to the Philippines and checked up on the banker's story, which was solid. He dug up details on at least $3.6 billion of identifiable government-swallowed foreign loans, which had ended up with President Ferdinand Marcos and his closest associates.

As all this happened across the developing world, an army of bankers, lawyers and accountants was lobbying inside the US, to make it more attractive to these rising tides of dirty money, successfully turning it into a secrecy jurisdiction in its own right, just as Hudson's memo had suggested. Meanwhile, the offshore industry continued to capture legislatures in small tax havens, to perfect the global dirty-money system. Playing all three corners of the triangle – source countries being drained of wealth, increasingly offshore-like economies receiving the wealth, the offshore conduits handling its passage – turned global private banking into one of the most profitable businesses in history.

'The rise of Third World lending in the 1970s and 1980s,' Henry explained, 'laid the foundations for a global haven network that now shelters the world's most venal citizens.' Henry's calculations suggested that at least half of the money borrowed by the largest debtor countries flowed right out again under the table, usually in less than a year, and typically in just weeks. Third World public debts were matched almost exactly by the stock of private wealth their elites had accumulated in the US and other havens, and by the early 1990s there was enough flight wealth in Europe and the US to service the entire debt of the developing world – if only its income were taxed modestly. For some countries like Mexico, Argentina and Venezuela, the value of their elites' offshore illicit wealth was several times their external debts. Today the top 1 per cent of households in developing countries own an estimated 70–90 per cent of all private financial and real estate wealth. The Boston Consulting Group reckoned in 2003 that over half of all the wealth owned by Latin America's wealthiest citizens lay offshore. 'The problem is not that these countries don't have any assets,' a US Federal Reserve official said. 'The problem is, they're all in Miami.'

In 1982 Mexico's President José Lopez Portillo gave a speech to parliament, outlining the challenges facing the country. 'The financing plague is wreaking greater and greater havoc throughout the world. It is transmitted by rats and its consequences are unemployment and poverty, industrial bankruptcy and speculative enrichment.' He blamed 'a group of Mexicans . . . led and advised and supported by the private banks that have taken more money out of the country than the empires that exploited us since the beginning of time.'[30] Lopez Portillo vowed to ignore the IMF, nationalise the banks and introduce exchange controls – but within ten days an alliance of bankers, business people and conservative Mexicans had made him back down. The IMF and the Bank for International Settlements in Switzerland, ignoring Mexico's offshore flight wealth, ordered Mexico and other debtor nations, 'Put your house in order.'

Economist Michael Hudson described how he was hired in 1989 by a Boston money management firm to organise a sovereign debt fund investing in the government bonds of developing nations.[31] Huge risk premiums then meant that Argentine and Brazilian dollar bonds were yielding almost 45 per cent, while Mexican bonds were yielding 25 per cent. In its first year the fund, incorporated in the Netherlands Antilles, became the world's second best performing of its kind. Hudson found out what was happening. 'The biggest investors were political insiders who had bought into the fund knowing that their central banks would pay their dollar debts despite the high risk premiums,' he said. Some of the biggest investors were people in top positions in central banks and governments. 'We realised who has all the Yankee dollar claims on Latin America,' he said. 'It was local oligarchies with offshore accounts. The dollar debt of Argentina in the early 1990s was owed mainly to Argentinians operating out of offshore banking centres. The major beneficiaries of foreign debt service were their own flight capitalists, not bondholders in North America and Europe.'

This trick turns out to be a routine practice conducted by so-called 'vulture funds'. Wealthy foreign investors buy up distressed sovereign debt at pennies on the dollar – typically at a 90 per cent discount – then reap vast profits when those debts are repaid in full. One trick is to make sure that influential locals are secretly part of the investor group buying the discounted debt: these locals will then do battle inside the developing country governments to make sure the debts get paid in full. Their involvement, of course, must be hidden behind a shield of offshore secrecy, so that the impoverished nation's citizens can never find out how their nation's wealth was stolen.

Economists have not ignored these issues entirely, but they almost always break them down into discrete, country-level local problems that only blame corrupt local elites. These matter, of course – but such analyses obscure what all the disasters have in common. Offshore.

And in the relatively few instances when offshore erosion *has* been considered, it has been taken as an inconvenience, to be addressed with Band-Aids. As one IMF report put it: 'Offshore banking has most certainly been a factor in the Asian financial crisis. A special effort is therefore needed to help emerging economies . . . to avert financial crises through dissemination of internationally accepted prudential and supervisory standards.'[32]

The IMF is arguing here in an illogical circle. By helping local elites effectively place themselves above the law and creating new temptations to mischief, the offshore system neuters the chance of the prudent regulation and supervision that is needed to protect those countries against that very same offshore system. Imagine if those elites had to keep their money at home, or at least account for their wealth, pay appropriate taxes on it, and submit to appropriate laws. Very soon they would understand why good government was in their direct interests.

The saddest part of all this is that it should have been obvious to anybody who gave it a moment's thought.

As well as all this, there is something more systemic, and hard-wired into the global economy, which puts developing countries at an even greater disadvantage than most people think. It concerns the old question of double taxation, and it needs a brief detour.

Let's say a European bank or company invests in Africa. One might have thought the African country could simply tax the investor's local earnings. As I've mentioned, countries sign double-tax treaties with each other to avoid earnings getting taxed first at source in Africa, then again in Europe. Under a treaty like this, the African country may well agree not to tax the company's local earnings – fearing that otherwise European companies will simply invest elsewhere. There is clearly a power relationship here.

Even with this treaty, however, the European corporation has not solved its problem yet. The treaty may have knocked out the African tax charge on its earnings, but if it sends these untaxed earnings back to Europe they will often still be taxed there. So it sends the earnings to a third country – what is known as a conduit or treaty haven – which will have a wide network of treaties, including one with Africa. This treaty will ensure the African country does not tax the income – and the treaty haven *also* agrees not to tax the earnings, serving as a stepping stone for the corporation's profits to emerge along carefully constructed tax-free pathways from Africa into the wider world. 'Like two closely marked football players passing the ball to a third one who is unmarked,' explains Professor Sol Picciotto, a tax haven expert, a conduit haven 'can create major gaps in the defences of tax authorities.'

The havens justify themselves as useful tools to avoid this double-tax problem, and to smooth investment flows, but there are other ways to avoid double taxation, and to ensure that investment flows to where it is needed, and as we have seen, this system has a massive consequence: double *non*-taxation.[33] In this example, both Africa and Europe are legally deprived of tax revenues, courtesy of offshore.

There are over 2,500 tax treaties in place around the world: an extensive but very poorly understood counterpart of the global trading and investment regime. Two bodies set rules and models and standards in this field: the OECD, a club of rich nations, and the UN, where poor countries have a stronger voice. Unsurprisingly, the OECD dominates – and it works hard to ensure that its treaty models, which tilt the playing field in favour of rich countries at the expense of poor ones, is dominant. It also works hard to undermine its competitor, the United Nations. John Christensen, the former Jersey adviser turned transparency campaigner, remembers Britain's representative standing up at a UN tax meeting in Geneva in 2009, in what looked like an intervention coordinated with the representative from Liechtenstein.

'He kept on interrupting,' Christensen said. 'It was a general assault on developing countries being better able to represent their interests, about providing more resources to the UN Tax Committee. He was the cheerleader. Twice the chair had to tell him "please let us speak". People there were *really* angry with him: we could all see he was blocking progress to protect the UK's and the United States' interests.'

These donor countries are happy for civil society to be occupied with debating levels of aid, when potentially larger sums are at stake in this unnoticed arena. Nobody has ever studied this at a global level, but if we consider that $18 *trillion* flowed in 2008 through the Netherlands, just one of many conduit havens, it is not unreasonable to imagine that tens or even hundreds of billions of dollars of tax revenue are at stake here for developing countries, dwarfing flows of foreign aid. And this, let us not forget, is the *legal* business. This is not part of the illicit flows numbers outlined above: it should be added to it. South Africa's finance minister Trevor Manuel explains the incoherence of the aid debates effectively. 'It is a contradiction to support increased development assistance, yet turn a blind eye to actions by multinationals and others that undermine the tax base of a developing country.'

Tax havens help explain why international investment flows often look so strange. The two biggest sources of foreign investment into China in 2007 were not Japan or the US or South Korea, but Hong Kong and the British Virgin Islands.[34] Likewise, the biggest source of foreign investment into India, at over 43 per cent of the total, was not the US or Britain or China, but the treaty haven of Mauritius, a rising star of the offshore system.[35] And herein lies another strange tale.

Although French-speaking, Mauritius has a long history of British colonial involvement, and is intricately linked to the City of London today.[36] It set up its offshore centre in 1989 with help from the City of London, Jersey and the Isle of Man and is ideal as an offshore centre in many respects: it is politically stable, boasts a cheap, well-educated and multilingual labour force and is in the perfect time zone to serve Europe, Asia and Africa. Though formally independent, it is a member of Britain's Commonwealth, and its final appeal court is the Privy Council in London.

Rudolf Elmer, who worked as a senior offshore practitioner in Mauritius from 2006 to 2008 for Standard Bank, said, 'I was trained up for Mauritius in Jersey and the Isle of Man before being sent there'. There is a lot of British influence: the major banks like Barclays and HSBC have built huge operations and multi-storey buildings in Cyber City south of Port Louis [the capital]. Six years ago there were only five – today, I estimate about forty.'

Mauritius also has over forty tax treaties with major economies in Asia, Europe and Africa. 'City of London investment companies run business through Mauritius to finance projects in Africa and in Asia with countries that have a tax treaty in place with Mauritius,' Elmer said. 'It is a hot spot. It will become very prominent.'

Not only does Mauritius channel foreign investment in and out of countries like India, it also hosts another common offshore activity known as 'round-tripping'. A wealthy Indian, say, will send his money to Mauritius, where it is dressed up in a secrecy structure, then disguised as foreign investment, before being returned to India. The sender of the money can avoid Indian tax on local earnings, and also use the secrecy to do nefarious things – such as constructing a local market monopoly by disguising the fact that a seemingly diverse and unrelated array of competitors in a market is in fact controlled by the same interests. The construction of secret monopolies via offshore secrecy is pervasive in certain sectors and helps explain why, for example, mobile telephony charges are so high in some developing countries.

Local elites lobby for these treaties, despite the harm they can cause. 'The India treaty with Mauritius is pure treaty shopping,' said David Rosenbloom, a US tax expert. 'Why do the Indians tolerate it? We, the United States, have a treaty with Bermuda, which is ridiculous. Bermuda doesn't even have a tax system. Countries do bizarre things. A lot of it is political. It defies rational thought.'[37]

9

Ratchet
The roots of crisis

The practice of usury – lending money out at excessive interest rates – has a nasty historical taint. The prophet Ezekiel included it with rape, murder and robbery in a list of 'abominable things'; the books of Exodus, Deuteronomy and Leviticus forbid it, and Plato and Aristotle called it immoral and unjust. In Dante's *Inferno* 'lewd usurers' sit in the seventh circle of hell, and the Koran states that 'whoever goes back to usury will be an inhabitant of the Fire'. When the ancient Greeks deregulated interest rates, indebted Athenians ended up being sold into slavery. One can argue about the relative evil of usury, but in a deregulated market the poor and vulnerable inevitably pay the most. Annualised rates of 400 per cent or more are not uncommon.[1]

Historically, the United States regulated lending rates carefully. In 1978, however, a new era began when the First National Bank of Omaha started enrolling out-of-state Minnesota residents in its BankAmericard Plan. At the time the state of Nebraska let banks charge interest up to 18 per cent a year, while Minnesota's usury limits were 12 percent. Minnesota's solicitor general wanted to stop the bank charging higher interest rates. Could the Nebraska bank 'export' the 18 per cent rate to Minnesota residents? The Supreme Court ruled that it could, and Wall Street noticed. If one state removed interest rate caps, they could export this deregulation across the United States. In March 1980 South Dakota passed a statute eliminating its anti-usury interest rate caps entirely. The statute was, according to Nathan Hayward, a central player in this drama, 'basically written by Citibank'.

Dakota whizzed the laws through in a few weeks. US banks could now, by incorporating in South Dakota, roll out credit card operations across the country, with no interest rate caps. Then came Delaware. The tale of its Financial Center Development Act of 1981 is an account of ten to fifteen powerful people who came together to pass an enormously significant piece of legislation, from which many of them, along with friends and colleagues, reaped huge wealth.

David Swayze, a grizzled and affable lawyer who was chief of staff to Delaware's then governor, Pierre S. 'Pete' du Pont, picked up the story. 'What Citibank did [in South Dakota] was not lost on the other money centre banks,' Swayze said. 'They wanted some – but they didn't want to be in South Dakota. It's cold out there.' Hayward, who is du Pont's second cousin and was a member of his cabinet at the time, continued the story. 'Pete inherited a state that was in bad financial shape. There had been a continuous stream of red ink and the deficits were hidden with tricks and budget games.' After being elected governor in 1976 du Pont had overseen an improvement in state finances and he was a cert for re-election. 'We weren't on a cocaine high,' said Hayward, 'but we were beginning to feel pretty good.'

In early June 1980 a group from Chase National Bank came to the venerable University and Whist Club ('Delaware's premier fine-dining club') in the state's commercial capital Wilmington, to meet Delaware officials.[2] The link was Henry Beckler, an ex-Chase man at the Bank of Delaware, and he had already persuaded Chase to manage some of its foreign operations out of Delaware. 'Henry Beckler's son and my son went together to school,' said du Pont. 'When you put a statute like this together you have to talk to the banks. He was very important. He asked them what things we should be putting in there.'

Du Pont, who is reminiscent of an ageing, less handsome Mitt Romney, comes from a family that has dominated Delaware politics for over a century, and seems to have been a surprisingly passive player, given his position. His memory of the episode was not so fresh, and he is clearly not a detail guy: three or four times when asked to describe what had happened he replied vaguely, ending by saying something like, 'It was good, it was very good.' When challenged about Delaware allowing certain kinds of corporations that provide iron-clad secrecy, he offered no detailed rebuttal, just, 'I don't think that's right. It all works nicely.' But he did put his finger on one important element of the process: the small-town groupthink that let it happen. 'One of the nice things about Delaware is that it's a small state,' du Pont said. 'We all have the same ideas.'

Hayward says the aim of the June meeting was 'to listen to New York bankers who were friends of the Delaware bankers who had helped us. They said, "We'd love it if Delaware allowed market rate banking."' The Chase team wanted changes rushed through in a few weeks, well ahead of the November 1980 gubernatorial elections. That was too tight. But what happened next was remarkable. Confirmed by several interviewees, by a 1981 *New York Times* investigation[3] and by du Pont's official biography, it is a testament to the ability of elites in small offshore jurisdictions to create and sustain a consensus in their favour.

Frank Biondi, a powerful Democrat lawyer,[4] and Chuck Welch, du Pont's general counsel, went to see Hayward. '(They) said that the locker room on this was very small,' Hayward remembers. 'If the idea got out in public, the Democratic candidate for governor, a downstate farmer named Bill Gordy, is going to grab onto this and the Democrats in the House and Senate will make this a big campaign issue. We'll lose the battle before we even get suited up in our armour.' Du Pont was popular and the Republicans weren't that worried about the state election, but they did fret that if the story got out, it might affect the campaigns of other Republican candidates, including US presidential nominee Ronald Reagan.

'Gordy was one of the unsung heroes of the whole story,' Hayward continued, 'a good old pig farmer. Frank [Biondi] and Chuck Welch got into a helicopter in Wilmington and went to see him and said, "Bill, we want you to know what we're working on. We're here to ask you to keep your mouth shut and not make it an issue in the campaign." Bill Gordy, God bless him, said yes.' The entire Democrat establishment in Delaware seems to have bought into the silence. And not just them. 'If you go back and read the *News Journal*,' said Hayward, 'you will not find one mention of it in the press in the campaign season.'[5] This proposal was circulating among Delaware's entire top business and political elite, including a couple of populist legislators who saw usury as a threat to the basic consumer. 'We had all these major bankers in Delaware through the whole summer,' said Glenn Kenton, another key player, reeling off names like Citicorp's CEO Walter Wriston and Chase's president Tom LaBreque. 'Nobody found out about it. It's just an amazing thing.'

Still, even inside this rarefied secret circle, resistance did materialise. 'The most significant counterforce, though not overt, was the local banks,' said Swayze. 'In the cold citadels of privilege there was a fear the big banks would run rings around them.' Wall Street began to apply pressure. Chase stiffened Delaware spines at a meeting at the Wilmington Club in June, threatening to give up and plump for South Dakota.[6] 'The banks would come down and say, "Now if we come [and build these institutions], are you guys, meaning the government, you're not going to cut us off at the knees here?"' du Pont explained. He agreed to form an informal task force to look into Chase's plan and promised to reply by September.

In the end, Wall Street and Delaware's bankers settled on a compromise. To protect local banks, they promised clauses to prohibit outsiders from touting for local retail business. By mid-August the local banks were on board and the task force turned to the legislative process. A special session of the legislative assembly was called outside normal procedures to insulate this from the democratic process. As the *Delaware Lawyer* explained it, the special session's purpose 'was to prevent the proposal from becoming encumbered in the "horse trading" that typically occurs in the regular session'.

While bigger states saw laws regulating economic activity as complex moral, political and economic issues, Delaware was seeing them instead through offshore lenses: as pieces of sovereignty that could be sold to make locals rich.

Chase had opted for Delaware rather than South Dakota, partly because it did not want to follow in Citicorp's slipstream. 'Chase said, "We're not going to the same place Citicorp is going,"' Kenton remembered. Citicorp, he added, had said, '"We're only out in South Dakota because we had to go someplace. But if you are going to open up [in Delaware], count us in too."'

As Wall Street interest grew, Biondi suggested talking to JP Morgan, where he had some connections. It did not issue credit cards, but Delaware hoped other business could be done. 'We went up to see Morgan and we said, "What do you want?"' Kenton explained. 'And they said, "We're just getting the heck taxed out of us up here and we need to have a low-tax environment."' So Delaware served up the offshore classic: a regressive state tax structure – the richer you are, the lower your tax rate. They set the bank franchise tax at about 8 per cent on income under $20 million, then 6 per cent on $20–25 million, and so on, until the really big incomes got away with just 1.7 per cent. The goal, as Swayze put it, was 'sheltering the indigenous banking community against competitive threats on the one hand, and attracting and growing the business of newly created Delaware bank subsidiaries of non-Delaware bank holding companies on the other'.[7] As for the lost tax dollars from the banking behemoths – well, American taxpayers elsewhere could pick up the tab for that.

Biondi's firm Morris, Nichols, Arsht & Tunnell represented both Chase and JP Morgan, and both he and his firm are frank about their role in the bonanza. 'The Chase Manhattan and JP Morgan banks hired Morris, Nichols's Frank Biondi to draft the law,' the firm's official history notes, 'and help convince the state legislature to adopt it.'[8] Biondi himself added: 'Did I lobby the state legislature? You're damn right I did.' So Chase and JP Morgan, in effect, wrote the law through their local representatives. The *New York Times* noted later that it was drafted without any written analysis by a Delaware official, and that Biondi's drafts got their primary reviews from other bank attorneys.[9] Biondi denies any conflict of interest, saying he disclosed his connections to all parties.

On 4 November 1980 du Pont was re-elected governor of Delaware, and the draft legislation was unveiled in public two months later, on 14 January. Du Pont's administration gave the legislative assembly the deadline the banks demanded: pass the bill by 4 February, or the deal was off.[10] The bill sailed through on 3 February, and du Pont signed the Delaware Financial Center Development Act two weeks later. Delaware was to remove interest rate ceilings on credit cards, on personal loans, car loans and more. Banks would have powers to foreclose on people's homes if they defaulted on credit card debts; they could establish places of business overseas or offshore, and they got a regressive state tax structure to boot. And crucially, because Delaware law could now be exported to other states, this was to be rolled out across America. Two hundred years of legislation capping interest rates in the United States was now a dead letter.[11]

Despite the timing – the bill was pased less than a week before Ronald Reagan took office as US President – all interviewees stressed that this came purely from Delaware and the New York bankers, not from Washington. 'Lawmakers quickly realized,' wrote du Pont's biographer, 'that the Financial Center Development Act was favoured by almost everybody in the state's power structure – and by the powers most likely to contribute significantly to their future election campaigns.'[12]

Out-of-state banks flooded into Delaware, and the credit card industry took off. Within months the credit card giant MBNA had opened its first office in a vacant supermarket; within a decade it had over $80 billion in outstanding credit card debt. 'Every night helicopters took off from here carrying receipts and paperwork from all the credit card businesses,' said du Pont. 'It gave us twenty-five years of growth, and revenues growing every year.' Before 1980, Delaware's revenue from the bank franchise tax had amounted to just $3 million per year; by 2007 it was taking $175 million.[13]

Two months after the bill's passage, the *New York Times* summed up. 'To bankers and their supporters the law is modern and comprehensive, drafted in a thoughtful manner,' it wrote.

To some state officials, legislators and consumer advocates, both in Delaware and elsewhere, the bill was stampeded through the Delaware Legislature, is one-sided and, as one critic put it, a banker's 'dream'.

Bankers say the possibility that the Delaware plan could be enacted in other states is a sign of healthy competition among the states and a reflection of the current emphasis on states' rights. Their critics say it illustrates the ability of powerful private interests to pass laws with national ramifications by singling out and exploiting the weakest and most malleable states.[14]

The same *Times* article noticed something else. 'Many legislators say they did not read the 61-page bill before agreeing to sponsor it and did not understand the complicated measure before voting on it.' Harris B. McDowell, the majority whip for the Democrat-controlled state senate, said he was told at the last minute. 'I confess I have no expertise in the banking area,' he said. 'I am mystified by the bill.' He voted for it on a promise that it would create jobs. Others said the only hearing for the bill, which lasted just three hours, was handled and timed in ways that prevented many legislators from attending, and inhibited rebuttal. Delaware's Consumer Affairs Department never saw the bill before its passage, a deliberate exclusion that Kenton defended by saying that he and du Pont shared the 'bias' that 'banks should charge what they want in fees. I didn't see any sense in running that fundamental principle by anybody who doesn't agree with it,' he added.

This pattern will be familiar to offshore legislators worldwide. In Delaware bankers had found a malleable legislature, used special legislative tricks to stymie bothersome objectors from other stakeholders, worked hard to keep objectors in the dark, reassured bamboozled legislators that all would be well and created ring-fences giving special exemptions to outsiders not available to locals. Most important was a typical offshore feature that made all these things possible: 'It's small, you can get the leadership together because of that,' Biondi said. 'The leadership was accessible at the governor's office but also in the legislature and in the business community.' Du Pont made exactly the same point. 'I used to say to them,' he said, 'if you've got a problem, you come on in, and around this one table we can put all the people we need to solve your problem, whatever it may turn out to be. And we'll talk about it. We're small enough. We can move fast. We can get things done.'[15] Swayze agreed, and added a detail. 'There were significant forces in the New York legislature opposed to this,' he said. 'Delaware took advantage of the fact that New York couldn't turn the dreadnought around in the harbour. We're small; we take advantage of opportunities, and we can fill that void.' In other words, we can give the bankers what they need faster than anyone else. Delaware's legislature is for hire.

Once Delaware fell, the banks used it as a crowbar to prise open other states. Thomas Shriver of the Pennsylvania Bankers' Association warned that Delaware is 'a very viable option if the Pennsylvania Legislature doesn't enact a bill we have proposed'. Robert Erwin, head of Maryland's Consumer Protection Division, warned that if other states gave in to the 'pressure' from Delaware, 'then it becomes a game of Russian roulette among the fifty states, trying to outdo themselves'.

With interest rates caps removed, the credit card industry took off, and Americans splurged. By mid-2007, as the global financial crisis emerged, US consumers owed nearly a trillion dollars on their credit cards[16] – not to mention loans taken out against homes to pay credit card bills. Not a single one of the players interviewed for this book showed any sign of doubt that the Financial Center Development Act was a very good thing.

The respected liberal lawyer Thomas Geoghegan pointed to the significance of this episode. 'Some people still think our financial collapse was the result of a technical glitch – a failure, say, to regulate derivatives or hedge funds,' he wrote.

No, the deregulation that led to our Time of Troubles was of a deeper, darker kind. The problem was not that we 'deregulated the New Deal' but that we deregulated a much older, even ancient, set of laws . . . the laws against usury, which had existed in some form in every civilization from the time of the Babylonian Empire to the end of Jimmy Carter's term, and which had been so taken for granted that no one ever even mentioned it to us in law school. That's when we found out what happens when an advanced industrial economy tries to function with no cap at all on interest rates.[17]

This probably overstated the case – there is no single explanation for the latest crisis – still, Geoghegan identified an important contributing factor. The elimination of usury caps spilled out into a wide variety of financial fields. A comment from Paul Tucker of the Bank of England, in a widely referenced 2010 paper on financial stability in the wake of the crisis illustrates its effects on one such field.[18] He explored so-called money market mutual funds, major players in the shadow banking system that underlay the crisis, and which I will discuss later.

Almost any history of the past few years will give money funds a fairly central role. Money funds began their life in the US, as a response to now long abolished caps on interest rates that the banks could pay on deposits. They have become a gigantic part of the US financial system; at about $3 trillion, being roughly the same size as the transactions deposits of commercial banks.

These funds became a major supplier of short-term funding to banks, helping them hide their true financial positions and making the financial system more fragile. Credit card debt, money market funds and numerous other instruments that fuelled the borrowing binge and the crisis – the deregulation of interest rates had effects that are incalculable.

Having helped deregulate and boost the supply of debt, Delaware also set about getting a share of the demand side. It did this by setting itself up as a major player in the securitisation industry – the business of parcelling up mortgages and other loans, including those on credit cards, and repackaging the debt and selling it on. Once again, Delaware did this simply by establishing the exact legal framework that corporations desired.

The Delaware Financial Center Development Act of 1981 itself contained a section exempting 'affiliated finance companies' from all state taxes. These companies act like banks but aren't formally banks so fall outside banking regulations. Along with structured investment vehicles and their like, they are a core part of the global shadow banking system that dragged the world into economic crisis from 2007. They were especially prominent in the US, notably in Delaware. In 1983 its International Banking Development Act got Delaware into the new offshore game of international banking facilities. When that was enacted, Chase and several other banks promptly moved foreign offshore activities to Delaware.

Biondi outlined several other statutes that followed, and his role in them. 'I wrote those bills with my boys here,' he said. The 1986 Foreign Development Act built on the 1983 legislation designed to let foreign banks take advantage of Delaware's regressive bank franchise taxes. New tax legislation in 1987 enticed banks who wanted to get into dealing securities. 'My staff and I wrote it,' Biondi explained. 'We represented Morgan, Chase, Citicorp, Bank of New York and Bankers Trust.' Biondi's team also wrote the Bank and Trust Company Insurance Powers Act of 1989, authorising banks to sell and underwrite insurance.[19] The Statutory Trust Act of 1988, giving huge flexibility to people setting up such trusts and 'the protection of trust assets from creditors', made Delaware the top jurisdiction for setting up so-called balance sheet CDOs (collateralised debt obligations), which allowed banks to offload their assets onto other investors, another important contributor to the crisis.[20] A new act in January 2000 allowed limited liability partnerships, a major contributor to the degradation of corporate governance, which I will soon explore in detail. There was also the Asset-Backed Securities Facilitation Act of 2002, which further opened the securitisation spigots. All these helped Delaware become, as one expert put it, 'the jurisdiction of choice in securitisation'.[21]

Delaware has also played a central role in transforming global banking from its traditional fare of funnelling savings into productive investments, towards more speculative, risky, fee-based banking models. 'Delaware recognised the quantum shift in the financial services industry toward fee-based activities,' said Swayze, 'and it provided the legislative and regulatory framework to accommodate that shift.'[22]

Now here is the big point. I do not claim this story as an explosive new revelation about the cause of the mortgage and financial crisis, important though it was. This was just one among many tangled roots of the global disaster. My point instead has been to show what a tax haven is: a state captured by financial interests from elsewhere. The next story, from thousands of miles across the Atlantic Ocean in Jersey, rhymes almost perfectly with Delaware's.

In June 1995 the director of Jersey's Financial Services Department met a partner in Mourant du Feu & Jeune, a member of the so-called Offshore Magic Circle, the ten or so law firms most active offshore. They discussed a corporate form known as the limited liability partnership (LLP). A letter from Mourant du Feu & Jeune to the president of the Finance and Economics Committee then began to circulate in Jersey political circles, dated 9 October 1995.

'My firm has been working with the UK partnership of Price Waterhouse (PW) and English solicitors, Slaughter and May, to find a method of obtaining some limited liability protection for the part-ners' personal assets without completely restructuring PW's business and losing the cultural benefits of a partnership,' the letter said. After surveying several jurisdictions, it continued, Jersey was deemed the most suitable. 'We are therefore seeking support of your Committee for the introduction of a Special Limited Partnership Law in Jersey during 1996.' In short, firms wanted to write a new law for Jersey, and a draft law had already been prepared in London.

The letter urged Jersey's powerful Finance and Economics Committee to consider the law by December, then have it debated in the States (the island's parliament) the following January or February.

'We would also propose that we would prepare any necessary subordinate legislation required in connection with the Special Limited Partnership Law,' it added. 'We appreciate that this is a very short time scale.' Suggesting that Jersey's PR firm Shandwicks and the PW media team get to work, it also said, 'It would be very important for PW and I believe, Jersey's finance industry, that the correct messages are sent to the media.'

The big four accounting firms – Price Waterhouse (now PricewaterhouseCoopers – PWC), Ernst & Young, KPMG and Deloitte Touche – are giants. PWC employed over 146,000 people and generated $28 billion in revenues in 2008, making it the world's largest professional services firm. Auditors also occupy a very special place in the global economy. Their audits are the main tools through which societies know about, and regulate, the world's biggest corporations: in a sense, they are the private police force of capitalism.[23] Audit failures lie behind most great corporate scandals: Enron, WorldCom, and most of the collapses behind the latest financial crisis. Because of the extreme dangers bad audits pose to corporate capitalism in general, and to you and me in particular, governments try to regulate this profession with extra care.

Since the middle of the nineteenth century limited liability has been part of the grand bargain at the heart of corporate governance. If a limited liability company goes bust, owners and shareholders may lose the money they invested, but their losses (liabilities) are limited to that: they are not liable for additional debts the corporation has racked up. This concept was controversial when it was introduced – it was feared that it would erode standards of accountability – but it was justified on the grounds that protection would encourage people to invest and boost economic activity. But there was a caveat: in exchange for the gift of limited liability, corporations must agree to have their accounts properly audited, and these audits published, to open a true and fair window into what they are up to. It was an early-warning system, to keep the risks manageable.

A general partnership is very different from a limited liability company. Investors in a partnership are experienced professionals who should know what they are doing, and they have *un*limited liability: when things go wrong they are personally liable for all losses: creditors can theoretically take even the shirts off partners' backs. Since they have given up the right to shift losses onto the rest of society, partners are held to less stringent standards of disclosure. Partners were also subjected to 'joint and several' liability: a partner is liable not only for his or her own mistakes, but also for the mistakes of others in the partnership.[24] All this helps focus auditors' minds on doing their job properly – and policing their colleagues too.

Konrad Hummler, the managing partner of Wegelin Private Bank in Switzerland – which is an unlimited liability company – explains what it is like to operate under such rules.[25]

Partners who have [joint and several] unlimited liability have a solidarity; the dynamic within the group is totally different. On so many boards – and I have quite some experience of this – one doesn't dare to ask the right questions. This [unlimited liability] is the only way of doing business where you dare to ask the really difficult questions – mostly the simplest questions. I will say, 'Listen, Mr Chairman, I still don't understand the case.' The chairman will say, 'You obviously haven't read your papers properly.' At this point I don't stop the discussion, but I say again, 'Mr Chairman, I still don't understand this bloody thing.' That's the difference. Because of your unlimited liability, you think twice.

Joint and several unlimited liability for partners in audit firms is clearly, given their special role in policing modern capitalism, a very good idea.

What was being proposed in Jersey, however, was different again: a law allowing *limited liability partnerships*. An LLP for accountancy firms is an example of having your cake and eating it: an LLP partner not only gets the benefits of being in a partnership – less disclosure, lower taxes and weaker regulation – but limited liability protection too. And if a partner breaks the rules or is negligent, other partners who are not involved aren't accountable for the consequences. This law was the product of what Professor Prem Sikka of Essex University calls an auditor's ultimate aim: 'to use the state to shield it from the consequences of its own failures'. For those involved, it is the best of all worlds. For the rest of society, it is the worst.

The draft Jersey LLP Act was worse still. LLPs would not need to have their own accounts audited or even to say on their invoices or letterheads that they were registered in Jersey. It had no provisions for regulating audit firms or investigating misdemeanours, and it offered other audit stakeholders – that is, the public – almost no rights. To get these astonishingly generous concessions from the public at large, these multi-billion-dollar global corporations would have to pay a one-off fee of just £10,000, then £5,000 a year afterwards.

As with the liberalisation of usury provisions in Delaware, the Jersey proposal was a delayed reaction to the ideological revolution associated with Ronald Reagan and Margaret Thatcher: a shift away from the view that competitive markets need robust regulation to a childlike faith in self-regulation by market actors. Big accountancy firms had already secured LLPs in the US after first influencing the Texas legislature in 1991; within four years nearly half of US states had them. Limited liability provisions 'took away the most powerful incentive for self-policing by the corporate professions of law and accounting', wrote the tax expert David Cay Johnston, and 'help explain the wave of corporate cheating that swept the country'.[26] Already there was evidence from the US that when LLPs are introduced, less time is allocated to each audit, and quality suffers. It is nearly impossible to identify a smoking gun in cases like this, but these concessions were undoubtedly important factors in the Enron and WorldCom disasters and in the destruction of Enron's auditor, Arthur Andersen LLP.

In Britain, following high-profile audit failures such as BCCI, Polly Peck and many others, auditors had already squeezed major concessions out of the government, having won the right in 1989 to be limited liability companies[27] – though few audit companies converted, since most did not want to have to publish their accounts. A British House of Lords decision in 1990 worsened matters, ruling that auditors owed no 'duty of care' to individual stakeholders injured by audit failures.

Still, the UK was holding out against an LLP law, and for once was doing the right thing. 'The UK . . . wanted to tell the world, "You can trust London,"' said Sikka, who researched the Jersey LLP affair. 'If it is imposssible to sue the auditors, that makes it harder to look clean.' The accountants had other ideas. 'I think the calculation was that if the UK fell, the rest of Europe would fall, and the former British colonies would also fall into place. They thought, "If the UK gets going, everything else is won."'

The accountants' strategy was simple: find an easy-to-influence legislature offshore, win LLP concessions there, then threaten to relocate if the UK refused to create its own law. First they approached the Isle of Man, then Guernsey, but were turned down. Then they came to Jersey, which has, as Jersey Senator Stuart Syvret put it (and like Delaware), 'a legislature for hire'.

A month after that initial letter, Price Waterhouse and Ernst & Young announced the proposed Jersey LLP legislation. Senior Jersey politicians had assured them that the bill would be 'nodded through', as one insider noted. But not everybody was happy. Jersey's senior law draftsman complained that the new law was like 'getting a completed crossword and being asked to write the clues'. Syvret remembers first coming across the proposed law. 'I knew bugger all about accountancy, and suddenly it was on our desks and we had to debate it in two weeks.' He and Gary Matthews, one of the few other legislators to smell a rat, set about educating themselves about LLP laws. Matthews contacted a British parliamentarian, Austin Mitchell, who in turn called Sikka. When they understood what the new law meant, Matthews put it bluntly. 'This law is poison.'

Sikka remembers Matthews and Syvret first contacting him as they scrambled to get up to speed. 'Gary Matthews said, "They want to rush this through parliament and I don't understand a word, and other people I've spoken to don't understand it either,"' Sikka said. 'I'd been there on holiday but had taken no interest in this funny little island until that fateful call from Gary Matthews. The more we looked into it, the more rotten the place looked.'

Matthews and Syvret were up against a well-resourced and motivated establishment on an island whose very political structure makes dissent extremely hard. Jersey has no political parties. The fifty-three members of the States are directly elected, but in three separate groups: twelve senators, twenty-nine deputies, and twelve parish constables (connétables). Elections are staggered over time so there has never been a general election or a change of government. There is no tradition of government versus opposition; there is instead a permanent regime that evolves over time. This dramatically weakens opponents of an establishment consensus. 'When bad men combine,' the conservative thinker Edmund Burke wrote, 'the good must associate; else they will fall, one by one, an unpitied sacrifice in a contemptible struggle.'

Without political parties, good men and women are isolated, then picked off.

'Democracy doesn't work here,' said Geoff Southern, one of the few dissident deputies in the States. 'There are fifty-three members, but nobody can stand up and say, "Vote for us and we will do this" as a bloc. Instead, it's, "I am a good bloke – vote for me." Manifestos are just candyfloss.' Jersey politics is about personalities, not issues; without shared platforms States members tend to look after themselves rather than embrace common agendas to reflect the public interest. 'For the last 200 years the establishment has cultivated the notion that party politics is wicked, divisive and harmful,' Southern said. 'The media spreads it. If you did a survey, I expect two-thirds would say they think party politics is a bad idea. Propaganda is everywhere. The media here is like in Soviet Russia.'

Voter turnout reflects the absence of local democracy. The 33 per cent turnout in the November 2005 election would have put Jersey in 165th position of 173 countries in a world ranking: marginally better than Sudan and far below the 77 per cent European average since 1945. Poorer voters especially face endless little hurdles. Much of the Portuguese-origin working-class subgroup that makes up nearly 10 per cent of the population is unaware they even can vote, Southern said; voters must re-register every three years, and he has found dead people on his voters' rolls.

The *connétables*, by virtue of the parochial system through which they emerge, are intrinsically conservative and inexperienced, and vote with the establishment every time. They tend to be small shopkeepers, farmers, guest-house owners and plumbers, but can get into major positions of power, and into the finance sector. When it comes to decisions on whether Jersey should adopt a global standard of banking regulation, they are unable to judge responsibly. A *Wall Street Journal* article at the time noted this: 'Jersey is an island that until two decades ago lived off boat building, cod fishing, agriculture and tourism. It is run by a group who, although they form a social and political elite on Jersey, are mostly small-business owners and farmers who now find themselves overseeing an industry of global scope involving billions of dollars.' The article went on to report the judgement of John Christensen, who was Jersey's economic adviser at the time: 'By and large they are totally out of their depth.'[28]

Christensen now remembers a legislature made up largely of small-town politicians with no understanding of the complex currents of international finance, who simply passed legislation through on the nod. 'When I talked to the politicians on the Finance and Economics Committee,' he said, 'time and time again I talked about proposals coming forward. They said, "I'm being honest, John: I don't understand the detail, but I trust the lawyers and the bankers when they say it is necessary."' The similarities with what members of the Delaware legislature were saying in 1980–1 are remarkable. It is as if a vast global financial centre has been tacked onto a couple of small-town parish councils in England or a smaller US county. 'They can argue at enormous length about the budget for the local pony club,' said Christensen, 'but a new limited liability law or a new trust law will go unchallenged. It's the captured state.'

Syvret also noticed that Senator Reg Jeune, one of the most powerful politicians on the island and a major supporter of the LLP legislation, was simultaneously a consultant to Mourant du Feu & Jeune, the lawyers who had brought in the legislation in the first place, and so had a direct financial interest in supporting it. 'I thought "Whoa! This is extraordinarily brazen,"' said Syvret. 'When the States Assembly convened I stood up and said that Jeune had a conflict of interest – a financial interest. Jeune looked as though somebody had shot him. He staggered out of the chamber.'[29] Syvret came under ferocious pressure from the Jersey establishment to apologise. He declined, was pressed again, and refused again. Another top politician threatened him with 'serious implications' if he did not recant, adding, 'which is a pity, since you had such a lot to offer'. The politician emphasised the word 'had' – which Syvret took as a threat. He stood his ground. 'I just wasn't going to take that crap,' he said. He was suspended from the assembly, and in States deliberations in his absence he and Matthews were referred to as 'the enemy within'. Sikka, for his part, was called an 'enemy of the state'.

Senator John Rothwell, responding to Matthews' concerns, pointed to the Jersey establishment's approach to ethics. 'The island has done extremely well in projecting an image of low-profile respectability,' he said, 'but people in the finance industry, having heard speeches in the House about ethics of government, are getting rather twitchy about what members might embrace.'[30] Rothwell, a public relations adviser by trade, knew exactly what he was saying. Oppose the LLP law and the financial services industries will see Jersey as unreliable, and the money will go elsewhere.

Matthews' and Syvret's robust challenges slowed the fast-track passage of the legislation, but did not stop it: it was finally enacted in November. In elections that year, well-financed candidates stood against Matthews under banners reading DON'T ROCK THE BOAT, and Matthews was vilified in public. He lost his seat and was unable to get a job afterwards. He left for England and his marriage fell apart. As Sikka put it, 'They put that man through the mincer.'

On the surface Jersey feels terribly British, and the island's rulers always say it is a well-regulated, transparent and cooperative jurisdiction. The reality is shockingly different. It is a state whose leadership has essentially been captured by global finance, and whose members will threaten and intimidate anyone who dissents. In a later chapter I will show just how repressive places like Jersey can be.

After the LLP law passed in Jersey, the accounting firms next opened a front in London. They publicly threatened to relocate to Jersey if the UK did not enact its own LLP legislation. Sikka fought to stop it. 'We told the politicians, "You can't concede this – these firms have held you to ransom,"' he said. He wrote in *The Times* how harmful such legislation would be, and that the Jersey card was clearly a bluff: the big firms would never close up in London, sack their clients and staff, renegotiate contracts and reopen there. 'If the government were to concede a liability cap to auditors, it would hardly be able to deny the same to producers of food, drink, medicine and cars. None of this would be welcomed by consumers.'

The *Financial Times* saw the real agenda too. They 'want to keep the threat of moving "off-shore" as a cosh with which to threaten the (UK) government if it fails to come up with a workable LLP law.' But the accountants got most of the British financial press behind them, criticised Sikka and wielded that old favourite: that Britain's government was 'anti-business'. The campaign worked. Britain passed its own LLP law in 2001 and the accountants stayed. 'It was the work that Ernst & Young and Price Waterhouse undertook with the Jersey government,' an Ernst & Young partner crowed, 'that first concentrated the mind of UK ministers . . . I've no doubt whatsoever ourselves and Price Waterhouse drove it onto government's agenda because of the Jersey idea.'[31] As Sikka put it, 'the Jersey sprat had served its purpose, now that the UK mackerel had been landed.'

The UK legislation was not quite as bad as the Jersey law – it involved more disclosure, for example – and perhaps Sikka's campaigning helped. Yet it still drastically diluted auditors' incentives to take care with their accounting. Ernst & Young became an LLP in 2001; KPMG went in May 2002; PricewaterhouseCoopers made the move in January 2003; Deloitte & Touche followed that August. A host of lawyers, architects and others joined in, getting the tax perks and limited disclosure available to partnerships, but with limited liability.

Canada took on LLP in 1998; it has been followed by New Zealand, Australia, South Africa, India, Singapore and Japan – to name just a few. These changes can only have contributed to the latest financial crisis. Had auditors personally faced getting into big trouble when they or their partners screwed up, they might not have been so hasty to sign off on all the off-balance-sheet financing.

The Jersey and Delaware episodes are stunningly similar, despite happening fifteen years and an ocean apart, and concerning entirely different people and laws. Deep truths about global finance are at work here. 'Someone comes up with a new idea, but onshore regulation blocks it,' said Robert Kirkby, technical director for Jersey Finance, echoing what Delaware's insiders had boasted of. 'You can lobby onshore, but there are lots of stakeholders, you have to get past them all, and it takes a long time. In Jersey, you can bash this thing through fast. We got the leading edge years ago. We can change our company laws and our regulations so much faster than you can in, say, the UK, France or Germany.' Talking in March 2009, in the depths of the financial crisis caused substantially by reckless deregulation, Kirkby went out of his way to praise Jersey's new unregulated funds regime and its specialisation in securitisation – that pooling and repackaging of mortgages and other assets into securities to sell on to investors which has caused such mayhem. 'We're able to put the criteria in place, the regulation is lighter,' Kirkby said.

I have no objection to deregulation in principle, as long as it is the process of genuine – and I mean genuine – democratic bargaining that considers the needs of all affected stakeholders, at home and overseas. But what we have in Jersey and Delaware is rampant, uncontrolled deregulation, harnessed to the interests of a few insiders and large corporate players. Just as European nobles used to consolidate their unaccountable powers in castles, to better subjugate and extract tribute from the surrounding peasantry, so financial capital has coalesced in these fortified nodes of unaccountable political and economic power, capturing local politics and turning these jurisdictions into fast and flexible private law-making machines, defended against outside interference and protected by establishment consensus and the suppression of dissent.

Offshore is not just a place, an idea, a way of doing things, or even a weapon for the finance industries. It is also a *process*: a race to the bottom where the regulations, laws and trappings of democracy are steadily degraded, as one arrangement ricochets from one fortified redoubt of finance to the next jurisdiction, and the offshore system pushes steadily, further, deeper, onshore. The tax havens have become the battering rams of deregulation.

Most people have not yet understood these deep truths about offshore, because of two related confusions. The first stems from efforts to use technical criteria to define secrecy jurisdictions: tax rates, forms of secrecy, and so on. But these are just outcomes of the deeper truths. Our maps of offshore need to identify, first of all, these strongholds of financial power. A definition like my loose one – that secrecy jurisdictions are 'places that seek to attract business by offering politically stable facilities to help people or entities get around the rules, laws and regulations of jurisdictions elsewhere' – helps us see what we are looking for. A second confusion is to think that this is about physical geography, when it is really about political jurisdiction and trust-based networks. The future that the offshore system promises has a distinctly medieval quality: in a world still nominally run by democratic nation states, the offshore system is more like a network of guilds in the service of unaccountable and often criminal elites.

Jersey and Delaware should serve as a warning to larger economies about what happens when the offshore ethic isn't challenged.

The Delaware story is one part of an explanation of how offshore contributed to the latest financial crisis, and the Jersey example helps explain why nobody saw it coming. A few more examples now will flesh out the picture a little more.

One of the major factors underlying the recent global economic and financial crisis is debt. Why has so much of it built up in the world's richest economies? An article in the *Financial Times* in June 2009 headed DEBT IS CAPITALISM'S DIRTY LITTLE SECRET provides one answer. 'The benefits of economic growth have gone into the pockets of plutocrats rather than the bulk of the population,' it said. 'So why has there been no revolution? Because there was a solution: debt. If you couldn't earn it, you could borrow it.' And the infrastructure was put in place to make this happen. The tax havens are a big part of that.

As the 1990s progressed, occasional expert warnings about systemic, debt-related threats from offshore *did* emerge. The IMF pointed squarely at the problem in 1999 when discussing the interbank market, where banks lend to each other. 'A large part of the growth in OTC [over-the-counter] trading of derivative instruments may have involved offshore banks,' the IMF said.[32] 'The interbank nature of the offshore market implies that, in the event of financial distress, contagion is likely . . . Offshore banks are likely to be highly leveraged, that is less solvent, than onshore banks.' The report, which contains plenty more along these lines, frets especially about lax offshore regulation. It was a direct warning long before the crisis struck.

That report followed soon after the implosion of the hedge fund Long Term Capital Management (LTCM), a classic slice-and-dice offshore structure which nearly destroyed the US banking system in 1998, after the fund took on massive risks, covered by near-paranoid secrecy. LTCM's managers were in Greenwich, Connecticut; the hedge fund was incorporated in Delaware; and the fund it managed was in the Cayman Islands. Yet none of the agonised analyses that followed took any serious interest in the offshore angle.[33] And the pattern just keeps being repeated.

The latest financial crisis was incubated in the so-called shadow banking system – a vast economic sector containing all manner of special purpose entities (shadow banks) that borrow money to lend out again at a profit – which falls outside normal bank regulation. SPEs do this partly by separating themselves legally from the regulated institutions that sponsor them, thus going off their balance sheets. The shadow banking system is not traditionally described as either offshore or onshore, but an in-depth 2008 study on special purpose entities by the Swiss-based Bank for International Settlements is very clear about where the dangerous shadow banks are actually located. 'The most common jurisdictions for US securitisations are the Cayman Islands and the state of Delaware,' the BIS said. 'The most common SPE jurisdictions for European securitisations are Ireland, Luxembourg, Jersey, and the UK.'[34] Every last one is a major secrecy jurisdiction that uses a simple business model: ask the financial institutions exactly what they need, then shape the laws accordingly and without democratic debate.

The BIS report calls Cayman offshore and Delaware onshore.[35] It is exactly this misunderstanding – confusing physical geography with political geography – that has led to widespread claims that secrecy jurisdictions had nothing to do with the gigantic mess we are now in. The Bank for International Settlements, along with every other major international financial institution, needs to understand what offshore is and how it works.

Among the only academic experts to have seriously examined offshore's role in the financial crisis is Jim Stewart, senior lecturer in finance at Trinity College, Dublin. In reports in July 2008[36] Stewart investigated the Dublin International Financial Services Centre (IFSC), a secrecy jurisdiction set up in 1987 under corrupt Irish politician Charles Haughey with help primarily from City of London interests. A showcase for high-risk wild-west financial capitalism, the Dublin IFSC emerged the year after London's giant deregulatory Big Bang and currently hosts over half the world's top fifty financial institutions. It became a big player in the shadow banking system, and now hosts 8,000 funds with $1.5 trillion in assets. Perhaps most alluring of all Dublin's lures, Stewart said, is its 'light touch regulation'.[37]

In June 2007 two Bear Stearns hedge funds incorporated in the Cayman Islands announced huge losses, presaging the company's collapse. Bear Stearns had two investment funds and six debt securities listed on the Irish stock exchange, and operated three subsidiaries in the Dublin IFSC through a holding company, Bear Stearns Ireland Ltd, for which every dollar of equity financed $119 of gross assets, an exceedingly high and dangerous ratio. The accounts of Bear Stearns Ireland Ltd state that it was regulated by the Irish Financial Services Regulatory Authority, and EU directives state that the host country is responsible for regulation. Yet in an interview the Irish regulator said he considered his remit extended only to 'Irish banks.' So Bear Stearns was effectively regulated nowhere, and the Irish regulator did not feature in any media analysis of its insolvency. In his reports Stewart cited nineteen funds in difficulties in the crisis and added, 'almost always, the IFSC link is not discussed'.

Several German banks which got into trouble also had funds quoted in Dublin. These included IKB, which got €7.8 billion in German state aid, and Sachsen, which got €17.8 billion of emergency funding and €2.8 billion in state aid. 'And yet none of the accounts or prospectuses for any of the years examined mentioned regulation or the Irish regulator,' Stewart continued. 'Within Ireland the Financial Regulator has been quoted as saying that they have no responsibility for entities whose main business is raising and investing in funds based on subprime lending.' The *Financial Times* analysis of the episode laid the blame almost entirely on the structure of the German banking system.

In Ireland, Stewart noted, if the relevant documents are provided to the regulator by 3 p.m., the fund will be authorised the next day. Yet a prospectus for a quoted instrument is a complex legal and financial document – a debt instrument issued by Sachsen Bank ran to 245 pages. The regulator could not have assessed it in the two hours between 3 p.m. and the normal close of business. In Luxembourg, Stewart noted, a new law states that a fund can enjoy pre-authorisation approval if the fund manager 'notifies' the regulator within a month of launch. It is the captured state, over again.

In April 2010 the US Securities and Exchange Commission (SEC) opened a fraud probe into Goldman Sachs, alleging that it had misled investors over a CDO called Abacus 2007-AC1. Goldman agreed to pay $550 million to settle the charge, without admitting or denying the allegation. The deal's structure is worth noting:

Issuer: Abacus 2007-AC1, Ltd, Incorporated with limited liability in the Cayman Islands
Co-Issuer: Abacus 2007-AC1, Inc., a corporation organised under the laws of the state of Delaware[38]

McClatchy's, the only mainstream media organisation to investigate the deal's offshore nature, found 148 such deals by Goldman Sachs in the Cayman Islands over a seven-year period. In fact, every big Wall Street player used the Caymans for this business. These deals 'became key links in a chain of exotic insurance-like bets called credit-default swaps that worsened the global economic collapse by enabling major financial institutions to take bigger and bigger risks without counting them on their balance sheets . . . sheltered by the Caymans' opaque regulatory apparatus.'[39]

It was not so much the Caymans' opacity that attracted the large players – though that helped – as its 'flexibility'. When tax haven supporters say they promote 'efficiency' in global markets, this is the kind of thing they are talking about. This 'efficiency' really means 'flexibility': their political capture by financial capital.

Rudolf Elmer, a senior accountant in a Swiss bank's Caymans office until 2003, takes the story further. Supervision in the Caymans was especially lax, he said. 'Even if you have the right regulatory framework, you need the brainpower to audit the banks and companies. There is a general lack of this in the offshore world. You get a lot of high-risk issues running through the islands being covered by junior auditors in CIMA [Cayman Islands Monetary Authority].'

One of Elmer's office's functions was take out cheap short-term loans and invest the proceeds in longer-term assets with higher rates of return. This is an easy way to make tax-free money, but it is dangerous too: you must roll over short-term loans every few days, replacing one loan with another. But when lending dries up, as it did in 2007, you must still repay the short-term loans fast – but suddenly nobody will provide new loans to replace them. You can fall into default very quickly. This is exactly what brought down the British bank Northern Rock in 2007. Yet the Caymans regulator, Elmer said, took an extremist laissez-faire approach to these so-called maturity mismatches. 'This short-term and long-term problem,' Elmer said, 'from a regulatory point of view we couldn't have done that in the UK or Switzerland. The Cayman Islands Monetary Authority should have picked that up.'

Elmer was involved in two CIMA audits. During the first one he and his local CEO talked for an hour or so with an official. 'The CIMA person said, "Is it the same as it used to be?" The CEO said, "Yes, it is the same." The CIMA guy said, "No problem." The Cayman regulator knew our CEO well, and he knew he would tell him the truth. Personal relationships were key.' A subsequent audit was more extensive, and lasted about a week. 'You have to be very experienced in that sort of thing,' said Elmer. 'Two junior auditors came in and made a lengthy report, which had little content. I went through those audits, and from a regulatory point of view they were not sufficient at all.' No further action was taken. 'It was quite crucial for [our] group to use Cayman and BVI [British Virgin Islands] vehicles,' he said. 'It boils down to three things: tax, regulatory and legal advantages. You have a lot of freedom.'

This extreme freedom, turning the secrecy jurisdictions into hothouses for risky new banking products, contributed massively to the crisis of the world's major economies.

An IMF paper from October 2010[40], looking at how shocks from the Greek crisis were transmitted around the world, contains a fascinating picture. It shows a welter of countries and draws a maze of interconnections between them, showing the funding flows related to Greece. In a circle at the centre sit the countries right in the thick of Greek contagion: those with the densest connections which served as the hot-money transmission belts for crisis. Every one of the 15 jurisdictions, barring France and Germany whose banks were most heavily involved in Greece, is a major secrecy jurisdiction.

The growth of debt in world economies has yet more offshore origins. There is space here only to sketch a few of the most important ones.

In 2009 the IMF published a detailed report explaining how tax havens, combined with distortions in onshore tax systems, cranked up the global debt engine by encouraging firms to borrow rather than finance themselves out of equity. These practices, it said, 'are pervasive, often large – and hard to justify given the potential impact on financial stability'. Amid all the noise from G20 leaders about tax havens in 2008 and 2009, the IMF concluded, this dangerous aspect had gone entirely unnoticed.[41] The core principles the IMF outlined are simple. A corporation borrows money from offshore, then pays interest on that loan back to the offshore financing company. It then uses the old transfer pricing trick: the profits are offshore, where they avoid tax, and the costs (the interest payments) are onshore, where they are deducted against tax. This trick is central to the business model of private equity companies. They buy a company that someone has sweated for years to create, then load it up with debt, cutting the tax bill and magnifying the returns.

Leveraged buyouts – always involving offshore leverage – accelerated fast ahead of the crisis: the amount raised by private equity funds rose more than sixfold from 2003 to over $300 billion in 2007, by which time their share of all US merger and acquisition activity had risen to 30 per cent. Reports praise private equity companies for excellent 'value creation'. Sometimes private equity companies do create real value, but the core feature of their business model is not value creation, but value skimming. A big tax bill is slashed, the company's shares or value rise, managers' remunerations become fatter, wealth is shifted away from taxpayers to wealthy managers and stockholders. Nowhere in any of this does anyone produce a better or cheaper product. And in the process extra debt is injected into the financial system. Plenty of good firms have gone bust as a result of offshore debt-loading, which the *New York Times* in 2009 described as 'a Wall Street version of "Flip This House."' More than half of the companies that defaulted on their debt that year were either previously or currently owned by private equity firms.[42]

A lot of innovation – I'm talking about *useful* innovations to make better and cheaper goods and services, not the City of London's innovations that simply shift wealth upwards and shift risks downwards – happen in small and medium-sized enterprises. But the offshore system works directly against this. It subsidises multinationals by helping them cut their taxes and grow faster, making it harder for the innovative minnows to compete. And when small innovative firms do emerge they become targets for predators who seek to 'unlock value' from 'synergies' created by bringing the small firm into the bigger, more diversified one. Some synergies may be useful – economies of scale, for instance – but too often the predator unlocks value simply by being better at obtaining abusive, unproductive offshore tax privileges. Some make their best profits by seeking out and harvesting small, genuinely innovative companies that haven't yet managed to unlock those abuses for themselves.

This harvesting removes nimble, competitive and innovative firms from the marketplace and relocates them inside large corporate bureau-cracies, curbing competition and potentially raising prices. Debt rises, and ordinary people pay more tax or see their schools and hospitals fall into disrepair. And if the predators leave their earnings offshore they can defer tax on them indefinitely. Deferred taxation is, as I have mentioned, effectively an interest-free loan from the government, with no repayment date. In other words, more debt.

Consider what happens when this multinational corporation is a bank. Like multinationals on steroids, banks have been particularly adept at going offshore to grow fast: by using tax havens to escape tax, to avoid reserves requirements and other financial regulation and to gear up their borrowings. Banks achieved a staggering 16 per cent annual return on equity between 1986 and 2006, according to Bank of England data,[43] and this offshore-enhanced growth means the banks are now big enough to hold us all to ransom. Unless taxpayers give them what they want, financial calamity ensues. This is the too-big-to-fail problem – courtesy of offshore. But that is *still* not all.

This next point takes a little bit of explanation. Many blame the recent crisis not just on deregulation but also on global macroeconomic imbalances, as funds have flowed from countries with export surpluses, like China, India, Russia and Saudi Arabia, into deficit countries like the United States and Britain. This has led to overconsumption and borrowing in the deficit countries. Now look at Global Financial Integrity's estimate that illicit financial flows out of developing countries have been running at up to a trillion dollars a year. Again most has flowed out of large developing countries like China and Russia and Saudi Arabia, and into large OECD countries like Britain and the United States. Illicit flows in the other direction are much smaller, so the net result is a flow worth hundreds of billions of dollars each year into rich economies and secrecy jurisdictions.[44] The unrecorded and hardly noticed illicit flows add to the recorded imbalances.

Consider what these illicit flows involve. Take, for example, a practice known as reinvoicing. Say a London trader buys a cargo of oil worth $100 million from an exporter in Moscow. The exporter invoices the London importer for $120 million, asking that $20 million of that is quietly deposited in her London account. Russian trade statistics will record the $120 million flowing in, even though only $100 million should have flowed in. The missing $20 million is completely invisible to the boffins who compile the trade statistics, though it represents a very real illicit financial flow from Russia to the United Kingdom which has tangible effects. That $20 million will be reinvested in, say, London housing, where the Russian can earn tax-evading rental income. This illicit inflow does nothing to increase productivity but instead distorts the British housing market and boosts bank profits from their mortgage operations. House prices in Britain rise; first-time buyers find it harder to get on the property ladder; a housing bubble inflates further; and debt builds up in the economy.

There is more. In May 2009 Andrew Haldane of the Bank of England summarised a seminal paper on the financial crisis very simply. 'If there is a unifying theme, it is informational failure,' he said. 'This has been a crisis born of, and prolonged by, lack of information.'[45] Financial markets seized up in 2007 because nobody knew, or trusted, what the other players in the market were doing, or what they were worth, or what or where their risks were. And there is nothing – *nothing* – like the offshore system to generate opacity.

Secrecy jurisdictions specialise in bamboozlement. That is what they do. Along with secrecy and a curmudgeonly reluctance to cooperate with foreign jurisdictions, they provide endless incentives for corporations – especially financial ones – to festoon their affairs across strings of jurisdictions, usually a complex mix of onshore and offshore, to fox the regulators. As the IMF noted, with typically polite and stilted understatement, the offshore system encouraged 'increased complexity and opacity of financial arrangements' which 'may hamper financial supervision'. Impenetrable offshore trails, sliced, diced and trailed around the world, increased the distance between lenders and borrowers until bankers no longer knew who their ultimate clients were. It is hardly a surprise that the Royal Bank of Scotland in 2003 offered a gold credit card with a £10,000 spending limit to one Monty Slater in Manchester, England. Monty Slater was a shih-tzu dog.

John Maynard Keynes summed up the problem as well as anyone. 'Remoteness between ownership and operation is an evil in the relations among men, likely or certain in the long run to set up strains and enmities which will bring to nought the financial calculation.' This is the flaw in the grand bargain at the heart of the globalisation project. In giving freedom to finance, people in democratic nation states lost their freedom to choose and implement the laws and rules that they wanted. They handed these freedoms to the world's financiers in exchange for a promise: that the efficiency gains from those free financial flows will be so enormous as to make that loss of freedom worthwhile. The tax havens helped bring this calculation to nought.

10

Resistance

In combat with the ideological warriors of offshore

In April 1998 the Organisation for Economic Cooperation and Development, a club of rich countries that includes the world's most important secrecy jurisdictions, made an astonishing admission: that tax havens cause great harm. Tax havens and associated offshore activities, an OECD report acknowledged, 'erode the tax bases of other countries, distort trade and investment patterns and undermine the fairness, neutrality and broad social acceptance of tax systems generally. Such harmful tax competition diminishes global welfare and undermines taxpayer confidence in the integrity of tax systems.'[1] Offshore is not only a place, a system and a process, it is also a collection of intellectual arguments. The OECD's new project was the first serious and sustained intellectual assault on the secrecy jurisdictions in world history.[2] At the time, there were widespread protests against the obvious evils of globalisation, yet campaigners focused many of their arguments on trade and all but ignored the offshore system. The OECD's initiative, which contained a lot of baffling discussion of international tax, hardly registered on protesters' agendas.

The report was allowed to emerge for several reasons. First, the evidence had become impossible to ignore: the use of tax havens was 'large, and expanding at an exponential rate'. Second, the report targeted mostly small Caribbean islands that were not OECD members and glossed over the role of OECD countries.[3] Also, several OECD countries who were not tax havens pushed the report hard. But there was another important reason why the report got through: tax havens are so steeped in indifference to big intergovernmental bodies that although the OECD had flagged the report for two years, almost nobody offshore had paid it enough attention to mount a serious effort to stop it emerging.

John Christensen was in Jersey when the report came out. 'Virtually nobody there took it seriously except me,' he said. 'Bankers were saying, "OECD who? Isn't that some sort of customs organisation?"' Daniel J. Mitchell of the right-wing Heritage Foundation in Washington, one of the secrecy jurisdictions' most vocal supporters, had a similar reaction to the Paris-based OECD. 'I thought, "Ah, just a bunch of crazy European socialists."'[4] Still, Mitchell decided to write a couple of things on the report for the Heritage Foundation, and began to see that it mattered. And the OECD's follow-up report in 2000 contained a primed bomb: a blacklist of thirty-five secrecy jurisdictions, and the threat of 'defensive measures' against havens that did not shape up. More alarming for Mitchell, it was not only 'European collectivists' who backed the OECD, but the Clinton administration too.

'Our side was caught with our pants down,' Mitchell said in an interview in Washington. 'Heritage, a big full-service think tank, doesn't focus on just one thing. I thought we ought to have a group to have a go at this.' So he got together with Andrew Quinlan, a friend from college, and Veronique de Rugy, a Paris-educated libertarian academic, to create a small outfit called the Center for Freedom and Prosperity (CF&P) with a subgroup, the Coalition for Tax Competition, whose aim was to protect 'the cause of tax competition'. They located it at the Cato Institute, a well-funded free-market think tank in Washington.

Anti-tax sentiment in Washington in those days was rife. A Delaware senator, William Roth, had been whipping up a storm against the US Internal Revenue Service (IRS) under a declared Republican strategy to 'pull the current income tax code out by its roots and throw it away so it can never grow back'.[5] In an effective piece of political theatre, Roth, a manic supporter of tax cuts for the wealthy, got IRS agents to testify at hearings behind screens like mobsters, with their voices electronically distorted. His people regaled the hearings with stories about IRS agents in flak jackets storming houses and forcing teenage girls to change their clothes at gunpoint. The IRS had no right of reply and most of the claims were untrue.[6] Roth also bombarded politicians with emails about the OECD reports, wrote scary op-eds in national newspapers with headlines such as GLOBAL TAX POLICE and publicly insulted the OECD. Hostilities had begun in the offshore world's first big battle of ideas.

To understand the intellectual underpinnings of offshore finance, it seems appropriate to start with Daniel J. Mitchell, one of the secrecy jurisdictions' noisiest and most active defenders. He is a man of striking warmth and great personal charm. In his blog 'International Liberty: Restraining Government in America and Around the World', he declares that 'I'm a passionate Georgia Bulldog,' and continues, 'so much so that I would have trouble choosing between a low-rate flat tax for America and a national title for the Dawgs. I'm not kidding.' His blog notes that Britain's left-of-centre *Observer* newspaper called him a 'high priest of light tax, small state libertarianism' and adds that this was 'the nicest thing anyone's ever said about me'.

Mitchell's world of beneficial tax competition emerged from a 1956 paper by the economist Charles Tiebout, who explored what happens (only in theory, you understand) when markets are perfect and free citizens flee in hordes from one jurisdiction to another at the drop of a tax inspector's hat. This is not, of course, how the world works. Libertarians and defenders of tax competition simply stretched Tiebout's ideas like rubber, to make an intellectual shield for the havens.

Mitchell began to take a serious interest in politics in the Reagan era, emerging from George Mason University fascinated by conservative economists such as James Buchanan and Vernon Smith, who explored a branch of economics known as public choice theory, which rejects the notion that politicians act on behalf of people or societies and instead looks at them as self-interested individuals. Its followers' distaste for government dovetailed with Mitchell's budding libertarian outlook and his admiration of Reagan. He worked with Republican Senator Bob Packwood, then for the Bush/Quayle transition team, before joining Heritage.

His vision is of a world where government is pared back to just a few core roles like providing security, leaving the rest to the market. 'Some people fantasise about supermodels,' he said. 'I fantasise about having government at 5 per cent of GDP.' (This is quite an ambition: currently, most OECD governments take in tax revenues equivalent to 30–50 per cent of GDP.) He portrays himself as an academic. During our interview he retreated several times behind a disclaimer along these lines: 'I just work with theories; I have not worked in the real world of business.'

Mitchell's speciality is a calculated tone of arched-eyebrows incredulity when discussing people or ideas that he disdains, and his sound bites are carefully crafted to appear utterly reasonable. His short, peppy Internet videos are clear, simple and striking, and he sprinkles them with homespun wisdom, along with repeated use of words like 'freedom' and 'liberty' and digs at his adversaries. 'International bureaucrats', 'intrusive governments' and 'Europeans' (especially the French) are particular bogeys – uttered in tones of theatrical horror. 'Let me give you some frightening numbers,' Mitchell said in a bouncy presentation to the Freedom Conference at the anti-tax Steamboat Institute in Colorado in August 2009. Citing a seventy-five-year projection that raised the spectre of whopping tax rises, and reeling off statistics about the free-spending habits of George W. Bush (whom he dislikes), he predicted that 'we will have a bigger government than any European welfare state – even France and Sweden . . . I don't know if that means we have to stop using deodorant and train our army to surrender if there's a war, but we are going to be a European welfare state.'

Before the OECD report emerged Mitchell said he did his best to avoid international tax. 'My bread and butter was fiscal policy issues – tax cuts versus tax increases, that kind of thing,' he said. 'For me, international tax – transfer pricing, interest allocations and so on – was almost as bad as excise taxes on milk in Mongolia.' In those days there was no real ideology of tax havenry: few people understood how important the offshore system was becoming, and in the age of rapid globalisation almost nobody questioned it. Fortunately for Mitchell, the OECD had tried to avoid looking like it was victimising smaller jurisdictions by couching its initiative not so much as an attack on tax havens, but on harmful tax *competition* – the race to the bottom between states to attract footloose capital by offering zero taxes and other lures. This focus gave Mitchell an immediate advantage in Washington, letting him complain that the OECD was a big bureaucracy that opposed competition.

This question of competition is one of the main arguments that tax havens deploy to justify their existence, and it is well worth exploring. Mitchell articulates the arguments as well as anybody. 'International bureaucracies and politicians from high-tax nations are launching a coordinated attack against these jurisdictions. The high-tax nations of the world want to set up something equivalent to OPEC,' Mitchell thundered in a Washington presentation in 2009, flashing up pictures of sinister-looking men in Arab headdresses. 'It is an effort by high-tax nations to form a cartel that will enable the politicians to put in place worse tax policies.'[7] He continued:

Say you only had one gas station in a town. That one gas station could charge high prices; it could maintain inconvenient hours; it could offer shoddy service. But if you have five gas stations in a town, all of a sudden those gas stations need to compete with each other. They have to lower prices, they have to be attentive to the needs of consumers. We've seen the same thing internationally, with governments.

Imagine you are a governor of Massachusetts. You'd love to shut down New Hampshire – because it's competition. Obama and the rest of the collectivists on the left hate tax havens because they are outposts of freedom. Because of globalisation, labour and capital are a lot more mobile than they used to be. If governments are trying to impose high tax rates, [people] actually have options to move either themselves, or their money, across borders. Just like if you have one monopoly gas station in town, and all of a sudden new gas stations open up, you can decide, 'I'm no longer going to shop at that gas station that was ripping me off; I can shop at the gas station that is actually giving me a better deal for my money.'

In other words, tax competition is beneficial and you can't fight it anyway. At first glance these arguments seem reasonable, but look closer and they collapse in a puff of nonsense. Here's why.

Competition between companies in a market is absolutely nothing like competition betweeen jurisdictions on tax. Think about it like this: if a company cannot compete it may fail and be replaced by another that provides better and cheaper goods or services. Such 'creative destruction' is painful, but it is also a source of capitalism's dynamism. But what happens when a country cannot compete? A failed state? That is a very different prospect. Nobody would, or could, as Mitchell put it, 'shut down New Hampshire'. What does it actually mean for a country to be competitive? Governments obviously do not compete in any meaningful way to police their streets. They do, perhaps, compete to educate their citizens better – but this kind of competition results in higher taxes to pay for better services.

The Geneva-based World Economic Forum (WEF) provides a more comprehensive definition of states' competitiveness: 'the set of institutions, policies and factors that determine the level of productivity of a country'. It uses twelve competitiveness 'pillars' including infrastructure, institutions, macroeconomic stability, education and the efficiency of goods markets. One could quibble with these, but it is a sensible enough selection. Most of the pillars require raising appropriate levels of tax. In fact, the most competitive countries on the WEF's measure are the higher-tax countries. There is plenty of variation, of course: Sweden, Finland and Denmark, the world's three highest-taxed countries, were ranked fourth, fifth and sixth most competitive in the 2009–10 index, while the US, with lower (but still not very low by world standards) taxes, is second. But the really low-tax economies like Afghanistan or Guatemala are the least competitive.

Dig further into the data, and other interesting facts emerge. Countries that spend a lot on social needs – something Mitchell opposes – score best on the competitiveness scale.[8] Higher taxes help countries spend more on education, health and other things that help their workers compete. What applies to tax applies to laws and regulation too. A jurisdiction may enjoy a 'competitive advantage' by being a heroin smuggling entrepôt or offering lax enforcement on child sex tourism, but in any sensible comparison with other countries such features cannot be seen as positives.

Mitchell also claims that secrecy jurisdictions tend to be wealthier than other states, and takes this as evidence that offshore is a good thing. This is like an argument that points to the private jets, yachts and palaces owned by a rich dictator and his cronies as evidence that corruption generates wealth. Yet in one area, Mitchell is probably right.

Around the world tax rates have been tumbling for years. Corporate tax, for example, fell from nearly 50 per cent in 1980, Mitchell says, down to just over 25 per cent today. This is in large part the result of competition between jurisdictions; with tax havens as the cutting edge. 'When I go in for my salary review, I always say it's because of the great papers I write for Cato that is forcing governments all over the world [to cut taxes],' Mitchell says. 'But the real story is tax competition . . . and tax havens are the most powerful instrument of this tax competition.'

It is a hard point to prove, but it is reasonable to suppose that while the world has fixed on ideologies as the driving force behind global tax-cutting and financial deregulation, tax competition may have been the bigger force. Many economists see this is a non-story, though. Although tax *rates* have fallen, tax *revenues* have been fairly steady. Since 1965 personal income taxes in rich-world OECD countries have remained remarkably stable at 25–26 per cent of the total tax haul,[9] and total corporation taxes have even risen slightly, from 9 to 11 per cent. Some say this proves that tax competition does not matter. But look behind the numbers, and an interesting picture emerges.

Though rich countries have preserved their overall tax revenues, corporations and rich folk have paid much less as a share of these. Corporate profits, on which their tax liabilities are assessed, have increased sharply.[10] Meanwhile, the rich have not only seen their wealth and income soar, but they have shifted their income out of personal income tax categories and into corporation tax, to be taxed at far lower corporate rates. For example, the richest 400 Americans booked 26 per cent of their income as salaries and wages in 1992, and 36 per cent as capital gains. By 2007 they recorded only 6 per cent as income, and 66 per cent as capital gains.[11] The same has been happening across all high-income categories and in all OECD countries since at least the 1970s. So falling corporation tax rates are being masked by rich people's tax avoidance.[12] In contrast, the working population has seen its personal income taxes and social security contributions rise over the last thirty years, as their wages have stagnated. Mitchell is right to say that tax competition is real, and it bites.

Look at how tax competition hits developing countries, and a bigger story emerges. One of the only studies ever made was a short IMF paper in 2004, which noted that 'little attention has been paid to how international tax competition has been affecting developing and emerging-market economies. This paper takes a first look at those issues.'[13] Its results are remarkable. Tax rates have fallen at least as fast as in rich countries, if not faster – and furthest of all in sub-Saharan Africa. But tax revenues fell sharply too: in the eleven-year period from

1990 to 2001 corporation tax revenues in low-income countries fell by a quarter. This is especially troubling because developing countries find it much easier to tax a few big corporations than millions of poor people, so corporate taxes are a bigger deal for them.

One reason for falling corporate tax revenues has been special tax incentives. In 1990 only a small minority of poor countries offered these incentives; by 2001 most of them did. The IMF's first detailed study of these in July 2009 concluded that tax incentives, which are supposed to attract foreign investors, slash tax revenues but do not promote growth.[14]

Tax, not aid, is the most sustainable source of finance for development. Tax makes governments accountable to their citizens, while aid makes governments accountable to foreign donors. Many Africans know this very well. 'I have made revenue collection a frontline institution because it is the one which can emancipate us from begging,' said Yoweri Museveni, president of Uganda, which collects taxes worth only about 11 per cent of GDP. 'If we can get about 22 per cent of GDP we should not need to disturb anybody by asking for aid; instead of coming here to bother you, give me this, give me this, I shall come here to greet you, to trade with you.'[15]

Tax competition is destroying developing countries' tax revenues, making them more dependent on aid. Brazilians talk about tax competition in terms of a *guerra fiscal* – tax war – which reveals far better what is really happening. US Senator Carl Levin echoes the sentiment. 'Tax havens,' he said, 'are engaging in economic warfare against the United States.' It is more accurate to say that they are helping a minority of Americans in their campaign against the working population, yet there is something more subtle at work here. When a multinational company from a rich country invests in a low-income country, the tax treaty between the two countries will dictate which country gets to tax which bits of the income. But the global tax treaty system, under the OECD's influence, has over time shifted the right to tax multinationals away from poor countries towards rich ones. So when Uganda, say, gives a tax holiday to Big US Coffee Inc., the corporation makes more profits, which it then either shelters offshore or brings home to be taxed in the United States. This also helps explain why rich countries have maintained their corporate tax revenues in the face of tax competition: because they have been securing a higher proportion of the tax on profits made through international trade, at the expense of low-income countries.

Mitchell has another presentation: 'The Moral Case for Tax Havens'.[16] A video from October 2008 gives a flavour.

The vast majority of the world's population lives in nations where governments fail to provide the basic protections of civilised society. [Cue pictures of Kim Jong-Il, Robert Mugabe and Vladimir Putin, looking sinister.] Tax havens help protect these people from venal and incompetent governments by providing a secure place to hide their assets.

One reason why Switzerland has such an admirable human rights policy of protecting financial privacy is that they strengthened their laws in the 1930s to help protect German Jews wanting to guard their assets from the Nazis. [Cue photos of Hitler saluting from a car, and a Gestapo officer rounding up scared women.] What about the Argentine family who face the risks that their life savings could be wiped out overnight by devaluation?

Put it offshore, he says, and money is safe. Again, his arguments are persuasive – right up to the point where you stop to think about them.

First, as I explained earlier, Mitchell's story about the origins of Swiss bank secrecy is no more than an appealing fiction. And even if a country is misruled, why should it only be the wealthy elites who get to protect their money by going offshore? If a country has unjust laws, then providing an offshore escape route for its wealthiest and most powerful citizens is the best way to take the pressure off the only constituency with real influence for reform. Keep their money bottled up at home, and pressure for change will come fast. Even then, there is no need for offshore secrecy to protect your money. If I am a Tanzanian with a million dollars in London earning 5 per cent, and I ought to pay tax on that income at 40 per cent, then I owe my government $20,000 in taxes for that year. Britain could tell my government all about my money, but that would still give Tanzania no power under any international agreement to confiscate my million dollars. An Argentine family can protect its money from hyperinflation by shifting it to Miami, but secrecy plays no part in this protection. Put it in a normal bank account, exchange information on the income and pay tax on it. The principal remains quite safe.

On the question of people needing to protect their cash from tyrants, Mitchell might like to answer this. Who uses secrecy jurisdictions to protect their money and bolster their positions? The human rights activist screaming in the torturers' dungeon? The brave investigative journalist? The street protester? Or the brutal kleptocratic tyrant oppressing them all? We all know the answer.

Ah but, Mitchell then retorts, 'Your personal data may be sold to kidnappers who then grab one of your kids.' Transparency threatens homosexuals in Saudi Arabia and Jews in France 'victimised by corrupt and/or despotic governments. Without the ability to protect their assets in so-called tax havens, these people would be at even greater danger.' The answer, he says, is to 'place your money in a bank in Miami, since America is a tax haven'.[17] This carries a veneer of truth, but no more. Kidnappers don't need tax data to know that someone has money. And the very wealthy have bodyguards and are relatively rarely kidnapped: the lower and middle classes are usually the victims. More importantly, though, good tax systems promote better governance (and hence less kidnapping), as all the research indicates. By helping elites loot their countries, secrecy jurisdictions are causing exactly the problems Mitchell says he is worried about.

When we get to the question of freedom. Mitchell is quite clear. The high-tax welfare state, he says, is 'a prison for the human soul. It's making pets out of all of us. It's going to put us in a little cage, control our freedom, control our lives – that's what we need to fight against.' Tax is bad, and tax havens are the answer. In this world view personal property is inviolable, and tax is theft. 'It makes sense,' Mitchell says, 'to protect your family's interest by putting your money some place like Hong Kong, where the politicians from your country can't find out about it. And if they can't find out about it, they can't steal it.' Leaving aside the fact that this sounds like a general incitement to criminal tax evasion, it is worth asking whether or not tax *is* theft.

Property rights, as the philosopher Martin O'Neill pointed out, emerge from a general system of legal and political rules that includes the rules of taxation. To say tax is theft, then, is to use a system of which tax is a central part as your weapon against taxation. It is to argue in an illogical circle. Corporations too emerge from states, legally speaking. 'The state is the only institution in the world that can bring a corporation to life,' explains Joel Bakan in his best-selling book *The Corporation*. 'It alone grants corporations their essential rights, such as legal personhood and limited liability ... Without the state, the corporation is nothing. Literally nothing.'[18] To say that corporation tax is theft is again simply illogical.

Offshore, you can find any number of other illogical eddies, ironies and contradictions. Secrecy jurisdictions routinely say their role is to promote efficiency in financial markets, but the cloak of secrecy they provide directly contradicts the idea of efficient markets, which require transparency. In an article entitled 'Why Do I Have to Deal with People Like Dan Mitchell?' the Berkeley economist Brad deLong pointed to several of Mitchell's articles – including one praising Iceland for its tax-cutting deregulated economic policies just before Iceland's economy collapsed – and one entitled 'A Better Way To Chastise France,' urging the United States to eliminate witholding taxes on all dividends paid to foreigners, so as to suck tax-avoiding capital out of 'oppressive high-tax nations'. So Mitchell contradicts himself: tax havenry does 'chastise' other nations, after all.

Monetary policy is another area where offshore cheerleaders get into a muddle. Generally, such folk have supported monetarism, which argues that you tackle inflation and unemployment by managing the quantity of money. Yet it is ironic that this doctrine began its rise with a paper by Milton Friedman in 1956, the very year when the Eurodollar market and the offshore system properly took off. But the offshore system directly undermines monetarism: in a world where capital flits effortlessly to unregulated offshore worlds and banks can create money willy-nilly, governments struggle to control their money supplies. 'The use of quantity of money as a target,' Friedman himself finally conceded in 2003, 'has not been a success.'

Tax avoidance is another case in point. Tax havens endlessly promote themselves as delivering tax efficiency to corporations, but tax avoidance is inefficient. 'If tax abuse is needed to ensure an investment is viable,' notes the accountant Richard Murphy, 'it's a misallocation of resources to do it.'

Another offshore favourite is the old claim that tax cuts actually increase revenue, partly because people will be less inclined to avoid taxes. Therefore tax competition, which drives down rates, must be a good thing. This has been bundled together in many US Republican

minds with another big idea embraced by the anti-government libertarian world of offshore: that it is essential to cut taxes to starve the
beast of big government. Or, as the anti-tax zealot Grover Norquist
memorably put it, government should be cut 'down to the size where
we can drown it in the bathtub'.[19] There is a problem with this, of
course. Some people think tax cuts boost revenue; starve-the-beasters
think tax cuts are useful ways to cut revenue; They can't both be right.
Bob McIntyre of Citizens for Tax Justice explains how he thinks the
two conflicting theories have thrived side by side for over a quarter
of a century. 'It's simple,' he said. 'On Mondays, Wednesdays and
Fridays Republicans say that cutting taxes raises revenues. On Tuesdays,
Thursdays and Saturdays they say cutting taxes reduces revenues so
much that it forces government to cut back – to starve the beast. And
on Sundays they rest.' In truth, most serious analysts don't believe
that tax rates, on their own, make all that much difference. Obviously,
real business people invest and hire workers where there is demand
for their products, strong infrastructure and a healthy and educated
workforce. Most studies show that for most types of business corporate tax rates are a relatively minor factor in deciding on location.
Tropicana won't grow oranges in Alaska just because it is offered a
tax break there. In the golden age of 1947–73 the US economy grew
at nearly 4 per cent a year, while the top marginal tax rate was between
75 and over 90 per cent.[20] Those tax rates did not cause that growth,
but high taxes clearly didn't choke it either.

And if tax cuts are the answer to reducing tax evasion, as Mitchell
suggests, then he might like to explain the great global eruption of
international tax evasion and the sudden plague of capital flight from
the 1970s onwards – just as tax rates went into free fall worldwide.
This is the real story: when tax havenry exploded and finance became
freer, tax evasion and capital flight followed.

By 2000, as the OECD project on tax havens' harmful tax competition rolled forwards, Mitchell and his allies were bombarding
Washington with letters, emails and presentations. Almost nobody
was articulating the counter-arguments, and the OECD was soon on
the defensive. Then the havens themselves began to mobilise. In January
2001 the secretary general of the Commonwealth invited the OECD
to set up a joint working group, with equal representation for small

member states – that is, the tax havens. This group festooned the OECD project in red tape, and the whole thing got bogged down in arcane haggling. The havens also set up a body called the International Tax and Investment Organisation to coordinate their defences, and linked up with Mitchell and the Center for Freedom and Prosperity. Then George W. Bush came to power.

President Clinton's Treasury secretary, Larry Summers, had backed the OECD, even proposing sanctions against the havens in his last budget. Bush's first Treasury secretary, Paul O'Neill, initially seemed unsure about the issue, even saying, to Mitchell's alarm, 'I support the priority placed on transparency and cooperation.' The Center for Freedom and Prosperity ramped up the pressure. They organised eighty-six congressmen and senators, including big hitters like Jesse Helms and Tom DeLay, to urge O'Neill to ditch the OECD project. Milton Friedman, James Buchanan and other conservative economists signed up. Letters flooded into the Treasury. Mitchell thundered about the 'Parisian monstrosity', and a Cayman Islands official popped up at the United Nations to rail against 'big brother' and the 'big bully syndrome'. The lobbyists neglected to mention that the Caymans was effectively governed from London. The Commonwealth reheated Mitchell's critiques in Washington and lambasted the OECD as a bullying, coercive bureaucracy.[21]

The Caribbean havens also persuaded the powerful Congressional Black Caucus to act, and to send O'Neill a letter warning that the OECD initiative 'threatens to undermine the fragile economies of some of our closest neighbors and allies'. They made no mention of the effects these jurisdictions had on vastly bigger African nations, of course, or of the fact that the main Caribbean beneficiaries from offshore activities were rich white bankers, lawyers and accountants.

Mitchell also pounced on something else. No OECD country – not Switzerland, not Luxembourg, and certainly not the United States or Britain – was on the blacklist. 'The OECD, a rich man's club of industrialised nations, is launching this anti-tax haven jihad, but they omitted to blacklist their own members,' he said. 'They are a bunch of racist hypocrites. Powerful white-governed nations in Europe are targeting less powerful nations in places like the Caribbean. Somebody needs to tell the bureaucrats in Paris that the era of colonialism is over.'[22] This time Mitchell had a point, and he soon got his breakthrough. On

10 May 2001 O'Neill wrote in the *Washington Times*, a conservative newspaper set up by the cult leader Reverend Sun Myung Moon and a regular mouthpiece for tax havens, that the OECD's mission was 'not in line with this administration's priorities'.[23] The United States, O'Neill continued, 'simply has no interest in stifling the competition that forces governments – like businesses – to create efficiencies'. The article looked almost as if Mitchell had written it himself. The United States, O'Neill added, 'does not support efforts to dictate to any country what its own tax rates or tax systems should be'.[24] It was the offshore contradiction to end them all. 'Don't interfere with our rights as sovereign states!' the havens cry while interfering merrily in other nations' sovereign laws and tax systems.

The OECD's project was dying. As Marty Sullivan of *TaxAnalysts* put it, the initiative 'slowly dissolved into a series of toothless pronouncements, a mixture of cheerleading and scorekeeping. The OECD started to abandon its confrontational approach.' The OECD watered down its blacklist criteria: tax havens were now 'participating partners' and escaped the blacklist merely by promising to shape up, and only needed to do so if everyone else – including the hard nuts like Switzerland or Britain or the United States or newly independent Hong Kong – did too. In other words, it would never happen.

Two months after O'Neill's letter, Senator Carl Levin, fighting a lonely rearguard action, estimated that the US was losing $70 billion annually from offshore evasion: 'a figure so huge that if even half that amount were collected it would pay for a Medicare prescription drug program without raising anyone's taxes or cutting anyone's budget'. When Levin noted that fewer than 6,000 of more than 1.1 million offshore accounts and businesses were properly disclosed to the IRS, O'Neill's response was simple and clear. 'I find it amusing.'[25]

A July 2001 OECD deadline to avoid defensive measures came and went, and the organisation later publicly said it had no intention of pursuing them in the future. Mitchell's colleague Andrew Quinlan subsequently warned, for good measure, that just ten days of lobbying could shut down the OECD's US funding. The end result is neatly summarised by Jason Sharman, who wrote a well-researched book about the episode. 'The OECD,' he wrote, 'had to give up its ambition to regulate international tax competition.' The tax havens had won.

*   *   *

A lot of the tax havens' arguments hinge on the scope of state power.

Democracies have long supported the principle of progressive taxation, as outlined by Scottish economist Adam Smith: 'It is not very unreasonable that the rich should contribute to the public expense, not only in proportion to their revenue, but something more than in that proportion.' But in the United States, as in many countries, the principle of progressive taxation – something accepted since Adam Smith – has evaporated. The richest 1 per cent of Americans paid just over 40 per cent of all federal income taxes in 2009. The right-wing Tax Foundation claimed this 'clearly debunks the conventional Beltway rhetoric that the "rich" are not paying their fair share of taxes'. Yet in 2009 the richest 1 per cent owned almost half of all financial assets in the country and rising. This is not about high taxes on the wealthy, but about stratospheric wealth and inequality. And the 40 per cent refers only to income taxes – rich people usually convert most of their income into capital gains, which is taxed at far lower rates. Then there are payroll taxes and state taxes, which tend to fall on low- and middle-income people more heavily than the rich. For the 400 richest Americans, their effective tax rate was far lower: just 17.2 per cent, and falling. Count offshore tax evasion by the wealthy, which income statistics don't see, and the picture skews further. 'A quarter-century of tax cuts,' wrote the tax author David Cay Johnston, 'has produced not trickle down – but Niagara up.'[26]

During my long interview with Mitchell in Washington we went out to a modest eatery near the Cato Institute offices, where we bumped into Richard Rahn, a Cato staffer and former board member of the Cayman Islands Monetary Authority. Rahn is a gruff, serious man who wears an eyepatch, and when Mitchell introduced us with great bonhomie, Rahn scowled back, declined to shake hands, muttered something about 'European commies,' and stalked out. A year or so later I looked Rahn up, and he agreed to talk. This time he was more personable: after first hawking me around the Cato offices as a crazy European curiosity, he then handed me a little maroon passport-sized booklet, containing the US Declaration of Independence and the US Constitution. 'It looks like an EU passport, doesn't it?' he rasped, twinkle-eyed. 'One, of course, is an instrument of oppression. The other is a document of freedom.

'I have ancestors who fought in the American Revolution,' he said, sitting me down in his rather spartan office. 'Genetically I don't like foreign governments.' After making me buy Mitchell's book for twenty dollars (I already had a copy but didn't want to spoil Rahn's mood) we began to talk.

Rahn did not strike me as an accomplice for wealthy interests but someone acting, at least in part, on deep personal conviction. 'You people upset me . . . I often wonder if you people are evil, or just ignorant,' he declared. 'Tax oppression is causing misery around the world.' He said this was well established in the literature and cited some recent Bulgarian studies to back his case. 'When international bureaucrats want to attack places for not imposing bad taxes,' he continued, 'well, I think that fits into my definition of evil.' He described a 'conspiracy of the international bureaucratic class' to raise taxes – not so much an organised plot but a constant effort to raise revenues to feed the bureaucrats' own well-being and privileges.

Perhaps there is a *little* truth in this. But his next point is worth tackling, for it is a foundation for the intellectual edifice of offshore. 'Capital is the seedcorn of economic growth. Without capital, there is no growth. It is suicidal to tax your own seedcorn.' Along with this argument comes the tax havens' Exhibit A in their own defence: that they help smooth and promote international flows of capital, channelling it efficiently to capital-hungry developing countries, where it can grow productively and benefit everyone. Rahn's seedcorn contention contains a kernel of truth: capital certainly can and does promote investment and economic growth. Helping it flow efficiently, at first glance, seems like a good idea. But here is where the arguments fall apart.

First, financial capital isn't the only kind of capital. Social capital – an educated and experienced workforce, a trustworthy business climate and so on – matters more. Seedcorn is just one factor in a good harvest, along with rain, good soils, fertiliser – and the manpower, knowledge and confidence to put it all together. 'Access to capital is not, in fact, the decisive constraint on economic growth,' wrote the economist Martin Wolf. 'It is social and human capital, as well as the overall policy regime that matter.'[27] These, of course, need tax dollars.

Second, tax isn't only about revenue, the first of the four Rs of taxation. The second R is redistribution, notably tackling inequality. This is what democratic societies always demand, and as the painstakingly researched book *The Spirit Level* attests, it is inequality, rather than absolute levels of poverty and wealth, that determines how societies fare on almost every single indicator of well-being, from life expectancy to obesity to delinquency to depression or teenage pregnancy. The third R is representation – rulers must bargain with citizens in order to extract taxes from them – and this leads to accountability and representation. The fourth is repricing – changing prices to do things like discourage smoking. Secrecy jurisdictions directly undermine the first three, if you think about it, and possibly the fourth too.

Then there is the small matter of the evidence. One might think that capital should flow from rich countries, where it is plentiful, to low-income countries, where it is is scarce, promoting productive investment, growth and better lives for all. In the real world, this has not happened. The low-income countries that have been growing the fastest, like China, tend to be those that have exported capital, not imported it.[28] Countries need, above all, sound institutions, good infrastructure and the effective rule of law, exactly what the offshore system has been undermining.

This is not such a surprise. A country can only absorb so much capital, just as an acre of land can only take so much seedcorn. Capital loans to low-income countries haven't found their way into productive investment, but instead have washed back into private bank accounts in Miami, London and Switzerland, leaving public debts behind. Waves of financial capital, processed 'efficiently' offshore, have led to financial crisis after crisis. In many low-income countries, as the economist Dani Rodrik puts it, 'capital inflows are at best ineffective, at worst harmful'.

And that is not all. Much of the world's wealth derives from what economists call rents, the kind of unearned income that flows effortlessly to oil-rich rulers. 'Oil is a resource that anaesthetizes thought, blurs vision, corrupts,' as the Polish writer Ryszard Kapuscinski put it. 'Oil expresses perfectly the eternal human dream of wealth achieved through lucky accident, through a kiss of fortune and not by sweat, anguish, hard work. In this sense oil is a fairy tale and, like every fairy tale, it is a bit of a lie.' Nearly every sane economist since Adam Smith has agreed that it is very good, and very efficient, to tax rents at very high rates. One kind of rent comes from market monopolies or oligopolies, such as those enjoyed by pharmaceutical patents, by government-sanctioned licences afforded to the big four accounting firms, by taxpayer-guaranteed international banks and by the one and only Fédération Internationale de Football Association (FIFA), the super-wealthy international governing body of world football.

The global headquarters of most major players in all these highly profitable industries are located offshore, most especially in Switzerland, directly against every notion of economic efficiency. FIFA, for example, used its monopolistic position to force poor South Africa to place it in a special tax bubble for the 2010 World Cup, in order to shift its revenues out of the country. This is an organisation whose luxurious $200 million Zürich headquarters lies just a few hundred metres from where I am writing this.

Offshore is not only about tax, of course. It is about regulation too. Herein lies a range of different arguments advanced by offshore in its defence.

The simplest and commonest offshore argument is to deny responsibility for problems and use the just-a-few-rotten-apples defence: that the system is basically clean, but occasionally bad ones get through. Immediately after the collapse of BCCI the president of the Cayman Islands Bankers' Association, Nick Duggan, said, 'BCCI is a unique worldwide situation and does not reflect on the local banking community at all.'[29]

Another argument is like the one on tax: tax havens promote efficiency by driving financial innovation and being what the offshore writer William Brittain-Catlin calls a 'seller of novelties on the financial market, a sweetshop for capitalism, developing new flavours'. The recent financial crisis has exposed what most of this financial innovation really involves. Innovative forms of abuse are to be resisted, not encouraged.

The next offshore argument involves deflection. Anthony Travers, chairman of the Cayman Islands Financial Services Authority, uses this technique widely. In a 2004 article in *The Lawyer* entitled 'Framing Cayman' he sought to explain why some of the biggest economic scandals in world history – BCCI, Enron and Parmalat, in each of which Cayman played a pivotal role – were in fact not the Caymans' fault at all.[30]

Parmalat was brought down by its Cayman-based finance subsidiary Bonlat Financing, which had fraudulently claimed to hold nearly

€4 billion in assets. According to Travers, the missing Bonlat billions 'never existed at all, save in a document forged in Italy by a corrupt Parmalat executive. If that is the nature of the fraud in relation to Bonlat, how precisely is the "part" of the Caymans "substantial"?' In other words, though the Caymans was central to the fraud, it is blameless because the fraudsters were actually elsewhere. He said a similar thing about BCCI. 'Had BCCI not been so licensed [as a deposit taker] by the Bank of England, at a time when the Caymans banking regulator was on secondment from the Bank of England, its subsidiary would not have been licensed in the Caymans.' As for Enron's 692 opaque Caymans subsidiaries, 'these were on the balance sheet consolidated subsidiaries which owned the overseas Enron operating assets, thereby lawfully deferring US taxation,' he said. Their profits were 'properly accounted for and audited'. Enron's Caymans limited partnership LJM No 2, Travers continued, was 'a victim and not a perpetrator'; the perpetrators were Delaware limited partnerships. In other words, the frauds were carried out elsewhere. And he added, 'None of the financial recklessness that has brought about much of the current global crisis occurred in or involved the Cayman Islands.'[31]

The breathtaking audacity of Travers' claims is leavened by the fact that his arguments contain a truth: the frauds could not have happened only in the Cayman Islands. They required culprits elsewhere too. 'The charlatans responsible for this type of behaviour,' Travers notes, 'are far closer to Westminster than the Caymans.' Quite so. But he is deliberately missing the point: that this is how the offshore system works! Offshore structures always serve citizens and institutions elsewhere – so the beneficiaries are always elsewhere. This is why it is called offshore. Plausible deniability is the whole game. The fraudsters may well be elsewhere, but offshore is what makes the fraud work. Secrecy jurisdictions are to fraudsters what fences are to thieves. Such arguments from Cayman are like someone fencing stolen property blaming the police for not stopping the criminals in the first place. The Caymans is a place 'which has pledged to meet the highest and quite new international standards of tax transparency', Travers said, but added a more menacing note. 'If it were not for a quirk in the laws of defamation,' he said (noting that jurisdictions cannot sue for libel), 'comment of this sort would be actionable.'

*   *   *

On 11 September 2001, two months after the OECD's tax haven project died, al-Qaeda attacked the United States and a new tale of hypocrisy and deception began, which continues up to today. After the attacks George W. Bush's administration suddenly wanted better cooperation and transparency from secrecy jurisdictions on terrorist financing, though it wanted to leave offshore tax evasion alone. The problem was how to do this, given that the two practices involve exactly the same jurisdictions, structures and techniques. The answer came in the form of one of the slyest offshore tricks ever devised.

The best way for countries to share information with each other is through so-called automatic exchanges of information – where they tell each other about, for example, their taxpayers' financial affairs as a matter of course. This happens routinely inside Europe and between a few other countries, and although the system is leaky – it needs sharpening up to cover all sorts of loopholes – it works well enough. Privacy is not invaded. Tax authorities keep the information to themselves, just as doctors keep details of their patients' haemorrhoids and venereal diseases confidential. Doctors and tax authorities need such information and can share it with others who need it, but they don't publicise it.

But there is another way of sharing information, 'on request': a country will agree to hand over information about another country's taxpayers, but only on a case-by-case basis, only when specifically asked, and only under very narrow conditions – the requester must be able to demonstrate exactly why they need the information. In other words, when the information is requested, the requester must already know, more or less, what it is. No fishing expeditions – or general trawls to find tax cheats – are allowed. You can't prove criminality until you get the information, and you can't get the information until you can show criminality. *Catch-22*'s Captain Yossarian would have appreciated the double bind. On request information exchange is a fig leaf. It lets tax havens claim they are transparent, while continuing business as usual.

This model, of course, is the one that got the Bush administration's endorsement. Instead of real transparency, we got very conditional transparency – only when there is permission to be transparent. On request has become the OECD's model too.

It is hard to know how much information is exchanged on request globally, but Geoff Cook, chief executive of Jersey Finance, confessed in March 2009 that in the seven years since Jersey signed a tax agreement with the US, it exchanged information with American investigators on just 'five or six' cases.[32] Compare that to the million-plus US offshore accounts and businesses Senator Levin identified, and clearly the system is a nonsense. Moreover, requests for information can take months or years to process, and the assets under investigation can be shifted elsewhere in hours or even minutes. It gets worse. After the financial crisis struck in 2007 the OECD, by now at the mercy of the secrecy jurisdictions, set up another piece of sleight of hand to respond to public pressure. At the urging of G20 leaders it compiled a blacklist of tax havens. The way to get off the blacklist was to sign twelve agreements to share information with other countries, using the OECD's hopeless on request standard.

The OECD claimed that a major crackdown was under way. 'What we are witnessing is nothing short of a revolution,' boomed OECD Secretary General Angel Gurría. 'By addressing the challenges posed by the dark side of the tax world, the campaign for global tax transparency is in full flow.' Newspaper articles ran headlines like BANK SECRECY IS DEAD, and British Prime Minister Gordon Brown declared the aim was to 'outlaw tax havens'.

By 7 April, just five days after the G20 declared that banking secrecy was dead, the OECD blacklist was empty. The OECD had exonerated 32 tax havens which had merely *promised* to sign enough of the OECD's useless agreements to qualify. At the last count a third of these were with Nordic states, including such global economic giants as Greenland and the Faroe Islands, and another third or so with other tax havens. As usual, nobody bothered about the developing countries, which suffer most from offshore abuse. India, China, Brazil and countries in Africa were entirely left on the sidelines.[33]

'The blacklist has been a sad joke,' said Professor Michael McIntyre, who knows this area better than almost anyone. 'The OECD programme has provided a patina of respectability to countries that are actively assisting taxpayers in evading taxes in their home country.'[34] The blacklist was a whitewash. After a temporary setback during the recent financial crisis, the offshore system is now growing again at ferocious speed. And the OECD insists to this day that its next-to-useless on request form of information exchange is 'the accepted international standard'.

Rich governments cannot be trusted to do the right thing on tax havens and transparency. Many will demand more transparency and international cooperation even as they work to frustrate both. They will call for reasoned debate as they engage in character assassination, secret deals and worse. They will talk the language of democracy and freedom the better to defend unaccountable, irresponsible power and privilege. However, civil society is beginning to stir. The current leaders are Global Financial Integrity in Washington and the Tax Justice Network (TJN) in Europe, whose expertise has been invaluable for this book. John Christensen, the TJN's director, remembers holding an expert briefing on offshore for staff in the Senate buildings in Washington DC, and seeing a senior congressional staffer with tears in her eyes. Battling to get any traction on offshore issues in the face of ferocious Washington right-wing counter-lobbies, 'She said she had waited for years for civil society to take an interest in this.' Much greater mobilisation is now required.

How do all these fallacies – the OECD's information exchange standards, the contradiction of tax cutting to increase revenues and tax cutting to starve the beast, and Mitchell's offshore incoherencies – continue to thrive? Author Jonathan Chait provides a good answer. 'The lesson for cranks everywhere,' he wrote, 'is that your theory stands a stronger chance of success if it directly benefits a rich and powerful bloc, and there's no bloc richer and more powerful than the rich and powerful.' The last word here goes to Bob Mcintyre of Citizens for Tax Justice, who has spent much of his life battling the armies of lobbyists in Washington. 'There are so few of us,' he sighs wearily, 'and so many of them.'

11

The Life Offshore

The human factor

In 2009 I met a former private banker, Beth Krall, to explore a question that had been nagging me: how do private bankers who shelter the wealth of gangsters and corrupt politicians justify what they do?

We met one Sunday in the bustling cafe at Kramer Books off Dupont Circle in Washington DC, where she was living. She had left private banking and joined the non-governmental sector. Dressed in a striking black and white coat, she still looked very much the stylish international financier. Aged forty-seven, and with nearly twenty-four years in the banking business, Krall (which is not her real name) was still coming to terms with her past life. She hated what she had seen and was clearly unsettled by exposing the horrors she had experienced, but she adamantly refused to reveal any of the client details she had sworn to protect. She was wary of disrupting the many friendships she had made in the industry and was careful about what she would, and would not, say.

Krall's last offshore posting was in the Bahamas, an island archipelago with over 300,000 residents which has been an important offshore centre since the golden age of American organised crime in the early decades of the twentieth century. A few months earlier a practitioner in the Caymans had warned me to watch out for my personal safety if I went 'asking all these questions' in the Bahamas. Krall said she was unsure what might happen to her if she went back, as she was partly breaking the private bankers' code of silence. 'I don't want to have concrete shoes put on me,' she said without smiling. One reason for her fear was something that had angered her in the first place: so many of the people she dealt with were powerful members of society in their home countries. One case involved 'very prominent people in world politics'.

Unusually for foreign bankers in the Bahamas, Krall had got closely involved in the Junkanoo celebrations, a mixture of Latin American and Caribbean carnival traditions which a dedicated website calls 'the greatest cultural event of not only the Bahamas, but also the world at large'. She seemed distressed at the thought that fellow members of her Junkanoo group – not to mention many other friends she had left behind in Nassau – might judge her criticism of its offshore industry 'anti-Bahamian', and when we spoke she was working up the courage to tell them why she could not go back. She was still redefining her relationship with the offshore values within which she had made her career: that secrecy is good; whatever brings in the money is good; and if you break the code of silence you are sloppy or treacherous.

Krall was born in Leicester in England and took her banking exams straight after school, starting in Britain's Midland International Bank in 1980 before moving to a partly state-owned Swedish bank and then, in 1987, to Chase Manhattan in Luxembourg to work in its back office – the administrative side. Chase was a paying agent for certain bond issues, and Krall toiled in the vaults in the coupons department, making sure Eurobond holders got paid. 'We were dealing with those "Belgian dentists" who keep bonds under the mattresses,' Krall remembers. 'Sometimes they all came in at once – what we called the coupon bus would arrive. They came from Belgium, Germany, the Netherlands, filling the lobby, spilling out the door, getting angry, waving their coupons and getting their cheques.' The vaults held, among other things, *enveloppes scellées* (sealed envelopes) relating to 'Henwees' – HNWIs or high net worth individuals. 'We didn't know what the hell was in there,' she said. 'The private bankers and relationships managers put those things in there – we never had an inkling.'

Working fourteen to sixteen hours a day, including some weekends, was common enough, and the pressure was intense. 'It is almost a culture of fear. The client loses money? Oh my God, are you in trouble! We were stressed to the max. There were deadlines within deadlines. The corporate politics was insane: high pressure, devious, mean, cut-throat and backstabbing.' She moved to a Brazilian bank, Banco Mercantil de São Paulo, and then on to Cititrust in the Bahamas, where she ran evaluations and accounting for their mutual funds business. From this point, Krall declined to identify her employer.

She became a client relationship manager with the private banking arm of a well-known British bank in the Bahamas. They worked with what are euphemistically known as managed banks or shell banks, an offshore speciality. These have no real presence where they are incorporated, so they can escape supervision by responsible regulators. A shell bank will typically be operated through an agent in a tax haven jurisdiction – perhaps a famous global bank – which provides a reassuringly solid name and address to back the shell but which will otherwise carry no responsibility or even real knowledge of what the shell is actually up to. So a shell bank might be incorporated in the Bahamas, for example, but its owners and managers could be anywhere.

Shell banks handle business that many banks will not touch. As US Senator Carl Levin put it, 'These banks are generally not examined by regulators, and virtually no one but the shell bank owner really knows where the bank is, how it operates or who its customers are. One shell bank owner told us that his bank existed wherever he was at the moment.' Advertisements offer to set up shell banks for just a few thousand dollars, promising things like 'no intrusive background checks' or a 'European jurisdiction' and 'fast set-up time'. The bank Krall worked for provided a well-known name to reassure the Bahamas regulator. I asked Krall how much due diligence her British bank did on these entities. 'Ha ha. Yeah,' was her initial reply. 'These banks would send quarterly statements to the Bahamas Central Bank, but it wasn't our job to monitor them.'

Krall remembers that there were brass plates up in the reception area of her British bank saying BANCO DE X, perhaps an Argentinian bank using the Bahamian address and phone number of the British bank on their headed notepaper. The Bahamas regulator could not find out what was going on back in Argentina, and vice versa, the classic offshore technique. Predictably, some of these banks failed, despite being audited and passed by one of the big five accounting firms. Krall, who speaks Spanish, remembers taking calls from angry depositors when banks and funds with which her bank was involved collapsed. 'People were on the phone in tears, with their life savings gone, and I was saying to them, "There is no point coming on a plane to look for the money because there is no money here."' The money never *was* there.

The terrorist attacks on 11 September 2001 prompted the US to legislate against shell banks. A bank in the Bahamas must now employ two senior bankers and keep its books and records there to be judged real enough to do business. 'That means a bank maybe with a room or suite in a building, with two people in it – that's a bank now,' Krall said. She directed me to the current website of a Bahamas-based trust company which will provide you with exactly that: the appearance of being a real bank – including two staff members as directors and a place to keep the books and records. Such a set-up can allow business almost as usual, yet still tick the regulators' boxes.

Krall moved to a big European bank, again as a client relationship manager – in effect, someone who finds wealthy clients and keeps them happy. Trawling for business, she was routinely pointed towards Latin America, where she travelled frequently. 'On the immigration form you would write that you were going for pleasure, though your suitcase would be full of business suits and portfolio evaluations, or marketing materials and presentations explaining the advantages of a trust in the Bahamas.' The client's name didn't appear on their portfolio evaluation: in fact, the bank would not even record it as the account name. 'You'd cut off the account name and number so it was just a list of securities and holdings – you could never attach it to anyone.' It was nerve-racking, sometimes, going through airports, but she always got through unchallenged.

Krall said she rarely, if ever, had the feeling she was doing anything wrong, despite often helping clients break the law. Part of what she called 'managing not to check into your conscience' was that there were always cases where you could believe you were helping someone. For example, countries like Brazil have forced heirship, which dictates who in a family gets the assets after parents die, and an offshore trust may be a way to get around this. Krall cited a case she knew of in another country where forced heirship would have granted the assets to a playboy son, instead of to the family's preferred beneficiary, a daughter with special needs.

Krall would cold-call top lawyers and asset managers, hoping to get into what is known in the trade as the beauty parade – the line-up of obliging banks that clients and their representatives will look at to manage their riches. The key is to build a relationship of trust, mixing the good and the bad. With good trust you offer a solid, safe return on assets; bad trust is confidence that you will keep their identities secret and break laws on their behalf. In pursuit of these elusive relationships Krall went to polo games, the opera, orchestral concerts in Rio de Janeiro and umpteen working breakfasts, lunches and dinners in the most expensive restaurants in town.

Despite her growing qualms, Krall ended up working for a boutique Swiss private bank in the Bahamas. This was no ordinary bank and was the only bank where she actually saw a suitcase full of cash. 'My bank never once had a client walk through the door,' she said. 'The bankers and their clients go on big-game hunting trips, or to the ballet in Budapest. That is where it happens.' From her tone, she made the 'it' sound like some sordid sexual act. The real business operated out of Switzerland, and the Bahamas was purely a 'parking space' or transit point for money, an extra layer of secrecy. A major driver was, of course, the imperative to receive and store the proceeds of crime.

'I felt I was prostituting my personality just to get money in the bank,' she said. 'I came to realise that the system I was involved in contributes to the perpetuation of poverty in the world.' She thought a bit, then added, 'But I did enjoy the adrenaline. When it fuels you, you don't question what you otherwise would.'

Her colleagues hailed from old European aristocratic circles. While Krall was perfectly good at her job and had close working relationships with top lawyers, asset managers and so on, a gap remained. 'They went to parties with royalty, with ambassadors,' she said. 'I wasn't in their circle.'

At the time laws in the Bahamas were being tightened a little, following a feeble global crackdown, and she moved sideways in the bank to work as a compliance officer. These days, offshore bankers make a big show of their know-your-customer rules to keep out the bad money. Depositors may have to supply a certified copy of a passport, for example, and divulge where their money came from. Jurisdictions like the Bahamas and the Cayman Islands put these requirements into their statutes, and banks employ compliance officers like Krall to enforce this. That, at least, is the theory.

In her new job Krall began to learn of the many devious routes around the rules. 'You would ask for the source of funds, and they could tell you anything. You didn't ask for documentation.' Another compliance officer Krall knew was expressly forbidden from seeing certain files. A loophole in Bahamas law allowed an institution to waive due diligence checks on clients as long as the business was referred from a financial institution in a jurisdiction where the legislation is supposed to be good. Once in a while a bank would uncover a money-laundering case to show it was enforcing the law. They were happy to do this, Krall said, provided it did not expose anyone the bank did not want to upset.

Offshore, legal frameworks that distinguish between the criminal and the legitimate have eroded away and been replaced by networks of trust that distinguish between the well established and respectable, on the one hand, and the unknown and dubious on the other. Individuals with sums to launder or invest with minimal taxation want to know that they are dealing with people who can be trusted not to have moral qualms. If the bankers don't know someone, they will have to jump through many hoops; if you are a long-standing and trusted client the rules fall away. These trust-based networks, deferential to the aristocracy of wealth and privilege and resistant to formal laws, are the ultimate comfort for banks' wealthy clients. The similarities with Mafia codes of behaviour are no coincidence at all.

'These banks are competing with each other, but they also scratch each other's backs', Krall said. 'The heads of these banks are part of a circle of friends and business associates, where the whole social circle revolves around it – a social structure intertwined with a business relationship. They will pass business between each other. The law says you must report suspicious activity to the Financial Intelligence Unit [FIU] or the police,' she continued. 'But in a very small place everyone knows everyone and their cousin. I couldn't trust a report being handled confidentially or through proper channels. There is a huge chance that someone in the FIU or the police will be close to people in the bank where you work . . . and this could cause me harm for raising the issue.'

Krall was supposed to check for suspicious movements through the accounts – of which there were plenty. She raised many red flags. 'They [her managers] would say, "This was a commission."' Were these bribes? Commissions on what? 'I went back, and never got an answer.' One Swiss-based trust company which had a relationship with her bank displayed almost nothing on its website bar some photos of a nice fountain in Geneva. 'The crap they brought to us was unbelievable. There is no way a responsible trustee should take this on. You would have no idea who the trust settlors were, what the assets were or where they came from. I objected strongly, but the bank took them on.'

Her qualms grew over time and she began to find herself in a very lonely place. 'I couldn't even tell my boyfriend – I was supposed to abide by bank secrecy,' she remembers. 'He knew I was very very stressed about things I couldn't speak about, and that was all he could know. He has lots of patience but it wasn't easy for him, with someone walking through the door at the end of the day, pale, drained and sick, with stuff going on he can never know about.' Some other compliance officers with whom she talked also felt their powerlessness. 'There was a fear abroad,' she remembers. 'You have this dilemma – the difficult news you will give to directors may not be appreciated . . . Most people want to do their job, protecting the bank and country from the taint, as well as doing their ethical, moral and legal duty. You go into the job with that mindset.'

I chatted to Krall about my own recent experiences in the Cayman Islands: about what had happened when I revealed to one of my first interviewees in the Caymans that I had links to an organisation that had been critical of tax havens. That meeting had ended within minutes. I had been referred to this interviewee by a mutual friend, and after our meeting my friend had received several emails from her stressing how 'uncomfortable' she felt afterwards, and requesting promise upon promise that I would never identify her.

People I met almost always seemed to find it distasteful, or changed the subject, when I asked questions such as how one might balance the prosperity of the 50,000-odd islanders against the interests of 350 million North Americans, 600 million Latin Americans and the same number again in Africa. Even more surprising to me was that despite the confidence with which I hold my own views, I found myself feeling shy, almost ashamed, expressing them on the Cayman Islands. Krall recognised this feeling immediately. 'When I was planning to leave the Bahamas, friends were introducing me to other private banking opportunities,' she said. 'The thought of continuing in that profession made me feel disgusted to the point of being physically nauseous, yet here were my dear friends, working in exactly the same industry, being helpful. How could I say to them directly there was no way I could do that work any more, while they were still in it? I felt that "unclean" feeling from every direction: unclean for having done that kind of work and yet unclean with feeling as though I was being, somehow, not truly and openly honest with my friends.'

Stephanie Padilla-Kaltenborn, an American mother of two and an old friend of mine, who lived until recently in the Cayman Islands, soon became aware of the unspoken limits of curiosity and candour when she moved there. 'It's a feeling when you live there that there's something under the surface and I did *not* want to look. I knew the answers would be more complicated than I could deal with. You cannot talk to people. It's a strange invisible line you can't cross. It's a semi-chosen state of mind, a self-censorship.'

Visiting the Caymans in 2009, I was chatting with a former senior Caymanian politician at his house, when a thickset dark-skinned Caymanian, probably in his forties, wearing a blue polo shirt, khaki shorts and sunglasses, walked in and introduced himself as 'the Devil'. I still do not know his name, though my sober and well-connected host vouched firmly for him. The mystery stranger said he had serious credentials in international law enforcement, so – this was all I could think of – I tested him by bringing up a photo on my phone that I'd recently taken of Robert Morgenthau, the Manhattan district attorney and a legend in the business. Not a sophisticated test, for sure, but my stranger passed it without hesitation.

He said he had spent years probing some of the global sins that freewheel through the Cayman Islands, and chatted about several cases, many of which I'd never heard of. One concerned Imad Mugniyah, whom I later discovered to be a senior Hezbollah official killed in Syria in 2008; another was a Cayman company fingered in the transfer of missile technology to Iran – later I checked with the US Office of Foreign Assets Control and discovered this was still a very live investigation. He touched on some Cayman operations of the international arms dealer Victor Bout which never reached the media. He spoke of Cayman hedge funds, mutual funds, special purpose vehicles, and described these sectors as being riddled with crime, though he declined to go into any detail. At this point he gave me a health warning.

'If we discuss this with you, you will end up like Salman Rushdie. There are things here not to be discussed. I mean it,' he said. 'This is a wicked, vicious place.' He said he had become too interested in certain stones that would normally, and deliberately, have been left unturned, and this had made him an enemy of the establishment. This, he said, was why he called himself the Devil – for that was how they treated him now.

'You have to have a deep soul,' he continued. 'They carry out economic isolation – they destroy your credibility and your integrity. They will strip you of your dignity. We operate here under a code of silence – *omertà*. They will tell you this is not so. There is a cabal here . . . These people in firms get together – it is an informal thing – and say this guy is causing trouble. You will get hints. Be careful.' Powerful Masonic and other networks are at play. The cabal does not include Caymanian politicians, he said, but added, 'They will give the politicians a call and tell them what to do.' My host – the only dissident I encountered on the island – interjected, adding that this cabal was 'spoken of in terms you'd speak of a ghost'.

'The very difficult part of this,' the Devil said, 'is that a few people here – those people who have committed what the international community would consider unlawful acts . . . they sit on boards; they have high status, and they are looked on as statesmen.'

Cayman boasts of its intrusive know-your-customer laws, which are fairly strong – on paper. Yet it was just as Beth Krall had found it in the Bahamas: the rules fall away if you are a trusted part of the network. 'If I do not have a relationship [with an institution] they will want to know even my underwear size,' the Devil said. 'But if you have an established relationship with a bank over time, the rules don't apply to you. If you are established as a well-to-do person, your credibility isn't questioned.' His words reminded me of an internal memo at the Riggs Bank brought to light in 2004 by the US Permanent Committee on Investigation. 'Client is a private investment company domiciled in the Bahamas,' it said, 'used as a vehicle to manage the investment needs of beneficial owner, now a retired professional who achieved much success in his career and accumulated wealth during his lifetime for retirement in an orderly way.' The 'retired professional' was Chilean torturer-in-chief and former dictator Augusto Pinochet.

Later I recounted the Devil's story and Krall's tale to an accountant who had worked in the Caymans, who nodded fiercely when I mentioned the reference to Salman Rushdie. 'Yes, yes, it's serious,' he said. 'It's not naive to take these threats seriously. You will be the first to go to prison if something goes wrong.' He told me about several mysterious offshore deaths, including that of a Swiss banker, Frederick Bise, who was found dead in 2008 in the boot of a burning car in West Bay on the Cayman Islands, with injuries from a blunt instrument.

My interlocutor, a former hedge fund administrator, compliance officer and chief accountant, described how he slowly grew to see what was going on. 'I started feeling bad three or four years after I arrived,' he said. 'We ran business through the accounts which was kind of dubious. You'd get information here and there and put it together, but you could not ask questions. Even if you had indications, you could not speak up. I did speak up, and the result was that I got less information at meetings. Information was sort of pre-discussed. I felt that a kind of show was going on.' He came under suspicion and was overloaded with work: 1,200 hours of overtime in a year, with no compensation. 'The CEO said, "This is part of your job."'

We replaced 40 to 50 per cent of our staff within two years. People who do not fit into the system for any reason are pushed out. Ask questions, and you can get fired or given so much work until you resign. It is not done obviously: they won't call you into meetings and say, 'Stop asking questions.' These are highly intellectual, well-educated people – they have their own way of communicating. You learn to read between the lines. They will not say, 'I am threatening you.' They will say, 'This person does not fit into the picture.' I have been in the business for years, and I know what they mean.

To stay in the Caymans, you need a work permit. Any expatriate who causes trouble – be they a seconded police official, lawyer, regulator or auditor – can have their work permit revoked by the Cayman Protection Board, which grants permits. Foreigners in the Caymans are made painfully aware of their vulnerability on this.

Most people working offshore only see fragments of the big picture so do not understand what is going on.

For example, if there is a trust set up in the Caymans, and the securities portfolio is in Switzerland, you will get very little information in the Caymans. You won't know the reason why things happen. The ones who commit the crimes – those people who set up the trust or the special purpose vehicle – will often sit in New York or London. The employees in many cases are honest people, trying to do their best; it will be the lawyer or the CEO or the chief operating officer who knows the truth.

'If you blow the whistle and stay on the island – and this is general in offshore centres – you don't have whistle-blower protections at all. If you speak up in one place, the network works in a way that you will never get work again. It is suicide – physically and economically. There is *no way* you would find protection,' he said, chopping the palm of one hand with the other for emphasis. 'Have you seen the John Grisham film *The Firm*? It's worse. It's not only the lawyers, it's the whole political environment.'

Before visiting the Caymans in 2009 I contacted the island authorities to request interviews, and told them I had done work for the Tax Justice Network (TJN), an expert-led organisation that strongly criticises secrecy jurisdictions like Cayman. On my arrival, government spokesman Ted Bravakis said there was 'no willingness to engage' and added that the decision to shun me had been taken 'at the highest levels of government'. Earlier, I had sent an email to a senior official in the Cayman Islands regulatory apparatus, asking for an interview. The official subsequently (and inadvertently) copied me into an email criticising efforts by his predecessor, Tim Ridley, to get me interviews. 'I do wish Tim would stop hawking this chap around as if to say he is doing us a favor,' he wrote. 'We are going to prepare a factual anodyne piece in writing but will decline any on the record interview.' I replied, suggesting that he may not have meant to copy me in on the mail. 'Quite so,' he replied, then put his finger squarely on an important truth. 'I have no problem with you understanding how the world at large regards the comments of TJN,' he said. 'I say so directly at every opportunity and meet with uniform agreement.' In his 'world at large' – the offshore environment – there is no opposition to the establishment consensus, it seems.

There is something about island life that stifles dissent and encourages the pervasive groupthink that he displayed. In his novel *Snow Falling on Cedars* David Guterson captures the essence of this generic island spirit. 'An enemy on an island is an enemy forever,' he wrote. 'There is no blending into an anonymous background, no neighbouring society to shift toward. Islanders are required by the very nature of their landscape to watch their step, moment by moment.' The social and political inhibitions islanders feel, he continued, 'are excellent and poor at the same time – excellent because it means most people take care, poor because it means an inbreeding of the spirit, too much held in, regret and silent brooding, a world whose inhabitants walk in trepidation, in fear of opening up'.

In the island goldfish bowl you cannot hide. The ability to sustain an establishment consensus and suppress troublemakers makes islands especially hospitable to offshore finance, reassuring international financiers that local establishments can be trusted not to allow democratic politics to interfere in the business of making money. This groupthink did not originate in the island havens – these are merely fortified nodes in bigger global power networks led by Britain and other large powers – but they have come to host and protect concentrations of anti-government, kick-the-poor attitudes that originate elsewhere, and allow them to flourish unchecked.

John Christensen, Jersey former economic adviser-turned-dissident, describes encountering extremist right-wing offshore attitudes when he returned to his native island in 1986 after working overseas as a development economist. It was the year of the City of London's Big Bang of financial deregulation, and he found the tax haven amid a spectacular boom. Old houses, tourist gift shops and merchant stores in Jersey's beautiful capital St Helier were being knocked down and replaced by banks, office blocks, car parks and wine bars. He went to an employment agency and they told him he could have any job he wanted. The following day he had three offers.

He began work with an accounting company, working with over 150 private clients. The firm performed reinvoicing, the practice I have described in which trading partners agree on a price for a deal, then record it officially at a different price in order to shift money secretly across borders. It is fiendishly hard to work out how much money flows through reinvoicing. Global Financial Integrity in Washington estimate that about $100 billion is drained from developing countries each year just from this practice. That is about the same size as all foreign aid from the rich world. 'This was about capital flight, shifting capital out and evading tax – the really nasty stuff,' Christensen said. 'I saw this stuff coming in daily.' The accountancy firm provided a fax number, headed notepaper, a bank account and a veneer of exceedingly British solidity and respectability.

Christensen worked there for twenty months, mostly handling clients based in countries linked historically to Britain, including South Africa, where much of the work involved evading anti-apartheid sanctions, Nigeria, Kenya, Uganda and Iran. 'I was an insider, and I worked systematically through hundreds of client files,' he said. 'I could gradually put the bits together: "Ah yes, so this client is a politician disguising his identity," and so on.' He learned that a very senior right-wing French politician was using his influence to secure planning permission on behalf of developers for a series of property deals across France. The Jersey link meant nobody in France could find out what he was up to. Generally, he said, junior offshore operators are unaware of what they are handling, because the laddering through various jurisdictions hides the trails. 'You don't get that information from a cursory look at the file,' Christensen said. 'I got hold of this guy's name by talking to an office in France. They told me, "I'll have to speak to the senator about that." If you work there long enough, they get to know you and get comfortable telling you things. The market rigging, the insider trading – I was sitting there thinking, "Holy shit, this is dynamite." These were very prominent families. This would be on the front pages if it got out.'

Christensen, like Krall, won't reveal precise details. 'I signed oaths and contracts for life,' he said. 'If I transgressed those I could be thrown into a pit for ever.'

Reinvoicing is just one more workaday business procedure in the world of secrecy jurisdictions. 'They thought this was good business practice,' he continued. 'They rationalised it in all sorts of ways: foreigners were protecting their money from political risk or unstable currencies; people in Africa are poor because they don't work hard enough or they are corrupt; countries are poor so we send them aid money. That kind of thing. They didn't want to think about economic systems.'

He worked with client after client as the river of money flowing into Jersey became a tide. When he expressed unease about the origins of some of it, much of it from Africa, he was brushed aside. One Friday, ahead of the habitual office binge-drinking session, his section supervisor told him she didn't want to discuss these things and didn't 'give a shit about Africa anyway'. 'Her attitude was typical. Profitability was sky-high, and nobody made the connection between their actions and criminality and injustice elsewhere. None of the financial intermediaries involved – banks, law firms, accountants and auditors – bothered to report or even question illicit transfers.' He met an old childhood acquaintance, now a chartered accountant, drunk in a pub.

I told him about India, Malaysia, trekking and so on, and he switched off immediately. No interest. He was in a bubble. Last night's party, which car I was driving, who's screwing whom – that was it. I can't tell you how much of a shock it was to come back. There were really extreme views I was picking up on in Jersey: deep racism, sexism, the repressive feel, the awful in-your-face and aggressive consumerism I'd never seen before, and an almost fanatical hatred of any progressive ideas.

There was this 'Don't speak out' mentality. In London all my mates had taken anti-racism and stuff like that as normal. Back in Jersey I got, 'You don't do that here, sonny.'

Progressive legislation has taken years to seep into Jersey from the outside world. Britain abolished its anti-sodomy laws in 1967 but Jersey only repealed its law, under pressure from Britain, in 1990. Birching, done away with in Britain in 1948, only left the Jersey statute books in 2005, again under outside pressure.

Soon after arriving Christensen turned up at a cocktail party on a motorcycle and was assailed by a guest, a senior Jersey business figure. 'He was saying that a crash helmet is an infringement on your liberty. He was anti-seatbelts, anti-tax and anti-government. He would say apartheid was good for black South Africans; that we should re-establish colonialism: that "these people" had been much better off under white governments.' Christensen clashed with Sir Julian Hodge, a pillar of the Jersey banking establishment, 'a mega-apologist for apartheid; a mega-pusher for empire; a libertarian beyond anything I've met'. He remembers a stand-up row at a public meeting with the Reverend Peter Manton, a Jersey senator and Anglican minister, who had also said publicly that 'the blacks' in South Africa were better off under apartheid than anywhere else. (Manton was subsequently prosecuted for sex offences and has died.) At a government committee meeting exploring sexual discrimination and equal opportunities for women a senior politician made a show of falling asleep and snoring. Another politician, who ran his own business, went further. 'I can still picture it,' Christensen remembers. 'He said, "If any of my girls got pregnant I would sack them immediately. Nobody wants to see a pregnant girl behind the desk." That is how he referred to all women – girls.'

Offshore sometimes feels like a *Boys' Own* fantasy of the world, in which white men sort things out over Scotch whisky and see the rest of the world as a consumable resource. Christensen continued:

The ruling classes realise they don't need to worry about the Democrats coming to power in the US, or Social Democrats coming to power in Germany, or Labour coming to power in Britain. They realised they didn't need to fight the fight at home. They already had this flotsam and jetsam of the empire strewn across the globe, with their red post boxes and British ways of life, and incredible subservience to the English ruling class. In Jersey I was amazed by how fawning the local politicians were to outsiders with money. There was this idea: 'We can take over our own little places, and the locals will be grateful to us. The checks and balances aren't there; the press isn't there; and they resent interference from outsiders.' Happy days. The City gentlemen had found a way around the threat of democracy.

In small jurisdictions – not necessarily islands – it is also easy for collective inferiority complexes to emerge, where residents come to see themselves as plucky defenders of local interests against the predations of bigger, bullying neighbours. From such mistrustful self-regard it is but a short step to a libertarian, leave-us-alone world view that sees any self-advancement at the expense of outsiders as valiant resistance against tyranny. This of course dovetails closely with offshore's 'It's not our problem – fix it yourselves' ethical framework, which holds the rights of citizens and governments elsewhere to be inconsequential, which sees democracy as a tyranny of the masses and which holds the very idea of society in disregard, even contempt.

Providing facilities for foreign tax evasion clearly fits this framework, as does a general hatred of tax. This can go to extreme lengths. In court papers filed in New York in February 2010 the British private equity tycoon Guy Hands revealed that after moving to the British Crown Dependency of Guernsey to legally avoid tax, he had 'never visited' his school-age children or his parents in England since he left, in order to preserve his non-resident tax status.[1] Konrad Hummler, a vocal senior Swiss banker, calls Germany, France and Italy 'illegitimate states' because their taxes are too high. Tax evasion, or what he calls 'Swiss-style saving outside the system', is, he says, a legitimate defence by citizens attempting to 'partially escape the current grasp of the administrators of a disastrous social welfare state and its fiscal policies'.[2]

Offshore attitudes are characterised by amazing similarities of argument, of approach and of method, and some striking psychological affinities in a geographically diverse but like-minded global cultural community. A peculiar mixture of characters populates this world: castle-owning members of ancient continental European aristocracies, fanatical supporters of American libertarian writer Ayn Rand, members of the world's intelligence services, global criminals, British public schoolboys, assorted lords and ladies and bankers galore. Its bugbears are government, laws and taxes, and its slogan is freedom.

Government is 'a self-seeking flea on the backs of the more productive people of this world', wrote Matt Ridley, a best-selling science writer and old Etonian son of the fourth Viscount Ridley, lord steward of the royal household. 'Governments do not run countries, they parasitise them.' Ridley went on to become non-executive chairman of British mortgage lender Northern Rock, which used a tiny charity for people with Down's syndrome without its consent as the registered beneficiary of a Guernsey-based structured investment vehicle named Granite that had issued the best part of $100 billion worth of commercial paper. Granite helped Northern Rock keep mortgage loans off its balance sheet, leading to its collapse at the leading edge of the 2007–9 global financial crisis and a massive taxpayer bailout.[3] Northern Rock's Granite vehicle was neither onshore nor offshore; it had a foot in both camps. And this reflects an important point about the offshore world view: while it is in secrecy jurisdictions where these attitudes flourish so vigorously, they mainly originate among the onshore ruling classes.

The concentration of extremist attitudes in Jersey was self-reinforcing, as Christensen explains. 'Most liberal people like myself left,' he said. 'My socially liberal friends from school, almost all of them left Jersey to go to university, and almost all of them didn't go back. I can't tell you how dark it felt. I have never been a depressed person but I went into a big one there. Everything I valued seemed of no significance. There was no one I felt I could turn to.' He almost left but was persuaded to stay by academic researcher Mark Hampton, who was putting together a new framework for understanding tax havens and convinced him how important it was to understand the system from the inside. 'I went undercover,' Christensen said, 'not to dish the dirt on individuals and companies, but because I couldn't understand it – and none of the academics I spoke to could either. There was no useful literature.' He did not even tell his brother what he was doing. Christensen kept this up for twelve years, working in several different companies before becoming Jersey's economic adviser.

'I had to suppress everything so I devised this strategy of keeping myself busy with other things.' He became president of the Jersey Film Society, raced high-speed catamarans and started a family. Though he never made a secret of his distaste for the system, his capers – such as founding the island's first and only Jean-Claude Van Damme appreciation society – meant that politicians saw him as a lightweight and therefore not a threat. When he was appointed economic adviser in 1987 he began to feel the full force of what it means to stand out against an all-embracing consensus. Occasionally, he said, the pressure was so severe that he actually lost his voice.

Tension gets me around my neck. At times, in meetings and round-table discussions with the Finance and Economics Committee and other government committees, there were moments when I was literally choking with anger. It took real strength to stand up and say, 'I'm sorry, I don't agree with this.' I felt like the little boy farting in church. I felt so lonely during those committee meetings; nobody ever supported me . . . Dissenting in committee means saying, 'I'm not interested in my career here.' I was cutting my own throat.

Three local sayings encapsulate Jersey: 'Don't hang your dirty linen out in public;' 'Don't rock the boat;' and 'If you don't like it, there's always a boat in the morning.'

Jersey is riddled with elite, secretive insider networks, typically linked to the financial sector. After being appointed economic adviser Christensen found that many people who came to see him wanted him to join their Masonic lodge, and gave him the secret signal. 'It was a finger twisted back on itself in a handshake,' he said.

These were mainly people I knew vaguely, who would come into my office. Blah, blah, general talk, then quite openly, 'Are you interested in joining this lodge?' I always said I would consider it, and I never did. The type of people doing this were bankers, senior merchants and senior politicians. You don't look at people's hands; you feel a lump there when you shake. For me it felt slightly dirty – covert, as if we were all part of some dirty deal, a schoolboy thing.

'Their thinking is very much of the old boy network – you are either one of us or you are against us,' he continued. 'It means they can trust you to do the right thing without having to be told – an insidious meaning of the word "trust". I ended up being labelled untrustworthy, I frequently heard of them calling me "Not One of Us." Once it was said to my face.'

Even the media was captured by the consensus. The dominant newspaper in Jersey was owned for many years until 2005 by a company chaired by Senator Frank Walker, who was also head of the powerful Finance and Economics Committee and one of the most vociferous cheerleaders for Jersey's finance industry. As the *Financial Times* said in 1998, 'That is akin to Gordon Brown [then UK chancellor] or Oskar Lafontaine [Germany finance minister] owning all their country's national newspapers. Few on Jersey see it as odd.'[4] Walker left the newspaper in 2005 and it does now carry dissenting views and plenty of decent reporting, yet its overall editorial tone and content mix staunchly favours the tax haven industry.

Patrick Muirhead, an experienced former BBC radio journalist who spent time as the anchorman of Jersey's nightly ITV news until 2004, described the atmosphere.

In an island of 90,000 souls, one is only removed from another by the smallest step of separation. My co-host's home became a popular salon for politicians and decision makers. In such an atmosphere of closeness, any meaningful challenge becomes impossible. 'You rub people up the wrong way,' she said, primly dismissing my methods. After I left, my integrity, professional ability and popularity were trashed by a hostile and defensive Jersey media and island population.[5]

Unaccountable elites are always irresponsible, and I got my own flavour of Jersey's mouldy governance on the very first day of a visit in March 2009, when the *Jersey Evening Post* carried a front-page story headlined STATES IN SHAMBLES. 'The States resembled a school playground yesterday as foul language and personal insults flew across the chamber,' it related. Senator Stuart Syvret, a popular but controversial local politician, had complained publicly in the States Assembly, Jersey's parliament, that the health minister was whispering in his ear. Syvret, the newspaper reported,

stood up and said: 'On a point of order, I am sorry to interrupt the minister. But the minister to my right, Senator Perchard, is saying in my ear, "You are full of f*****g s**t, why don't you go and top yourself, you bastard."' Senator Perchard immediately responded by saying: 'I absolutely refute that. I am just fed up with this man making allegations.' The BBC, which was broadcasting the sitting live, had to apologise for the language.

Syvret has been a regular victim of efforts to suppress dissent. 'Any anti-establishment figure here is bugged,' said Syvret. 'There is a climate of fear. Anyone who dares disagree is anti-Jersey, an enemy of Jersey. You are a traitor, disloyal. There is all this Stalinist propaganda.' A few weeks after my visit eight police officers arrested Syvret and held him for seven hours while they ransacked his home and personal files, including his computer. The next day Syvret's blog administrator told him someone had been clumsily trying to hack his passwords. When I phoned him soon afterwards his answering machine message, hinting at his mischievous character, said, 'Don't be frightened by the police bugging. Speak freely, as you are not breaking the law, unless you are my smack dealer, in which case you know where the new drop-off point is.' His blog describing his incarceration summed up the atmosphere: 'Come to Sunny Jersey. The North Korea of the English Channel!'

In October 2009, having been accused of leaking a police report about the conduct of a nurse, Syvret fled to London and claimed asylum at the House of Commons, saying he could not get a fair trial in Jersey. British Liberal Democrat MP John Hemming put Syvret up in his flat, declaring that 'we should not allow him to be extradited, to be prosecuted in a kangaroo court'.[6] When Syvret returned in May 2010 to fight an election he was arrested at the airport. 'This is a society with no checks and balances, run by an oligarchy,' Syvret said. 'It is a one-party state, and it has been for centuries.'

It is hard to construct coherent intellectual justifications for hosting secretive offshore finance, so the usual technique is to engage the messenger, not the message. Attacks on dissidents mostly consist of mean-spirited slurs and innuendoes: this person is ignorant, motivated by envy, economically illiterate, unreliable or mentally unbalanced; this person cannot be trusted. Dr Mark Hampton, a lecturer at Portsmouth University who used to be involved in field trips to Jersey, remembers how helpful the authorities were until he publicly criticised Jersey's offshore status and became more visible in the media. Field trips were no longer welcome 'because Hampton is at Portsmouth', a colleague told him. 'They started giving negative briefings about me,' Hampton said. 'They started calling me things; they suggested I had a dodgy PhD, that I was fabricating things, that I was a "whip-persnapper". They refused to call me doctor. I'm not big on status – my students call me Mark. It was no big deal, but this was all part of the chipping away at my professionalism.'

Geoff Southern, a dissident deputy, said he now tries to avoid pointing in public. Last time he did he appeared in the *Jersey Evening Post* in a stunningly Hitler-like pose. He and his friend Senator Trevor Pitman wearily describe being labelled 'destroyers of Jersey' or 'the enemy within'. They are accused in public of being driven by personal bitterness; hints are dropped about darker motives. When we spoke, Southern and Pitman's wife Shona, another deputy, were being prosecuted for helping elderly and disabled residents fill in requests for postal votes, albeit in breach of an arcane electoral law. They were later found guilty and fined. The amorphous finance industry is, locals say, ultimately behind the attacks. 'The finance industry is like an amoeba,' said another

Jersey politician, who declined to be identified. 'You attack it, and it
absorbs that, and attacks back. It is the parasite in the island. It has taken
it over. It controls us and decides on everything that happens here.'

At the Smugglers' Inn on Jersey's beautiful south-west coast, I sat with
John Heys, a tour guide at the world-famous Durrell Zoo, and his friend
Maurice Merhet, a former printer and pig farmer, now retired, who still
speaks the Jèrriais dialect, which is very like the variety of French spoken
in nearby Normandy. The two old friends had spoken out – in letters to
the *Jersey Evening Post* and in other public forums – and have been decried,
publicly and regularly, as traitors. 'We live in a dictatorship,' Heys said,
jabbing his finger at the table. 'This is not a democratic country. John
Christensen is public enemy number one. We call them the Junta, and
people are afraid to stand up against them.' Some of Merhet's family
have told him not to associate with Christensen. 'They say he's no good
for Jersey; he's a traitor, that kind of thing.' Both described the same
climate of fear that Syvret had: the dread of being squeezed out of a
job, of never getting anywhere, of being blacklisted. 'The ministers here
are gods,' Merhet continued, 'and the gods are answerable to them.'

Heys showed me an email from a government minister to a dissident friend who had, in a cheeky Christmas message to the minister,
pointed out the large sums stashed away in Jersey amid global poverty.
The minister responded – mistakes included:

Hi Traitor

Please refrain from sending me your unsolicited garbage . . . I am surprised
you still decide to live in this 'tax haven' island . . . ifs its so bad why do
you not leave to live somewhere else . . . good riddance I would say . . .
but perhaps NOT because you get a damm good living here no doubt
perhaps funded by banks and your morgage lender . . . in fact my family
have lived in Jersey for several generations and I am so very proud of
it but to listen to traiterous idiots like you makes me furious.

I would not have the nerve to wish you a happy christmas in fact I
hope you continue to to live a miserable existence in your traiterous world

Do not respond

To the casual visitor, Jersey looks and feels very British. But it is very,
very different from the Britain I know.

*   *   *

In tiny states everyone knows everyone else, and conflicts of interest and corruption are inevitable. Jersey insiders will talk about this for hours, especially the corruption. Sometimes conflicts of interest are embedded in the political structure itself. In Jersey the attorney general, William Bailhache, for years prosecuted cases in courts presided over by his brother Sir Philip Bailhache, the bailiff. The bailiff of Jersey, who is appointed by the Queen, is simultaneously the senior judge of the Royal Court of Jersey and president of the States Assembly. In other words, one person oversees judicial impartiality while also being responsible for projecting an image of political stability and respectability. The dominant group thus becomes synonymous with the interests of the entire population. There are no independent think tanks or universities, a small and vulnerable civil service, no clear divisions between the legislature, the judiciary and the executive, and no second chamber to scrutinise the States' deliberations. When Christensen was economic adviser, the public could not attend committee meetings or examine their agendas or policy papers, and there is no written record of parliamentary debates on major laws.[7]

These problems extend to the governance of the finance industry. In Jersey there are no credible and truly independent processes for scrutinising or regulating offshore finance. A 2002 publication from the Association of Accountancy and Business Affairs, one of the most detailed academic analyses of Jersey's politics, put it concisely. 'Most Jersey politicians are in business,' it said. 'They lobby for business and promote business interests. They draft, refine and pass legislation. They have also sat on regulatory bodies, effectively acting as "gate-keepers" adjudicating on complaints and malpractices. Politicians sit on the boards of the companies that they are supposed to regulate.'[8]

Close relationships are inevitable on such a small island, but it is precisely because of this that Jersey needs extra checks and more transparency, to weigh against the inbuilt tendency towards conflicts of interest. This is especially important when Jersey plays such a major role in international finance. This affects you and me. Skittish financiers dislike places that are chaotically corrupt, as do onshore regulators. Secrecy jurisdictions steeped in sleaze confront this by putting on a strenuous performance of rectitude, a theatre of probity that involves repeatedly projecting the essential message – 'We are a clean, well-regulated, transparent and cooperative jurisdiction' – burnished by carefully selected comments and praise from toothless offshore watch-dogs like the Financial Action Task Force or the OECD. This theatre also depends on a refusal to engage with critics. As a top Caymans official put it when I requested an interview, 'There is no value to us in being seen to engage with you, rather the contrary.'⁹ Christensen and his colleague Richard Murphy have a standing challenge to the Jersey establishment to engage in televised debates about the offshore industry on neutral ground. No senior figure in Jersey has ever accepted.

Perhaps the biggest weapon deployed against local critics is the job market. A middle-aged Jerseyman, who asked me not to identify him, said his career crashed after he spoke out against the offshore corruption he had become entangled in. 'I have all the qualifications,' he said, 'and I couldn't get a job in a law firm to make tea now.' Syvret echoes the point. 'The finance industry – if you piss them off, your career is finished.'

Angola or Kuwait are oil-dependent states; Jersey is a finance-dependent state. Economists talk of the 'Dutch disease' that afflicts mineral-rich countries: when revenues flood in, price levels rise and locally made goods, notably manufactures and agricultural products, cannot compete with cheaper imports. These sectors wither. Meanwhile, talent leaches into the dominant sectors, and politicians lose interest in the thorny challenge of keeping other areas afloat, because it is far simpler and more lucrative to latch on to the sources of easy cash. Although Jersey's finance industry only employs about 13,000 people directly, perhaps a quarter of the workforce, it now accounts for over 90 per cent of government revenue and has crowded out the other sectors, just as oil has devastated other areas in Angola. Jersey house prices rose fivefold from 1985 to 2001, then 60 per cent more until by mid-2008 the average house price in Jersey was £508,000 ($960,000), nearly two and a half times the cost of the average house in Britain, itself in a house-price bubble. In the nine years to 2006 bank deposits and fund values in Jersey doubled, while incomes in agriculture and manufacturing fell by 20 and 35 per cent respectively. Agriculture and manufacturing have shrunk to just 1 per cent of the economy each, and tourism is fading fast.

A former guest-house owner remembered how his business ended, as finance muscled in. 'We were selling up; a couple of the banks came round to look at buying our place. They were saying, "Sell now, you've no chance in hell in making it work here."' Christensen also noted how the whole character of the place had changed. 'Jersey was a bucket-and-spade tourist destination,' he said. 'Interesting people were always coming across from the mainland: good bands, comedians, great shows. Really lively stuff. Now the bankers bring across string quartets.'

As with oil economies, those at the top get rich fast and those at the bottom see their wages stagnate or fall. 'There is this powerful standard image in most people's minds: that Jersey is full of gin-swilling millionaires, so the population are all a load of rich bastards who deserve a kicking,' Syvret said. 'In reality, most people in Jersey are politically powerless and it's the entrenched oligarchic elites who are the swines at the trough.' The economic inequalities translate into political inequalities, magnifying the pressures on dissidents.

Rosemary Pestana, a tough and fearless trade union activist, described what it is like to live without money in Jersey. A single mother with three children, she is registered as disabled – with a heart problem and arthritis – and lives in a rather dishevelled apartment block in downtown St Helier opposite a muddy derelict area. For thirty-five years she has worked as a part-time cleaner at the Jersey General Hospital, earning £13,000 a year – about a fortieth of the average house price – which she tops up with £8,000 in income support. Just to survive, she said, you need about £400 a week – but the minimum wage brings in £230 before insurance and tax, so many people have two jobs. The quirks of labour law makes strike action unusually hard here.

In her cramped and cluttered kitchen she remembered her childhood. 'It was hard then, but I don't think it was as hard as it is now.' Even when her parents split up the children stayed in school, with occasional day trips and holidays. 'You couldn't do that now.' She outlined the cost of getting medical treatment. Jersey has no British National Health Service, and patients must pay fees to doctors. Jersey's *Annual Social Survey* for 2009 noted that the cost of going to doctors and dentists had become so high that more than half of islanders were not having routine health checks.[10] 'I love my island,' Pestana said. 'But I want it back.'

Christensen used to control Jersey's retail prices index (RPI), which had an important real impact on the inequalities. Many things like rent or water were linked to the index, and if prices went up, employers would have to pay ordinary people more. 'I guarded the index carefully from political interference, which was constant,' he said. Once, in 1991, one of Jersey's most senior politicians stopped him in a corridor. 'He thought of me as a little boy. He said, "How is your dear mother?" and then went, "Now look here. This inflation is causing a problem – what can we do about it?" I said I expected it would start turning downwards this time next year. He said "that isn't going to help – we have to do something now." I said no. He never spoke to me again.' The Jersey Chamber of Commerce pushed inquiry after inquiry into the RPI. Each time, Christensen was vindicated. He generally got on well with his boss Colin Powell, a British civil service mandarin, but they did clash. One Christmas Christensen got a cartoonist friend to draw Powell as a wizard about to sacrifice a goat at Stonehenge, with the caption 'The Retail Price Index is announced.' Powell was not amused.

A Jersey law makes it fiendishly hard for most non-financial businesses to set up, even though foreign workers can turn up on the boat and quickly find jobs. 'If you control demand for labour but don't control supply there is only one possible outcome,' said Christensen: 'downward pressure on wages.' When Christensen was in Jersey, there there was no minimum wage or unemployment benefit, all of which suits the finance industry perfectly as it keeps costs down. When he gave the *Jersey Evening Post* an interview arguing for a minimum wage, the Chamber of Commerce made an official complaint.

Extreme economic inequalities are tolerated offshore, and often welcomed as incentives for the poor to work harder. It is an ethos memorably summarised by economist J. K. Galbraith as 'the "horse and sparrow" theory of income distribution and tax: if you feed a horse enough oats, some will pass through to the road for the sparrows'. Soak the poor is a constant theme as Jersey seeks to stay ahead of other jurisdictions in its race to attract capital. In 2004 Jersey cut corporation tax from 20 per cent to zero, except for finance, which pays 10 per cent. This blew a hole in the budget big enough to finance Jersey's entire benefits system, so they made hundreds of redundancies and introduced a tax on consumption, hitting the poor especially hard. Shona Pitman, a States deputy, calls this the 'tax-the-poor-to-save-the-rich' approach. 'Jersey has the social structure of a Hilton hotel,' explained Jerry Dorey, a Jersey senator: 'a collection of alienated individuals who are just here to make money.'

In Jersey super-wealthy people and corporations can actually negotiate the tax rates they pay. For most of the 1990s wealthy people wanting to take up residence sent their lawyers directly to Christensen's office to negotiate their rates. Jersey would insist on a minimum annual tax payment, and the millionaire or billionaire would then simply remit the amount which, when calculated at Jersey's flat 20 per cent tax rate, produced this sum. Christensen's predecessors had settled on £25,000–30,000 tax; Christensen raised this to £150,000, which meant remitting income of £750,000 each year to Jersey. If you had worldwide income of £10 million, say, your effective tax rate was 1.5 per cent. A similar principle applied to corporations.[11] For a Jersey international business company the top rate starts at 2 per cent and falls from there, depending on how much profit it plans to book in Jersey.[12]

The millionaires tend to keep their heads down. A down-at-heel 1950s office block near St Helier town centre above the New Raj curry house is the home of the broadcasting empire of wealthy pornographer and newspaper owner Richard Desmond. Closer to the edge of town, a property next to Christensen's old school has served for years as a base for Hugh Thurston, an accountant who looked after some of the financial affairs of former British Prime Minister Margaret Thatcher and her family, and of the giant arms multinational BAE Systems. A retired property developer who did not want to be identified said, 'I pay a quarter in tax terms of what the guy who collects my bins does. I play golf all day while he probably can't even afford to pay for the house he lives in. Living in Jersey is like that: if you've got the money, you get the cream'.[13] Six of Jersey's ten current ministers are multi-millionaires. 'This is a parliament of wealthy people,' said the dissident Jersey deputy Geoff Southern. 'I think there is still a resentment that peasants have got into power.'

One winter night in 1996, towards the end of his time in Jersey, Christensen opened the books for a reporter from the *Wall Street Journal* who was investigating a fraud ring involving a Swiss bank operating out of Jersey that had been ripping off American investors. The story, headlined OFFSHORE HAZARD: ISLE OF JERSEY PROVES LESS THAN A

HAVEN TO CURRENCY INVESTORS, ran on the *Journal*'s front page several months later. Jersey's finance industry and politicians went into spasm. This was one of the first times Jersey's supposedly clean and well-regulated finance sector had been challenged in a serious global newspaper. The end of the article quoted a senior civil servant everyone in Jersey was sure was Christensen. He knew that in talking to the reporter he had effectively resigned.

'From then on they would have done anything to get rid of me, but I had tenure. Only way they could do it was to find me guilty of professional misconduct or in bed with a choirboy. The tension was incredible.' He did not leave immediately. His second son was born the following month and he had to work out a long notice period. Leaving wasn't so easy either. 'The lure of being a big fish in a small pond, it's extraordinarily seductive,' he said. 'I could so easily have bought a fifty-two-foot Swan yacht, cruised through a nice career and got a gong at the end of it.' Now he is a dissident, the barbs continue to fly across the English Channel. 'Grapes come no sourer than those trodden by Mr Christensen, who once worked in Jersey and was passed over for promotion,' the *Jersey Evening Post* thundered later. 'Ever since, he has worked unceasingly to undermine the Island that foolishly slighted him.' A quote from Jersey published in France's *Le Monde* newspaper in April 2009 called him a 'traitor to the nation'. Insiders in the Jersey establishment have confirmed that it is semi-official policy to attack him in exactly these terms.

Offshore thrives on narrow self-interest combined with a culture of collusion. Its defenders are neurotically quick to impute mean motives and a hidden agenda to their critics. But men angling for promotion do not usually speak to the *Wall Street Journal* to get it.

Finance can take advantage of insularity, timidity and moral short-sightedness, but the soak-the-poor ethos of the Jersey establishment derives ultimately from the offshore industries and their onshore controllers, not from innate island character. Offshore repression can happen in larger jurisdictions too. Rudolf Elmer, a Swiss banker who had worked for banks in several offshore centres before becoming a whistle-blower on some of the corruption he had seen, felt the pressure in Switzerland, a country of eight million people.

In 2004 Elmer noticed two men following him to work. Later, he saw them in the parking lot of his daughter's kindergarten, then from his kitchen window. His wife was followed in her car. The men offered his daughter chocolates in the street and late at night drove a car at high speed into the cul-de-sac where he lived. The stalking continued, on and off, for over two years. He worked for a Chinese company at the time, and at one point the stalkers wore Chinese T-shirts with dragons on the backs. His previous employer, Julius Baer, denied any involvement; there has been no determination as to who sent the men. The police said there was nothing they could do. In 2005, they searched his house using a prosecutor's warrant, and he was imprisoned for thirty days, accused of violating Swiss bank secrecy, which is, as he put it, 'an official violation, like murder'.

'I was thinking of suicide at this stage,' he said. 'I would be looking out of the window at two a.m. They intimidated my wife, my children and my neighbours. I was an outlaw. I was godfather to a child whose father is in finance. He said I have to stop – "you are a threat to the family."' A close relative was pressured by his superior at work to avoid contact with Elmer; after one such warning he left the office in tears. 'I was bloody naive to think that Swiss justice was different,' Elmer said. 'I can see how they might control a population of 80,000 people in the Isle of Man, but eight million? How can a minority in the banking world manipulate the opinion of an entire country? What is this? The Mafia? This is how it works. Jersey, the Cayman Islands, Switzerland: this whole bloody system is corrupt.'

Right-wing ideologies that for years have been beyond the pale in the larger democracies have been allowed to grow without restraint offshore. As offshore finance has become increasingly influential in the global economy, re-engineering onshore economies in ever more significant ways, so such attitudes have flourished, gaining strength and confidence within the larger economies. This is evident in the intransigent arrogance of bankers, who, having nearly brought the world economy to its knees, still ask for more and threaten to relocate else-where if they are regulated or taxed too much. It is visible in the demands of the super-rich, who have come to expect and demand tax rates below those of their office cleaners. When Irish musician Bono, for years the world's most prominent poverty campaigner, shifts his financial affairs offshore to the Netherlands to avoid tax and is still warmly welcomed in society, the battle seems lost. America, the great democracy, is now in thrall to the world views of unaccountable, abusive and often criminalised elites, in large part thanks to offshore finance.

Having colonised the economies and political systems of the large nation states where most of us live, offshore finance has gone a very long way towards capturing our attitudes too.

12

Griffin

The City of London Corporation

One of the few people to have sounded a clear early warning about the impending financial crisis from 2007 was Gillian Tett of the *Financial Times,* a former Cambridge anthropology student who slipped sideways into financial journalism. In 2004 a colleague drew her a diagram of the City of London, the collective term for Britain's global financial services industry, and she saw that a big part of the City was being ignored.[1] 'To understand how a society works,' she said, 'you need to not just look at the areas of what we call social noise – i.e. what everyone likes to talk about, the equity markets and M and A [mergers and acquisitions] and all the high-profile areas everyone can see. But you need to look at the social silences as well.' She had spotted what would later become infamous as the shadow banking system: the structured investment vehicles, asset-backed commercial paper conduits and other then-unknown and largely unregulated structures whose assets, by the time the crisis struck in 2007, were greater in size than the entire $10 trillion US banking system,[2] and which nearly brought the world economy to its knees.

That social silence is now, we think, well understood, but the City of London is surrounded by a far more ancient silence which almost nobody talks about even today. 'When I started working in this area a long time ago, I was startled that there was no research on the City of London, even on the left,' said Robin Ramsay, a British political writer. 'Societies have no-go areas, and you are about to enter into one of those great no-go areas of British politics.' I was introduced to this area by two independent-minded characters: Maurice Glasman, a north London Jewish academic, and a young Anglican priest named Father William Taylor. They are the only private citizens in living memory to have seriously and directly confronted the City of London Corporation, the municipal authority for the City of London. The social silence they found hides what strikes me as one of the strangest stories in the history of global finance.

In the late 1990s Father Taylor got involved in a campaign against a property developer in Spitalfields, a poor inner-London zone wedged against the City's north-eastern flank. He knew the area well: after leaving university in 1988 his bishop had told him to get some parish experience before considering being ordained, so he had worked in Spitalfields for a time as a driver delivering fruit and vegetables. Margaret Thatcher had then just started her third term as prime minister and, following Big Bang financial-services liberalisation in 1986, developers were looking to expand the financial district beyond the City's boundaries. Neighbouring Spitalfields was a tempting prospect. 'The free market was reigning supreme,' Taylor remembers. 'I felt this was a problem, and I felt the Church should have something to say about it.'

Spitalfields still hosts some of Britain's most atmospheric and ancient street markets: Brick Lane, Petticoat Lane and Old Spitalfields Market itself. Immigrant histories and cultures crowd up against one another here: Irish, Huguenots, Jews, Bengalis, Maltese and many others. 'All these groups that were claiming to tell the history of Spitalfields,' he remembers. 'Migrant communities, conservationists living in their old Georgian houses, old cockney geezers in the pubs and markets, and now this new group – the developers and planners – the professional agents of capitalism. This was a contested community.' Taylor was gripped.

On 1 May 1997, the first day in power for Tony Blair's Labour government, Taylor became chaplain of Guildhall University in the City of London. Labour immediately gave the Bank of England its operational independence, a gift of economic and political power to the City that the *Independent* newspaper called 'the most radical shake-up of the Bank in its 300-year history'.[3]

Local campaigns in Spitalfields against the developers' juggernaut had been smouldering for years but in February 2000 they flared up again when the developers submitted plans to replace over half of Spitalfields Market with an office block.[4] Taylor discovered that the consortium behind the developers, which had suddenly gained a ferocious new momentum, had an unusual shareholder: the City of London Corporation, the world's oldest continuous municipal government. 'I could not work out how a public authority could act as a developer outside its jurisdiction,' Taylor said. 'I became interested – what exactly *is* the Corporation of London?' He resolved to find out.

At Guildhall University Taylor met Maurice Glasman, a senior lecturer in political theory. Born in 1961 as the grandchild of poor Jewish immigrants, Glasman imbibed from his mother a socialist world view, coloured by the scars of family history. 'I was brought up with the Holocaust like I was there.' He was an expert on the work of the thinker Karl Polanyi, an opponent of mainstream economic theories who emphasised how deeply economies are embedded in societies and cultures, something which had been all but forgotten by the 1980s. Glasman had been at Guildhall University since 1995. He and Taylor discussed their shared thoughts and confusions, chatting about commodification, the notion that everything has a price. 'When people consider it necessary to sell their own organs to pay for the treatment of their brain-damaged children, and that is argued to be a moral good, you will understand what is meant by commodification,' Glasman said. 'It means the selling of things in the market that were not produced for sale. The human kidney was not made for sale – and neither were school playing fields and public libraries.' The City, of course, was where all this was happening. 'Prostitution, people trafficking, where was the Church in all of this?' Glasman remembers asking Taylor. 'In all other European countries the Church was speaking out about the unregulated free market; in Britain they were talking about homosexuals and women priests.'

Taylor had a campaign, Spitalfields Market Under Threat (SMUT), which brought together local community and religious groups, and they got a court order to halt the development plans, which a SMUT official said looked like a 'huge corporate claw reaching into the market from the City'. Construction was interrupted, yet the developers did not seem to flinch. Taylor and Glasman were curious about the Corporation of London. 'My first thought,' Glasman remembers, 'was, "This is a local authority. How can it have spare money?" All the others are cash-strapped.' The more they learned, the more they realised that the Corporation wasn't like other local authorities. In fact it was unlike anything the two men had ever encountered.

At its broadest, the term 'City of London' refers to the financial services industry located in and around the British capital. More precisely, the City, or the Square Mile, is a 1.22-square-mile[5] slab of prime central London real estate that stretches from the Thames at Victoria Embankment, clockwise up through Fleet Street, the Barbican Centre, then to Liverpool Street in the north-east, then back down to the Thames just west of the Tower of London. Smaller clusters of financial services activity exist elsewhere in Greater London: the hedge funds in Mayfair a few underground stops further south-west, and the newer Canary Wharf, three miles east along the Thames, which hosts the over-spill from the overloaded Square Mile. Neither of these upstarts, nor other small financial centres in places like Edinburgh or Leeds, are real rivals to the Square Mile.

Early on weekday mornings, waves of humanity flow into Liverpool Street Station then ebb again in the evenings as they return to dormitory suburbs cross London and beyond. By nightfall most of the City's 350,000-odd workforce – four-fifths employed in financial services – has left, leaving fewer than 9,000 resident souls, plus security guards, cleaners and night workers. Move eastwards from the City into Spitalfields and the tidy, well-kept streets suddenly give way to scruffier zones speckled with signs of real deprivation. The City is an island of wealth surrounded by historically poor areas.

London has more foreign banks than any other financial centre: by 2008 it accounted for half of all international trade in equities, nearly 45 per cent of over-the-counter derivatives turnover, 70 per cent of Eurobond turnover, 35 per cent of global currency trading and 55 per cent of all international public offerings.[6] New York is bigger in areas like securitisation, insurance, mergers and acquisitions, and asset management, but much of its business is domestic, making London the world's biggest international – and offshore – financial hub.

London was once the seat of the world's greatest empire, and expertise accumulated over centuries has clustered here. Its position in Europe between Asia and the United States and the English language are formidable advantages. Another source of power is its offshore structure. Since the 1950s financial services companies have flocked to

London because it lets them do what they cannot do at home. As we have seen, it was the creation of the unregulated offshore Euromarkets in London from the late 1950s onwards, which emerged exactly as Britain's formal empire collapsed, that created an escape route for US banks, and others, seeking to get around the burdens of New Deal regulation. When the US introduced the Sarbanes–Oxley regulations in 2002 to protect Americans against the likes of Enron and WorldCom, the City did nothing. Every Russian firm listing overseas chooses London not New York, partly because of Britain's permissive govern- ance standards.

'Even as the debris of [colonial] deconstruction went overboard,' wrote historians P. J. Cain and A. G. Hopkins, 'the gentlemen of the City had already changed course and were heading towards new horizons, where global opportunities – above the nation state and beyond empire – beckoned.'

The Big Bang of 1986 enhanced London's offshore status, as thrusting Americans muscled in, demanding stratospheric salaries, buying up British banks and shaking up the City's gentlemanly club of Old Etonians and landed lords in top hats. New City values penetrated rapidly into wider British society, and regulatory competition from 'light-touch London' became a crowbar for lobbyists around the globe: 'If we don't do this, the money will go to London,' they would cry, or, 'We can already do this in London, so why not here?' The City emitted anti-regulatory impulses around the world, deregulating other economies and their banking systems as if by remote control. The British empire, it seemed, had faked its own death.

Time and again, US banking catastrophes can be traced to those companies' London offices. The unit that blew up the insurance company American International Group (AIG), putting the US taxpayer on the hook for $182.5 billion, was its 400-strong financial products unit, based in London. In June 2008, as world oil prices soared amidst uproar about market manipulation, former regulator Michael Greenberger noted in testimony to a Senate committee that the US Commodity Futures Trading Committee (CFTC), the regulator for energy derivatives, had been pursuing a 'continuous charade that a US-owned exchange located in Atlanta and trading critically import- ant US-delivered energy products should be regulated by the United Kingdom, whose regulation of these markets is self-evidently lacking'.[7] The court-appointed examiner looking into the collapse of Lehman Brothers in September 2008 found it had used a trick called Repo 105 to shift $50 billion in assets off its balance sheet, and that while no US law firm would sign off on the transactions, a major law firm in London was delighted to oblige.[8] Three-quarters of US *Fortune 500* companies, and all of its big banks, have London offices today.[9]

Yet another attraction is secrecy. Britain does not follow the Swiss approach to bank secrecy, which makes its violation a criminal offence, it uses other mechanisms. Denis MacShane, a former UK Foreign Office minister, remembers criticising bank secrecy at a European seminar. His opposite number from Luxembourg, he said, 'turned and gently asked, "Have you ever examined UK trust law? All our bankers and financial lawyers say that if you really, really want to hide money, go to London and set up a trust."'[10] Under UK law offshore companies can be directors of UK companies; it is usually impossible to know who the real owners are.[11]

Having gone out of its way to welcome wealthy Arabs in the 1980s and rich Japanese and oil-rich Africans in the 1990s, the City has more recently, with the help of conduit havens like Cyprus, aggressively courted Russian oligarchs, providing them with bolt-holes beyond the reach of Russian law enforcement. By April 2008 a hundred companies from the former Soviet Union's Commonwealth of Independent States (CIS) were listed on the London stock exchange, which had hosted trading in almost US$950 billion in securities from CIS-based companies.[12] Some 300,000 Russians live in London; Russians own top UK football clubs; and one, Alexander Lebedev, owns the *London Evening Standard* and *Independent* newspapers. Many others are attracted by Britain's lax tax laws and the City culture of 'Don't ask, don't tell'. In February 2010 Alexander Zvygintsev, Russia's deputy prosecutor-general, said that 'Londongrad', as it is sometimes known, was 'a giant launderette for laundering criminally sourced funds'.[13]

In January 2009 US law enforcement fined the British bank Lloyds TSB $350 million after it admitted secretly channelling Iranian and Sudanese money into the American banking system. Robert Morgenthau, the Manhattan district attorney, explained how Lloyds would routinely strip out identifying features from payments from Iran so that wire transfers would pass undetected through filters at

US financial institutions.[14] The US has a long tradition – even if it has been little in evidence of late – of sending bankers to jail and cracking down on banks after scandals. Britain is different. 'In this country bankers don't go to jail,' said political writer Robin Ramsay. 'Someone threw an egg at [top banker] Fred Goodwin's house. That's it. There are no consequences in London.' Paris-based investigating magistrate Eva Joly summarised the overseas view: 'the City of London, that state within a state which has never transmitted even the smallest piece of usable evidence to a foreign magistrate'.

London's next offshore attraction is its so-called domicile rule. The concept of domicile was originally developed to help colonials identify themselves wherever in the empire they lived. An English colonial administrator in India would be *resident* in India, but *domiciled* in England. England was their 'natural' home, and they were subject to English law. An Indian in London, by contrast, would remain domiciled in India, and never fully British. In 1914 the tax rules were twisted to let those resident but not domiciled in England escape tax on their worldwide income – they would only be taxed on what was actually earned in Britain. A rule originally created to discriminate against foreigners now discriminated against ordinary British residents.[15] And that is essentially the situation today. A 'non-dom' hedge fund owner can make sure all his income is booked outside Britain and escape tax on it.

About 60,000 non-doms live in the UK now, including Greek shipping magnates, Russian oligarch football club owners, Saudi princesses and the Indian steel magnate Lakshmi Mittal, many of whom pay very low taxes. Just to add another layer of absurdity to the system, many resident non-domiciles were born in this country, including Lord Ashcroft. Born in Sussex and a member of the House of Lords, his heart belongs to Belize, at least for tax purposes.

In 2006 a *Sunday Times* investigation found that the UK's fifty-four billionaires living in Britain, not all non-doms, paid income tax totalling just £14.7 million on their estimated £126 billion combined fortunes – and two-thirds of that was paid by inventor James Dyson – a real entrepreneur, who makes vacuum cleaners.[16] Had they earned, say, 7 per cent on those assets and paid 40 per cent income tax, they would have paid over $3.5 billion in tax – about 250 times more. The celebrity entrepreneur Sir Richard Branson – who owns his business empire through a maze of offshore trusts and companies, said in 2002 that his company would be half its size if he hadn't legally avoided tax via offshore structures.[17] The British media treats Branson with awe.

The City plays another curious, quasi-offshore role in the global economy: many institutions that regulate or influence global commerce are located here. Yards from the lord mayor's Mansion House sits a modernist wedge-shaped building looking like a glass-covered cruise liner on stilts. This is the headquarters of the International Accounting Standards Board (IASB), which sets the rules for how companies around the world publish their financial data. Over one hundred countries use its standards, and the US is currently converging its standards with the IASB's. Its rules let multinational corporations scoop up all their results from different countries and consolidate them into a single figure, perhaps broken down by region. A corporation might publish its total profits from, say, Africa, but there is no way to unpick the numbers to work out the profits in each country. Given that over 60 per cent of world trade happens inside multinational corporations, this is massive opacity. Essential information about trillions of dollars' worth of cross-border flows simply disappears from view. Under IASB rules you often cannot even find out who really owns a lot of companies, and as multinationals become ever more complex, this problem just gets worse.

Richard Murphy, a chartered accountant who has done more than anyone to put this onto the public agenda, describes the problem in a nutshell. 'A company gets its licence to operate in any territory from the government that represents those people. It has a corporate duty to account in return. This is the essence of stewardship and accountability, concepts that the IASB has deliberately forgotten. Instead we have companies pretending they float above all these countries. They don't.' If the IASB made multinationals break their financial information down by country and disclose what they do everywhere they operate, this would vastly increase the transparency of markets, informing investors about where their money was being used, helping governments understand how they were being fleeced through offshore strategies and how competitive markets were being distorted, helping citizens understand who is really operating in their countries, and giving economists a treasure trove of new information to help them understand how international markets work.[18]

The IASB is not a public rule-setting body, accountable to demo-cratic parliaments; it is a private company registered in Delaware, financed by the big four accountancy firms and some of the world's biggest multinationals. This is an example of what Professor Prem Sikka of Essex University calls the privatisation of public policymaking. Through the IASB, hosted by the City of London Corporation, these giant businesses write their own disclosure rules. Armies of citizens have marched against Standard Oil, ExxonMobil, Union Carbide, WalMart, Halliburton, Fox News, McDonald's, and so on, yet who ever marched against the IASB?

But the City's biggest role in the global offshore system is in its relationship with running Britain's spider's web. In the second quarter of 2009 the UK received net financing of US$332.5 billion just from its three Crown Dependencies Jersey, Guernsey and the Isle of Man.[19] In June 2009 the web as a whole held an estimated US$3.2 trillion in offshore bank deposits, about 55 per cent of the global total, according to data from the Bank for International Settlements – and that is just bank deposits. Remember, this British offshore web provides the City with three things. First, the tax havens scattered across the world capture passing foreign business and channel it to London just as a spider's web catches insects; second, it is a storage mechanism for assets; and third, it is a money-laundering filter that lets the City get involved in dirty business while providing it with enough distance to maintain plausible deniability.

But to return to the very peculiar City of London Corporation. You could read every page on its website for days, and still not find a satis-factory answer to the question 'What *is* it?' except that the Corporation is the local government of the Square Mile. Consequently, it is often ignored.

The first odd thing about the Corporation is something it admits freely: it is 'committed to maintaining and enhancing the status of the City as the world's leading international financial and business centre . . . and to establish contact with decision-makers and people of influ-ence worldwide.' The Corporation's head is the Lord Mayor of London, not to be confused with the mayor of London who heads the much larger Greater London municipality, containing the tiny City but with no jurisdiction over its non-municipal affairs. 'The Lord Mayor's principal role today is ambassador for all UK-based financial and profes-sional services,' the Corporation states, 'in private meetings and speeches, the Lord Mayor expounds the values of liberalisation.'[20]

An official City report into one such occasion gives a flavour of the institution's ambition and reach.[21] The lord mayor, then a former head of PricewaterhouseCooper's China office, visited Hong Kong, China and South Korea in October 2007, accompanied by the lady mayoress, the sheriff and his wife, and a forty-strong business delegation. The aim of the visit, during China's 17th National Party Congress, the City report said, was to:

- Lobby for China to maintain its course of economic and financial liber-alisation, and encourage South Korea to adopt more open policies.
- Promote London as a global financial centre offering world class finan-cial and business services.
- Explain the UK's liberal approach to regulation and corporate governance . . . lobby for liberalisation and improved market access in China's banking, insurance and capital markets sectors; including highlighting the restrict-ive implications of Ordinance 10 [which is designed to curb illicit finan-cial flows and requires Chinese government approval for companies to list overseas][22] and the benefits of closer engagement with international players.
- Encourage South Korea to adopt more liberal policies, notably in legal services, and to follow up on Seoul's ambitions to become a regional financial hub.
- Explain the UK's liberal approach to trade policy and regulation; and to encourage a critical mass of similarly thinking countries.

The City's messages 'were clearly heard and appreciated at a high level in all our Chinese destinations,' the report said, 'not least London's emergence as the world's leading global financial centre'. In a meeting with senior officials from Tianjin, the Chinese city chosen as a pilot for national financial reform, Mayor Dai Xianglong 'placed great value on deepening cooperation with the City of London, which he dubbed "the holy place" of international finance and globalisation'.

This is a municipal authority for fewer than 9,000 souls whose job is, *officially,* not only to protect and promote the City's financial services, but also to promote financial freedom and liberalisation, *and* to fight these battles around the world. The global deregulatory impulses from London's light-touch regulation are complemented by active lobbying. The Corporation is perhaps one of the most potent players in global financial regulation. Few have noticed. Through myriad subtle levers and influences, it exerts an invisible influence on Britain's financial regulators and politicians. Stuart Fraser, chairman of the City's powerful Policy and Resources Committee, asserted in 2010 that he is probably the most effective lobbyist in Britain.[23]

Among many other things, the City is a powerful coordinating force for financial services. Labour MP John McDonnell is one of very few politicians to have confronted directly the Corporation's potent lobby in parliament. 'The City Corporation is a good example of a formalised network of old boys,' McDonnell said. 'When the port comes around, they decide on who goes where in the City, and this spills out into other networks.' When British Chancellor Alistair Darling introduced a bankers' bonus tax into the pre-budget report in 2009, he felt the force of this lobby. 'I received lots of calls, actually, from lots of bankers, and curiously they appeared to be speaking from one script,' Darling said. 'They didn't like it – of course they didn't. They said this was causing them to think long and hard about London and all the rest of it.'[24]

The Corporation shapes and sustains a consensus in favour of the financial interest. It seeks to influence legislation at home and abroad. The Corporation's fingerprints are all over the Financial Services and Markets Act of 2001, which declared that Britain's then regulator, the Financial Services Authority, should not 'discourage the launch of new financial products', that it must avoid 'erecting regulatory barriers' and 'avoid damaging the UK's competitiveness'. Yet even this doesn't quite capture what is going on. For if you delve deeply enough, as Taylor and Glasman did, you find that the Corporation is so ancient and mystifying that barely any outsiders understand it.

The Corporation's website is a warren of tunnelling links and un-expected connections. There are the 108 livery companies, dating back a thousand years, which include the Worshipful Companies of Broderers and Cordwainers (the current Lord Mayor, Nick Anstee, is an honorary liveryman of the Plaisterers' Company).[25] Then there are the offices and officers of government: you will find sheriffs, aldermen, the Court of Common Council and 'Rules for the Conduct of Life'.

The Lord Mayor's Show, replete with gilded coaches, elderly men in long satin robes and much arcane ritual, happens every November, watched by half a million people on the streets of London and millions more on the BBC. The world's oldest civic procession, the show is 800 years old: it was referenced by Shakespeare, and was the first event ever broadcast on live television. Over 6,000 people worked on the 2010 show.

Over centuries the Corporation has carved out for itself a political domain that lies to a fair degree outside the laws and democratic institutions of the rest of Britain. Like the best social silences, this is not exactly secret; the outlines are there if you know where to look.

The City of London has existed since what some City tour guides call missed time or, as some historians put it, time immemorial – a term taken to mean that its origins extend beyond the reach of memory, record or tradition – or, more precisely, before King Richard I was crowned in 1189. There is no direct evidence, Corporation executives note, of the Corporation actually coming into existence. Corporation spokesmen say, only half in jest, that the City dates its 'modern period' from 1067. 'The City of London is the oldest continuous municipal democracy in the world,' the Corporation boasts. It predates parliament and its constitution 'is rooted in the ancient rights and privileges enjoyed by citizens before the Norman Conquest in 1066'.

If something dates from time immemorial, Glasman says, then it is outside the normal legislative remit. The City's powers have waxed and waned over the centuries but overall it has remained a political fortress withstanding tides of history that have transformed the rest of the British nation state. Its special privileges stem ultimately from the power of financial capital. Britain's rulers have needed the City's money and given the City what it wants in exchange. The Corporation itself hints at this:

The right of the City to run its own affairs was gradually won as concessions were gained from the Crown. London's importance as a centre of trade, population and wealth secured it rights and liberties earlier than other towns and cities. From medieval to Stuart times the City was the major source of financial loans to monarchs, who sought funds to support their policies at home and abroad.[26]

Britain's entire political system derives, in a sense, from the City of London Corporation. The House of Lords – its parliamentary upper house, filled with elderly worthies – was originally modeled on the City's Court of Aldermen (elder men); the House of Commons, the lower house, was based on the City's Court of Common Council. The prime minister's office was strongly modelled on the office of the lord mayor, elected by the Court of Common Council, which refers to itself as the Grandmother of Parliaments. 'The City still acts as a state within a state,' Glasman continued. 'There are, in effect, two Cities called London. One is a real City; the other place called London is home to eight million people.' Each year the chancellor speaks at the Guildhall and the lord mayor's Mansion House, where he is expected to justify how he has been serving the interests of finance.

Modern Britain has no written constitution but some historians talk of an ancient constitution involving old rights, privileges and liberties. This is a way of talking about spheres of power and influence and the ebb and flow of relationships between different pillars of the realm over the centuries. Glasman describes four pillars of the ancient constitution: the King as its head, the Church as its soul, the parliament as the country and the City as the money – only subordinate to the Crown and parliament up to a limited point, intertwined with them in complex relationships. When William the Conqueror invaded England in 1066 and the rest of the country gave up its rights, the City kept its freehold property, ancient liberties, and its own self-organising militias – even the King had to disarm when entering the City.[27] When William commissioned the Domesday Book – a survey of the kingdom's assets and revenues that determined taxation – the City of London was excluded.[28]

At the Protestant Reformation 500 years later, the English Church became subject to the Crown, and in the centuries that followed, the power of the monarch declined, parliament steadily lost its aristocratic character and broadened the suffrage to include almost all adults. But the City kept its privileges. It was, a nineteenth-century reformer said, 'like some prehistoric monster which had mysteriously survived into the modern world'. Monarchs, firebrands and demagogues who tried to roll back the City's special rights and privileges had occasional successes, but most came to a sticky end, and the City vigorously reasserted its rights afterwards. You can see one such sticky end on a guided tour of the Mansion House, the lord mayor's elegant Georgian town palace just across the road junction from the Bank of England on Threadneedle Street. Inside, a magnificent triumphalist stained-glass window depicts William Walworth, lord mayor of London, slashing to death Wat Tyler, leader of the Peasants' Revolt in 1381.

King Henry VIII's powerful adviser Cardinal Wolsey enraged the City by introducing progressive taxation and forcing the nobility to cough up large 'benevolences,' even taking all the armour and plate of the City's livery companies. The City helped engineer Wolsey's demise in 1529 with accusations such as 'he having the French pox presumed to come and breath on the king'. The City never forgot that, and in 1571 instituted the post of city remembrancer to remind the King of his debt. The remembrancer, the world's oldest institutional lobbyist, remains a potent force in the British state today, 'a conduit between Parliament and the City'.[29] The only non-parliamentary person allowed into the Commons chamber, he sits unobtrusively facing the speaker, and his role is to have 'day to day contact with officials in government departments responsible for developing government policy, the drafting and promotion of legislation and responsibility for relations with both Houses of Parliament and their Committees'. The remembrancer, currently a man named Paul Double, is charged 'with maintaining and enhancing the City's status and ensuring that its established rights are safeguarded'.[30] A previous remembrancer boasted that his operating principle was to 'oppose every bill which would interfere with the rights and privileges enjoyed by the Corporation'. At the time of writing in 2010 its most recent public memoranda included one arguing against European efforts to rein in the activities of hedge funds,[31] and another largely seeking to absolve over-the-counter derivatives of helping to cause the financial crisis and arguing against severe restrictions on them.[32] True to the City's offshore status, the remembrancer's office has a major international role too. It deals with the City's diplomatic corps, and collaborates closely with the royal household on state banquets and dinners to honour visiting heads of state and government.

Glasman remembers once visiting the Guildhall Library to ask for the City of London's charter. A charter is a grant of authority by a sovereign power and is the means by which cities, corporations and other artificial bodies are created. Charters transform mere collections of individuals into self-governing institutions. The body that grants the charter is implicitly superior to the recipient, so a chartered city, for example, is subservient to the nation state. Glasman remembers the Guildhall librarian chuckling at his question. 'No, there isn't one,' the librarian said. 'It was a great moment,' Glasman said. 'And I thought, "Well, that's my career sorted out."' Without a charter, the City stands in a state of permanent ambiguity relative to the British constitution.[33] As with gravity, you can only see its true nature in the effects it has on the bodies around it.

Sitting in his cluttered north London kitchen, Glasman pulled out quotation after quotation to illustrate how the City has carved out for itself privilege after privilege, in order to ensure the rules governing the rest of Britain stop at the City borders. The Statute of William and Mary from 1690, for example, 'confirming the Privileges of the Corporation,' states:

All the charters, grants, letters patents, and commissions touching or concerning any of their liberties or franchises, or the liberties, privileges, franchises, immunities, lands, tenements and hereditaments, rights, titles, or estates of the mayor and commonalty and citizens of the City of London, made or granted to any person or persons whatsoever . . . be and are hereby declared and adjudged null and void to all intents.

Plenty of law made in Westminster applies to the Corporation, but many acts of parliament specifically exempt it, either fully or in part. Hence the City is connected to the British nation state but remains a constitutional elsewhere. In this the City resembles Jersey or the Cayman Islands, the offshore jurisdictions that are its satellites. For skittish global capital, this matters. Any challenge to the City faces the mystique of history and the extravagant skills and powers of the many servants of finance. This globe-encompassing futuristic financial services centre, whose influence reaches silently into people's homes from Baltimore via Birmingham to Borneo, is founded upon an ancient constitutional platform that seems as impregnable as it is unique.

The City's flamboyant ceremonies are not just colourful relics; they impress and reassure the City's friends and allies in part because so few appreciate their meaning, and they reinforce the City's power. As an old Corporation handbook states, these ceremonies 'are not idle forms or shows put on merely for entertainment. They embody and make visible rights and privileges.' In 1884, the year reformers introduced a bill to merge the City with Greater London, the Lord Mayor's Show was, as a City researcher described it, 'the single most magnificent and politically charged Show to be staged to date'.[34] The biggest banner read LONDON WOULD NOT BE LONDON WITHOUT THE LORD MAYOR'S SHOW – implying, of course, that London would not be London without an unreformed City. Servants were removed from the Guildhall banquet to make room for more politicians; a City slush fund brought people in from the provinces to protest at public meetings on the bill; and a smear campaign was launched against the 'deluded dupes'[35] who led the reform movement. The reform was shelved.

This was not the first time reform had been tried. In the seventeenth century London received tens of thousands of rural refugees from brutal land reforms known as the enclosures, and the Crown asked the Corporation to extend its ancient legal protections and privileges to new areas of London. The Corporation refused, and instead shipped its excess population off to the Ulster Plantation and the Corporation of Londonderry in what is now Northern Ireland,[36] establishing a large Protestant community there. Glasman calls this the 'great refusal', the moment the City turned its back on England and when London history properly became a tale of two cities.

There is a mayor and a lord mayor precisely because London is two cities: a large, vibrant and troubled population centre plus a supremely wealthy offshore island in its midst. The people of London lack a unitary municipal authority while business, particularly finance, has the most ancient political institution in the kingdom at its disposal.

Glasman works with London Citizens, a network of 140-odd London civic and faith groups seeking to improve London's political governance and community organisation, substantially inspired by the Chicago-based community organisers from whom Barack Obama learned about political organisation. Neil Jameson, London Citizens' executive director, contacted the City Corporation after the 2007 financial crisis erupted. 'We were looking into the causes of the crisis, and all the roads seemed to lead to our neighbours, whom we didn't know much about,' he said. The Corporation was rather stand-offish. 'My first impression was an attitude of "We don't mind giving you money, but a relationship is pushing it."' Jameson was irked that while the lord mayor travelled the globe representing the City, he was ignoring a large and deep-rooted London civic organisation representing London's citizens. He invited the Corporation to a London Citizens event in 2009, and its strange, stilted reply illustrates the Corporation's almost allergic stance towards ordinary Londoners. 'We welcome London Citizens as we welcome any group,' it said. '"Formal visit" has no meaning in this respect . . . for the avoidance of doubt, this does not mean any form of recognition or negotiation.'

A relationship of sorts has emerged, but Corporation officials regularly walk out of meetings only to reappear minutes later, and when London Citizens issued calls for a living wage for cooks, cleaners and other workers in the City, a 20 per cent cap on interest rates and the use of City resources for affordable housing in London, the Corporation complained it had been 'ambushed'.

Back in the eighteenth century the City lobbied ferociously against war with the rebellious colonies in America, warning against inflicting 'a deep and perhaps fatal wound to commerce and . . . the principle of liberty'.[37] The King expressed 'utmost astonishment that any of his subjects should be capable of encouraging the rebellious spirit . . . in North America'. When American independence was declared, the official City record reports that 'the news was received in the City with the greatest joy'. When the state press-ganged civilians into the navy as it prepared for war with France, the lord mayor boasted that 'the press gangs did not dare enter the City'.[38]

In 1917, as working class men died in the fields of France, Herbert Morrison, secretary of the fledgling London Labour Party, captured a renewed mood for reform. 'Is it not time London faced up to the pretentious buffoonery of the City of London Corporation and wipe it off the municipal map?' he asked. 'The City is now a square mile of entrenched reaction, the home of the devilry of modern finance and that journalistic abortion, the stunt press. The City is an administrative anachronism.'[39] For much of the last century the Labour Party, the party of Britain's working class, had a pledge in its manifesto to abolish the Corporation and fold it into a unified London government. 'The traditional Labour position,' Labour MP John McDonnell told me, 'was to control the finances of the country in the long-term interests of its people.'

After the Great Depression, and the spilling of more working men's blood in the Second World War, a fearsome new public mood was abroad, almost unique in British history. 'The British State,' Glasman wrote, 'for the first and only time in its history adopted a substantive idea of the economy and subordinated the fiscal economy to needs.' Prime Minister Clement Attlee, true to the Labour Party manifesto, made no secret of his goal.

Over and over again we have seen that there is in this country another power than that which has its seat at Westminster. The City of London, a convenient term for a collection of financial interests, is able to assert itself against the Government of the country. Those who control money can pursue a policy at home and abroad contrary to that which has been decided by the people. The first step in the transfer of this power is the conversion of the Bank of England into a State institution.[40]

The Bank of England was set up in 1694 as a private institution capitalised by wealthy Protestant City interests, in large part to provide credit for building the navy. The emergence of the bank and the creation of the national debt ushered in a financial revolution that led quite quickly to the emergence of mortgage markets, Lloyds insurance, a stock exchange, a financial press and the rapid expansion of overseas trade. The financial sector constituted what P. J. Cain and A. G. Hopkins called the 'governor of the Imperial engine'.

Attlee got his wish: the Bank of England was finally nationalised in 1946. Yet even this apparent victory was not all it seemed, for the bank had powerful cards to play: not only its control over the nation's money, but also the Attlee government's commitment to empire. As writer Gary Burn explained, this commitment 'ensured that sterling's international role became the single most defining economic project of the immediate post-war era'. In the end, nationalisation was a mirage. The bank continued to be run by essentially the same court of Old Etonian merchant bankers, and, as the bank itself admits, the act that nationalised it made 'no mention whatsoever' of the bank's role or purpose.[41] The government got powers to issue 'directions' to the bank, but admitted in 2010 that 'thus far, the power has not been used'.[42] As *The Economist* said soon after nationalisation, 'The nationalised bank of 1946 will not differ in any fundamental way from the privately owned bank of 1945.'[43] This marked the full extent of efforts to restrain the financial interest.

Attlee and Morrison failed to unify London; the pro-City Conservative Party returned to power in 1951; and the subsequent royal commission of 1957, which sparked a big shake-up of local government across Britain, opens with the memorable words: 'Logic has its limits and the position of the City lies outside them.'[44] By 1963, as the empire faded and Eurodollar's bigger bang was reinvigorating the City, the bank was so firmly on top that Lord Cromer, the Bank of England's governor, forced new Prime Minister Harold Wilson to throw away half his election promises and slash government spending. Wilson reacted furiously, shouting on one occasion, 'Who is prime minister of this country, Mr Governor, you or me?'[45]

In 1965 it was not the Corporation but the far bigger London County Council which got abolished. Another effort was launched in parliament in 1981 to abolish the City and 'give the City of London the same type of democratic local government which the rest of the country has had for many years'.[46] It was thwarted. By then, Margaret Thatcher was prime minister, and almost the entire political class was losing faith in manufacturing and genuflecting towards the City. Everything was for sale: school playing fields, telephone companies, railways and marketplaces. The City was at the forefront of a global trend of financialisation: the re-engineering of manufacturing firms as highly leveraged investment vehicles and, soon, the packaging of mortgages into assetbacked securities for trading on global markets.

The Bank of England, like other financial regulators, answers to parliament, not to the Corporation, but its physical location at the centre of the City reflects where its heart lies. It shares the City's view, established over centuries, that the path to progress lies in deregulation and freedom for financial capital, with the City at the forefront. In 1991 the bank's directors decided to work out more explicitly what the bank is *for*, and they came up with three main aims. Two were the usual central bankers' goals: to protect the currency and to keep the financial system stable. The third is, as governor Eddie George put it, to 'ensure the effectiveness of the United Kingdom's financial services' and advance a financial system 'which enhances the international competitive position of the City of London and other UK financial centres'.[47] That word 'competitive' strongly suggests a mission to promote the UK as an offshore centre.

This policy to promote and protect the City as an offshore centre is a kind of industrial policy: antithetical to the free market principles the City and its supporters claim to represent. Meanwhile Glasman is infuriated that a vital, wealthy part of the city he loves – this exuberant English melting pot that welcomed his refugee grandparents – has been substantially roped off, outside civic government. Like the earlier reformers, he and Taylor want to see the City Corporation merged into the rest of London, where among other things its formidable assets could be put to good use tackling poverty.

Political theory has great difficulty noticing the Corporation, let alone appreciating its significance. Mainstream modern publications about the City gloss over its free-floating status.[48] Political theorists know that every other power form has been subordinated to the state, and it is easy to assume that capital became dominant by acting within the state, rather than outside it. Marxists, primed not to be too concerned about how financial capital organises itself, mainly consider the City in the context of a broader clash between manufacturing and financial capital. The followers of philosopher John Rawls have focused on the social compact – the relationship between rulers and ruled – but have paid relatively little attention to the role of institutions or history. Globalisation has led to whole fields of research into the actions and interactions of economic actors in markets, but political institutions are usually discussed only at an abstract level. Much research has explored the role of corporations, but corporations get their licence to operate from the state – they are creatures of state power. The City of London Corporation is something else. It may be the grandmother of parliaments. It is most certainly the granddaddy of old boy networks.

With its politics of personal proximity, its bonds of shared identity and principle, and its elaborate ceremonial, the City manages to be at once vastly powerful and barely visible. It is, in Glasman's words, 'an ancient and very small intimate relational institution, which doesn't fit into anybody's preconceived paradigm of modernity. Here is a medieval commune representing capital. It just does not compute.'

* * *

As Glasman and Taylor tangled with the Spitalfields developers they stumbled across another odd thing. The City is divided into twenty-five subdivisions, or wards, only four of which have a resident population to speak of; the rest is mostly commercial real estate. Through his contacts Taylor discovered that a developer was negotiating to buy the land under a primary school in Portsoken, the poorest of the City's four residential wards, and to close the school. So he decided to stand for the ward elections in December 2001, to campaign against the closure. This, he discovered, was the only contested election in all of the City; every other candidate in the elections that year was unopposed. Ahead of the election, some City councillors asked him to stand down – in fact, they told the electoral officer that he *had* stood down. Yet he stood his ground, and the Portsoken residents elected him.

As Taylor, with Glasman's help, enquired into the City's electoral practices, they discovered a private member's bill passing through the House of Commons, almost entirely ignored by the news media.

One might have expected the election in 1997 of the Labour Party, Britain's bulwark of the left since the 1920s, to usher in a new, more confrontational era for the City and its offshore satellites. Blair's incoming chancellor Gordon Brown had promised in 1993 to 'end the tax abuses which reach to the heart of our public finances by indulging the super-rich at the expense of all the rest of us . . . a Labour chancellor will not permit tax reliefs to millionaires in offshore tax havens.' Yet in 1992, ahead of the previous general election, Labour leader John Smith had launched the so-called Prawn Cocktail Offensive – a tour of City dining rooms to persuade the captains of finance to accept a new Labour government. Michael Heseltine of the ruling Consevative Party mocked Smith's subservient approach. 'The right honourable and learned gentleman has become a star attraction in the City,' Heseltine said. 'Lunch after lunch, dinner after dinner, the assurances flow. Not a discordant crumb falls on to the thick pile . . . All those prawn cocktails for nothing. Never have so many crustaceans died in vain.'

Soon afterwards, Labour suffered its fourth consecutive defeat since Margaret Thatcher's election in 1979, and Smith died of a heart attack in 1994. His replacement, Tony Blair, finally transformed the Labour Party into an institution that the City could learn to love. In this work Blair was ably assisted by Herbert Morrison's grandson Peter Mandelson. In 1996 Blair quietly dropped Labour's decades old pledge to abolish the Corporation of London, replacing it with a vague promise to 'reform' the City. Few people in Britain even noticed the capture of Britain's last major bastion of real opposition to the financial sector.[49] When Blair was elected the following year by a landslide, the Corporation could rest assured that its position was safe.

Michael Cassidy, then chairman of the Corporation's powerful Policy and Resources Committee, explained Blair's approach as 'A two-way deal: Labour are naturally keen to get closer to the Corporation.'[50] Labour MP John McDonnell described what it looked like from inside the party:

You have been eighteen years in opposition and you are desperate to get into power, no matter what. Blair and Brown made a Faustian pact to give the City its head. The idea was to let them do their profiteering and just take the tax benefit. It was not a relationship on our terms; it was simply 'Give them what they want.' I don't think Brown understood what he was doing. It was simply a whizzo scheme to stabilise their government.

Not only that, but the Labour Party's proposed 'reform' – that private members' bill Taylor and Glasman had noticed – was no compromise but an astonishing capitulation to the Corporation of London. On the face of it the bill was a non-event: it merely streamlined and shook up voting rights in the Court of Common Council, the Corporation's municipal governing body.[51] Yet behind this lay an extraordinary fact. While the City's 9,000-odd human residents had one vote each, businesses in the City could vote too, with 23,000 votes between them. The corporations could easily outvote the human beings.

Blair's reform proposed to dilute the power of the residents even further. They would still get their 9,000 votes, but the business vote would be expanded to 32,000, giving the companies, as the *Guardian* noted, 'carte blanche to run the City'. Businesses would be assigned voting rights according to how many employees they had but without any requirement to take their workers' wishes into account. Management – representing the money –would be voting, not ordinary employees.[52] Thus Goldman Sachs, the Bank of China, Moscow Narodny Bank and KPMG have been voting in British elections. Glasman consulted several academics to find out if they knew of anything resembling this elsewhere: other examples of 'a workforce with no civic personality', as he put it. The response he got was invariably one of puzzlement. 'Nobody knew what the fuck I was talking about,' Glasman remembers.

Just as Switzerland's system of *concordance* has emasculated potential political opposition there, and Jersey's no-party politics embeds the dominant view of a political elite captured by the interests of finance, so the Corporation of London has institutionalised the death of opposition politics in the City.

In May 2002 Taylor lodged a petition against the City reform bill, and in October 2002 this was heard by the Law Lords, the highest court in the land. Taylor and Glasman were summoned to present their case.[53] Nobody supported them except a few MPs[54] like John McDonnell, who had fought a lonely rearguard action against the bill in parliament, helping delay it for four years. He remembers putting in amendment after amendment to slow it down. He was offered a post on the Northern Ireland Select Committee – something they knew he had long coveted – if he would drop his opposition. He refused. Tony Benn was one of their few supporters.[55] 'We are considering a corrupt proposal,' Benn said in an earlier debate. 'We are being asked to legalise the buying of votes for political purposes.' The City of London, he said, 'is an offshore island moored in the Thames, with a freedom that many other offshore islands would be glad to have'.[56]

Glasman described the scene as he and Taylor faced the Law Lords, confronted by serried ranks of scriveners, aldermen, recorders, barristers and other representatives of the City Corporation's pomp and might, all under the hawkish eye of the chair, Lord Jauncey of Tullichettle. Tom Simmons, the Corporation's chief executive, started proceedings by describing the Corporation's ancient majesty: how it was no ordinary local authority but a potent and self-funded lobbying network, able when necessary to draw on massive financial and political firepower, through corporations and their trade associations, and its own resources, to defend the privileges of the financial sector.

Not only the Labour Party, Simmons explained, but also Britain's third force, the Liberal Democrats, had dropped their pledges to abolish the City Corporation 'largely I think as a result of the good work that the Corporation was doing'. (The Conservative Party – the party of wealth and privilege – never made such a pledge, and at the time of writing is in a coalition government with the Liberal Democrats.) 'We employ consultants in Brussels to actually look out for things on the horizon which could impact on the City,' Simmons continued. 'When this arises we work with the various trade associations in the City to ensure somebody has picked up the baton and is running with it and that the City's views are properly represented. Just before a country assumes the presidency of the European Union, we normally visit the capital of that country to seek to build alliances so we can actively promote issues.' He spoke of the Policy and Resources Committee, whose head 'is prepared to take up cudgels on behalf of the City anywhere in the world on any subject which is of concern to the City'.

Then it was Taylor's and Glasman's turn to speak. Glasman made a long, complex presentation drawing out historical patterns, and exploring the nature of power, democracy and accountability. The only precedent he had been able to find for the City's system of corporate voting was, he said 'with the voting rights given to the owners of chattel [slaves and cattle] in the antebellum American South at the time of the American Revolution' – the 'slavery franchise', as he put it. At the very least, it should be the workers, not the companies, who voted.

He remembers Lord Jauncey turning to his colleagues and letting them know that this was a serious matter. 'They all started scurrying around,' Glasman said. 'Some left the room. They were passing pieces of paper to each other.' In the end, Taylor and Glasman's petition did not affect the thrust of the bill, which passed into law fairly intact. They could claim a small victory: the Law Lords demanded that the process for making voting appointments should be 'open and clear'.

Taylor's position as a City councillor gave him access to records that revealed something else. The City Corporation runs three special funds. One is the City Bridge Trust, which the City parades widely and which makes charitable donations worth around £15 million per year.[57] Then there is the City Fund, derived from rental and interest income plus money from central government, which covers the Corporation's day-to-day running costs as a municipal authority. The third fund is the interesting one: City Cash. The City admits it exists but will not say how much money is in it, saying only that it is 'a private fund built up over the last eight centuries' and that it earns income from 'property, supplemented by investment earnings'.[58] It has well over £100 million available to spend each year, presumably from income on its assets, but its accounts are opaque. The Corporation says its assets are worth about a billion pounds – three billion for all three funds – but it won't say what those assets are, so we can't check. It funds many things, including monuments and ceremonial – it funded the City Corporation's stake in the Spitalfields development and several other current projects outside the City boundaries.[59] It has also helped finance certain free-market think tanks. Its other big role is to finance lobbying around the globe, running permanently staffed operations from Brussels to Beijing.[60]

Glasman remembers first becoming aware of City Cash. 'I thought, "So what the fuck is this?"' he said. He rang them up to ask about the City's Cash. They said they would never give a full account of their assets, "because as a City established from time immemorial which has never been in debt, we are not required to give any public accounting."' Glasman was astonished. 'It was just "piss off – you don't know what you are dealing with." And I thought, "OK, now I am really going to get involved."'

Jason Beattie, an experienced political reporter from the *London Evening Standard*, also got interested. 'I smelt a rat,' Beattie said. 'The City with a vast property empire somewhere — and we don't know what they own?' He tried freedom of information (FOI) requests, a standard journalistic tool that forces reluctant British government departments to yield information. 'I FOI'd them to hell and I got nowhere,' Beattie remembers. And when he started asking questions, he encountered the biggest public relations team for a local authority he had ever came across. 'It was a very slick operation. It was clearly a fishing exercise. They wanted to know where I was coming from. After that, it was just rejecting, rejecting, rejecting my FOIs.' The Corporation's website reveals how it is able to do this. The FOI Act of 2000, it admits, 'applies to the City of London as a local authority, police authority and port health authority **only**' – emphasising the last word in bold.[61] In other words, everything is open to examination – except the money. Which is the part that matters.

Taylor found out some information, since being a common councillor gave him access to some of the books. 'I found this bizarre and fascinating . . . I was puzzled by the City driving all these changes on the City fringe with no real way to hold it to account.' After being rebuffed many times, he discovered that City Cash is vested in 'the Mayor and Commonalty and Citizens of London', though when he asked what this meant, he was told that 'valuable time and resources would be committed unnecessarily' to define what 'citizens' means. As to the details of the assets underlying the funds, he got little.

The Corporation admits to owning the Conduit Estate, covering some of the most valuable parts of London's West End, bordering the world-famous Regent and Oxford Streets.[62] Glasman said he had seen indications – nothing solid – that it also owns real estate holdings in New York, as well as property in Hong Kong and Sydney. The Corporation denies this, saying that City's Cash assets lie 'nearly all, if not entirely, within the UK.'

Taylor sees a big part of the City's power as its ability to dispense political patronage – a scholarship here, a subsidy or charitable donation there, or a choice position at the lord mayor's banquet, perhaps next to a visiting foreign president. Taylor would dress in a clerical frock coat and get invited to grand dinners and lunches with the likes of French President Nicolas Sarkozy and Brazil's Luis Inácio Lula da Silva. 'Don't underestimate the power of dinners and fine claret,' Taylor said. 'Being invited to these banquets will often settle down any revolutionary urges.' He recalled one occasion in February 2009, in the depths of the recent financial crisis, that showed him how hard it was, in the face of this ceremonial, to stand up and object. After each of the lord mayor's foreign visits the chief commoner ritually proposes a vote to congratulate him for a successful visit; the chairman of finance then seconds it and a show of hands in the Court of Common Council grants unanimous approval. When the lord mayor returned from a visit to the tax haven of Cyprus, Taylor opposed the vote of congratulations. He was the only member in living memory to do so.

'I said, "I am not persuaded that this is in the interests of the citizens of London. This system is causing chaos in the world,"' said Taylor. 'Somehow the oxygen went out of the room. People were sucking in air through their teeth. It reminded me that I had joined a club, not a political body.' He was taken aside and told he was being discourteous. 'They said, "This is not what we do in the City." I felt I was doing something naughty and shameful. But I felt compelled to do it. This was a consensus that needed to be interrupted.' He even had to force a correction to the minutes of the meeting, which claimed the vote had passed unanimously. Still, he rarely found people in the Corporation unpleasant. 'Only one or two people would spit at me, as it were,' he said. 'On the whole people were very genial and friendly. That's where it gets dangerous: you become part of it, then it's easier not to say anything.'

Taylor has spent years pondering the City of London Corporation – what it means, spiritually and theologically. Drawing on Walter Wink's notion that spirituality and evil are embedded in the structure of contemporary institutions, Taylor sees something more than human greed at work. 'We are in the grip of something quite demonic. Institutions keep it alive, and it's part of all of us. I see it as a demonic spirit.' He calls the spirit Griffin, the mythical creature which appears in many of the City's ceremonies.[63] 'It is a very intelligent demon,' he continued, 'a dangerous thing. I felt myself in personal danger at times.' I pressed Taylor on this, but he became reticent and sat quietly for a moment, apparently wrapped in his own thoughts. Then he ventured, 'Maybe some things are best not talked about. I do think that it is spiritually very dangerous: the Corporation of London is a very dangerous place. I don't want to say that so-and-so is evil. People who work there are not bad people. We're all part of it.'

Taylor also recognises another, very different side to the City: an honourable history of serving as a check to arbitrary royal powers. The City could stop monarchs and demagogues from riding roughshod over citizens' ancient liberties. Before the seventeenth century it was 'the custodian of the ancient liberties of the English people and the champion of common law against encroachment by the state', as Glasman puts it.

City officials are proud of this history, though they play it down too, for fear that the citizenry will notice. 'There is a sense they know exactly what they are, but they don't want anyone else to know,' Taylor said. This was brought home to him in 2002, when he was at the City's Guildhall Club for the Queen's golden jubilee. Assembled City dignitaries in top hats and frock coats were watching the royal procession on the BBC, waiting for the Queen to enter the City for a Guildhall luncheon. To enter the City the Queen waits at the City boundary for the lord mayor to accompany her before proceeding, a telling marker of the differences between the City and the rest of the country.

'We were just about to practise singing "For She's a Jolly Good Fellow"; we were going to sing this to her at lunch,' Taylor remembers. 'There is a shot of the Queen sitting at Temple Bar, waiting for the lord mayor. She didn't seem to be doing anything, just sitting there.' BBC commentator David Dimbleby remarked on how out of place this formality seemed in the modern world, and everyone in the Guildhall Club laughed. 'It said a lot to me,' said Taylor. 'Dimbleby was saying, "Isn't this extraordinary that the Queen has to wait?" and there was this great guffaw in the Guildhall Club. They were saying, "This is our little secret . . . don't you get it?" The City does have at its heart something very beautiful – this ancient story of the power of the citizenry within the ancient constitution, which flows through the memory of the City.'

I asked Taylor how he reconciled this beautiful side with his notion of a demonic spirit inside the same conceptual framework. He answered immediately. 'A demonic spirit is a fallen angel. That is the problem. It is not serving its intended purpose. It has become suborned to another purpose. In its ceremony the City continues to articulate the power of the citizenry but it has been completely taken over by the money men. I conceptualise the city not as an evil thing in itself, but as a thing that has become perverted from its true vocation.'

For me, this double personality hinges on the word 'freedom'. As John Maynard Keynes understood, freedom for financial capital can mean bondage for citizens and their democratic representatives. The deception, as practised by George W. Bush and so many others, is to pretend that the two freedoms that oppose each other are in fact the same thing. The City has fought viciously against encroachment on its liberties, yet the archives reveal no comparable concerns about the evils of the slave trade or the depredations of the East India Company. Liberty has meant the liberty to trade on terms satisfactory to the City. Over time, the defence of freedom has become the defence of freedom for the interests of money – against the interests of the rest of the country when necessary.

'Most painful for me is that the Church is not more engaged in this,' Taylor continued, broadening his focus to the modern global economy. 'They haven't understood the great dangers we face. The damage was done at the beginning of the modern world, and in the role the Church took in its relationship with capitalism and colonialism. It lost its balls, lost its mojo – it lost its ability to critique.'

His forthright views haven't, it seems, done him any favours. 'In another age he'd have risen far up the Church,' said Glasman. 'William discovered the City, and it drove the Church in London a bit potty. It caused mayhem to his career.' Taylor spent some time unemployed in London, finishing his doctorate, before finally getting a post in late 2009 as vicar of a small back-street parish in Hackney in north-east London, where he now works.

In 2005 Britain's then chancellor Gordon Brown introduced his Better Regulation plan, scorning the 'heavy hand' of regulation and exalting 'a million fewer inspections every year . . . a risk based approach to regulation to break down barriers holding enterprise back'.[64] Financial regulation would have 'not just a light touch but a limited touch'; this would 'move us a million miles away from the old assumption . . . that business, unregulated, will invariably act irresponsibly'. The new model of regulation can be applied, he continued, 'to the administration of tax'.[65] The light or limited touch now extends to official 'independent' commissions for reform, which are led by trusted members of City networks, operate under narrow terms of reference, and always end up advocating some tinkering – nothing more – to the status quo.

An official review in 2008 of the Crown Dependencies and Overseas Territories was led by Michael Foot, a former Bahamas central banker and chairman of a financial services company, the Promontory Financial Group, whose website boasts that its client roster includes 'banks of all sizes, securities firms, insurance companies, investment advisers, private equity firms, hedge funds, broker-dealers and exchanges – in short, financial companies of every stripe'. The Foot review was tasked with investigating 'the ability of each financial centre to weather the downturn and to remain competitive in the future'.[66] In other words, how to protect the British spider's web? At no point was the harm wreaked on the rest of the world taken seriously. Later, a British parliamentary committee to review the Crown Dependencies concluded that while their interests do sometimes conflict with Britain's, the mother country's duty to represent the Crown Dependencies internationally 'is just that: a duty and not an option'.[67]

When the government launched an inquiry in 2008 into the financial crisis, every single one of the team's twenty-one members had a background in financial services:[68] four were from the City Corporation itself, including the lord mayor and two former lord mayors. The review was led by Sir Winfried Bischoff, a former Citigroup chairman. This was like asking oil companies to decide how to regulate the oil industry, and it was hardly a surprise when the report recommended no real changes. 'This is finance reporting to finance,' said professor Karel Williams. 'In the old days when you had these reports – Macmillan in the 1930s, Radcliffe in the 1950s, Wilson in the 1970s – all these reports had a broad range of social constitutencies: industrial employers, trade unions, academics. All of this vanishes with Bischoff.'

Something profound has changed in Britain. 'Nobody is willing to take on the City,' said McDonnell, 'even now, after everything that has happened.'[69]

In 2009 the OECD published a detailed study examining so-called regulatory capture, where government regulators are taken over by sectional interests like banks. 'We found there was a huge number of connections of people who had gone through the revolving door to the banks and back again, with alarming speed,' said David Miller, who led the research. 'The biggest banks had the most concentrated connections, and the countries that had the biggest connections were the UK, the US and Switzerland.'[70]

To discover how far the City consensus has penetrated the British body politic, I sought out an insider. Through an intermediary I arranged to meet a senior officer of HM Revenue and Customs (HMRC), Britain's tax authorities, who was involved in taxing big corporations. We met in Pizza Express in central London.

'The policy used to be: try to tax offshore profits at the same rate as onshore so as not to encourage people to put business offshore,' he said. 'But in the last ten years this has been skewed hugely towards the multinationals.' After the Labour government came to power, the whole culture in HMRC changed. Taxpayers became 'customers'. HMRC used to assign a 'case director' to investigate multinationals; this is now a 'customer relationship manager' charged with building a happy connection. After a review in 2006, promising better 'customer service' and 'greater mutual respect and trust', average times spent on international investigations fell from thirty-seven to eighteen months.

'We used to have a priority to collect tax,' my informant said, 'now we have a priority to have a good relationship. We have got into a situation of persuading ourselves that it is a win-win to have businesses pay their taxes voluntarily, rather than have us take them to litigation.' A UK parliamentary committee in October 2008 found that a quarter of multinationals paid no corporation tax at all in 2005-2006. When we spoke in 2009, just 600 staff members in HMRC's Large Business Service were responsible for 700 groups of companies. Given that a big multinational can muster a hundred lawyers or more for one tax case, this is a true David and Goliath job. '[The big companies] won't give up without going to court,' my informant said wearily. 'And they will go to court every time.'

He described how businesses he was investigating went over his head if they thought he was trying too hard. Sometimes one of his superiors, he said, 'reaches down and gets involved in cases no one like that should ever get involved in'. This is a disaster for the integrity of the British state. Under the leadership of HMRC head Dave Hartnett, the culture shifted perceptibly. 'He knew that the best way to remain top dog is to make sure Gordon [Brown] doesn't get too many whinges from business at his breakfast meetings.'

The financial sector is especially hard to tax. Banks use their privileged offshore positions to avoid tax on themselves and to create, fund and sell tax-avoidance schemes to others. HMRC discovered one dividend stripping scheme, Dave Hartnett, HMRC head, said, that 'could have wiped out the whole corporate tax base in the UK for the financial sector'.[71] The Wall Street Journal reported, for example, on a company set up in 2003, co-owned by Barclays PLC and Wachovia Bank in the US. It had no employees, no products and no customers, just a mailing address in Delaware.[72] This company did pay British taxes – but then the co-owners found a legal way to claim to each of their home tax authorities that they had paid all the tax themselves.[73] Barclays PLC had 315 tax haven subsidiaries in April 2009.[74] Banks churn out arrangements like this – partnering with other companies and sharing the resulting tax advantages – routinely.

'All the tax breaks end up with the banks, or they lever the tax breaks to get a huge competitive advantage,' said Richard Brooks, a high-profile tax writer. 'Tax avoidance played a key part in generating the financial crisis,' he said. 'To put it simply, the securitisation vehicles, which were so profitable that banks couldn't generate enough of them, were often such good deals because of the tax avoidance central to them. It was a key part of cranking up the engine.'

The culture of tax avoidance permeated British society. An Oxford

University study found that only three of its business interviewees said they would worry about negative press coverage from avoiding corporation tax. 'It has become so normal within the banks and the accounting firms,' Brooks said. 'You do what it takes to avoid the tax. If it's about the rights of chickens, you will get celebrity chefs jumping on the problem; if it's about tax avoidance, nobody cares.' The consensus is now so widespread that Britain's tax authorities sold off nearly 600 of their own buildings in 2001 to a company, Mapeley, registered in Bermuda to avoid tax; the National Audit Office concluded eight years later that the deal would probably cost £570 million more than originally anticipated.[75] In 2009 it emerged that the government minister in charge of cracking down on corporate tax avoidance had set up a business in Bermuda to avoid tax.[76]

Then there is the Commonwealth Development Corporation (CDC), the former government-owned development finance agency set up sixty years ago to promote agriculture and industry and alleviate poverty in some of the poorest parts of the empire. Now partially privatised and renamed CDC Group plc, it is chaired by Richard Gillingwater, dean of the City of London's Cass Business School ('the intellectual hub of the City of London').[77] In 2004 it restructured itself, selling off a 60 per cent stake to a limited liability partnership for just £373,000. CDC now operates more like a fund of funds in the private equity market, and a parliamentary report in 2008 concluded that it had accumulated a £1.4 billion cash pile and remarked on its 'extraordinary levels of pay in a small publicly owned organisation charged with fighting poverty'. It said compliance with CDC's declared ethical business principles could not be verified; CDC had very high and rising administrative costs; it did not consult the development agency that owned it as it was supposed to do; and it was not reporting properly its non-financial information 'such as its contribution to reducing poverty'. Only 4 per cent of its resources were invested in small and medium-sized enterprises – which was its whole point. The report concluded, 'there is limited evidence of CDC's effects on poverty reduction'. At the last count, CDC had 78 subsidiaries in tax havens such as Mauritius, Bermuda and the British Virgin Islands.[78]

Paying tax should be at the centre of debates about corporate responsibility, but it is ignored. Lord Oakeshott of the Liberal Democrat Party noted in 2009, 'Too many boards right across Britain tick the green and diversity boxes, then reward their finance or tax director for cheating their customers, the taxpayer.'

The British supermarket giant Tesco illustrates another profoundly important facet of tax haven London. In April 2008 the *Guardian* wrote about Tesco's tax avoidance strategies. Reporting on tax avoidance is a massive, complex and costly job, and hardly sells newspapers, yet the *Guardian* went ahead. Unfortunately, it got parts of its story wrong, and Tesco launched a barrage of libel suits against the newspaper.[79]

English libel laws are among the comforts for those with dirty money who come to London. There is no constitutional protection here for free speech, like the First Amendment in the US; there is no defence in cases of high public interest; and unlike nearly everywhere else the burden of proof is deposited squarely on the shoulders of the defendant. An Oxford University study in 2008 revealed that libel litigation in England and Wales costs 140 times – yes, 140 times – the European average.[80] Of 154 libel proceedings identified in an official review in 2008, defendants won precisely zero.[81] Many true things have been self-censored from this book because of English libel laws; it is simply not worth risking my life savings and my family home. The libel laws, of course, suit the City's wealthy interests very nicely indeed. They are, in the words of commentator George Monbiot, 'a sedition law for the exclusive use of millionaires . . . an international menace, a national disgrace, a pre-democratic anachronism'. In the end a messy judgment was handed down in Tesco vs the Guardian, tilted in the newspaper's favour, and at the time of writing Britain's libel laws are under review. Effective change in the law would significantly weaken Britain's offshore empire.

Few newspaper editors now seriously cover the thorny issue of tax avoidance by multinationals – 'as intelligible to the average person as particle physics', as the *Guardian*'s editor Alan Rusbridger put it. Yet this tax avoidance is at the core of the relationship between money, governments and our democratic societies. Just when we need transparency, libel law in London is killing it.

Having helped transform the world economy, the City has wreaked havoc at home too. Apart from having carved itself out from important parts of British democracy, there is that same Dutch Disease problem that afflicts Jersey and oil-rich countries: crowding out other sectors like manufacturing or agriculture, and making it harder for them to compete with foreign goods. Here, in the birth-place of the Industrial Revolution, vast financial sector salaries empty manufacturing industries of their best-educated people, and politi-cians, hooked on the City's money-making machine, sneer at the dirty and difficult smokestack industries. 'Manufacturing, mining, fishing – all fucked, screwed, irrelevant,' said Robin Ramsay. 'The interests of a minority have come to dominate society.'

Between 1979 and 2011, as employment in UK manufacturing fell from 6 million to just under 2.5 million, its output stagnated while financial services output trebled.[82] Meanwhile, British banks aren't even lending to British industry: in the decade before the crash just 3 per cent of banks' net cumulative lending in the UK went to manufac-turing, while three- quarters went to home mortgages and commer-cial real estate. 'They have lent not for any productive purpose at all,' said Professor Karel Williams, author of a groundbreaking 2009 study of the financial sector in Britain's economy.

This is the finance sector working for itself and inflating asset prices in an unstable way. The story the industry itself is telling is a story about social contri-butions which presents finance as the goose that lays the golden eggs. When you look at it, none of it stands up to empirical scrutiny . . . If you check the figures and put them in context, the net social contribution is negative.[83]

Britain and the US, the two leaders of modern global finance, are now among the most unequal societies in the developed world. In Britain 0.3 per cent of the population owns two-thirds of the land; in famously unequal Brazil 1 per cent of the population owns only half of the land. In a UNICEF league of twenty-one industrialised nations measuring child well-being, the UK came last, marginally behind the USA. Britain's pensioners have Europe's fourth highest level of poverty and are worse off than their counterparts in Romania and Poland. Meanwhile, the 1,000 richest Britons had wealth of £335 billion by the end of Labour's term in 2010, up from £99 billion when Labour came to power in 1997. And that's just the wealth we know about.

Before the crisis that erupted in 2007, Britain had engineered another, more geographical pact with the City. The regions away from London, most especially the Northwest, Southwest, West Midlands and Scotland – but also large, poorer parts of London itself – were harmed by the City's growth, but they got generous dollops of tax revenue redistributed to them. It was not nearly enough to compensate for the hollowing out of industry, but it helped. Now, even that imperfect bargain has unravelled. A report into the City of London in June 2011 put it starkly. 'The financial crisis and the ensuing politics of austerity will traumatically terminate a redistributive social settlement which disproportionately benefited ex-industrial regions of the North and West that have no autonomous capacity to create private sector jobs. It consolidates the position of London as a kind of "City State" within the national economy.'[84] Meanwhile, City bonuses were £14 billion in 2010-11, nearly 40 percent higher than the average for 2000-2007, the boom years leading up to the financial crisis[85]. "In the new phase after 2008," the report continued, 'London finance had the disruptive power to resist any reform intended to help make finance safe, as well as to vigorously support a politics of austerity.'

Jim Cousins, a member of the UK Treasury Select Committee, is amazed at how Britain's policy towards finance has evolved. He said,

For thirty years this city has been engaged in a second empire project. We have run huge trade deficits for over thirty years . . . they dealt with that trade deficit by sucking in money from wholesale markets on the basis of better returns than could be got elsewhere. This was invented by Margaret Thatcher: the idea was that we would become financial dealers for oligarchs and oil people from around the world.

For nearly a century until the offshore explosion of the 1970s UK banks expanded their balance sheets cautiously, in line with spending in the economy, and combined they were worth about half of GDP. After 1970 everything changed. By the beginning of the twenty-first century their balance sheets had grown to over five times GDP. Under the City's new imperial project, money floods into London, then is repackaged and recycled out again, often via offshore satellites, to build glittering skyscrapers in Dubai, giant condominiums in São Paulo and games of financial bait and switch in New York.

'The government is guaranteeing up to £560 billion of what could be low-grade assets, most not in Britain itself,' Cousins said, speaking not long after the UK government had started a scheme forcing the

British taxpayer to back assets valued at this figure held by Lloyds Banking Group and Royal Bank of Scotland. 'Does anyone know how much this stuff is actually worth?' Britain has fallen into a trap. The National Audit Office has concluded, 'the UK bears the ultimate risk from potential liabilities'[86] arising from Britain's haven network, yet the City always warns: tax or regulate this, and the money will flit elsewhere. Cousins calls this 'the second empire project at its craziest'. Martin Wolf of the *Financial Times* calls it a 'financial doomsday machine . . . a machine to transfer income and wealth from outsiders to insiders, while increasing the fragility of the economy as a whole'.

Father William Taylor summed up the challenge that the values of the modern City of London, the values of offshore finance, present to us all. 'We need to repent of it,' he said. 'We are in the grip of a programme for our collective happiness that is illusory. It is a phantom, and it will enslave us.'

Conclusion
Reclaim our culture

They say that the *ancien régime* in France fell in the 18th Century because the richest country in Europe, which had exempted its nobles from taxation, could not pay its debts. France had, in one sense, become a failed state. In the modern world the nobles don't have to change the laws to escape their responsibilities: they go offshore. The latest financial crisis shows that state failure isn't something that only happens to developing countries: it can affect the very richest. And every time, offshore has lain close to the heart of the malaise.

To fix the problems, we must first understand the sickness. If there are just two ideas I'd want people to take from this book, it is these.

One is that the offshore system is perhaps the strongest determinant of how political and economic power works in this world. It helps rich people, companies and countries stay on top, for no good economic or political reason. It's the battleground of the rich versus the poor, you versus the corporations, the havens against the democracies – and in each battle, unless you're very rich, you are losing.

Next, I hope I've helped people grasp what offshore really is. The secrecy, tax breaks or other escape routes that Luxembourg or the British Virgin Islands provide are designed to attract money not from locals, but from foreigners, elsewhere. So the people who are actually affected by the laws of secrecy jurisdictions – those foreigners, elsewhere – are *always* separated from the people who make those laws. There is *never* proper democratic consultation when those laws are written. This is the whole point. These are laws by insiders, for insiders, shielded from democratic accountability: private, hidden law-making machines.

Offshore is, almost by definition, the smoke-filled room.

Understand these two things, and understand much of what you need to know about the economy of the modern world.

The time has come to tackle the offshore system in earnest.

Where to start? I won't pretend there is a magic bullet: there isn't. What I will do here is outline ten promising angles of attack. This isn't even a remotely complete list. I will avoid areas where others are already ably campaigning for reform – so I won't get into debates about, say, capital controls (a subject that many economists are, in my opinion, still too cowardly to explore, but which needs a proper airing now) and I'll sidestep financial transaction taxes (another area that seeks to throw sand in the wheels of hot money and cross-border finance, and which I generally support.) No, I will focus on a few areas I feel aren't being properly debated. My recommendations overlap, and the last ties them all together. Some are already, timidly, starting to be put into practice.

Let's start with **some financial reforms**. Severe pundit fatigue has already set in on this topic, so I will just make two short recommendations that have not been a part of the general clamour.

One. Policymakers, journalists and many others can start to understand and accept how tax havens have become the fortified refuges of financial capital, protecting it from tax and regulation and in the process contributing to the latest crisis in many and varied ways. The veil of silence and ignorance can be lifted and the message spread.

Two. Countries worried about the safety of their financial systems could compile blacklists of financial regulatory havens, based on the Jersey–Delaware notion of the captured state: *a place that seeks to attract business by offering politically stable facilities to help people or entities get around the rules, laws and regulations of jurisdictions elsewhere.* This black-listing would be easy enough once we understand what we are looking for. Ireland is a wonderful, special country, in so many ways. But when it comes to providing foreigners with lax financial regulations or tax trickery, it is a goddamned rogue state yet it still gets the kid gloves treatment. 'This is a member of the European Union or of the OECD,' the regulators will say, 'and we can't be rude about them!' Nonsense.

Be rude; be very rude. No more chickening out. Let's create some
real blacklists, based on objective measures of international responsibility, not hopeless and hypocritical blacklists based on what is politically convenient. New, <u>truly</u> independent bodies could do this. We can
blacklist other tax haven offerings too: on financial secrecy; on tax
trickery, and so on. The Tax Justice Network's Financial Secrecy Index
is a useful model here. Let's face it: what we are talking about here
is economic and financial warfare. With these blacklists, appropriate
prohibitions and regulations – many of them very simple – can be put
in place, to help countries reclaim their sovereignty and follow their
voters' wishes once more. Along with this another benefit would flow:
once the berserkers in the international regulatory system are cut
down to size, international co-operation on financial reform will
become much easier. This proposal will also help us guard not only
against repeating the errors that led to the latest crisis, but also those
of the next one – whose causes we may not even be able to imagine
yet.

Secondly, we can **pursue transparency.** Many and varied changes are
needed; here are two.

About 60 per cent of world trade happens inside multinational
corporations, which cut taxes by shuffling money between jurisdictions
to create artificial paper trails that shift their profits into zero-tax
havens and their costs into high-tax countries. The complexity and
cost of this system causes great harm. But these manoeuvrings are
invisible in corporations' annual reports. Under current accounting
rules they can scoop up all their results – profits, borrowings, tax
payments and so on – from several countries and consolidate each
into one figure, perhaps broken down by region. So a corporation
may publish its profits from, say, Africa, but nobody can unpick those
numbers to work out the profits for each country. You can't find the
information anywhere: trillions of dollars' worth of cross-border flows
simply disappear from view. So a citizen in a country cannot tell from
these reports even whether that corporation operates there, let alone
what it does, its level of activity, its profits, its local employment or
its tax payments. As multinationals become ever more complex, this
problem just gets worse.

Richard Murphy, an ex-KPMG accountant who has done more than anyone to put this onto the public agenda, summarised the problem. 'A company gets its licence to operate in any territory from the government that represents those people. It has a corporate duty to account in return. This is the essence of stewardship and accountability. Instead we have companies pretending they float above all these countries. They don't.' If multinationals had to break their financial information down by country and disclose what they do in each place, global markets would immediately become more transparent. A secret treasure trove of information vital to citizens, investors, economists and governments would come onshore and into view. Country-by-country reporting, as it is known, is already making progress in policymaking circles, particularly for the extractive industries.[1] It now needs major support, and must be expanded to include all businesses, especially banks.

Another essential step concerns how governments share information about the local incomes and assets of each other's citizens. If a person in one country owns an income-generating asset in another country, his or her tax authorities need to know about it. So governments need to share relevant information, subject to appropriate safeguards. But the dominant standard for exchanging information is the OECD's on request standard, a cheat's charter whereby a country already has to know what it is looking for before it requests the information from another, on a bilateral basis. Developing countries are particularly vulnerable here.

The OECD standard can be replaced by the far better alternative: automatic information exchange on a multilateral basis, whereby countries tell each other what their respective taxpayers own and earn without a request being necessary. Such a system exists in Europe: it works well and does not leak information though major loopholes need plugging to defend against Cayman trusts, Nevada corporations, Liechtenstein foundations, Austrian hidden *Treuhands* and various other secrecy facilities that infest the offshore system. Momentum is just starting to build for change here, and this can now be rolled out worldwide and vigorously supported. Britain's next government can signal its commitment by repudiating an appalling 2011 deal with Switzerland that would see Britain receive some money from British tax evaders in Switzerland, but which entrenches Swiss bank secrecy.[2] Sanctions and blacklists can be introduced to spur the shift.

*   *   *

Third, reforms can always prioritise the needs of **developing countries**.

The pattern always seems to be the same. A secrecy jurisdiction comes up with a new abusive offshore structure, and wealthy countries construct defences against it as best they can. But poor countries, without the relevant expertise, are left wide open to the new drain.[3]

Tax is the Cinderella in debates about financing for development. Overshadowed for decades by its domineering sisters – aid and debt relief – tax is now at last starting to emerge from the shadows. Tax is the most sustainable, the most important and the most beneficial form of finance for development. It makes rulers accountable to their citizens, not to donors, and the right kinds of taxes stimulate governments to create the strong institutions they need for getting their citizens and corporations to pay tax. 'It is a contradiction to support increased development assistance,' South Africa's finance minister, Trevor Manuel, said recently, 'yet turn a blind eye to actions by multinationals and others that undermine the tax base of a developing country.'

Three things can happen now. First, developing and middle-income countries can find a voice, to articulate their concerns about this global system for transferring wealth from poor to rich, and work together. A few countries like Brazil and India are beginning to construct serious offshore defences, and the time is ripe for this to become a mass movement. I am starting to detect early stirrings of action here. Speaking recently at a high-level United Nations meeting, one official said: 'the day is gone where there are rule makers and rule takers.'[4] Second, official development assistance in this area can rise dramatically: less than one thousandth of development aid is currently spent on helping countries improve their tax systems, and much of that is spent on ideas that may make poverty worse, not better.[5] Third, as citizens and civil organisations stop focusing exclusively on aid and start to revitalise the debates about tax and its role in fostering accountability, major change becomes possible. Aid can help, but when ten dollars are drained out of the developing world for every dollar going in, then we need new approaches.

If there were ever a movement that could unite the citizens of developing and wealthy countries in one cause, this is it.

* * *

The fourth big change necessary is to **confront the British spider's web**, the most important and most aggressive single element in the global offshore system. The City of London corporation – this offshore island floating partly free from Britain's people and its democratic system – must be abolished and submerged into a unified and fully democratic London. The City's international offshore web, a mechanism for harvesting and profiting from financial capital from around the globe, however dirty it may be, must be dismantled. It harms the people of Britain, and it harms the world at large. Britain is too subservient to the City and its offshore sector to be able to do this alone; pressure from outside is essential. Developing countries in particular need to appreciate how this economic system has a rather imperial flavour, and their own elites are deeply implicated. Alongside this new focus we need a greater understanding of the role of the USA as an offshore jurisdiction in its own right and the harm this causes, inside and outside the United States.

Here is another clever way to take the oxygen out of the British web – and out of tax havens more generally. This proposal's awful-sounding name – 'combined reporting with formula apportionment and unitary taxation' – masks a simple, powerful and straightforward approach to tax, which several U.S. states already use successfully. It is a way of taxing corporations based on the substance of what they do in the real world, rather than on the gymnastic legal fictions its accountants have cooked up.

Instead of the current approach of trying to tax each separate bit of a multinational as if it were a free-floating entity, tax authorities could treat the whole multinational group as a single unit, then allocate portions of its income out to the different jurisdictions where it operates, under an agreed formula based on real things like sales, payrolls and assets in each place. Each jurisdiction can then tax its portion at whatever rate it wants, so consider a US multinational with a one-man booking office in Bermuda and no local sales, and the vast majority of its operations in South Africa and Australia. Current rules let it shift billions of dollars in profits to Bermuda to skip tax, with South Africa and Australia getting short-changed. But under this alternative system, the formula would allocate only a miniscule portion of the income to the booking office in Bermuda (because it has such tiny sales, payroll and assets there), so only a miniscule portion of its overall income would be subject to Bermuda's zero tax rate. The rest would get taxed properly in South Africa and Australia. Countries can do this unilaterally – but better if many do. If it happened widely enough, a huge part of the tax havens' business model would disappear. And a lot of the political cover that corporations give to tax havens would disappear along with it. Again, developing countries could be particularly helped by this simplified approach to tax.

A fifth arena for change is **onshore tax reform**. Endless possibilities exist, and I will focus on just two promising solutions that have been largely overlooked. The first is a land value tax. This is huge, and it needs a very brief detour.[6] A street musician who sets up in the middle of the high street will earn far more than if s/he plays on the outskirts of town. The additional earnings on the best sites, over and above what s/he would earn on a just-worthwhile site, owe nothing at all to his or her skill or efforts, they are pure, unearned rental value.[7] If a government builds a major new railway line, property owners near the new stations will see their properties rise in value through no efforts of their own. For them it is a pure windfall: unearned rental value. Economists agree that the correct approach to unearned natural rents like these is to tax them at high rates (and use the proceeds either to cut taxes elsewhere or to spend more). A land value tax is a tax not on property ownership, but on land. Whether or not that piece of prime real estate is owned by a Russian oligarch hidden behind a Liechtenstein *anstalt*, its bricks are rooted firmly in the soil, and the tax can be levied. Because land cannot move, this tax is proof against offshore escape. It encourages and rewards the best use of land, and keeps rents lower than they would otherwise be.

A huge chunk of the profits of the financial sector derive ultimately from real estate business and land value. Tax land's rental value, and you capture a big slice of this financial business, however much of it is re-engineered offshore. When Pittsburgh became one of the few places in the world to adopt the tax in 1911, in the teeth of massive resistance from wealthy landowners, it had dramatic and positive effects: while the rest of America went on an orgy of land speculation ahead of the crash of 1929, prices in Pittsburgh only rose 20 per cent. Harrisburg's adoption of the tax in 1975 led to a dramatic inner-city regeneration. The tax is simple to administer, progressive (the poor pay less) and especially useful for developing countries.

A second, much-overlooked scheme concerns mineral-rich countries. Tides of looted or tainted oil money sluice constantly into the offshore system, distorting the global economy in the process. A radical and controversial proposal would up-end this by distributing a large share of a country's mineral windfalls directly and without discrimination to every inhabitant. With the money would flow political power: to the people. This has only been implemented in a few places like Alaska, but in many other mineral-rich countries, even poor ones, it is feasible. Doing so would drain hundreds of billions of dollars of stolen mineral-sourced loot from offshore centres and deliver tremendous immediate benefits for the populations concerned. Governments would still get their revenues – only via taxing their citizens. And tax builds accountability.

A corollary of onshore tax reform is **leadership and unilateral action**. After the 11 September 2001 attacks, US legislators tried to insert stronger anti-money-laundering provisions into the Patriot Act. In the halls of Congress civility collapsed, and shouting matches erupted between bank officials and congressional staffers.[8] Among other things, the bankers were defending offshore shell banks, which hide behind nominees and trustees so no one can know who their real owners and managers are. Senator Carl Levin, who led the transparency charge – after having had eleven bills shot down by Senator Phil Gramm – stuck to his guns and in the post-9/11 environment at last got his way. Remarkable new provisions stated that no US bank may receive a transfer from a foreign shell bank, and no foreign bank may transfer money to the US that it has received from a foreign shell bank. The result, as Raymond Baker explained, is that 'the thousands of shell banks that used to run loose have been reduced to perhaps a few dozen . . . With a stroke of the legislative pen, a major threat to economic integrity has been almost completely removed from the global financial system.' Already, the United States is amending its legislation to implement country-by-country reporting.[9] Companies want access to U.S. capital markets, and new transparency requirements won't stop them coming. International agreement is generally a good thing in cases like this, but leadership can work wonders too.

Too often, corporations or individuals threaten to relocate offshore if they feel they are taxed or regulated too highly, or asked to be more transparent, or to submit to criminal laws, or when offshore loopholes are to be closed and fearful government officials give the wealthy owners of capital what they want. Governments need to understand that these companies are usually lying: they never intend to relocate, but make the threats anyway. This is a form of deception for material gain, and we should call it by its real name: fraud. Confront it through leadership, and calling their bluff.

What is more, the latest crisis has made clear that much financial services activity is actually harmful, so if certain parts of the financial industry leave town so much the better. Good projects will always find financing, whether or not your country is stuffed with foreign financiers, and local bankers are better placed to supply it because they know their customers. Tax and regulate the financial industries according to an economy's real needs, ignore screams that capital and bankers will flit offshore, and you will tend to drive out the harmful parts, leaving the useful bits behind. Leadership and unilateral action can work wonders.

A seventh task is to **tackle the intermediaries and the private users of offshore**.

Rudolf Strahm, a Swiss parliamentarian, studied every historical episode when Swiss bank secrecy had been loosened in response to foreign pressure and concluded that pressure generally only ever works when applied to Swiss *banks*. Try to pressure the Swiss *government* and it will be seen as an attack on national pride, and will probably fail.

When a kleptocrat loots his country and shifts the plunder offshore, the banks, accountants and law firms that assist him are just as guilty as the kleptocrat. When a client gets caught and goes to jail, so should his relationship manager, accountant, trustee, lawyer and corporate nominee. A few organisations like the London-based Global Witness have sought to call the intermediaries to account, but we need a sea change in the world's approach. Get serious with these people.

Eighth, we can re-think **corporate responsibility**.

Societies grant corporations immense privileges, such as limited liability, which lets investors cap their losses and shift outstanding debts onto the rest of society when things go wrong. They have also been granted the legal right to be treated as an artificial person which can relocate to different jurisdictions almost at will, irrespective of where they really do business. They are granted a wealth of capital in the form of public infrastructure, educated and healthy workforces, the rules of law, and much more. In exchange for remarkable privileges like these, corporations were originally held to a set of obligations to the societies in which they were embedded, notably to be transparent about their affairs, and to pay tax.

The offshore system has undermined all this. The privileges have been preserved and enhanced, but the obligations have withered. Tax may now be brought squarely into corporate responsibility debates. We can make corporations accountable not only to shareholders, but to the societies that allow them to do business and provide them with the tools and confidence to do so. Tax can no longer be seen as a cost to shareholders, to be minimised, but as a distribution to society: a return on the investment that societies and their governments make in infrastructure, education, law and order and the other basic prerequisites for corporate activity. When this happens, a whole new arena will have been created in which the offshore system can be questioned and challenged.

Ninth, we can also re-evaluate **corruption**. I have already indicated how major corruption rankings of countries place many of the world's top tax havens – the repositories of trillions of dollars of stolen loot – at the clean end of the spectrum, and how the new Financial Secrecy Index has started the process of setting the record straight. But we can move beyond rearranging the geography of corruption, and reassess what corruption *is*. At heart, corruption involves insiders abusing the common good in secrecy and with impunity, undermining the rules and systems that promote the public interest, and undermining our faith in those rules and systems. In the process it worsens poverty and inequality and entrenches vested interests and unaccountable power.

Bribery does all these things, but many of the services tax havens provide do the same. The parallels between bribery and the business of secrecy jurisdictions are no coincidence: we are talking about the same underlying thing. Some people praise bribery as a way of getting around bureaucratic obstacles – without that backhander, they say, that container won't leave port. They are wrong to praise corruption. Bribery may benefit the payer, but it damages the system as a whole. Similarly, defenders of secrecy jurisdictions may argue that their services help private actors get around 'inefficiencies' in mainstream economies, smoothing the way for business to proceed. And they do. But what are those inefficiencies? They are, most importantly, tax, financial regulations, criminal laws and transparency, which exist for good reason. To help someone get around an obstacle is to corrode both the system and trust in the system. Bribery rots and corrupts governments, and tax havens rot and corrupt the global financial system.

Once we start seeing this we will no longer limit ourselves to pointing fingers at developing-country kleptocrats and rogue officials, but will begin to examine a much broader array of actors and their facilitating activities. And we will have found a rubric for the citizens of rich and poor countries to find common cause in fighting a global scourge.[10]

The final and most important element on my list is to **change the culture**. When pundits, journalists and politicians fawn over people who get rich by abusing the system – getting around tax and regulation and forcing everyone else to shoulder the associated risks and taxes – then we have lost our way.

Language can change. When someone claims that tax havens make global finance more efficient, we can ask, 'Efficient for whom?' When someone says countries should compete with each other on tax or financial regulation, or that policymakers should aim for a more competitive tax or regulatory system, one may ask, 'What kind of competition are you talking about? A race to the bottom on tax, secrecy or financial regulation? Or a race to the top, such as when corporations operate in competitive markets on a level playing field?' When we hear 'privacy' or 'asset protection' or 'tax efficiency' in the context of private banking, they can be asked *exactly* what is meant. When a private equity company shows record profits, we can be told how much of that comes from genuine productive improvement and how much from gaming the offshore system. When we hear a pillar of society say, 'We are a well-regulated, cooperative and transparent jurisdiction,' the investigator can assume the opposite and probe further. When magazines carry alluring advertisements from seedy offshore promoters who may be inciting clients to criminal behaviour, we can complain. When corporations talk about social responsibility, we can ask if they mean tax. When journalists need expert commentators to advise them about that tax story they are writing, they must understand that their interviewee from the big accountancy firm works for a business that makes a living out of helping wealthy corporations and individuals get around paying tax, and that their opinions will reflect a corrupt world view. They must always find alternative voices to balance their stories.

The world's international institutions and responsible governments can create and promote new guidelines and codes of conduct outlining responsible and irresponsible behaviour in the fields of international tax and regulation, with a special focus on offshore abuse. They could introduce general anti-avoidance principles into their tax laws so that complex and abusive trickery, while technically not breaking the details of legislation, can be disallowed. Tax evasion can become a predicate crime for money laundering, and tax offences, among others, could be included in international conventions such as the United Nations Convention Against Corruption. Professional associations of lawyers, accountants and bankers need to create codes of conduct which stress, among other things, that it is unacceptable for a member to help a client commit a financial crime, whether the crime occurs at home or overseas. The economics profession needs to reappraise its approach, in order to understand the effects of things such as secrecy and regulatory arbitrage. It could finally start to measure illicit, secret things, difficult though that may be.

We can recapture our language and culture from the forces of unaccountable privilege that have taken it away from us.

At the time of writing, heavy government spending around the world has staved off outright economic collapse following the meltdown in global finance, but at huge cost to taxpayers. 'Never in the field of financial endeavour has so much money been owed by so few to so many,' said Mervyn King, governor of the Bank of England. 'And, one might add, so far with little real reform.'

It is time for the great global debate about tax havens to begin in earnest. Whoever you are, wherever you live, and whatever you do, this affects you. Now there's a very simple step you can take when you close this book. To find out how you can get involved in amplifying this story to millions of people around the world, get involved as a supporter of one of the bodies dedicated to fighting this stuff. My personal favourite is the Tax Justice Network, but there are others. Offshore is at work nearby. It is undermining your elected government, hollowing out its tax base and corrupting its politicians. It is sustaining a vast criminal economy and creating a new, unaccountable aristocracy of corporate and financial power. If we do not act together to contain and control financial secrecy then the world I found in West Africa more than a decade ago, a world of suave insiders, impunity, international criminal complicity and desperate poverty, will become the world we leave to our children. A tiny few will have their boots washed in champagne while the rest of us struggle for our lives in conditions of steepening inequality. We can avert this future.

We can because we must.

Offshore after the Panama Papers

One afternoon in June 2016 I got a call from Donald Trump at my home in Berlin. My kids were making a racket so I had to put him on hold while I went downstairs to beg for quiet ('It's Trump on the phone!' did the trick quite nicely.)

He was chatty and frank and boastful and, well, just totally *Donaldish*. It was my fiftieth birthday; had I had the chutzpah I'd have asked him to sing me *Happy Birthday*. (I reckon he'd have done it.)

He opened with a question about 'the situation' in Germany: I quickly twigged that there was only one 'situation' in Germany for him: the immigration debates that have been raging here.

I'd been researching Trump's tax and business affairs for the U.S. magazine *Vanity Fair* and had been hoping to catch him using tax havens – something that I'd managed to do in an earlier article for them about Mitt Romney ahead of the 2012 presidential elections. *Vanity Fair*'s editor had read *Treasure Islands* and asked me to do some digging; and when I revealed that Romney was using unusual and peculiar tax haven vehicles, it damaged his campaign significantly.

I spoke to The Donald twice. Both times, when I asked him how exactly he'd deal with tax havens if he were to become president, he cut the call short (I imagined an adviser listening in and making urgent throat-cutting motions.*) But he did make some interesting observations about them.

---

* He promised to call me back, and a few days later he did.

'I don't use 'em,' he said. 'Over the years I have had many friends that have used that stuff, and honestly I think it's more trouble than it's worth. Highly overrated . . . They don't work and they cause lots of difficulty and nobody knows what's going on, and they are really not good . . . there is greater incentive in many ways to keep your money in the U.S.'

We don't know what he's up to because he hasn't released his tax returns, but his claim not to use tax havens, and his reasons, are plausible. That's for a simple reason: he is active in the U.S. real estate sector, which is a such a cloyingly rich pudding of loopholes and abatements that you can cut your federal tax bills to zero with relatively little effort. 'Real estate is the gold mine of gold mines for people who know how to manoeuvre through it,' says the veteran crime-fighting lawyer Jack Blum. 'The potential for shenanigans is virtually unlimited: much more than other sectors. The only other one that might come close is petroleum.'

The second point Donald made, unwittingly, reveals his apparent reluctance to lay out a detailed plan for tacking the tax havens. To be more precise, he said at the end of our first conversation: 'Nicholas, I would love to give you that answer right now. It is very easy to end it, by the way: you end it very easily. But I have to get going.'

Anyone who has read this far will know that tax havens are a multi-headed hydra and a far, far tougher adversary than Trump suggests. There is *no way* anyone could even begin to 'end' tax havens. Shrink them, perhaps.

This was made even more abundantly clear in April 2016 when the Panama Papers scandal erupted, reminding the world just how very hard it is going to be to tackle the issue.

The affair first began to unfold one evening in early 2015 when Bastian Obermayer, a journalist working for Germany's *Süddeutsche Zeitung*, opened his laptop at home. He saw a new message.

> [John Doe]: Hello. This is John Doe.
>   Interested in data? I'm happy to share.

A back-and-forth began.

There would be no meetings, ever, Doe said; and all communications would be encrypted.

Journalists need to be exceedingly cautious about these kinds of offers; caches of secrets can come with messy, twisted agendas and personal vendettas. They can even be sent as traps for reporters. Genuine whistle-blowers usually have a complex mix of reasons for spilling secrets; usually one of or a mix of revenge, anger, money, fear of getting caught in a scandal, blackmail, or ethical qualms.

John Doe, however, was crystal clear in describing to Obermayer what he said were his motivations: 'I feel that I must do it because I'm able. It's too important. There is just a mind-boggling amount of criminal activity going on here – I struggle to even wrap my head around it.'

Bastian Obermayer would soon team up with a *Süddeutsche Zeitung* colleague, the similarly surnamed but unrelated Frederik Obermaier, to pursue the leak.

> [Obermayer]: How much data are we talking about?
> [John Doe]: More than anything you have ever seen.

A relationship of trust was established, and the data began to flow. Soon they had 50 gigabytes, on several USB sticks. In pure data terms, that was 30 times the size of the Wikileaks diplomatic cables. But still more came; soon, they had 250 gigabytes, then 1,000. In the end they got 2,600 gigabytes: at least an order of magnitude larger than any leak to any journalist in world history.

This was far too big for one newspaper to handle. So they turned to the International Consortium of Investigative Journalists (ICIJ,) which had already established a track record of international collaborations of journalists. The ICIJ, in turn, began to work with over 350 journalists from eighty countries to try and make sense of the avalanche of data, which came from a Panamanian law firm called Mossack Fonseca – known in the offshore world as Mossfon.[1] The leak included details on more than 200,000 offshore companies and thousands of trusts, created in twenty-one different tax havens. There were emails, incorporation documents, bank account details, company owners, discussions of the workings of trusts, financial transactions and more.

One of the first things to become clear was the complexity, which is inherent in the system. The secrecy is often achieved by festooning a structure's financial affairs across multiple tax havens, so that if you find out details of one part, you still can't understand the whole. This fragmentation also applied to Mossack Fonseca itself, which had branches and subsidiaries in numerous countries.

'The trick is not only used by Mossfon but also by numerous other companies and involves working as seamless, vertically integrated top-down organisations until the minute that a cop or investigator comes along,' explained Jack Blum. 'Then they disintegrate into a series of unconnected entities, and everyone swears they don't know anything about anyone else in the system. It's like a jigsaw puzzle that's assembled but suddenly falls apart when someone starts investigating.'

The bamboozlement and hornswoggling embedded in the structure of the offshore world is one important part of why Trump would find it so hard to deliver on his boast to 'end' the offshore system 'very easily'.

But the Panama Papers revealed the bigger reason too. The revelations underlined, again and again, the core problem: that tax havens are projects of the world's rich and powerful people. And there's no group richer and more powerful than the rich and powerful. Even if you didn't believe *Treasure Islands*, the Panama Papers made this crystal clear. *That*'s the big challenge Trump would have to overcome, if he were serious: how to stop the rich and powerful from protecting the tax havens.

When the ICIJ began deciphering the data, the big names started mounting up. In their book *The Panama Papers: Breaking the Story of How the Rich & Powerful Hide Their Money*, Obermayer and Obermaier recount how quickly the ICIJ's collaborative Panama Papers encrypted forum began to fizz with excitement: 'Every time you post something in the forum, it's another head of state,' comments ICIJ Deputy Director Marina Walker dryly on the forum.

It is remarkable how many Arab heads of state move their money abroad – every single one of them, more or less.

With our data, we are again finding it hard to keep track of the countless emirs, dictators, princes and sheikhs. A number of these govern in countries that display stark levels of inequality. They enjoy unimaginable luxury while at least part of the population is living a hand-to-mouth existence. A number of African and Middle Eastern countries are being sucked well and truly dry by their corrupt elite.

Key associates of Vladimir Putin emerged, along with the family of Chinese President Xi Jinping – who in 2004 had called on officials to 'rein in your spouses, children, relatives, friends and staff, and vow not to use power for personal gain'.

The Prime Minister of Iceland was forced to resign, along with several other Icelandic politicians, after his and his wife's secret offshore holdings were revealed. There are, as Obermayer and Obermaier explain it, 'Drug lords. Financial fraudsters. Mafiosi. Arms smugglers. Tax evaders. Sanction breakers. Pretty much every type of fraudster.' There is a child rapist and a child prostitution ring, covered up by the very deliberate turning of offshore blind eyes. The Papers even seem to have helped provoke a bout of fighting between Azerbaijan and Armenian forces over the disputed enclave of Nagorno-Karabakh, as leaders on each side sought a diversion to cover up the exposure of their financial misdeeds.

Then there were the banks. Obermaier and Obermayer naturally probed the German ones. 'We search for Deutsche Bank. Thousands of hits. Dresdner Bank? Same result. A number of regional banks also get thousands of hits each,' they said. 'Our data sketches out how entangled almost all German banks were or are in the offshore system.'

Pretty much every big bank, it turns out, was in there: most commonly because they were setting up anonymous shell companies for German clients, many of whom were evading tax.

Deliciously, the Papers unearthed a fundraising bid to Mossack Fonseca from my friends at the Center for Freedom and Prosperity. 'We hope you can support this effort with a donation,' they wrote to Mossack Fonseca, outlining a drive to raise $247,000 for an eight-month campaign to derail some anti-tax haven measures in the US Congress. Senator Carl Levin, who has led the anti-tax haven push, said: 'I consider tax havens the enemy . . . they help to starve us of resources that we need for all the things we do. And this center is out there helping them to accomplish that.'[2]

All this skulduggery, plus oceans more, was exposed at a firm which, by its own estimate, has just a 5 per cent world market share in this line of business.[3] The Panama Papers have only scraped the surface of the truth. Making matters worse, many of the outrages potentially exposed by the Panama Papers scandal remain covered up. Apart from a heavily restricted set of data available on the ICIJ's website, the leaks aren't publicly available – and in many countries, oligarchic ownership of local media has kept many secrets hidden. For instance, Panama, a former province of Colombia, is widely known to host huge assets linked to Colombian elites and drugs cartels – but the Panama Papers hardly made a stir in Colombia.

The Papers also revealed in detail another side of the offshore story: the inner workings of what I call the 'captured state'. Ramón Fonseca, one of Mossfon's founders, was (until the scandal broke) adviser to the Panamanian president Juan Carlos Varela, with a seat in the Cabinet, and he was a deputy chairman of the governing Panameñista governing party. The Panamanian press has even speculated that Varela had wanted to make Fonseca Minister for Public Security but backed down under US pressure.

Mossack Fonseca has shaped, and even written, laws in other 'captive states'. The Pacific island of Niue, with a population of 1,100, signed a 20-year deal giving Mossfon exclusive rights to register offshore companies. The smaller a state is, of course, the easier it is to capture its politics; and by 2001 Mossfon's business was paying 80 per cent of Niue's budget revenues. That same year, the US State Department warned that the microstate was linked with 'the laundering of criminal proceeds from Russia and South America'.

Mossfon later told Agence France-Presse that it chose tiny Niue partly because it would face no competitors. 'If we had a jurisdiction that was small, and we had it from the beginning, we could offer people a stable environment, a stable price.' That word 'stable' means insulated from local democracy – or 'captured' by the private offshore players.

Since writing *Treasure Islands* I've investigated the offshore histories of seventeen of the world's most important havens and I found the same underlying pattern in every single one.[4] A tax adviser once boasted to me that he had obtained a tax advantage for one of his clients by choosing a tiny jurisdiction – he wouldn't tell me which – and persuading them to tweak their legislation in a particular way, in his and his client's favour. It was a formality, he said. This is how it is done. You generally don't even need to resort to bribery, the legislators know that listening to the tax advisers' lobbying is often a good way to bring in new sources of mucky money. A 'good' one, they know, can be a gold mine – at least for some. The Mossack Fonseca files simply confirm the long-established pattern: tax havens are captured states.

The biggest British part of the Panama scandal, of course, concerned David Cameron, prime minister at the time. As the scandal broke he said he had 'no shares, no offshore trusts, no offshore funds: nothing like that' – but it soon emerged that he'd owned shares in the Blairmore unit trust in Panama, set up by his father Ian. David said he sold his shares for £31,500 in January 2010, just before becoming prime minister, for a profit of £19,000.

The British media briefly became obsessed with the question of whether or not the arrangements had helped Cameron dodge tax. But this was the wrong question to be asking. Neither Cameron's involvement with Blairmore, nor the Panama Papers scandal, was really about tax. They were about something much bigger.

To understand this, let's consider why, in 1982, Ian Cameron set up this fund in Panama. There seem to be two main reasons. First, the usual tax haven ones: low or zero taxes at a local level (though the Camerons would surely have paid their UK taxes) plus the option of secrecy, and libertarian laws and rules for how funds can invest their money, escaping rules[5] that are supposed to protect 'unsophisticated' investors. Those rules are in place for good reason: to prevent people investing their savings in shark-tank vehicles, insane risk-surfers, or criminal enterprises.

The second reason is more specific: why, of all tax havens, did he choose Panama, one of the world's muckiest and most crime-fuelled havens? What could Panama offer that was more attractive to him than other tax havens? A March 2006 prospectus for Blairmore Holdings, Inc. gives us a clue: 'Investor Due Diligence Forms . . . must be completed pursuant to Bahamian legislation.'

The Bahamas rivals Panama in terms of its tolerance of criminality. Those 'due diligence' rules – that is, the rules about checking up on who the warm-blooded investors in these funds actually are – are deliberately not enforced in the Bahamas. It's been one of the Bahamas' selling points for many years. The US State Department, in a blistering assessment in 2013, said:

The Bahamas is a transshipment point for cocaine bound for the United States and Europe. The major sources of laundered proceeds stem from drug trafficking, human smuggling, and illegal gambling. There is a significant black market for smuggled cigarettes and guns. Money laundering trends include the purchase of real estate, large vehicles, boats, and jewelry, as well as the processing of money through a complex web of legitimate businesses and international business companies (IBCs) registered in the offshore financial sector. Drug traffickers and other criminal organizations take advantage of the large number of IBCs and offshore banks registered in The Bahamas to launder significant sums of money, despite strict know-your-customer and transaction reporting requirements.

That word 'strict' must have got in there by accident. Investors can escape the Bahamas' skimpy checks altogether if they either apply through an 'approved' financial institution – giving them a world of criminal banks to choose from – or if they fund their investments via accounts held in their name at a financial institution in an 'approved' jurisdiction. The list of approved jurisdictions includes the Bahamas' partner in crime, Panama.

This set-up reminds me of Beth Krall's description (mentioned in Chapter 11) of how, if you're a small-time investor, you'll have to jump through all sorts of hoops to deposit your money or invest in funds offshore – but if you're a long-standing client and part of the trusted circle, the rules simply fall away.

Choosing a Panama–Bahamas structure, rather than a more obviously British one, gives a fund greater opportunities to hoover up money from Latin America and elsewhere – with the maximum reassurance of secrecy and minimal regulatory scrutiny. I doubt very much Ian or David Cameron broke any laws in their home country – but they may have stood alongside many who did.

The Panama Papers revelations were far bigger than tax: this was about the Camerons' complicity in this charmed, crime-fuelled elite fortress-world of offshore.

One of the most intriguing new analyses of this world comes from Brooke Harrington, an American sociologist at the Copenhagen Business School. She went as far as to train to become a wealth manager, so as to penetrate the inner circle of offshore society. 'Tax avoidance was only the tip of the iceberg,' she recalled later. 'I didn't realise how much bigger the problem is. What wealth managers do [extends] much more generally to law avoidance . . . That is the sort of thing that can potentially topple governments.'

A wealth manager described to Harrington how she'd flown with the CEO of her company from Switzerland to meet a client outside Europe. At Zurich airport, the wealth manager realised she'd left her passport at home and wanted to race back to get it. However the CEO assured her, despite her protests, that she wouldn't need it. Harrington recounts what the wealth manager told her:

So we get on the plane in Zurich, and no one checked our documents. And then when we arrived at the client's location, and there was just a limo waiting to take us directly to him. Nobody asked for our passports, even when we returned to Switzerland on the client's jet. The CEO was right. These people, our wealthiest clients, are above the law.

Similarly, in 2005 I interviewed Arkady Gaydamak, a Russian billionaire who had been the subject of an international arrest warrant. A Global Witness report cited sources who suggested he may have visited Britain after the warrant was issued.[6] I asked Gaydamak if he could still travel to countries he wasn't supposed to go to, including Britain. He replied simply with: 'Do you think I am not able to go where I want to? Technically it is very easy.'

Harrington had read *Treasure Islands* fairly early on in her research and found it chimed closely with what she'd found offshore, from the structures and techniques, to the often extreme-libertarian, anti-social attitudes, which were particularly pronounced among a group of 'really hardcore neoliberals'. She estimated these hardcore neoliberals made up maybe a fifth or a sixth of the people she spoke to. 'They were completely unreflective about what they were saying,' she explained. 'They felt great about what they were doing: as in, "the welfare state is a really terrible thing because it denies poor people the dignity of self-determination, the dignity of bootstrapping themselves into the middle class".' But what Harrington soon picked up on, was that much of what she was being trained in was a series of tools that essentially benefited men at the expense of women.

'You get lots and lots of stories like, "Oh I had Sergey Smith as a client, and Mrs. Sergey was interested in having her share of his estate – but we weren't going to let that happen, ha ha ha." There is a great deal of clubby chortling about these things, and everyone sort of joins in: because the audience is mainly men too. It reminds me of that American frat boy saying: *Bros before Hos*. Why is this such a sport?'

Not only is the global system of tax havens transferring wealth and power from poorer to wealthier sections of our societies, and from poorer to richer countries, but it is also shifting wealth and power from women to men, on an industrial scale.[7] For example, in March 2016 there was talk of a cut in Britain's top rate of income tax, from 45 to 40 per cent. After looking at some official numbers I discovered that such a cut would hand £3.3 billion directly to men, and £428 million directly to women. That's 89 per cent for men, but only 11 per cent for women. (And don't get me started on offshore 'asset protection' strategies in divorce proceedings.)

Such views were embedded in the training manuals for the Society of Trust and Estate Planners (STEP), a little-known but massively influential body in the offshore world, which an experienced offshore tax adviser recently described to me recently as 'a snake with many heads'. STEP now has over 20,000 members in 95 countries. Harrington was astonished by the politics of these training manuals. 'I don't think they realise how outrageous some of the statements are,' she said. 'The cluelessness of it all. Just the sheer smug shamelessness of it all. Imagine the most noxious neoliberal. It's what Monty Python's Upper Class Twit of the Year would say, in all seriousness.'

It seems likely that the German-born Jürgen Mossack, one of the two founders of Mossack Fonseca, is one of these 'hardcore neoliberals' that Harrington refers to. He's given few interviews but Mossack seems to have imbibed some of the see-no-evil worldview. In a 2016 interview he wielded the classic offshore defence of his company's practices: when you create large numbers of companies, he said, it's like selling cars. Some will end up in the hands of bad guys, and they'll run people over, but that's not the manufacturer's fault. This is hardly a good comparison: car manufacturers don't design vehicles with the prime purpose of running people over.

His father, Erhard Mossack, was a *Rottenführer* in the murderous *Totenkopf* (Death's Head) division of Hitler's Waffen-SS. Most of the division's members were recruited as concentration camp guards, and the *Totenkopf* was involved in widespread war crimes. Erhard Mossack was arrested by the US Counterintelligence Corps (CIC) in 1946 and seems to have become a US intelligence 'asset' afterwards. In their book, Obermayer and Obermaier quote from Mossack's CIC assessment: 'Indoctrinated through and through with Nazi ideology. As a typical Hitler Youth leader, he still lives in his world of Nazi slogans and is a remarkable example of a German youth under Hitler.' In 2015, the two *Süddeutsche* journalists asked the BND, the German intelligence services, for any archive material on Erhard Mossack. The BND refused to provide it, saying that disclosure might 'endanger the welfare of the Federal Republic of Germany or one of its regions'.

Who knows what kind of world view Jürgen Mossack imbibed from his father: the facts, though, are that his actions as a co-founder of Mossack Fonseca, and his public justifications for those anti-social actions, are typical for the offshore world.

David Marchant is a specialist in offshore fraud who runs a well-regarded investigations company called Offshore Alert, and he is all too familiar with the peculiar societies and world views that predominate in these kinds of places. He describes himself as 'cold and calculating and unemotional' when doing his job: there's no need to embellish, he says, because the facts are amazing enough on their own. Yet he became quite animated when I asked him about how far this world has been penetrated by criminals and shady characters.

'You come to the realisation what a dirty, dirty industry international finance is,' he said. 'Whether it is some low-life obvious crook, or whether it's [the world's biggest banks]: it is just inherently dirty.' Marchant speaks a lot at conferences and struggles to persuade people of this, he said. Many people believe that people and big companies are generally honest and not involved in illegal activity; they might be involved in occasional scandals, or have rogue officials. 'If you subscribe to that belief, you might think, "man, this guy, he is over the top." But it really isn't.'

He gave the example of a relatively new wheeze in town, known in Cayman as the Segregated Portfolio Company (SPC).[8] These are basically ways of setting up large numbers of hedge funds on the cheap. This is about as good an idea as helping people set up banks or insurance companies on a shoestring – a recipe for the worst elements in society to get up to mischief. It's reminiscent of the antics of Jerome Schneider, who used to advertise in conferences and in-flight magazines that he would set you up as the owner of an offshore bank for just $60,000. Not long before he went to prison in the US in 2004, Schneider said he expected that 'every single one' of his clients could be prosecuted or sued for evading tax.[9]

The basic idea of these newer SPCs is that you set up an 'umbrella platform' which provides all the directors, auditors and other overheads – and then you set up individual hedge funds under that umbrella. Each hedge fund is legally segregated from the others, so if one blows up it won't affect the others. And by sharing all those overheads, you cut costs dramatically. But of course those shared officers will be handling a multitude of different portfolios – so are hardly likely to be able to take their duties seriously, even if they wanted to.

The secret of all hedge funds is Other People's Money, or OPM. First, you find a way to persuade people to invest in your fund – and then you cream off official fees, hidden fees, plus a hefty slice of any profits your fund might make. If the fund tanks, but you've set it up the right way, you still get those fees. So if you *own* a hedge fund, you can hardly lose. If you *invest* in hedge funds, you can lose it all. In a devastating analysis in 2012, investment industry veteran Simon Lack estimated that since the late 1990s, *investors* in hedge funds had made $30 billion in total worldwide profits, less than they could have got from bank deposit interest. Meanwhile, hedge fund *owners* had creamed off $566 billion in fees from those poor investors – that's to say, 95 per cent of all the profits. As the sardonic old financial sector adage goes: 'Where are the customers' yachts?'

When you make this sharky business model available to all the world's small-time crooks, the problem shifts beyond raw greed and uselessness, into something worse. As Marchant explained, 'They are appealing to the lowest common denominator – with the inevitable disastrous results.'

The trick to securing OPM is to tell a story that's convincing enough to persuade unsuspecting punters to send you their savings. The victims, in Marchant's experience, are typically retired British expatriates. Offer them the chance to invest in something as grand as a hedge fund, and persuade them that playing with the big boys makes them a 'sophisticated investor', you're already a long way towards tickling and teasing their retirement funds into your offshore Ponzi scheme.

'Every bloody loser out there – any individual who decides on a whim "Oh, I wouldn't mind owning my own offshore hedge fund", it could be you or me – could do so easily,' says Marchant. The sort of people who set these things up, in his experience of investigating, 'are complete riff-raff, criminals. I've come across situations where all of the portfolios have been fraudulent, even though they are unrelated, and with different frauds in each one.'

These SPCs have mutated and spread in recent years, with variants popping up under different names in Cayman, the British Virgin Islands, Jersey, the Isle of Man, Malta, Luxembourg, Switzerland and elsewhere. While writing this section, I opened a Youtube video and was presented with an advertisement for one of these vehicles, run out of Malta, where they're known as Recognised Incorporated Cell Companies (RICCs). Presumably Google Adwords must have been running its creepy spiders over my chapter draft and picked up references to this stuff. I clicked on the advert for this SPC (I won't give the name because I hate the thought of advertising it) and was whisked to a beautiful, glossy, chrome-styled beige-gold website, which gushes: 'Imagine a tier-one hedge fund solution on a solid legal and regulatory platform that appeals to institutional investors. A trading infrastructure with all the autonomy and sophistication that appeals to you . . . but none of the high costs.' They provide, among many other things, 'initial anti-money laundering due diligence, with ongoing checks as required' – whatever that means. All this, they promise, is yours for just €10,000; a tiny fraction of what it would normally cost.

A slick video shows looping arrows and boxes indicating ownership and control; the main umbrella platform, it says, is regulated by the UK's Financial Services Authority (now the Financial Conduct Authority, in fact) with a line snaking out to 'your hedge fund', where FSC/FCA regulation was not indicated. This platform is serviced by such upstanding names as PwC, Nomura International, Royal Bank of Canada, Bank of America Merrill Lynch, and a bunch of lesser known players. I asked Marchant about this firm; he didn't know it but said it looked similar to others he'd probed.

* * *

This new and apparently fast-growing niche in the offshore ecosystem, however, pales into insignificance when compared to the next thing I want to write more about: the wild, woolly, slippery and ancient world of trusts.

A rapid re-cap, for those who've forgotten how they work.

A classic trust is a triangle. A wealthy grandfather, say, gives away a billion dollars' worth of stuff into a trust, where it is handled by a trustee, typically a lawyer, who is bound by a set of instructions from the rich old man to manage those assets on behalf of, say, his lucky grandchildren – the beneficiaries.

That 'stuff' could be anything; an apartment in Paris or Chelsea; gold bars in a vault in Singapore; a racehorse or a yacht or a Picasso painting; a portfolio of FTSE 100 shares; Giuseppe's Pizza company sporting a bloated Swiss bank account; or a Panamanian company that owns a bunch of other shell companies in other tax havens, each of which owns other stuff in a bunch of other places. Or all of the above, and more.

Trusts pose two challenges for society.

First, they can create impenetrable secrecy. Trusts aren't legal entities that need to be registered somewhere to exist; they are just agreements. You could, in theory, set one up merely on the basis of some words and a handshake. Usually, trusts don't disclose to anyone the people who matter – in this case the old man, the lawyer and the grandchildren – nor do they disclose Guiseppe's Pizza Co. and those other assets,[10] or the nature of those instructions to the trustee.

That is impenetrable enough, particularly if those players and assets are strung out across several tax havens. The second problem, however, goes deeper; worsening the secrecy and creating a host of new problems. Notice, in this example, that Grandfather has *given away* the assets, but the grandchildren haven't received them yet. They may well be allowed by the trust to *live* in that apartment in Chelsea, groom and nuzzle and ride that racehorse, or hang that Picasso on their living room wall. But legally, they don't *own* them. That's the whole point of the trust.

And this raises a big question. If Grandad doesn't own those assets, and the grandchildren don't own them either, then who does? Certainly not the trustee: she's just the manager, bound by tight laws and rules that don't allow her to snaffle the assets for herself.

To cut a long story short, trusts manipulate the very concept of ownership, so that *nobody* really owns them. These are 'ownerless' assets.[11] And if you don't own those assets, then it can be very hard for your tax authorities to tax you on their income, or for your creditors to get hold of them when you've defrauded them, no matter how many expensive lawyers they hire.

It's hard to know how big this problem of 'ownerless' assets is, but a couple of numbers may give an idea. Colin Powell, the outgoing chair of the Jersey Financial Services Commission, told me in 2009 that he thought there were some 300–400 billion dollars' worth of assets in Jersey trusts alone. That figure is probably higher now – and Jersey is just one of maybe ninety significant tax havens in the world. More broadly, there's a 2014 paper by the US National Bureau of Economic Research that estimated that around 5 per cent of all US household wealth is held in trusts.[12] If you were to apply that share to the estimated $250 trillion in world household wealth, it would suggest $12.5 trillion in wealth is held in trusts. That's the same order of magnitude as the estimated $7.5–36 trillion of wealth held in tax havens.

There's a huge overlap between trusts and the offshore world – and a large share of these assets in the overlap are 'ownerless'. This means, among other things, that inequality is generally worse than the statistics suggest. If you can't assign an owner to an asset, you can't say it belongs to a particular income group, and so you can't slot it into the inequality data[13].

And in the world of trusts, things are getting worse, fast. Adam Hofri-Winogradow, a Senior Lecturer at the Hebrew University of Jerusalem Faculty of Law, talks of the 'stripping of the trust' amid a race to the bottom among jurisdictions. He talks of a 'global revolution in trust law' which is happening 'at an exhilarating speed'.[14]

And here's another little fact about trusts.

The ICIJ has a searchable database that includes some data from the Panama Papers and other leaks. I entered the word 'trust' into the database and got 1,630 results, an underestimate given that many trusts don't have 'trust' in their name. More than three-quarters of these – 1,236, to be exact – were incorporated in the Cook Islands, a tiny, former British protectorate of 11,000 people in the south Pacific, now essentially an offshore satellite of New Zealand.

No country has burrowed further into the rabbit hole of trusts than the Cook Islands; John Doe of the Panama Papers scandal calls it a 'financial fraud mecca'. The Cook Islands specialises in 'asset protection' so strong as to enable what Harrington calls 'debt avoidance'. They taught her about it on her wealth management course. She explains:

People can get sued and lose, or incur debts they can't cover, but if their assets are in a Cook Islands trust, they can say, 'Meh, I don't feel like paying. Come and get me.' It's one of the things you learn about in wealth management training: how to help clients avoid paying what they owe, such as debts that the courts might impose in a commercial dispute, or in a divorce case.

In interviews with Cook Island practitioners I asked 'Are you really saying what I think you are saying? Are you really saying you can skip out on the debts?'

I was horrified: horrified and fascinated. I'd ask things like 'Can't they sue for fraud? I would never dream of trying something like this because I would imagine I would lose.' They said: 'No, no, this is how you do it.'

One user of Cook Islands trusts was Kevin Trudeau, a telegenic US populariser of cancer prevention pills, facelifts-in-a-bottle, and other bogus health products and get-rich-quick schemes. The US Federal Trade Commission won a $37.5 million judgement against Trudeau for bamboozling many people over one of his weight-loss books – yet try as it might, it simply could not break into his Cook Islands trust to get the money. To try and recover assets from the Cook Islands you need to fly your lawyers out to fight it in Cook Islands courts, where your odds of winning are approaching zero. Even the mighty US justice system could not break into this South Pacific offshore flyspeck.[15]

Harrington flew to the Cook Islands herself and suffered a terrifying break-in into her hotel room at night where she was sleeping with her young child.

She filed a report with the police then walked down to the harbour, where a Maori fisherman was cleaning his catch. He could see she was troubled; he interrupted his work to ask what was wrong.

When she explained, he laughed and said that since the financial services industry had grown so powerful on the island, crime had soared. 'It was as if the business of evading the law had created a kind of contagion, corrupting island life even in aspects that had nothing to do with finance,' she said. He told her, 'We trusted each other. Native culture has a special set of values; we are supposed to be protected. All of that has gone out of the window . . . Everyone calls us the Crook Islands now.'[16]

There is a big lesson here for other jurisdictions like Britain that are dominated by an overseas-focused and increasingly offshore financial sector. Financial centres looking for foreign, or offshore, business face two opposing incentives. On the one hand, they want to appear safe, trustworthy, clean and well regulated. 'Your money is safe with us.' On the other hand, they also want to attract as much dirty money as possible.

They reconcile these two with an offering to the world's hot money that goes like this: 'We won't steal your money – but we'll turn a blind eye if you steal someone else's.' The idea is to have your cake *and* eat it.

The Maori fisherman understood clearly that this approach simply doesn't work. You can't get involved in offshore and ring-fence your own economy and politics from the murk. It will, inevitably, leak into and corrupt your own system.

Offshore has so thoroughly corrupted the banking fraternity and the British establishment that they now seem, essentially, untouchable. Rowan Bosworth-Davies, a former British fraud detective, spent many years watching the steady degradation of London's laws as they tried to play the offshore card. He described giving a talk to some senior British bankers in 2003, warning of the dangers of openly tolerating criminality in the financial system. Afterwards, he says, a board member of a major high street bank told him, 'If you think Her Majesty's Government is ever going to prosecute people of my class, you are utterly mistaken. We are a protected species.'

'The most prestigious names in the British banking and finance,' said Bosworth-Davies, 'routinely engage in criminal activities on a scale that would make any Mafia family proud.'[17] Marchant, the fraud investigator, has the same impression. When he investigates offshore schemes, he said, he routinely treats the inclusion of titles like 'Sir' or 'Lord' in the documents as red flags. If a scheme feels the need to flaunt a peerage or two, there's a good chance it needs to whitewash something.

Following the Brexit vote, will Britain, removed from the moderating, social democratic European bath, come under the sway of those 'anti-regulation fantasists', and tumble headlong into an unreformable, butler-to-the-rich, offshore gated wonderland?

* * *

The best way to ponder the future is, very often, to remember the past, for that's where the deep, structural forces of change come from.

The Panama Papers is just the latest of a long, long string of offshore scandals, says James Henry, the former McKinsey's chief economist and author of the book *Blood Bankers*. He's one of few people to have watched this offshore stuff for decades from a critical economist's perspective, and says you only really understand the system through what he calls 'investigative economics' – that is, by sitting down with spreadsheets of data, then getting on planes and diving into the wild, roiling turmoil of the thing; hanging out with the bankers, accountants, lawyers, finance ministers, rich people and drugs pilots who make up the blood and guts of the system.

'There is almost a banality about the exposés,' such as the Panama Papers and Luxleaks, he says, reeling off a long list of past scandals including exposures of BCCI, HSBC, and a couple of others that were arguably each as bad as, if not worse than, Mossack Fonseca's escapades. But what is striking is the sheer, exuberant growth of the thing. 'When I started looking at this in 1985 there were 10–15 significant havens: in the Channel Islands, Caribbean, and Switzerland. Now there are over 90, depending on how you define them. There's a risk that we lose sight of the fact that Panama is just one of them. It's become a commodity business.'

Henry now reckons there is now as much as $36 trillion stashed offshore. That's bigger than another widely publicised estimate by the French economist Gabriel Zucman, who uses a very different lens and finds 'only $7.6 trillion'.[18] Even with Zucman's smaller estimate, though, that many dollar bills laid end to end would stretch along the earth's orbit around the sun. As the business grows, metastasises, infects new jurisdictions, and pushes further into our mainstream economies, its political power grows.

But all is not lost; far from it.

Something has changed since *Treasure Islands* was first published in 2011. There is, at last, a new counterforce: a proper democratic fightback, fed by widespread public anger. I hear strangers talking about tax havens in queues at supermarkets and in pubs. World leaders are, at last, starting to listen.

Several streams feed this fightback. First is the financial crisis and its aftershocks, forcing governments to scramble to raise tax revenue from new sources. None makes a more tempting and legitimate target than secretive pots of often dirty offshore wealth.

Anger about rising inequality creates more interest; there's nothing quite like a tax haven to boost inequality in a society. And, as the IMF and many others are now beginning to see, more inequality means lower economic growth too.

A third stream, fed by the first two, involves a rising popular fury about our incompetent, economically illiterate, corrupt, banker-led elites. This anger has nurtured the Occupy movement, the UK Uncut tax protests, the Brexit campaign, and fed the rise of Donald Trump and Nigel Farage on the right and Bernie Sanders, Elizabeth Warren and Jeremy Corbyn on the left. The centre ground of politics is being hollowed out, all around the world.

Many pundits point to 'globalisation' as one of the root sources of this hollowing-out, and there's something to this. I'd prefer to sharpen the criticism and heap blame on a more specific ill: the dark, offshore heart of financial globalisation, which is helping to foster the rise of a parasitic financial sector that's hollowing out our economies.

There is another powerful stream feeding the fightback against tax havens, however. At last, we're seeing the beginnings of a coherent narrative and understanding of the offshore world, of the dangers it poses, and of its role at the heart of the globalisation project. Five years ago most people saw offshore as little more than a colourful freak show. Things have changed; its role is now increasingly widely understood as a high-energy, corrupting core component of financial hyperglobalisation. I'm confident that *Treasure Islands*, and groups like the Tax Justice Network, whose pioneering work inspired this book, have helped create a blueprint for understanding this peculiar, ever-metastasising phenomenon in its proper political and economic context for the first time. As our analysis has spread, so the old tax-cutting certainties are coming under attack, alongside new research demonstrating that not only has the orgy of tax-cutting on corporations and the rich since the 1980s accompanied a huge *rise* in tax cheating, but that the two are likely to be related.[19]

So we now have two opposing forces at work: the relentless onward march and proliferation of offshore, under its own race-to-the-bottom logic and armies of private enablers, versus a new counterforce, rising off the streets. And as a result of this counterforce, world leaders, pushed by their voters, are at last doing *something*. There's quite a bit to celebrate now.

On the secrecy side, the OECD, the club of rich countries, is putting into place a global mechanism for sharing banking information automatically across borders, moving beyond the old and failed 'on request' standard. Remarkably, most major havens have signed up, and first data starts to flow in 2017. The programme, known as the Common Reporting Standard, is full of holes though; Tax Haven USA isn't really playing ball, and places like the Bahamas and Panama are aggressively undermining it. I'm told these two countries, even after the Panama Papers scandal, are still sending delegations around the world to boast about how they won't play along and telling conferences of wealth managers and tax advisers: 'your secrets are safe with us.'[20] But it's a huge improvement on an appalling past and I'm optimistic that many holes will be fixed, in time.

A little behind this curve, countries are also setting up registries of the real, warm-blooded owners of secret shell companies. Again, Uncle Sam is not helping much, and countries like the Bahamas and Dubai are selling themselves as hold-outs against transparency. There's a list of loopholes here, too, not least a failure to get this shell company data published, or get to grips with the slippery, devious world of trusts. But there's real momentum behind this one.

A third improvement is country-by-country reporting, where countries require multinationals to open up their books about what they're up to in each country where they do business. Versions are now being rolled out, in the European Union, United States, with the OECD's blessing. Again, coverage is patchy and imperfect. But here, too, there's drive.

When the concepts underlying these three global programmes were first proposed by the Tax Justice Network a decade ago, they were ridiculed. These were crazy ideas, pie in the sky. Now these initiatives are official policy of the G20 group of the world's most powerful countries, and of the OECD.

Even Britain, that devious old offshore rogue, has been making some improvements. If there's one thing Cameron can be proud of, it's that he made *some* progress in cracking down on the secrecy that Britain and its spiderweb transmit around the globe. Though he didn't try nearly hard enough; Britain controls these places and it can, if it really wants to, *force* them to strike down their secrecy laws. He and his successors have (so far) chickened out, and merely promised to 'influence' and 'persuade' them to put in place some half-cock reforms. The offshore satellites have fought back hard against transparency – but they have at least made some concessions.

Secrecy is one thing. But tax is quite another. And here – particularly when it comes to taxing multinational corporations – Cameron and Osborne have gone exactly in the opposite direction. They have pointlessly slashed corporate tax rates, turning Britain into more of a tax haven than it already was; pulsing out new waves of corporate tax-cutting harm to every other country, and harming Britain too by savagely cutting its tax revenues. This gigantic handout now approaching £15 billion per year has attracted almost no useful corporate business either: as I've already mentioned, these handouts don't attract the real, genuine, embedded investments that countries want; they attract all but jobless accounting nonsense and profit-shuffling, which is good for the accountants (who have the government's ear) but no good for the economy. The corporate income tax is one of the most precious taxes there is, not least because it protects the main income tax: cut it far enough, and rich people will reclassify their income as corporate income and get out of paying their income taxes. This corporate orgy will be a disaster for Britain. The economic damage that's being done will now, of course, be masked by the Brexit shock – which will become an excuse for every economic failure for years to come.

More shocking than this, perhaps, is the so-called Luxleaks affair of 2014, which erupted after two employees of PwC in Luxembourg blew the whistle on a secret, industrial-scale tax-cheat factory that their employer was running for the world's multinationals. They leaked data to the ICIJ – the same body that handled the Panama Papers – and it provided a new window into some of the extraordinary schemes multinationals use to escape tax. Note that I didn't use the word 'avoid' here: this wasn't about 'legal tax avoidance', an awful term that I've used in this book but which I now think everyone should shun.[21] The legality of many of these schemes was indeterminate; that is, some would have likely have failed if they'd been properly challenged in court. Richard Brooks, a former corporate tax inspector who is now Britain's best known tax writer, said Luxleaks may have involved 'mass tax crimes' on an unprecedented scale.

Neither PwC, nor the multinationals involved, have been held to account for this scandal — and Jean-Claude Juncker, who essentially oversaw the construction of Tax Haven Luxembourg, is now President of the European Commission. The only people to have been punished are the two whistle-blowers, Antoine Deltour and Raphäel Halet, who got suspended prison sentences for spilling the beans, and the journalist, Edouard Perrin, who first handled the leak.[22]

All in all, the outcome of these grand, opposing forces pushing against each other – the growing offshore machine fuelled by the race to the bottom, versus the new democratic pushback – is messy. There is progress, and there is backsliding.

But there is one particularly worrying pattern discernible in this complex process. It concerns what one might call 'financial stability issues'.

I've described offshore as an ecosystem, with many niches. When there's a crackdown on one niche, as is happening right now on secrecy, the system shifts and coalesces into new shapes and other, often wilder niches come along to fill the holes left behind.

The bigger, supposedly better-regulated jurisdictions like Cayman, Jersey or Luxembourg are undergoing a long-term shift away from the more obviously dangerous things like hosting drugs money, Mafia activities and other purely secrecy-based shenanigans, into apparently more upmarket and lucrative areas like fund management, private equity, hedge funds, off-balance sheet financing and derivatives, and what one might call the shadow insurance system.

These kinds of activities are not yet significantly on the world's offshore radar. But they should be; the libertarian world of tax havens provides a discreet, hardly policed back door to financial deregulation for the world's biggest financial players. The financial stability risks they pose are unquantifiable – and I just have to stress, once again, how central the City of London is to this deregulatory, see-no-evil world.

Now and then, such matters poke their snouts briefly above the surface of this large, high-end swamp, then sink back into the offshore murk. One such matter concerns so-called 'off-balance sheet entities', which were heavily involved in the global financial crisis. To cut a long story short, the banks create these 'off-balance sheet entities' in order to get around regulators' restrictions on how much risk they take on. The risks are parked, of course, in the tax-free, regulation-free havens.

A Reuters investigation in 2015 revealed a widespread shovelling of these risks offshore, to London and to its offshore satellites. One bank alone, Wells Fargo, held $1.56 trillion (again, that's trillion with a 't') in off-balance sheet entities in the Cayman Islands, hardly noticed by anyone;[23] the Reuters analysis has long since been forgotten. So while it's true that there's a push to curb tax haven secrecy, and some tax shenanigans – there is rather less attention to the tax havens' roles in helping hide risks in our financial systems.

Still, since *Treasure Islands* was first published there have been some people who are starting to notice. 'It seems to be that every big trading disaster happens in London,' said Carolyn Maloney, a US Democratic lawmaker, at a hearing in 2012. At the same hearing Gary Gensler, then chair of the US Commodity Futures Trading Commission, which regulates derivatives, outlined the dangers of US firms setting up abroad to find 'lower regulatory regimes'. He compared London to other centres like the Cayman Islands and said that when crisis hit it wasn't the offshore miscreants who would foot the bill, but other poor saps in the US and elsewhere. 'So often it comes right back here, crashing to our shores.'

The US Dodd-Frank Act of 2010, responding to the global financial meltdown, contained powerful provisions in its early drafts to restrain offshore arbitrage in the wild-west global derivatives market, currently valued at nearly $700 trillion. Put simply, the provisions would have enabled the US regulator to regulate any such activities with a 'direct and significant connection' to the US economy, no matter where they were located.

But, like the giant fish in Ernest Hemingway's *The Old Man and the Sea*, this part of the package was gutted by wave after wave of attacks by bankers and other sharks, in league with UK Chancellor George Osborne, Swiss Finance Minister Eveline Widmer-Schlumpf, Michel Barnier, the European Commissioner for internal markets and services, and several others. What emerged at the other end of the legislative process was a near-lifeless skeleton.[24] The offshore Weapons of Mass Financial Destruction had been ring-fenced against the rules of society, with particular benefits flowing to a small circle of people in London and New York.

Some people think it's pointless to even try and tackle this shape-shifting monster. They compare these efforts to squeezing a balloon:

you compress it in one place but it will all just puff out somewhere else – but the volume stays the same.

The cynics are quite wrong, though. The crackdowns are more like squeezing a sponge. You'll displace plenty elsewhere when you squeeze, as people with a bigger stomach for risk and a deeper contempt for society, move their assets to wilder, woollier shores like Panama or the Bahamas. But the more risk-averse players will be persuaded to bring their money back into society. You won't get it all, but you can squash this sponge down.

And there's another good reason why these schemes will have teeth. The global culture has changed. A system that was tolerated or indulged a few years ago is becoming steadily less acceptable. That may discourage many users, but it is also making the system less and less safe for many of its secret users. They know that for the private enablers of offshore, it is getting harder now to ignore the damage. Some are now starting to question and doubt the morality of what they are doing – and the recent spate of giant offshore data leaks is no coincidence: long may it continue. Let's all now stand up for those whistle-blowers and figure out new ways to target the ever-growing private army of players who make the whole system tick.

Notes

Prologue

1. US Energy Information Administration (EIA). • **2.** The episode is covered in detail in Nicholas Shaxson, *Poisoned Wells: The Dirty Politics of African Oil*, Palgrave, 2007, Chs 4 and 5. • **3.** Valérie Lecasble and Airy Routier, *Forages en eau profonde*, Grasset, 1998. • **4.** Ibid. p252. • **5.** *'Scandale!*: How Roland Dumas got France Gossiping', *Independent*, 30 Jan 2001. • **6.** See Jean-Marie Bockel, 'Je veux signer l'acte de décès de la Françafrique', *Le Monde*, 16 Jan 2008.

1 Welcome to Nowhere

1. All these estimates should be considered as giving orders of magnitude only. The figures are impossible to quantify precisely, not least because there is no agreement on the meaning of 'offshore'. This statistic from French Finance Minister Dominique Strauss-Kahn, speaking to the Paris Group of Experts in March 1999, quoted in J. Christensen and M. Hampton, 'All Good Things Come to an End', *The World Today*, Vol. 55, No. 8/9, Royal Institute of International Affairs, 1999. The share has grown since then. • **2.** See Ronen Palan, Richard Murphy and Christian Chavagneux, *Tax Havens: How Globalisation Really Works*, Cornell University, 2010, p51. It cites BIS data showing offshore's share of banking assets and liabilities rising to around 65% in 1990, before falling to 51% in 2007. Also see Luca Errico and Alberto Musalem, *'Offshore Banking: An Analysis of Micro- and Macro-Prudential Issues'*,

IMF, Jan 1999, pp17–19. Figure was 54% in 1999. The figure is based on a relatively restrictive definition of offshore. • 3. Philip R. Lane and Gian Maria Milesi-Ferretti, 'The History of Tax Havens; Cross-Border Investment in Small International Financial Centers', IMF Working Paper, WP/10/38, Feb 2010. • 4. Data from Ronen Palan, The Offshore World, Cornell, 2003, and from David Bain, 'IMF finds "Trillions" in Undeclared Wealth', Wealth Bulletin, 15 Mar 2010, and from M. K. Lewis, 'International Banking and Offshore Finance: London and the Major Centres', in Mark P. Hampton and Jason P. Abbott, Offshore Finance Centres and Tax Havens, Macmillan, 1999. • 5. This loose definition is the result of collegiate discussions among members of the Tax Justice Network and others. It is similar to a definition offered by Richard Murphy of Tax Research UK. • 6. Ahmed Zoromé, 'Concept of Offshore Financial Centres: In Search of an Operational Definition', IMF Working Paper, WP/07/87, 2007. • 7. John Lanchester, 'Bravo l'artiste', London Review of Books, 5 Feb 2004, reviewing Neil Chenoweth, Rupert Murdoch: The Untold Story of the World's Greatest Media Wizard, Crown Business, 2002. • 8. Death and Taxes: The True Toll of Tax Dodging, Christian Aid, May 2008. • 9. The original figure was given in pounds: £400 million and £128,000. Average exchange rate for the year from www.oanda.com. • 10. Form 10-Q for Chiquita Brands International Inc, 5 May 2009, Quarterly Report, http://biz.yahoo.com/e/090505/cqb10-q.html • 11. 'One-third of biggest businesses pay no tax', Financial Times, 28 Aug 2007. See also 'One third of the UK's largest companies pay no tax', Tax Research UK, 28 Aug 2007, outlining reasons: these include pension payments, generous rules on interest payments, large capital allowances, international opportunities. • 12. http://www.economist.com/business/displaystory.cfm?story_id=319862&source=login_payBarrier • 13. Holding companies exempt from income taxes, introduced in 1929. • 14. Oliver Arlow 'Kim Jong-il Keeps $4bn "Emergency Fund" in European Banks', Daily Telegraph, 14 Mar 2010. • 15. From the Dutch Central Bank, cited in Jesse Drucker's U.S. Companies Dodge $60 Billion in Taxes with Global Odyssey, Bloomberg, 13 May 2010. Figure given is 12.3 trillion euros, which was around US$18 trillion according to average exchange rates on www.oanda.com. The Bloomberg story gives a $15 trillion conversion. • 16. Until the early 1990s, economic historians had viewed the British empire in large part as a corollary of the Industrial Revolution, which had made the empire both necessary and possible; empire was, to a large degree, a story about industrial capitalism and trade. The economic historians P. J. Cain and A. G. Hopkins transformed this view in 1993 with a two-volume book, British Imperialism, which recast the empire as fundamentally a story about financial capital, international credit and the City of London, the governor of the imperial engine. • 17. See Palan, Murphy and Chavagneux, 2010, p11. They estimate that the Crown Dependencies and Overseas Territories, plus the former empire, account for 37% of all banking liabilities and 35% of all banking assets; the City of London accounts for 11%. • **18.** Plenty of assets do flow to London, and have caused considerable harm this way. Assets from the Crown Dependencies and elsewhere are consolidated into Britain's national accounts, flattering a rather darker picture. • **19.** Michael Foot, *Final report of the independent Review of British offshore financial centres*, HM Treasury, Oct 2009. • **20.** 'Jersey Banking: The International Finance Centre', Jersey Finance Ltd, Fact Sheet, Aug 2009. • **21.** Martin A. Sullivan, 'Offshore Explorations: Jersey', 23 Oct 2007; 'Offshore Explorations: Isle of Man', 5 Nov 2007; 'Offshore Explorations: Guernsey', 10 Oct 2007, Tax Notes. Colin Powell, chairman of the Jersey Financial Services Commission, estimated in an interview with the author in 2009 that trusts in Jersey alone might involve another $300–400bn. • **22.** Seven, including the Falkland Islands and the British Antarctic Territory, are not havens. Ascension Island, which houses highly secretive US and British military bases, serves a quasi-imperial purpose, as a base to help project British power overseas. • **23.** In 2003, for example, a major money laundering trial collapsed after a key witness was forced to admit that he had been serving as an MI6 agent. • **24.** See, for example, 'Britain Imposes Direct Rule on Turks and Caicos', Associated Press, 14 Aug 2009. Plans are now afoot to prepare new elections for 2011. • **25.** Although Ireland lies in the eurozone, its emergence as a secrecy jurisdiction in the late 1980s was substantially linked to and promoted by interests in the City of London. • **26.** 'Users of "Tax Havens" Abroad Batten Down for Political Gale', *New York Times*, 26 Feb 1961. • **27.** See, for example, the Tax Justice Network's Financial Secrecy Index, 2009, which ranks the United States in first place. • **28.** 'The *Deepwater Horizon* switched from Panama to the Marshall Islands in 2005.' See US Coast Guard Report of Investigation into the Circumstances Surrounding the Explosion, Fire, Sinking and Loss of Eleven Crew Members Aboard the mobile offshore drilling unit *Deepwater Horizon* in the Gulf of Mexico April 20-22, 2010 http://scr.bi/qqvU97 • **29.** For Zeder and the Marshall Islands see *OIA Press Release: Fred Monroe Zeder*, US Office of Insular Affairs, 2008. Zeder was Bush's ambassador to the region; his private company Island Development was incorporated on 14 October 1986, four days before Zeder signed a treaty providing for $6m in aid for the Marshall Islands, of which $1.2m was used to help set up the ship registry. Zeder died in 2008. See 'Bush Friend, Former Ambassador: Company Wasn't Disclosed', Associated Press, reproduced in *The Victoria Advocate*, 30 Apr 1990. Khadija Sharife in the *London Review of Books* blog ('Offshore Exploitation', 9 June 2010) established that 'During a joint hearing to investigate the explosion and sinking of the *Deepwater Horizon*, Hung Nguyen, a captain in the Coast Guard, was surprised to learn from the US Interior Department's Mineral Management Service – the unit responsible for overseeing offshore exploitation – that "there is no enforcement". Each operator "self-certifies and establishes what they think is adequate". This system of self-regulation was formulated by Dick Cheney's Energy Task Force.' • **30.** *About the Liberian Registry*, an overview published by www.liscr.com. For the Standard Oil link, see Andrew Leonard, *Big Oil's slick trick*, Australian Business Spectator, 15 May, 2010. • **31.** Jeffrey Robinson, *The Sink: How Banks, Lawyers and Accountants Finance Terrorism and Crime – and Why Governments Can't Stop Them*, Robinson Publishing, 2004, p63. • **32.** 'Large US Corporations and Federal Contractors with Subsidiaries in Jurisdictions Listed as Tax Havens or Financial Privacy Jurisdictions', GAO, Dec 2008. • **33.** 'World Governments Chip Away at Bank Secrecy', German Press Agency, 12 Apr 2010. • **34.** Nicolas Sarkozy, just ahead of the G20 Pittsburgh summit, from '*Paradis fiscaux: bilan du G20 en 12 questions*', CCFD-Terre Solidaire, Apr 2010. • **35.** See 'List of Unco-operative Tax Havens', OECD, http://www.oecd.org/document/57/0,3343,en_2649_33745_30578809_1_1_1,00.html. The blacklist contained no entries in May 2009 after the OECD removed Liechtenstein, Monaco and Andorra. • **36.** There is some disagreement over its membership. See, for example, 'Offshore firms stay afloat while governments target tax havens', *Law Gazette*, 2 July 2009. • **37.** Source: Office of Management and Budget, *Budget of the US Government, Fiscal Year 2011, Historical Tables*, Feb 2010 (calculations by Citizens for Tax Justice). Also see http://www.progressive.org/node/1595. • **38.** 'Shifting Responsibility: How 50 Years of Tax Cuts Benefited the Wealthiest Americans', *Wealth for the Common Good*, Apr 2010. • **39.** http://www.telegraph.co.uk/news/worldnews/asia/northkorea/7442188/Kim-Jong-il-keeps-4bn-emergency-fund-in-European-banks.html • **40.** Dev Kar and Carly Curcio, *Illicit Financial flows from Developing Countries: 2000–2009*, a January 2011 report from Global Financial Integrity. http://iff-update.gfip.org/. This defines illicit money as 'illegally earned, transferred or utilised'. Economists from the Oxford Centre for Business Taxation have sought to discredit GFI's estimates, callling them 'drastically overstated', but their report making this accusation was comprehensively demolished by Dev Kar, a GFI economist (formerly an IMF senior economist), who has explained the blind spot in traditional estimates. Traditional models will estimate the magnitude of illicit outflows from a country, then estimate the magnitude of illicit inflows, and then subtract one from the other to achieve a net result. Kar explains, however, that the estimates should not be subtracted, but added. For further details, see 'Time to Bury the Oxford Report', Tax Justice Network blog, 16 July 2009, plus associated links, and Dev Kar, 'The Alpha, but Whither the Omega, of the Greek Crisis?', Task Force on Financial Integrity and Economic Development blog, 11 May 2010. • **41.** Capitalism's Achilles heel, whose headline $1.0–1.6 trillion figure was subsequently endorsed in 'Stolen Asset Recovery (StAR) Initiative: Challenges, Opportunities, and Action Plan', World Bank/UN Office on Drugs and Crime, June 2007. • **42.** See *Illicit flows: we finally reveal the official data*, Tax Justice Network blog, 23 Jul, 2009. In a long essay in May 2011 the celebrated economist J.K. Galbraith commented: 'What you cannot get – not at a meeting sponsored by the International Monetary Fund, not from the participants at the Institute for New Economic Thinking (INET) – is any serious discussion of contract law and fraud. I've tried, repeatedly. No one will deny, in response to the question, the role that fraud played in the financial debacle. How could they? But they won't discuss it either. Why not? Why is this one of the great taboo topics of our modern economic history?' See J. K. Galbraith's keynote lecture to the 5th annual 'Dijon' conference on Post Keynesian economics, meeting at Roskilde University near Copenhagen, Denmark, May 13, 2011. Transcript available at *James K. Galbraith: The Final Death (and Next Life) of Maynard Keynes*, Firedoglake, Aug 1, 2011.• **43.** Author's interviews with Blum, with sections from 'A Conversation with Jack Blum', *The American Interest*, Nov/Dec 2009. • **44.** 'Cyprus, Ireland and Switzerland Have Most Attractive Corporate Tax Regimes in Europe, Finds KPMG International Poll', 17 Dec 2007. • **45.** There is one notable exception: 'Business Unprepared as Fair Tax Follows Fair Trade into the Spotlight', SustainAbility, 14 Mar 2006, which examined the role of paying tax in the corporate responsibility debate. • **46.** See Hogan speaking on video embedded in 'Hogan Loses High Court Battle to Keep Financial Records Secret', *Sydney Morning Herald*, 16 June 2010.

2 Technically Abroad

1. Cain and Hopkins, pp50, 157; statements in June 1929 and 29 October by ambassador Robertson. The Argentinian beef industry relied almost exclusively on the British market for its exports. By 1929 Argentina generated about 12% of Britain's income from overseas investments. • **2.** Rodolfo Roquel, *Nosotros, los Peronistas*, Dunken, Argentina, p34. • **3.** http://www.vesteyfoods.com/en/vestey-group/vestey-group-history.html. • **4.** Phillip Knightley, *The Rise and Fall of the House of Vestey*, Warner Books, 1993, p27. • **5.** Leslie Bethell, *Cambridge History of Latin America*, Vol. 8. • **6.** Sol Picciotto, *International Business Taxation*, Weidenfeld and Nicolson, 1992, pp4–13. • **7.** Ibid. pp1–37. • **8.** Knightley, op. cit. 1992, p34. • **9.** http://hansard.millbanksystems.com/lords/1922/jun/29/lord-vestey. • **10.** 'Lord Ashcroft's "Unequivocal Assurance" That Finally Secured Peerage', *Guardian*, 18 Mar 2010. • **11.** http://www.irs.gov/businesses/small/article/0,,id=106537,00.html. • **12.** See Sol Picciotto, 'Offshore: The State As Legal Fiction', in Mark P. Hampton and Jason P. Abbott (eds.) *Offshore Finance Centres and Tax Havens. The Rise of Global Capital*, Macmillan, 1999, pp 43–79. • **13.** Vestey, Edmund Hoyle (1932–2007,) Blue Star Line obituary, Blue Star Line website. http://www.bluestarline.org/edmund_vestey2.htm • **14.** See 'Heirs and disgraces', *Guardian*, 11 Aug 1999.

3 *The Profitable Shield of Neutrality*

1. Described in Nicholas Faith, *Safety in Numbers: the Mysterious World of Swiss Banking*, 1982, p65. • **2.** Ibid. p68. • **3.** As described in Sébastien Guex, 'The Origins of the Swiss Banking Secrecy Law and its Repercussions for Swiss Federal Policy', *Business History Review*, 74, summer 2000; The President and Fellows of Harvard College, pp237–266; http://www.jstor.org/pss/3116693. • **4.** Ibid. p250. • **5.** Letter from the Federal Political Department to Swiss Embassy in Germany, 17 Nov 1932, cited in ibid. p251. • **6.** Bruno Gurtner, 'Swiss Secrecy Laws Had Nothing to Do With the Nazis', *Financial Times*, letters page, 26 Mar 2009. • **7.** 'Message du Conseil fédéral a l'assemblée fédérale concernant la revision de la loi sur les banques', *Feuille fédérale*, 13 Mar 1970, cited in Guex, 2000. • **8.** Jean-Marie Laya, *L'Argent secret et les banques Suisses*, Favre, 1977. • **9.** Switzerland strengthened this secrecy further. When France approached Swiss banks in 1937 for new credits, the Swiss agreed, but on two conditions. First, France should modify its import quotas in Switzerland's favour; second, the two countries should sign a treaty specifying clearly that France would scrupulously respect Swiss laws, regulations and administrative practices – and those included bank secrecy. Their French problem was neatly solved. • **10.** Author's interview with Guex in Lausanne, 29 Sep 2009. • **11.** 'The image of itself as a small master race that believed itself to be better than the rest of the world', in the words of Swiss politician Rudolf Strahm; see *A change of awareness has taken place*, Swiss Department of Foreign Affairs press release, 21 Apr 2009. • **12.** Jonathan Steinberg, *Why Switzerland?*, CUP, 1996, p128. • **13.** See Carolyn Bandel and Dylan Griffiths, 'Swiss Ratchet Up Tax Breaks As Europe Fights Deficits (Corrected)', Bloomberg, 2 June 2010. • **14.** A study in 2006 estimated that it had the greatest wealth inequality among all developed nations. Some larger industries did emerge later, particularly in industrial cities like Zürich, Basel and Winterthur, but workers' movements were still restrained when compared to, say, France. See 'Study Finds Wealth Inequality Is Widening Worldwide', *New York Times*, 6 Dec 2006. • **15.** Steinberg, 1996, p33. • **16.** Jules Landsmann cited in Faith, 1982, p18. • **17.** Data on banking flows during the Franco-Prussian War are scarce, but one account records deposits at one bank in Basel rising from 3.6m francs to 11.8m francs between 1869 and 1871. Adolf Jöhr, *Die Volkswirtschaft der Schweiz im Kriegsfall*, Verlag von Luhn & Schurch, 1912. • **18.** Tax rates rose in Switzerland too, but there was no war effort to pay for, and they remained far lower; foreign capital was granted exemptions in any case. • **19.** Steinberg, 1996, p64. Federal Councillor Kaspar Villiger in 1995 admitted publicly that the J was 'a German response to Swiss wishes'. Villiger also apologised for the attitude of the Swiss banks. • **20.** For example, Faith, 1982, pp92, 97. • **21.** Ibid. p99. The date or identity of the paper is not given. • **22.** Independent Commission of Experts (ICE) Switzerland – *Second*

World War, Vol. 17, 'Switzerland and Refugees in the Nazi Era', http://www.uek.ch/en/. By 1942, Switzerland legally hosted 9,150 foreign Jews, just 980 more than in 1931, although thousands more did get in unofficially, helped by sympathetic Swiss. Tom Bower, *Blood Money*, Pan Books, 1997, p22 and ICE, Vol. 17, summary. • **23.** On p72, Bower describes exactly such a plan, which eventually emerged on the eve of the liberation of Paris in 1944. • **24.** Ibid. pp41–2. • **25.** Faith, 1982, p119. • **26.** Steinberg, 1996, p68. • **27.** Bower, 1997, p83. • **28.** Martin Meier, Stefan Frech, Thomas Gees, Blaise Kropf, summary of 'Swiss Foreign Trade Policy 1930–1948: Structures – Negotiations – Functions', ICE Vol. 10, http://www.uek.ch/en/. • **29.** Bower, 1997, pp44–5. • **30.** Jean-Claude Favez, *Une mission impossible? Le CICR, les déportations, et les camps de concentration des Nazis*, Lausanne, 1988, cited in Steinberg, 1996, p70. • **31.** Bower, 1997, p51. • **32.** Ibid. p34. • **33.** Ibid. p74. • **34.** Ibid. pp64–5, Bliss letter to Lehman Arons, a US Treasury lawyer in London. • **35.** Ibid. p77. • **36.** 'Banking with the Nazis: Documents detail Swiss banks' ties with the Third Reich', Associated Press, 16 Oct 1996; Bower, 1997, pp78–9; Faith, 1982, pp105–6. • **37.** Widely cited, especially in Switzerland, in, for example, 'The Swiss Economy in World War II', www.swissworld.com, Federal Department of Foreign Affairs, General Secretariat, Switzerland. • **38.** Bower, 1997, p88. • **39.** Ibid. pp121–6. • **40.** Guex in *Business History Review*, 74, summer 2000, p264. • **41.** Roger P. Alford, 'The Claims Resolution Tribunal and Holocaust Claims Against Swiss Banks', *Berkeley Journal of International Law*, Vol. 20, No. 1, 2002. • **42.** According to the Swiss National Bank in 2009. • **43.** 'Swiss Banking Secrecy and Taxation: Paradise Lost?', *Helvea*, May 2009. The report only estimates evasion rates for Europe. • **44.** Andreas Missbach of the Berne Declaration, a Swiss non-governmental organisation, estimated in 2009 that the true stock of offshore private wealth in Switzerland was even higher: between $2.5 and $4.0 trillion. 'Highlights from the 2009 Summary of Deposits Data', *FDIC Quarterly*, Vol. 3, No. 4, 2009. • **45.** Interview with Strahm in Zürich, 21 Sep 2009. Strahm outlined a list of all significant changes to Swiss bank secrecy in Rudolf H. Strahm, *Warum wir so reich sind*, HEP Verlag A.G., Bern, 2008, p265. • **46.** Ken Stier, 'After UBS, Swiss Continue to Fight for Bank Secrecy', *Time* magazine, 5 Mar 2010.

4 *The Opposite of Offshore*

1. See the CIA's analysis of a countervailing view in R. Bruce Craig *Treasonable Doubt: The Harry Dexter White Spy Case*, Intelligence in Recent Public Literature By R. Bruce Craig. University of Kansas Press, 2004, Reviewed by James C. Van Hook, on www.cia.gov website. • **2.** Robert Skidelsky, *John Maynard Keynes: Fighting for Britain, 1937–1946*, Macmillan, 2002, pxv. • **3.** Robert Heilbroner, *The Worldly Philosophers*, Penguin, 1991, p253. • **4.** Robert Skidelsky, John Maynard

Keynes: Hopes Betrayed 1883-1920, Macmillan, 1992, p220. • **5.** Skidelsky, 2000, Vol. 1, p131. • **6.** John Maynard Keynes, *National Self-Sufficiency*, The Yale Review, Vol. 22, No. 4 (June 1933), pp. 755–76. • **7.** Heilbroner, 1991, p251. • **8.** 'A: The Secretary of the Treasury', Washington, 29 May 1937, from Henry Morgenthau to FDR, from Franklin D. Roosevelt Presidential Library. Given to the author in 2008 by his son Robert Morgenthau, then Manhattan district attorney. • **9.** Robert Skidelsky, *John Maynard Keynes: Fighting for Britain 1937–1946*, Papermac, 2001, p92. • **10.** Robert Skidelsky, *John Maynard Keynes: Fighting for Freedom 1937–1946* (the US edition), Penguin Books, 2002, p112. • **11.** Skidelsky, 2002, pxvii. • **12.** Ibid. • **13.** Lecture by J. Bradford DeLong, Econ 115 Lecture: Fall 2009: UC Berkeley, 29 Sep 2009 • **14.** Eric Helleiner, *States and the Reemergence of Global Finance: From Bretton Woods to the 1990s*, Cornell University Press, 1996, p4. • **15.** Skidelsky, 2002, pp340, 348. • **16.** Barry Eichengreen, *Europe's Post-War Recovery*, CUP, 1995, p99. • **17.** Skidelsky, 2002, p396. • **18.** Geoff Tily, The policy implications of the General Theory, *Real-World Economics Review*, Issue 50, 2009. • **19.** Helleiner chapter in Gerald A. Epstein, ed., *Capital Flight and Capital Controls in Developing Countries*, Edward Elgar, 2005, pp290–1. • **20.** Helleiner, 1996, p58. • **21.** Ibid. p59. • **22.** Ibid. p6. • **23.** Ha-Joon Chang, *Bad Samaritans*, Random House Business Books, 2007, p27. • **24.** See, for example, Dani Rodrik and Arvind Subramanian, 'Why Did Financial Globalization Disappoint?', *IMF Staff Papers*, Vol. 56, No. 1, 2009, pp 112–38. They seek other explanations, especially exchange-rate factors, for the disappointing performance of liberalised economies, but they do note the close correlation. Also see Monique Morrissey and Dean Baker, 'When Rivers Flow Upstream: International Capital Movements in the Era of Globalization', Center for Economic and Policy Research, Briefing Paper, Mar 2003. 'A striking feature of the distribution of current account surpluses and deficits among developing countries is that most of the countries that are experiencing high GDP growth have surpluses, and often large surpluses . . . The fact that most of these nations continue to experience rapid GDP growth, in spite of this large outflow of capital, suggests that the availability of capital has not been a major impediment to economic growth.' • **25.** See Martin Wolf, 'This time will never be different', *Financial Times*, 28 Sep 2009 • **26.** See the August 2007 Bank for International Settlements document for a description of how China's capital controls remain strong and binding. • **27.** 'Capital Inflows: The Role of Controls', IMF Staff Position Note, 19 Feb 2010.

5 *Eurodollar: The Bigger Bang*

1. See Catherine R. Schenk, 'The Origins of the Eurodollar Market in London: 1955–1963', in *Explorations in Economic History* 35, 221–238, EconPapers, 1998. • **2.** Ibid. p5. • **3.** Ibid. p7. • **4.** Anthony Sampson, *Who Runs This Place? The Anatomy of Britain in the 21st Century*, John Murray, 2005, p246. • **5.** David

Kynaston, *The City of London: Volume IV – A Club No More*, Pimlico, 2002, p94. • **6.** Ibid. pp80–1. • **7.** Ibid. p90. • **8.** Ibid. p54. • **9.** Ibid. p19. • **10.** Short biography of Hunold in Olivier Longchamp and Yves Steiner, 'The Contribution of the Schweizerisches Institut für Auslandforschung to the International Restoration of Neoliberalism (1949–1966)', presentation to EBHA – 11th Annual Conference. Geneva, 13–15 September 2007, published by University of Lausanne. • **11.** Richard Cockett, *Thinking the Unthinkable: Think-Tanks and the Economic Counter-Revolution, 1931–1983*, HarperCollins, 1994; pp100–21 explores the Mont Pelerin Society in detail. • **12.** Details are provided in Longchamp and Steiner, 2007. • **13.** Cockett, 1994, p108. • **14.** Macmillan report (which Keynes largely authored, also known as the Cunliffe Committee Report), 1929, reprinted 1979 by Arno Press Inc., point 50. • **15.** Gary Burn, *The Re-emergence of Global Finance*, Palgrave Macmillan, 2006, p97. • **16.** Kynaston, 2002, p76. • **17.** Burn, 2006, p26. • **18.** Ibid. p83. • **19.** Kynaston, 2002, p77. • **20.** Burn, 2006, p85. • **21.** Ibid. p86. • **22.** Kynaston, 2002, p506. • **23.** Burn, 2006, p102. • **24.** Kynaston, 2002, p578. • **25.** Ronen Palan, *The Offshore World: Sovereign Markets, Virtual Places, and Nomad Millionaires*, Cornell University Press, 2003, p29. • **26.** Quoted in Kynaston, 2002, p696–7. • **27.** Ibid. p697. • **28.** Mark Hampton, *The Offshore Interface: Tax Havens in the Global Economy*, Macmillan, 1996, p55. • **29.** Schenk, 1998, p235. • **30.** Burn, 2006, p113. • **31.** Burn, 2006, pp151, 158. • **32.** Kynaston, 2002, p396; Hampton and Abbott, 1999, p91 • **33.** Jane Sneddon Little, *Eurodollars: the Money-Market Gypsies*, Harper & Row, New York, 1975, p3. • **34.** Burn, 2006, pp10, 13. • **35.** Skidelsky, 2002, Preface and p98. • **36.** Burn, 2006, p142. • **37.** Ibid. p160. • **38.** Ibid. p161. • **39.** Ibid. p164. • **40.** Cited in Martin Mayer, *The Bankers*, W.H.Allen, London, 1976, quoted in Burn, 2006, p165. • **41.** Burn, 2006, p124. • **42.** Ibid. p125. • **43.** Western Europe: Those Euro-Dollars, *Time* magazine, 27 July, 1962. • **44.** Burn, 2006, p146. • **45.** Ibid. p140 and J. Orlin Grabbe, *The End of Ordinary Money, Part II: Money Laundering, Electronic Cash, and Cryptological Anonymity*, 1995. • **46.** Burn, 2006, p36. • **47.** Kynaston, 2002, p442, quoting Janet Kelly, *Bankers and Borders*, Cambridge, Mass., 1977, pp59–60. • **48.** Burn, 2006, pp122–3. • **49.** Ibid. p175. • **50.** 'Le Marché des Euro-Dollars correspondt-il aux besoins du système mondial des paiements?' *Le Monde*, 22/23 Oct 1967. Translated in the British National Archives, Letter from Petrie of 24 Oct 1967 to Messrs. Uffen, Hildyard, Woodruff, Ref. UE 4/44 in British national archives. • **51.** Robert Skidelsky, 'The World Finance Crisis & the American Mission', review of Martin Wolf, *Fixing Global Finance*, in *New York Review of Books*, 16 July 2009. • **52.** Helleiner, 1996, p21. • **53.** Ibid. p89.

6 *Construction of a Spider's Web*

1. See R.T. Naylor, *Hot Money and the Politics of Debt*, McGill-Queen's University Press, 2004, pp20–2. • **2.** Robinson, 2004, pp29–37. • **3.** For example, Baron

Grey of Naunton, 1964–8; Francis Edward Hovell-Thurlow-Cumming-Bruce, 8th Baron Thurlow, KCMG, 1968–72; Sir John Warburton Paul, GCMG, OBE, MC. • **4.** The Bahamas became internally self-governing in 1964, and fully independent in 1973, though remaining a member of the British Commonwealth. • **5.** See, for example, Oswald Brown, 'Restore Sir Stafford's portrait on the $10 bill', *The Freeport News*, 13 Feb 2009. • **6.** Oswald Brown, 'Restore Sir Stafford's portrait on the $10 bill', *The Freeport News*, Nassau, 13 Feb 2009 • **7.** See Marvin Miller, *The Breaking of a President 1974 – The Nixon Connection*, Therapy Productions, excerpt republished in Kris Milligan, *Crime, Big Business & Watergate*, The Mail Archive, 26 April, 1999. • **8.** 'The Bahamas: Bad News for the Boys', *Time* magazine, 20 Jan, 1967. • **9.** Such as in Naylor, 2004, p40. • **10.** This evidence has been marshalled principally by research work by Paul Sagar at the British National Archives. More research is needed to identify more precisely what happened. • **11.** Paul Sagar, the primary researcher for this material, provided the essence of this summary. • **12.** Thanks to Paul Sagar for this concise summary. • **13.** First impressions of the Cayman Islands; The Governor of the Cayman Islands to the Secretary of State for Commonwealth Affairs, George Town, 26 Jan 1972, Diplomatic report no. 216/72. • **14.** Ibid. • **15.** Interview with Bodden and in J. A. Roy Bodden, *The Cayman Islands in Transition: the Politics, History, and Sociology of a Changing Society*, Ian Randle Publishers (Kingston and Miami,) 2007, p105. • **16.** Letter from Rt. Hon. A. W. Benn MP, to Rt. Hon. Denis Healey MP, 3 June 1975. Ref 244/01. **17.** Author's interview with Scriven, Jersey, Mar 2009. • **18.** Interview with Powell, 12 Mar 2009, while he was chairman of the Jersey Financial Services Commission. Powell subsequently retired. • **19.** Richard Falle, *Jersey and the United Kingdom: a Choice of Destiny*, Jersey and Guernsey Law Review, 2004, published by www.jerseylaw.je, page last updated 28 Jul 2006. • **20.** Lee Kwan Yew approached the Bank of England for help but it gave little encouragement, preferring to focus on Hong Kong. See *From Third World to First: The Singapore Story 1965–2000*; Lee Kwan Yew, Singapore press holdings, 2000. • **21.** Widely reported, see 'Morgan Stanley fallout from Andy Xie costs more jobs', *Bloomberg*, 12 Oct 2009. • **22.** Robinson, 2004, p48. • **23.** *The Claims Resolution Tribunal and Holocaust Claims Against Swiss Banks*, Roger P. Alford, *Berkeley Journal of International Law*, Vol. 20, No. 1, 2002, p257–8. • **24.** Author's interview with Gill, George Town, May 2009. • **25.** The Confidential Relationships (Preservation) Law was amended in 2009, making the law somewhat less hardline, but the essential elements providing criminal sanctions against breaking secrecy remain in place. • **26.** Norman's Cay: Playground for Drug Smugglers, PBS Frontline, www.pbs.org 1995-2010. • **27.** Author interview with Johnson, George Town, May 2009. • **28.** See Seamus Andrew, Niall Goodsir-Cullen, *Accountability of Cayman Islands Directors*, published by SC Andrew LLP, London, 2008. • **29.** See *Companies and Partnerships*, published by Cayman Islands Financial Services, Cayman Islands government. Last accessed 27 Aug, 2010.

7 The Fall of America

1. As told to the author by Hudson in New York in 2008; the memo is repro-
duced on p33 of the 2004 paperback edition of Tom Naylor's *Hot Money and
the Politics of Debt*. • **2.** Raymond Baker, *Capitalism's Achilles Heel: Dirty Money
and how to Renew the Free-Market System*, John Wiley & Sons, Inc., 2005. Baker
is a world authority on illicit cross-border financial flows. Chapter Four
contains a long table headed 'Specified Unlawful Activities under US
Anti-Money Laundering Laws'. It lists 65 crimes – aircraft piracy, human
trafficking, alien smuggling, bank fraud, bribery, ocean dumping and so on
– which can be used as the basis for money-laundering charges under US
law. The table then cross-checks each crime against two columns: first, if
the crime underlying the money flow is committed in the US, and second,
if the crime is committed overseas. The table shows all 65 crimes triggering
US money-laundering laws if the crime is committed in America, but if the
crime is committed overseas, three quarters of them – including alien
smuggling, racketeering, peonage, slavery and nearly all forms of tax
evasion – are excluded from the 'prohibited' list. • **3.** See, for example, 'US
Bankers Attack IRS Deposit Interest Reporting Requirement', *Tax News*,
3 Dec 2002. • **4.** *Time* magazine, 2 Dec 1993. • **5.** See Naylor, 2004, p292. • **6.**
Blum, by correspondence, and ibid. p293. • **7.** Kennedy speech is at http://www.
presidency.ucsb.edu/ws/index.php?pid=9349. • **8.** The tax did not cover loans,
so many corporations simply switched from bond financing to lending. To
check bank loans to foreign countries, the US Congress enacted the Voluntary
Foreign Credit Restraint Program (VFCRP) in February 1965, broadening it
in 1966. US corporations were asked to voluntarily limit their direct foreign
investment. The programme was made mandatory in 1968. Capital controls
were relaxed in 1969 and phased out in 1974, after the US left the Bretton-
Woods system of fixed exchange rates. See, for example, 'An Introduction
to Capital Controls', *Review*, Federal Reserve Bank of St Louis, Nov/Dec
1999, p24. • **9.** This 'deferral,' as it is known, was not uniformly available.
The Kennedy administration enacted Subpart F of the code in 1962, which
defended against tax havens by curbing deferral of US corporate taxes in
certain situations, deeming the income of foreign subsidiaries and affiliates
of US corporations to have been distributed to the US parent and taxed in
the US even though this income is not actually distributed. • **10.** 'Ironically
the triumph of "monetarism" seemed to be occurring at just the time that
international linkages were reducing the Fed's ability to control the monetary base.' Helleiner, 1996, p136. • **11.** Ibid. p137 • **12.** Palan, 2003, p134. • **13.**
Robinson, 2004, p57. • **14.** The Federal Reserve Bank of St Louis, which
studied the new offshore IBFs, noted that the decline in Caribbean business
'suggests that the growth of business in this area was almost entirely intended
to bypass US monetary regulations'. See K. Alec Chrystal, 'International

Banking Facilities', St. Louis Fed, April 1984 • **15.** Hampton, 1996, p63. • **16.** Palan, 2003, p135. • **17.** Author's interview with Rosenbloom, 1 Dec 2009. • **18.** Portfolio Interest Exemption. • **19.** Author's interview with McIntyre. See also *Testimony of Michael J. McIntyre and Robert S. McIntyre On Banking Secrecy Practices and Wealthy American Taxpayers* before the US House Committee on Ways and Means Subcommittee on Select Revenue Measures, 31 Mar, 2009 • **20.** Ibid. • **21.** The US Foreign Account Tax Compliance Act (FATCA) of 2010 tightens up some aspects of the QI rules, making it harder for US tax cheats, but it leaves the secrecy for foreigners in place. See 'FATCA: New Automatic Info Exchange Tool', Tax Justice Network, 18 May 2010. • **22.** See Michael J. Mcintyre, 'How to End the Charade of Information Exchange', *Tax Notes International*, 26 Oct 2009, p194. • **23.** Much of the information comes from 'Failure to Identify Company Owners Impedes Law Enforcement', hearing of the US Senate Permanent Subcommittee on Investigations, 14 Nov 2006. Also see US *Corporations Associated with Viktor Bout*, prepared by Senate Permanent Subcommittee on Investigations, November 2009, www.levin.senate.gov • **24.** Ibid. p3. • **25.** See L. J. David, 'Delaware, Inc'., *New York Times*, 5 June 1988. • **26.** See *Incorporating in Nevada*, Corp 95, http://www.corp95.com/, accessed 25 Aug 2010. • **27.** The forms of secrecy are different: lack of corporate transparency in Delaware, and lack of financial transparency in Switzerland. • **28.** US Senate Permanent Subcommittee on Investigations, 14 Nov 2006. A new act was introduced in 2008, the Incorporation Transparency and Law Enforcement Assistance Act, aiming to beef up transparency in this area. At the time of writing, the bill was on the sidelines. • **29.** See Jeff Gerth, 'New York Banks Urged Delaware To Lure Bankers', *New York Times*, 17 Mar 1981. • **30.** Most accounts say it was Bedford Gunning Jr, but Hoffecker says it was Richardson. • **31.** See Rita Farrell, 'Delaware Justices Uphold Ruling on Disney Severance', *New York Times*, 9 June 2006. • **32.** See Bernard S. Black, 'Shareholder Activism and Corporate Governance in the United States', *New Palgrave Dictionary of Economics and the Law*, Vol. 3, 1998 pp. 459–65. • **33.** Senate Bill No. 58, *An Act to Amend Title 10 of the Delaware Code Relating to the Court of Chancery*, State of Delaware Division of Corporations, *http://corp.delaware.gov/*. • **34.** Matthew Goldstein, 'Special Report: For Some People, CDOs Aren't a Four-Letter Word', Reuters, 17 May 2010. • **35.** Dr Madhav Mehra, 'Are We Making a Mockery of Independent Directors?', World Council for Corporate Governance, http://www.wcfcg.net/ht130304.htm. • **36.** There are salient differences with the Cayman Islands. For example, most Cayman companies ('exempt' companies) are by Cayman law not permitted to do business in Cayman; not so in Delaware. Also in Delaware, typically federal but no state taxes are paid; in Cayman, no taxes are paid. • **37.** The true figure is closer to 18,000. • **38.** *List of Delaware Registered Agents,* State of Delaware Division of Corporations, http://corp.delaware.gov/agents/agts.shtml, accessed June 2010. • **39.** 2008 and 2007 reports at *2008 Annual Report: Serving Delaware and the World*, Delaware Division of Corporations, http://sos.delaware.gov/2008AnnualReport.pdf. • **40.** Chancery courts emerged out of English ecclesiastical courts and trust laws, where concepts of legal guardianship and fiduciary duty were paramount. This makes them useful for what Delaware's Court of Chancery does most of all: rule on the nitty-gritty of how corporations organise themselves internally, and what happens when things go awry – whether internal rules have been followed, management insiders are illegally abusing shareholders and whether corporate statutes have been applied fairly. • **41.** *Transcript of interview with Mrs Ngozi Okonjo-Iweala, Nigerian Finance Minister,* Interview by Paul Vallely, *Independent,* 16 May, 2006. • **42.** Transparency International is live to this issue and called in November 2008 for a 'second wave' of corruption campaigning to tackle these and other issues. As I write this, it is in the process of re-evaluating its stance.

8 *The Deep Drains of Development*

1. 'Interview: John Moscow', *Money Laundering Bulletin,* Apr 1997. • **2.** A range of estimates for the size of the narcotics trade exist. This one comes from 'The Global Narcotics Industry', Center for Strategic and International Studies, Washington DC. See http://csis.org/programs/transnational-threats-project/past-task-forces/-global-narcotics-industry. • **3.** Based on the current price of $75bn. • **4.** http://www.nytimes.com/1991/08/22/business/washington-at-work-a-crusader-driven-by-outrage.html?pagewanted=2?pagewanted=2. Blum also provided much support and advice for this book. • **5.** This section on BCCI is drawn mostly from Peter Truell and Larry Gurwin, *False Profits: The Inside Story of BCCI, the World's Most Corrupt Financial Empire,* Houghton Mifflin Company, 1992; from Robinson, 2004; from various newspaper and academic reports; and from the author's interviews with Robert Morgenthau and Jack Blum in 2008 and 2009. • **6.** For most of its life, Ernst & Whinney (now Ernst & Young) audited BCCI Luxembourg, while Price Waterhouse (now PWC) audited BCCI Cayman. • **7.** See Truell and Gurwin, 1992, p87. • **8.** Ibid. p189. • **9.** Ibid. pp193–7, 290–1; Robinson, 2004, pp79–81. Some of the capital was real money, but much of it was not. • **10.** Author's interview with Morgenthau, 4 May 2009. • **11.** Peter Truell and Larry Gurwin, *False Profits: The Inside Story of BCCI, the World's Most Corrupt Financial Empire,* Houghton Mifflin, 1992, p. 357. • **12.** Ibid. p84. • **13.** In 2009 Britain's Information Commissioners refused a Freedom of Information request by Prem Sikka to finally publish Price Waterhouse's 1991 'Sandstorm' report on BCCI. In an extraordinary and long-winded reply they argued, 'it is very clearly in the public interest that the UK maintains strong and effective relations with its international partners' – a clear defence of tax haven London. See Freedom of Information Act 2000 (Section 50), Decision Notice, 14 Dec 2009, Information Commissioners (UK). In an email to the author on 15 June 2010, Sikka said he remained committed to securing publication of the report. Sikka also provides a useful in-depth examination of the BCCI affair at Austin Mitchell, Prem Sikka, Patricia Arnold, Christine Cooper, Hugh Willmott, *The BCCI Cover-Up*, Association for Accountancy & Business Affairs, 2001. • **14.** Author's interview with Morgenthau, 4 May 2009; and 'More Offshore Tax Probes in Works: NY's Morgenthau', Reuters, 27 Apr 2009. • **15.** See Nicholas Shaxson, *Poisoned Wells: The Dirty Politics of African Oil*, Palgrave Macmillan, 2007. • **16.** French magistrates issued an international arrest warrant for Gaydamak in January 2001 and he moved to Moscow. In October 2009 he was convicted in absentia for arms trafficking, fraud and tax offences. Gaydamak said the magistrates used forged documents, and owed no French taxes because he had been resident in London at the time. Author's interview with Gaydamak, and *Le Monde*, 8 Dec 2000, cited in Global Witness, *All the President's Men: The devastating story of oil and banking in Angola's privatised war*, March 2002, p26. • **17.** The arms he helped finance did, it is true, hasten victory over UNITA, though not everyone would agree that helping supply arms constitutes 'bringing peace'. Gaydamak had recently bought the Israeli football team Hapoel and a basketball team, Betar Jerusalem, with, he said, political aims. • **18.** 'Time for Transparency', *Global Witness*, Mar 2004, p44. • **19.** Over $160m went to an account called Treasury Ministry of Finance in Moscow, though knowledgeable sources in Switzerland told me that despite its name, this account may have been a front, with other interests behind it. • **20.** *'Le règlement de la dette angolaise aurait donné lieu à des détournements de fonds'*, *Le Monde*, 3 Apr 2002: quoted in 'Time for Transparency', Mar 2004. I asked Gaydamak if the money had simply disappeared into private pockets offshore. No, he said. Instead of paying Russia in cash for the promissory notes, Abalone paid Russia in 'Russian obligations' – Russian debts he bought on secondary markets via these mysterious offshore companies and then redeemed to Russia – and Abalone had legally profited on those debt trades too. It was a 'huge stupidity', he said, to assume that he would pay Russia back directly, rather than via intermediary accounts. • **21.** Dev Kar and Devon Cartwright-Smith, 'Illicit Financial Flows from Africa: Hidden Resource for Development', *Global Financial Integrity*, 26 Mar 2010. • **22.** See Emily Crowley, DQWS '"Angolagate" Revisited', Global Financial Integrity, Task Force on Financial Integrity and Economic Development, 7 Apr 2010. • **23.** 'Angola: Statistical Annex and Angola, Recent Economic Developments', IMF data, various years. • **24.** The Soyo-Palanca Trust and the Cabinda Trust. • **25.** Some economists, many with ties to the financial services industry and to tax havens, have tried to dispute these numbers – none successfully. In fact, these numbers are quite compatible with the only comparable official estimate available, a World Bank study from 1994, which estimated total capital flight from developing countries at $155–377bn in 1992. Simply extrapolating this figure to 2006 dollars (using the IMF conversion rate of 287.2%) yields a figure of $443bn to $1.1 trillion. However, the growth rate has significantly exceeded the inflation rate. For counter-arguments and detailed discussions, see, 'Time to Bury the Oxford Report', Tax Justice Network, 16 July 2009. • **26.** Léonce Ndikumana and James Boyce, 'New Estimates of Capital Flight from Sub-Saharan African Countries: Linkages with External Borrowing and Policy Options', Political Economy Research Institute, 4 Aug 2008. • **27.** Although one might argue that the problem of climate change is a bigger threat. • **28.** http://www.free-domandprosperity.org/ltr/gramm-irs/gramm-irs.shtml. • **29.** James S. Henry, The Blood Bankers: Tales from the Global Underground Economy, Thunder's Mouth Press, 2003, p73. • **30.** Helleiner, 1996, p177. • **31.** Quotes are a mix of my interview and his interview in Counterpunch, http://www.counter-punch.org/schaefer03252004.html. • **32.** Luca Errico and Alberto Musalem, 'Offshore Banking: an Analysis of Micro- and Macro-Prudential Issues', IMF, Jan 1999. • **33.** Such as appropriate tax treaties and foreign tax credits. • **34.** Chinese Ministry of Commerce. Total for Hong Kong was $27.7bn; the next largest was South Korea, with $3.7bn. • **35.** See, for example, India gets 43% FDI through Mauritius route, Press Trust of India, 20 April 2009. • **36.** It was a French colony until Britain invaded during the Napoleonic Wars. • **37.** From my interview with Rosenbloom, by telephone, Dec 1, 2009

9 Ratchet

1. See, for example, 'High-Interest Lenders Tap Elderly, Disabled', Wall Street Journal, 12 Feb 2008. The article examined 'payday loans' and cited annual interest rates of up to 406%. • **2.** Some interviewees said May 1980, but Henry Beckler's résumé says 11 June 1980 – http://www.wtcde.com/Henry Beckler.pdf. • **3.** 'Others who might have raised questions about the bill, including other state officials, the press and the public, were intentionally kept in the dark, according to bankers and state officials.' 'New York Banks Urged Delaware to Lure Bankers', New York Times, 17 Mar 1981. • **4.** Biondi is a former president of the Delaware State Bar Association, a Democrat who has served as an adviser to both Republican and Democrat governors, and an attorney who has acted for business interests, the Teamsters union and many others. Delaware Grapevine, a local political website, called him 'a tough-minded political operative capable of delivering corporate contri-butions or muscling up votes'. • **5.** Interview with Hayward, and Hayward's comments in Larry Nagengast, Pierre S. Du Pont IV, Governor of Delaware,

1977–1985, Delaware Heritage Commission, 2006, p109. • **6.** 'Birth of a Banking Bonanza', *Delaware Lawyer*, fall 1982, p38. • **7.** David S. Swayze, Christine P. Schiltz, Parkowski, Guerke & Swayze, 'Keeping the First State First: The Alternative Bank Franchise Tax as an Economic Development Tool', *Delaware Banker*, fall 2006. • **8.** Adrian Kinnane, *Durable Legacy: A History of Morris, Nichols, Arsht & Tunnell*, Morris, Nichols, Arsht & Tunnell, Delaware, 2005, http://www.mnat.com/assets/attachments/MNAT_Book__Web_Version. pdf. • **9.** 'New York Banks', *New York Times*, 17 Mar 1981. • **10.** Nagengast, 2006, p113. • **11.** In 2010 the so-called Whitehouse Interstate Lending Amendment was introduced in the US Senate, co-sponsored by Senators Cochran, Merkley, Durbin, Sanders, Levin, Burris, Franken, Brown (O.), Menendez, Leahy, Webb, Casey, Wyden, Reed, Udall (Colo.) and Begich. It aimed to restore to the states the ability to enforce interest rate caps against out-of-state lenders. At the time of writing, it had made no progress. • **12.** Nagengast, 2006, p114. • **13.** A description of the Bank Franchise Tax, Delaware Department of Finance, http://finance.delaware.gov/publications/ fiscal_notebook_09/Section07/bank_franchise.pdf • **14.** 'New York Banks', *New York Times*, 17 Mar 1981. • **15.** Nagengast, 2006, p110. • **16.** 'Consumers Turn to Plastic as Home Loans Slow', Reuters, 11 Sept 2007. Credit card debt stood at $907bn, rising to $975bn by December 2008. 'US Credit Card ABS: 2006 Outlook', Barclays Capital, 26 Jan 2006; Mark Furletti, 'An Overview of Credit Card Asset-Backed Securities', Philadelphia Federal Reserve, Dec 2002; 'Fed report: Consumer Credit Card Balances Keep Plummeting', Creditcards.com. • **17.** This research was undertaken by myself and Ken Silverstein of *Harper's* in Delaware in 2009. As far as I know, nobody has ever explored this Delaware episode in depth and linked it to wider impacts, apart from the *New York Times* article cited in note 9 above. For Geoghegan quote see Thomas Geoghegan, 'Infinite Debt: How Unlimited Interest Rates Destroyed the Economy', *Harper's*, 1 Apr 2009. • **18.** Paul Tucker, 'Shadow Banking, Financing Markets and Financial Stability', Bank for International Settlements, 21 Jan 2010. Paul Tucker is deputy governor for financial stability at the Bank of England. • **19.** From Biondi interview and Swayze et al., and from David S. Swayze, Esq. & Christine P. Schiltz, Esq,. *Keeping the First State First: The Alternative Bank Franchise Tax as an Economic Development Tool*, in the Fall 2006 edition of Delaware Banker. • **20.** See, for example, *JP Morgan CDO Handbook*, 29 May 2001, p31 and Scott E. Waxman, *Delaware Statutory Trusts, Potter Anderson & Corroon LLP*. Biondi did not say he was involved in the Delaware Statutory Trust Act. • **21.** Scott E. Waxman, Nicholas I. Froio, Eric N. Feldman and Ross Antonacci, 'Delaware: The Jurisdiction of Choice in Securitisation', Potter, Anderson & Corroon LLP, http://library.findlaw.com/2004/May/19/133435.html. • **22.** David S. Swayze and Christine P. Schlitz, *The Evolution of Banking in Delaware*, published by Parkowski, Guerki & Swayze, http://www.pgslegal.com/CM/FirmNews/evolution-of-banking-in-delaware.asp. • **23.** See John Dunn, Prem Sikka, *Auditors: Keeping The Public in the Dark*, Association for Accountancy & Business Affairs, 1999, http://visar.csustan.edu/aaba/dunn&sikka.pdf. • **24.** The UK Companies Act of 1948, for example, required this. • **25.** Author's interview with Konrad Hummler, 4 Nov 2009. • **26.** David Cay Johnston, *Perfectly Legal: The Covert Campaign to Rig our Tax System to benefit the Super Rich – and Cheat Everybody Else*, Penguin, 2003, p15. • **27.** UK Companies Act of 1989. • **28.** Michael R. Sesit, 'Offshore Hazard: Isle of Jersey Proves Less than a Haven to currency investors', *Wall Street Journal*, 17 Sept 1996. • **29.** A letter in October 1996 from Colin Powell, chief adviser to the States, to Pierre Horsfall, president of Jersey's Finance and Economics Committee, suggests the uncertain official position at the time. 'Some might hold the view that there is nothing wrong with States members being directors of local companies,' it said. 'Indeed, for as long as States members are not full-time and salaried it is almost inevitable.' The solution put forward, Powell said, was to set up a commission to supervise the finance industry, though that, he conceded, might not change things much. 'The commission will include those who have a direct interest in the finance industry.' The answer was to make sure those in the Commission were not involved in particular areas where they had a conflict of interest, and to debate the matter further. • **30.** 'Finance: Damage Might Be Done to Jersey's Reputation', *Jersey Evening Post*, 15 Feb 1996. • **31.** 'Accountancy Age', 29 Mar 2001, p22, cited in Austin Mitchell, Prem Sikka, John Christensen, Philip Morris, Steven Filling, *No Accounting for Tax Havens*, Association for Accountancy and Business Affairs, 2002, http://www.taxjustice.net/cms/upload/pdf/AABA.pdf • **32.** Luca Errico and Alberto Musalem, 'Offshore Banking: an Analysis of Micro- and Macro-Prudential Issues', IMF, Jan 1999. Also 'Favourable regulatory treatment in OFCs increases the operational leeway of offshore banks for balance sheet management,' this IMF paper said, 'exemptions from reserve requirements on deposits; liquidity requirements; liability and asset concentration restrictions; capital adequacy thresholds; and stringent foreign exchange position limits, allow offshore banks to more freely manage their balance sheets.' • **33.** For example, in Roger Lowenstein, *When Genius Failed: the Rise and Fall of Long-Term Capital Management*, Fourth Estate, 2002, his otherwise excellent analysis of the episode almost entirely ignores the offshore element. • **34.** See, for example, 'Report on Special Purpose Entities', Bank for International Settlements, Sep 2009. • **35.** As the BIS report puts it, 'The onshore (Delaware) versus offshore (Cayman) decision will generally be driven by factors outlined in the previous section (on tax considerations of SPEs), while other (non-taxation related) considerations (such as clarity of legal regime, ease of incorporation, etc.) will generally be similar to those outlined for European SPEs immediately above'. Note that 'clarity of legal regime' and 'ease of incorporation' stem specifically from these jurisdictions' offshore status, as defined in this book.

• **36.** See Jim Stewart, 'Shadow Regulation and the Shadow Banking System: The Role of the Dublin International Financial Services Centre', *Tax Justice Focus*, Vol. 4, No. 2, Nicholas Shaxson (ed.), 18 Jul, 2008; Jim Stewart, 'Low Tax Financial Centres and the Subprime Crisis: The IFSC in Ireland', Presentation at Tax Justice/AABA research workshop, University of Essex, 3–4 July 2008; also draft version of Jim Stewart, 'Low tax Financial Centres and the Financial Crisis: The Case of the IFSC in Ireland', 15 May 2010. • **37.** Dublin's lures for shadow banks were not especially its low-tax regime – though that helped – but Ireland's wide array of tax treaties and the fact it ticks certain boxes that fund regulators require in their home countries, including that certain EU directives apply. Being within the euro currency zone is also crucial. • **38.** See the Abacus prospectus and Abacus indicative terms http://www.scribd.com/doc/30054003/Abacus-2007-AC1-INDICATIVE-TERMS. • **39.** 'Goldman's Offshore Deals Deepened Global Financial Crisis', McClatchy, 30 Dec 2009. • **40.** *Understanding Financial Inter-connectedness*, IMF, October 4, 2010, p19. • **41.** 'Debt Bias and Other Distortions: Crisis-Related Issues in Tax Policy', IMF Fiscal Affairs Department, 12 June 2009. • **42.** 2003–7 data from the IMF, and from 'Private Equity Fund Raising up in 2007: Report', Reuters, 8 Jan 2008. • **43.** Andrew G. Haldane, 'Small Lessons From A Big Crisis', Remarks at the Federal Reserve Bank of Chicago 45th Annual Conference 'Reforming Financial Regulation', 8 May 2009. For some excellent examples of these practices, see Gretchen Morgenson, 'Private Equity's Trojan Horse of Debt', *New York Times*, 12 Mar 2010, and Julie Cresswell, 'Profits for Buyout Firms as Company Debt Soared', *New York Times*, 4 Oct 2009. • **44.** The GFI studies present a range of estimates, with net flows into deficit countries worth hundreds of billions of dollars. See Chart 7 on p23 of Dev Kar and Devon Cartwright Smith, 'Illicit Financial Flows from Developing Countries 2002–2006', Global Financial Integrity, Washington, 2008. • **45.** Haldane, 8 May 2009.

10 *Resistance*

1. 'Harmful Tax Competition: An Emerging Global Issue', Organisation for Economic Cooperation and Development. • **2.** The last major attempt at attacking the havens had been the so-called Gordon Report published by the US Internal Revenue Service in January 1981. Hard-hitting though it was, the Gordon Report was launched a week before Ronald Reagan took office, and was buried almost immediately. Richard A. Gordon, special counsel for international taxation, 'Tax Havens and Their Use By United States Taxpayers – An Overview: A report to the Commissioner of Internal Revenue, the Assistant Attorney General (Tax Division) and the Assistant Secretary of the Treasury (Tax Policy)', report submitted 12 Jan 1981. • **3.** Though the 1998 report did not list the havens, the content was clearly aimed at smaller island centres. • **4.** Author's interview with Dan Mitchell, Washington, D.C., 16 Jan 2009. • **5.** See David Cay Johnston, 'Behind I.R.S. Hearings, a G.O.P. Plan to End Tax Code', *New York Times*, 4 May 1998. • **6.** Johnston, p148. • **7.** See Dan Mitchell 'The Liberalizing Impact of Tax Havens in a Globalized Economy', presentation at Capitol Hill, 23 Mar 2009, http://www.youtube.com/watch?v=ISfsYinqoaM&feature=related. • **8.** Paul de Grauwe and Magdalena Polan, 'Globalisation and Social Spending', Cesifo Working Paper No. 885, Mar 2003. • **9.** Tax revenues as a share of GDP, OECD, http://www.oecd.org/dataoecd/48/27/41498733.pdf • **10.** See 'A fair share: Has the tide turned for corporate profits?' *The Economist*, 27 Aug 2009. In 2006, for example, just ahead of the economic crisis, US corporate profits were higher as a share of national income, and wages and salaries were lower, than at any time since the Second World War. • **11.** See David Cay Johnston, 'Tax Rates for Top 400 Earners Fall as Income Soars, IRS Data', *Taxanalysts*, 2010. • **12.** Mitchell's own book quotes a seminal 2006 European study which baldly explains the problem: 'The effect [of falling tax rates] on incorporation is significant and large. It implies that the revenue effects of lower corporate tax rates – possibly induced by tax competition – partly show up in lower personal tax revenues rather than lower corporate tax revenues . . . there *is* reason (after all) to worry about tax competition.' 'Corporate Tax Policy, Entrepreneurship and Incorporation in the EU', CESifo Working Paper No. 1883, Dec 2006. Also see Lucas Bretschger and Frank Hettich, *Globalisation, Capital Mobility and Tax Competition: Theory and Evidence for OECD Countries*, in Elsevier, European Journal of Political Economy, 2002, and S. Ganghof, *The Politics of Income Taxation: A Comparative Analysis*, ECPR Press, 2006. • **13.** Michael Keen and Alejandro Simone, 'Is Tax Competition Harming Developing Countries More Than Developed?', *Tax Notes International*, 1317, 28 June 2004. • **14.** See Klemm, Alexander and Van Parys, Stefan, *Empirical Evidence on the Effects of Tax Incentives*, IMF Working Paper 09/136, IMF, 1 July, 2009. One such incentive was the tax holiday, which IMF economists said was 'widely regarded as the most pernicious form of incentive'. Britain had briefly tried this under Prime Minister Margaret Thatcher until it became clear it did not work: set up a ten-year tax holiday, and companies will pack up and leave after nine years and 11 months, or will transfer the business to another subsidiary and get another ten years. After such failures, Africa was nevertheless still encouraged to embrace them. In 1990 only one sub-Saharan African country offered tax holidays, but a decade later they all did. Often these holidays are available in special export-processing zones, which are a bit like small offshore jurisdictions lodged inside the state. When these zones pop up, wealthy locals who want to invest at home inevitably send their money overseas, dress it up in an offshore secrecy structure, then return it, slashing their tax bill in the process. • **15.** Todd Moss, Gunilla

Pettersson and Nicolas van de Walle, 'An Aid-Institutions Paradox? A Review Essay on Aid Dependency and State Building in Sub-Saharan Africa', Center for Global Development, Working Paper 74, Jan 2006. • **16.** Daniel J. Mitchell, 'Why Tax Havens are a Blessing', *Foreign Policy*, 17 Mar 2008. • **17.** 'The Moral Case for Tax Havens', Center for Freedom and Prosperity, Oct 2008, Youtube presentation, and 'Tax Justice Network Sides with Europe's Tax Collectors, Ignores Critical Role of Low-Tax Jurisdiction in Protecting Human Rights and Promoting Pro-Growth Policy', Center for Freedom and Prosperity, 7 Apr 2005. • **18.** Joel Bakan, *The Corporation*, Constable & Robinson Ltd., 2005, p154. • **19.** When tax writer David Cay Johnston challenged Norquist, noting that his views were at odds with those of most economists and taxes were needed to pay for civilisation, Norquist responded, 'We are not the successor of, we are not a continuation of, Western civilisation. We are a unique and different civilisation.' • **20.** Several graphs are available; this one illustrates it more clearly than most http://www.balloon-juice.com/wp-content/uploads/2009/03/graph.jpg. • **21.** Jason Sharman, *Havens in a Storm: The Struggle for Global Tax Regulation*, Cornell University Press, 2006, p85. • **22.** See The Moral Case for Tax Havens, Part II. • **23.** David Cay Johnston, 'Treasury Chief: Tax Evasion Is on the Rise', *New York Times*, Jul 19 2001. • **24.** *OECD Tax Haven Crackdown Is Out of Line, O'Neill Says*, Center for Freedom and Prosperity, 5 Nov, 2001. • **25.** 'Treasury Chief: Tax Evasion Is on the Rise,' David Cay Johnston, *New York Times*, July 19, 2001. • **26.** A new study in October 2008 based on unpublished IRS data found that the rich hide much more of their income than the poor do. Taxpayers earning true income between $500,000 and $1m a year understated their adjusted gross incomes by 21% overall in 2001, compared to just 8% for those earning $50,000 to $100,000. For poorer people, cheating was even lower. See 'Rich Cheat More On Taxes, New Study Shows', *Forbes*, 21 Oct 2008, http://www.forbes.com/2008/10/21/taxes-irs-wealth-biz-beltwaycz_jn_1021beltway.html. • **27.** Martin Wolf, *Why Globalization Works*, Yale Nota Bene, 2005, p283. • **28.** For useful explorations of this topic, see Morrissey and Baker, *When Rivers Flow Upstream*, Center for Economic and Policy Research, 22 Mar 2003, or Rodrik and Subramanian, 'Why did Financial Globalization Disappoint?', Mar 2008. • **29.** *Caymanian Compass*, 8 July 1991. • **30.** Anthony Travers, 'Framing Cayman', *The Lawyer*, 29 Mar 2004, http://www.thelawyer.com/framing-cayman/109308.article. • **31.** Anthony Travers, 'An Open Letter to President Obama From the Cayman Islands Financial Services Association', 5 May 2009. • **32.** Nick Mathiason, 'Tax havens batten down as the hurricane looms', *The Observer*, 29 Mar 2009. • **33.** See Richard Murphy, 'The TIEA programme is failing', 29 Mar, Tax Research blog, 27 Nov, 2009 and OECD, 'A Progress Report on the Jurisdictions Surveyed by the OECD Global Forum in Implementing the Internationally Agreed Tax Standard': progress made as at 10 May 2010' OECD,

May 2010. http://www.oecd.org/dataoecd/50/0/43606256.pdf. • **34.** Michael J. McIntyre, 'How to End the Charade of Information Exchange', *Tax Notes International*, 26 Oct 2009.

11 *The Life Offshore*

1. 'I Save Tax by Never Visiting my Family, Says Tycoon Guy Hands', *Guardian*, 5 Feb 2010. His children could visit him if they wanted, he said. • **2.** See 'Europe, US Battle Swiss Bank Secrecy', *Der Spiegel*, 20 May 2008. • **3.** Tax accountant Richard Murphy, who broke the story, called it a 'wholly artificial construction, seeking to shift liability and to avoid responsibility and abusing common sense decency'. As for the trustee, 'No surprise it has offices in London, New York, Delaware, Hong Kong, the Channel Islands and the Cayman Islands . . . this type of deal is constructed every day offshore.' See Richard Murphy, *Northern Rock – the questions needing answers*, Tax Research blog, 17 Sep 2007. • **4.** 'Doom-Mongers Huddle Over Island Under Threat', *Financial Times*, 11 Nov 1998. • **5.** Patrick Muirhead, 'Jersey's Culture of Concealment', *The Times*, 24 Apr 2008. • **6.** See 'Senator from Jersey accused of leaking police report wants asylum after fleeing trial', *Daily Mail*, 25 Oct 2009. A few months later the Ireland-born Lenny Harper, former Deputy Chief of the Jersey States police, who had crossed swords with the Jersey authorities over his investigations in a child abuse scandal, stated in an affidavit: 'I went to Jersey in 2002 full of expectation of the challenge that lay ahead. . . . I soon learnt that it was like nowhere else in the British Isles. There are no checks and balances on power and the abuse of it. . . . With such an absence of controls, such an absence of accountability, the ordinary decent people of Jersey are helpless. Intentionally or not, the system has allowed corruption to flourish to such an extent that those seeking to combat it are the ones open to scorn.' • **7.** That was the case then; things have admittedly improved: States' debates are now recorded on Jersey's Hansard, available online; ministerial agendas, and often minutes, of ministerial meetings are published online on the States website. • **8.** Austin Mitchell, Prem Sikka, John Christensen, Philip Morris and Steven Filling, 'No Accounting for Tax Havens', AABA, 2002. • **9.** Emails to author from the Cayman Official: two on 22 Apr 2009, one on 6 June 2009. • **10.** Andy Sibcy, 'At what cost?', *Jersey Evening Post*, 22 Dec 2009 There is public health provision, but no NHS. • **11.** The International Business Company was replaced by the so-called 0/10 tax regime, which operated unimpeded until January 2011 when the European Union, after long deliberations, judged it to be harmful under its Code of Conduct on business taxation. It is not yet clear what Jersey will replace this with. • **12.**

Companies can, if they prefer, set their own rates of tax, with a minimum of 2%, if they want to climb over the bar of the minimum rate specified in their country of origin. At the time of writing, Jersey is considering changes to its tax system. • **13.** See Cahal Milmo, 'Trouble in paradise as financial squeeze hits the expatriate lifestyle in Jersey', *Independent*, 10 Jul, 2004.

12 *Griffin*

1. Gillian Tett describes this in 'On the Money', *Guardian* interview, 31 Oct 2008, and in her book, *Fools Gold: How Unrestrained Greed Corrupted a Dream, Shattered Global Markets and Unleashed a Catastrophe*, Little, Brown, 2009 pp298–9. • **2.** Speech by Tim Geithner, 'Reducing Systemic Risk in a Dynamic Financial System', 9 June 2008. • **3.** 'A Chancellor Whose Record Has Divided the Economists', *Independent*, 22 Mar 2007. • **4.** See William Taylor, 'City Comes Against Market Forces', *Guardian*, 23 May 2001. • **5.** Select Committee on City of London (Ward Elections) Bill, Examination of Witness (Questions 1-19), 7 Oct 2002 • **6.** Megan Murphy, 'Banking: City Limits', *Financial Times*, 13 Dec 2009 and 'The City: A Guide to London's Global Financial Centre', *Profile Books*, 2008 pp261–73. • **7.** Michael Greenberger, 'Energy Market Manipulation and Federal Enforcement Regimes', testimony to US Senate committee, 3 June 2008, http://commerce.senate.gov/public/_files/IMGJune3 Testimonyo.pdf. • **8.** See 'Linklaters Sees Fallout From Repo 105', *Financial Times*, 13 Mar 2010, and 'Report of Anton R. Valukas, Examiner, Southern District Court', US Bankruptcy Court, Southern District of New York, in re Lehman Brothers Holdings Inc., 11 Mar 2010. The loophole was neither purely a UK or a US matter, but derived from arbitrage between the two jurisdictions. See Brooke Masters, FSA on defensive over Lehman failings', *Financial Times*, 18 Mar 2010. • **9.** 'Research and statistics FAQ', Economic Information and Analysis, www.cityoflondon.gov.uk City of London, accessed June 2010. • **10.** 'Reaction to the Tax Gap Series', *Guardian*, 14 Feb 2009. • **11.** Prem Sikka, 'UK company law is terrorism's friend', *Guardian*, 20 Jan 2010. • **12.** 'Number Of CIS Companies on London Stock Exchange's Markets Reaches 100 With Listing of Magnit', London Stock Exchange, 22 Apr 2008. • **13.** Will Stewart, 'Londongrad . . . Russia's Money Laundry', *Daily Express*, 27 Aug 2010, and 'Britain called crooks' haven,' *Sydney Morning Herald*, 28 Feb 2010. • **14.** 'Lloyds forfeits $350m for disguising origin of funds from Iran and Sudan', *Guardian*, 20 Jan 2009, and 'Lloyds TSB to Pay $350m to Settle Probe', Bloomberg, 10 Jan 2009. • **15.** See Richard Murphy, 'Response to the Treasury paper 'Reviewing the Residence and Domicile Rules as they Effect the Taxation of Individuals: A Background Paper'', Association for Accountancy and Business Affairs, Aug 2003. • **16.** Robert Winnett and Holly Watt, 'Britain:

world's first onshore tax haven', *The Times*, 3 Dec, 2006. • **17.** See Richard Wray, 'Naked truth about the brand king', *Guardian*, 27 Jul 2002. • **18.** This would cost little to do. Multinationals already hold all this information; all they need to do is publish it. At the stroke of a pen a vast secret trove of information vital to citizens, investors and governments would come onshore and into view. • **19.** Michael Foot, Final report of the independent Review of British offshore financial centres, HM Treasury, Oct 2009 http://www.hm-treasury.gov.uk/d/foot_review_main.pdf. • **20.** The Lord Mayor's International Work, City of London Corporation website, Accessed August 2010. • **21.** 'Report by the Rt Hon. the Lord Mayor (Alderman John Stuttard) on his Visit to China, Hong Kong and South Korea', City of London Corporation, 8 Nov 2007. • **22.** According to the document, the Lord Mayor was told that Ordinance 10 was designed to 'prevent the illegal transfer of assets overseas'. • **23.** In the Channel 4 *Dispatches* programme of 14 June 2010 it was put to Fraser that he was the most effective lobbyist in the country. He said, 'I guess that's probably right.' • **24.** Alistair Darling speaking on ibid. • **25.** See City of London, Livery Companies, Alphabetical list, www.cityof london.gov.uk/Corporation/LGNL_Services/Leisure_and_culture/Local_ history_and_heritage/Livery/linklist.htm • **26.** 'Development of local government', in Local History and Heritage, City of London Corporation website, accessed August 2010 • **27.** Reginald R. Sharpe, *London and the Kingdom* Vol II – Part 1, Bibliobazaar, LLC, 2008, p40. • **28.** Ibid. p42. Winchester was left out of the original survey too, but was later surveyed; the City never was. • **29.** UK Parliament Press Office communication with the author. • **30.** 'City Remembrancer's Office', under 'Council Departments', City of London Corporation Website, accessed 30 Aug 2010. • **31.** House of Lords European Union Sub-committee A (Economic and Financial Affairs and International Trade), 'Inquiry into Directive on Alternative Investment Fund Managers', memorandum from the City of London Corporation submitted by the Office of the City Remembrancer, Sep 2009. • **32.** House of Lords European Union Sub-committee A, 'Inquiry into the Commission's Communications on Ensuring Efficient, Safe and Sound Derivatives Markets', memorandum from the City of London Corporation submitted by the Office of the City Remembrancer, Jan 2010, published by UK parliament. • **33.** The Corporation of London's chief executive Tom Simmons stated, 'There is no charter that constituted the Corporation as a corporate body.' See Examination of Witness (Questions 20-39), Select Committee on City of London (Ward Elections) Bill Minutes of Evidence, www.parliament.uk, 7 Oct 2002. • **34.** Raymond Smith (ed.) *Corporation of London, Ceremonials of the Corporation of London*, 1962, cited in Timothy B. Smith, *In Defense of Privilege: The City of London and the Challenge of Municipal Reform, 1875-1890*, Journal of Social History, Vol. 27, No. 1 (Autumn, 1993), pp. 59-83. • **35.** Ibid. • **36.** Which King James 1 had granted to the City of London. The bowler hats and umbrellas of the Orange

Orders in Northern Ireland derive from their sponsorship by the Corporation of London. • **37.** Reginald R. Sharpe, *London and the Kingdom*, Vol. 3, Longmans, Green & Co., 1895, p151. • **38.** Ibid. p166. • **39.** I. G. Doolittle, *The City of London and its Livery Companies*, Gavin Press, 1982, p142. It has also been useful for the City that Fleet Street, until the 1990s the traditional home of the British media establishment, lies within the City boundaries. • **40.** C.R. Atlee, *The Labour Party in Perspective*, Gollancz, 1937, p179. • **41.** Eddie George, 'The Bank of England: How the Pieces Fit Together', *Bank of England Lectures*, 1996, p91. • **42.** Bank of England timeline, Bank of England website, http://www.bankofengland.co.uk/about/history/timeline.htm. • **43.** Burn, 2006, p68. • **44.** John Davis, *Reforming London: The London Government Problem, 1855–1900*, Oxford Historical Monographs, 1988, p51. The full quote is: 'If we were to be strictly logical we should recommend the amalgamation of the City and Westminster. But, logic has its limits and the position of the City lies outside them.' • **45.** Peter B. Flint, 'The Earl of Cromer Is Dead at 72'; Former Head of Bank of England', *New York Times*, 19 Mar 1991. • **46.** 'London Government Reform (Abolition of the Corporation of the City of London)', House of Commons Debates, 5 May 1981, Vol. 4, cc19–25, http://hansard.millbanksystems.com/commons/1981/may/05/london-government-reform-abolition-of. • **47.** Eddie George, *The Bank of England: how the pieces fit together* 1996, p91, in Bank of England Quarterly Bulletin: February 1996. • **48.** For example, Kynaston, 2002, which is regarded by some as the definitive work on the City, largely ignores the Corporation of London, and when it does it hardly strays beyond discussing the Corporation's role in City construction projects. • **49.** See, for example, Select Committee on City of London (Ward Elections) Bill, Examination of Witness (Questions 60-79), 7 Oct 2002. • **50.** See Fraser Nelwon, 'Labour Rift Over City Overhaul', *Independent*, 7 Apr 1996. • **51.** Select Committee on City of London (Ward Elections) Bill, Examination of Witness (Questions 1–19), 7 Oct 2002. • **52.** The voting is supposed to reflect the 'composition' rather than the 'wishes' of the workforce – a crucial distinction. Voters must be citizens of the UK or other Commonwealth or European Union country; they must be members of staff since 1 September whose main place of work is the City premises of the organisation which is appointing them, or a member of the board of directors or equivalent since 1 September, or have worked exclusively for the organisation for a total of five years or more at some time during their working career and either still work in the City or have done so within the last five years, or have worked mainly in the City for ten years or more regardless of the organisation at some time during their working career and still do so or have done within the last five years. See *The voting system for City of London Ward elections*, the City of London Corporation website www.cit oflondon.gov.uk. • **53.** Along with Taylor there was a second petitioner, a businessman, Malcolm Matson, who said he had been the victim of a 'secretive and undemocratic decision' to bar him from office after winning a seat in an earlier ward election, and was presenting his own petition. • **54.** Though varying degrees of support were provided by people including Labour MP Tony Benn and Martin Bell MP, who declared, 'It is strange that the government is not only acquiescing in but encouraging a piece of legislation that is profoundly undemocratic, anti-democratic and belongs not to the twenty-first century but to the eighteenth.' See *Statement of compatibility with the european convention on human rights,* Hansard, 24 Jan 2000 Vol 343. • **55.** Ibid. • **56.** Ibid. • **57.** Select Committee on City of London (Ward Elections) Bill, Examination of Witness (Questions 20-39), 7 Oct 2002 • **58.** *City of London Funds,* under 'council Budgets And Spending,' www.city oflondon.gov.uk, accessed 30 Aug, 2010 See also *City of London, Strategic Budget 2010/11,* City of London, 23 Feb 2010, http://217.154.230.218/NR/rdonlyres/8AAAC80D-CD37-48A3-BA98-3320DC61C115/0/StrategicBudgetBook_200910.pdf which contains a rough breakdown of the City's Cash, albeit short on detail of what the funds are actually used for. There is no information about the assets themselves. When the original version of *Treasure Islands* was written, the size of the City's Cash assets was not publicly available; this figure of 'about one billion' was provided by a spokesman of the City of London Corporation, in an email to me on February 9th, 2011. The spokesman wished not to be named in person. To be clear, his email provided the following quote: 'The total holdings of City's Cash are around £1bn, nearly all, if not entirely, within the UK. The reference to the City Corporation owing approximately 20% of the property in the Square Mile covers all three funds. Given that the published assets of the other two funds total approx. £2bn, that gives an overall total of approx. £3bn. These are the total assets of the City Corporation: there are no others.' I query the method of valuation of these assets, as these numbers seem small when referenced against the Corporation's income from its assets. • **59.** Developments are described in blog 'Mammon. From superhero to subzero', *Open Shoreditch,* 8 Feb, 2009. • **60.** City Cash also funds offices in Mumbai and Shanghai. • **61.** http://www.cityoflondon.gov.uk/Corporation/LGNL_Services/Council_and_democracy/Data_protection_and_freedom_of_information/access_info.htm. • **62.** See David Hencke and Rob Evans, 'Medieval powers in City trial of strength', *Guardian,* 5 Oct 2002. This was, apparently, the only mainstream media outlet that covered this issue in any depth. • **63.** City heraldry involves griffins and dragons, both guardians of treasure. For example, the Worshipful Company of International Bankers, a City livery company, has as its supporters the Griffins, the 'guardians of treasure'. See www.internationalbankers.co.uk/content/history.aspx • **64.** See *Chancellor launches Better Regulation Action Plan,* 24 May 2005, UK National Archives Press Notices. • **65.** See 'The Top Gamekeeper', *Guardian,* 6 Feb 2009. • **66.** 'Overview: Progress Report of the Independent Review of British Offshore Financial Centres', HM

Treasury, Apr 2009. • **67.** 'Crown Dependencies: Eighth Report of Session 2009–10', House of Commons Justice Committee, 23 Mar 2010, http://www.publications.parliament.uk/pa/cm200910/cmselect/cmjust/56/56i.pdf. • **68.** 'UK International Financial Services – the Future: A Report From UK Based Financial Services Leaders to the Government', HM Treasury, May 2009. • **69.** From author's interview with McDonnell, House of Parliament, London, 13 Oct 2009. • **70.** David Miller quoted on *Dispatches*, 14 June 2010; the study is 'Revolving Doors, Accountability and Transparency – Emerging Regulatory Concerns and Policy Solutions in the Financial Crisis', paper prepared for the OECD and the Dutch National Integrity Office, 6 July 2009, http://www.oecd.org/dataoecd/22/15/43264684.pdf • **71.** 'The Top Game-keeper, *Guardian*, 6 Feb 2009. • **72.** The WSJ – on Barclays and its Tax Trick, Tax Research blog, 30 June 2006. • **73.** 'Sand, sea and a double-dip: all you need to avoid millions in tax offshore', *Guardian*, 13 Mar 2009. • **74.** 'Where on earth are you? Major corporations and tax havens', Tax Justice Network, Revised Version April 2009. • **75.** Select Committee on Treasury (Fourth Report,) The Handling of the Joint Inland Revenue/Customs and Excise Steps Pfi Project, UK Parliament, 12 Feb 2003 and HM Revenue & Customs' estate private finance deal eight years on, UK National Audit Office, 3 Dec 2009. • **76.** See Robert Watts and John Ungoed-Thomas, 'Minister in charge of off-shore clampdown ran tax haven firm', *The Sunday Times*, 22 Mar 2009. • **77.** Cass Business School website, http://www.cass.city.ac.uk/about/location/index.html. • **78.** Death and Taxes: the true toll of tax dodging, Christian Aid, May 2008. The government admits to CDC having 40 offshore affiliates, using narrower criteria for offshore. See *Investing for Development: the Department for International Development's oversight of CDC Group plc*, Eighteenth Report of Session 2008–09, House of Commons Public Accounts Committee, April 30 2009. • **79.** The *Guardian*'s parent company had also participated in tax-avoidance schemes, as nearly all big companies do. This led, predictably, to calls from the City that the *Guardian* should censor its reporting on the subject. • **80.** See *Comparative Study of Costs of Defamation Proceedings Across Europe*, Centre for Socio-Legal Studies, University of Oxford, Dec 2008. • **81.** 'Libel Reform Campaign Welcomes Jack Straw's Commitment to Libel', Libel Reform Group, 23 Mar 2010. • **82.** *City State against national settlement: UK economic policy and politics after the financial crisis*, Centre for Research on Socio-Cultural change, by Ismail Ertürk, Julie Froud, Sukhdev Johal, Adam Leaver, Michael Moran, Karel Williams, June 2011. • **83.** 'An Alternative Report on Banking Reform', a public interest report jointly authored by a working group of practitioners and academics based at the ESRC Centre for Research on Socio Cultural Change, University of Manchester. Direct quotes are from Williams speaking on *Dispatches*, 14 June 2010. • **84.** *City State against national settlement: UK economic policy and politics after the financial crisis*, Centre for Research on Socio-Cultural change, by Ismail Erturk, Julie Fronad, Sukhder Johal, Adam Leaver,

Michael Moran, Karel Williams, June 2011. • **85.** See *Bonus Payments flat in 2010–11*, Office for National Statistics, http://www.statistics.gov.uk/cci/nugget.asp? id=2062 The years for 2000/2001 to 2006/2007 saw average bonuses of just over £10 billion. • **86.** Michael Foot, *Final report of the independent Review of British offshore financial centres*, HM Treasury, Oct 2009 http://www.hm-treasury.gov.uk/d/foot_review_main.pdf.

Conclusion

1. The World Bank says it 'meets the cost/benefit test' – see the World Bank submission to the IASB, in a letter from Charles A. McDonough, World Bank, to International Accounting Standards Board, published on www.ifrs.org, 28 June 2010. • **2.** Currently the most comprehensive source of updated information available on the topic of information exchange is a section entitled *On Exchange of Information for Tax Purposes*, Tax Justice Nework, http://www.taxjustice.net/cms/front_content.php?idcat=140. • **3.** 'Double Tax Treaties and Tax Information Exchange Agreements: What Advantages for Developing Countries?', Misereor, February 2010. • **4.** See UN Economic and Social Council (ECOSOC) ECOSOC/6473 2011 Organizational Session, 9th Meeting (AM) *Economic and Social Council sets out themes for next three annual ministerial reviews, 2011 humanitarian segment as it adopts five texts, April 26, 2011.* • **5.** 'Tax for Development', *OECD Observer*, Dec 2009 to Jan 2010. • **6.** Campaigns have been established to pursue this. See, for example, *Tax Justice Focus*, Vol. 6, No. 1, 2010, which explores land value taxation. • **7.** The example of the street musician is borrowed from Henry Law, 'A Tax That Is Not a Tax', *Tax Justice Focus*, Vol. 6, Issue 1, second quarter 2010, www.taxjustice.net. • **8.** Raymond Baker, 'Transparency First', *The American Interest*, July–Aug 2010. • **9.** The Dodd-Frank bill already requires companies to comply with country-by-country reporting for companies involved in the extractive (mineral) sectors. New legislation introduced by Senator Carl Levin in July 2012, an updated Stop Tax Haven Abuse Act, would, if enacted, require country-by-country reporting in all sectors, not just the extractive ones. • **10.** This last paragraph is taken from my article co-authored with Raymond Baker and John Christensen, 'Catching up with Corruption', *The American Interest*, Sept–Oct 2008.

Offshore after the Panama Papers

1. They gave the project a *Star Trek* codename: *Prometheus.* The ICIJ had already run some smaller leaks projects: *Voyager,* for the so-called Luxleaks scandal; *Enterprise for* another leak of explosive data from HSBC; and *Odyssey,* for an investigation into the World Bank. • **2.** 'How an obscure nonprofit in Washington protects tax havens for the rich', *Washington Post*, 10 June 2016. • **3.** The *Financial Times*, in an interview with Ramón Fonseca, noted: 'Mr Fonseca described his company as a big player in a highly competitive niche industry but that his global market share was only 5 per cent — a figure which, if true, suggests even the information contained in the 11.5m files is the tip of a very large iceberg.' 'Mossack Fonseca founder dismisses Panama Papers as "witch hunt"', *Financial Times*, 5 April 2016. • **4.** My co-authored reports can be found at www.financialsecrecyindex.com. Go to the full index and click on the country. I've written or co-authored reports on Switzerland, Hong Kong, USA, Singapore, Cayman, Luxembourg, Lebanon, Germany, Bahrain, Dubai, Japan, Panama, UK, Jersey, British Virgin Islands, Canada, Ireland. That last one, Ireland, is probably my personal favourite. • **5.** The Blairmore prospectus from 2006, exposed in the Panama Papers scandal, states: 'The Fund is not liable to taxation on its income or capital gains as long as such income or capital gains are not derived from sources allocated within the territory of the Republic of Panama. Dividends or participations distributed by the Fund shall not be liable to taxation in the Republic of Panama to the extent that such dividends or participations are derived from income not generated within the territory of the Republic of Panama.' Cameron stated that he owned the shares in Blairmore with his wife Samantha. http://global-documents.morningstar.com/documentlibrary/Document/ec3dcb9ffb02c630042fa1ac2c7d56de.msdoc/original See also Know Your Customer Requirements for Banks and Trust Companies, Rochelle A. Deleveaux, Legal Counsel, Central bank of Bahamas, 2002, and List of Banks and Trust Companies Licensed under the Bank and Trust Companies Regulation Act, 31 December 2005, just before the Blairmore prospectus was issued. As I write this, in July 2016, tax advisers tell me that delegations from the Bahamas are aggressively pitching for business around the world, selling themselves on the promise not to cooperate with emerging global transparency schemes. • **6.** https://www.globalwitness.org/sites/default/files/import/atpm.txt • **7.** See 'Top rate income tax cuts: 89 per cent go to men, 11 per cent to women', Tax Justice Network, 11 March 2016. Of course plenty of the wealth that flows to men flows to their families too, which includes women. But a lot doesn't. • **8.** Also known as Protected Cell Companies, and in Malta's case Recognised Incorporated Cell Company, or RICC. • **9.** 'Pioneer of Sham Tax Havens Sits Down for Pre-Jail Chat', David Cay Johnston, *New York Times,* 18 November 2004. (Schneider was brought down when he invited Jack Blum – my colleague whom I've quoted several times in *Treasure Islands* – to speak at one of his seminars. Blum wrote to the US Justice Department, prompting the investigation that led to his downfall.) Blum said that

'Schneider could operate openly for years, buying ads in the Wall Street Journal and the American Airlines flight magazine, shows the utter failure of tax law enforcement.' He said US law enforcement had known about Schneider for years, but had failed to act. • **10.** In Europe, at least, this is changing. At the time of writing, the EU had just issued proposals for a new directive that would require a central register of trusts. It is full of loopholes of course: not least that if you simply make sure the trustee is outside the European Union, you're out of scope. But it's a start, and I'd expect it to be beefed up over time. • **11.** Technically, the trustee is recorded as the 'legal' owner of the assets. But this is only a pale shadow of ownership: the trustee is just a manager, like the CEO of a company: they can't just run off with the trust assets. In very general terms the UK tax authorities, like others, try to tax trusts (including discretionary trusts) by taxing the trustee: an obvious way to get around that, of course, is to make sure the trustee is sitting off-shore. Most asset protection trusts are 'discretionary' trusts, where the trustees have 'discretion' as to *which* beneficiaries might get *which* assets or income, and *when* they get them. So a grandchild might only become entitled to a payout if they pass all their exams, or if they stay out of prison, or something. There might be as yet unborn children who could become beneficiaries one day: who knows? And a beneficiary might die before they are due a pay-out. So – because the trustee has this 'discretion' over who gets what, when, and how – you don't actually know, for sure, that any given beneficiary is entitled to anything, until there is an *actual* payout to them (after which they do finally own it). But before any payout you can't even definitively identify them as a beneficiary *at all!* Giles Corbin, a partner with Jersey-based law firm Mourant, said in 2013 that 'something like 90 per cent of Jersey trusts we draft' are those 'ownerless' discretionary trusts. See 'Jersey: 90% of our busi-ness is discretionary trusts', Tax Justice Blog, 12 June 2013. The blog cites a story on Expat Channel, with a screenshot, though the underlying link is bro-ken. The blog cites other evidence of their ubiquity, from other jurisdictions. • **12.** 'Wealth Inequality in the United States since 1913', Gabriel Zucman, Emmanuel Saez, NBER, October 2014. • **13.** See my co-authored document 'Inequalty: you don't know the half of it', Tax Justice Network, 19 July 2012. Some inequality experts do try and take hidden offshore wealth into account. The French economist Thomas Piketty told me in 2012: 'We tried always to be very clear that this is certainly a lower bound, not only for the level of inequal-ity, but probably for the trend as well.' He worked with Gabriel Zucman to try to incorporate offshore data into inequality data: See Gabriel Zucman's 2015 book *The Hidden Wealth of Nations*, which estimates $7.6 trillion offshore. The $36 trillion for the amount of offshore wealth is a figure provided by James S. Henry, in a range from $24 to $36 trillion, and first published in *Foreign*

Affairs in an article entitled 'Taxing Tax Havens: How to Respond to the Panama Papers', 12 April 2016. At the time of writing, Henry was in the process of producing background country-level data to support this global figure. I think Zucman's estimates are too low, for a couple of reasons. Most importantly, his estimates are based on measuring mismatches between assets and liabilities across borders: to over-simplify, if there's a mismatch then there's a 'missing offshore wealth' problem. But of course lots of assets *are* recorded as having an owner – it's just that they record the *wrong* owner, such as a trustee, who isn't usefully described as an 'owner'. These are 'missing' wealth but they won't show up as a mismatch because an owner is recorded. This 'wrong owner' issue is likely to also mean that Zucman's estimates for US assets held in trusts are too low. Not only that, but there are, broadly speaking, 'wealth management' trusts for private individuals, which is what Zucman is measuring – but there are also commercial trusts, whose assets are much bigger: according to one 2004 estimate (Langbein, J., 2004, 'Rise of the Management Trust', *Trusts & Estates*, 142, pp. 52–57) 20 times as large, though that seems excessive. See also 'Inequality: you don't know the half of it', Nicholas Shaxson, John Christensen, Nick Mathiason, Tax Justice Network briefing, 22 July 2012. Only a few measures of inequality try hard to incorporate this stuff. As ever, more research is needed here. • **14.** A 2015 paper he wrote explains: 'The law of trusts has spent the last twenty years rapidly shedding many traditional requirements, forms and restrictions which imposed liability on negligent trustees, protected vulnerable beneficiaries and prevented the use of trusts to avoid the claims of settlors' and beneficiaries' creditors,' he said. 'Most of the current reforms have welfare-reducing distributive consequences.' • **15.** A few other cases of Cook Islands trusts have made it into the public domain, via court cases, the Panama Papers, and earlier offshore leaks. Alongside a bunch of US Medicare fraudsters, there is also the Cordish real estate dynasty of Baltimore, which was found to have stashed at least $116 million in Cook Islands trusts; or Denise Rich, the former wife of disgraced sanctions-busting trader Marc Rich, who got a controversial presidential pardon from Bill Clinton at the end of his term in office; items in this trust contained a Swiss bank account, a Learjet and a yacht called *Lady Joy* (Joy is her middle name) which replaced an earlier yacht named *Artful Dodger*. The late Baron Elie de Rothschild of France, guardian of the French branch of the Rothschild banking dynasty, also set up at least twenty secrecy-cloaked Cook Islands trusts. There's no suggestion any of them did anything illegal; but that usually wasn't the point. The point was law *avoidance*. • **16.** The Harrington quotes are a composite of my telephone interview with Harrington, plus follow-up emails, and her article 'Inside the Secretive World of Tax Avoidance Experts', *The Atlantic, 26* October, 2015. • **17.** Interview with Bosworth-Davies,

3 March 2013. He gives a similar account in 'It's criminal to let the cheating bankers escape with impunity', *Independent*, 9 April 2013. • **18.** See 'Taxing Tax Havens: How to Respond to the Panama Papers', James S. Henry, *Foreign Affairs*, 12 April 2016, and Gabriel Zucman's *The Hidden Wealth of Nations*. • **19.** For a comprehensive look at the reasons why this might be, see 'Ten Reasons to Defend the Corporate Income Tax', Tax Justice Network, 18 March 2015. • **20.** For instance, a tax adviser, who wishes to remain anonymous, sent me a message via Skype on 5 August 2016: 'Panama govt orgs are travelling to Mexico and other Latam countries assuring intermediaries that Panama wont be exchanging info.' • **21.** Much if not most of what journalists call 'tax avoidance' (which, by definition, is not technically illegal) is not 'tax avoidance.' It is indeterminate: you don't know if a company has broken the law until there's a court challenge. The Big Four accountants flog these schemes or 'products' all the time. The UK Public Accounts Committee heard evidence in April 2013 from a senior PwC employee that they would approve a 'tax product' even if it only had a 25 per cent chance of being deemed lawful, if challenged. 'Tax avoidance: the role of large accountancy firms', 44th Report of Session 2012–13, together with formal minutes, oral and written evidence, UK House of Commons, 15 April 2013. Still, editors insist on the term 'tax avoidance' because their libel lawyers say it is safer. I'd argue that the correct response to a (very real) libel risk is not to publish a falsehood. I prefer legality-neutral terms like 'tax cheating, tax abuse, tax dodging'. But I, er, avoid 'avoidance'. • **22.** In June 2016 Deltour and Halet were convicted with twelve-month and nine-month sentences respectively; Perrin was acquitted. In August 2016 the Luxembourg prosecutor appealed in all three cases, seeking harsher punishments. This vindictiveness appears to be a case of self-harm, given that it is Luxembourg that is really on trial in this case. • **23.** Both Reuters articles, and others, are highlighted in the blog I wrote entitled 'Why Tax Havens will be at the heart of the next financial crisis', Tax Justice Network, 3 September 2015. Several academics are starting to investigate the role of tax havens in the area of financial stability. The only repository of articles in this area that I'm aware of is a section of the Tax Justice Network website, entitled Tax Havens & Financial Crisis. • **24.** For an overview of the issues, with numerous links, see a series of articles by the Tax Justice Network, including 'Derivatives WMD: lobbyists seeking to remove "burdensome" safety catches', 25 June 2013, and 'Letter on Offshore Derivatives: Stop the Offshore Race to the Bottom', 11 March 2014. See also a series of more technical statements on this from Americans for Financial Reform, and 'U.S. banks moved billions of dollars in trades beyond Washington's reach', Reuters, 21 August 2015.

Acknowledgements

This book could not have been written without the help of a great many people around the world. First I must thank John Christensen, who has worked tirelessly with me on this book, and who deserves much of the credit. (Any mistakes, though, are mine.) Alongside him stand several leaders in this field, each of whom has provided remarkable help and insights and each of whom has contributed in a range of ways. This group, in alphabetical order, includes Jack Blum, Ray Baker, Richard Murphy, Ronen Palan, Sol Picciotto and David Spencer. Special mention must also go to Paul Sagar and Ken Silverstein for their terrific contributions on the history of the British spider's web and on Delaware, respectively.

A number of others deserve great thanks too, for their time and their help in specific areas. They are Jason Beattie, Rich Benson, Richard Brooks, Michèle, Elliot and Nicolas Christensen, Sven Giegold, Maurice Glasman, Bruno Gurtner, Mark Hampton, Jim Henry, Dev Kar, Pat Lucas and her merry team, Mike McIntyre and his brother Bob, Andreas Missbach, Matti Kohonen, Markus Meinzer, Prem Sikka, Father William Taylor and Geoff Tily.

Karolina Sutton, Dan Hind, Kay Peddle, Will Sulkin and the staff at Random House: you all deserve special thanks too. Second last, and by no means least, a particular thank you to the Joseph Rowntree Charitable Trust, and the Tax Justice Network, who made all this possible. And finally, I would like to offer my thanks, appreciation and respect to all those in the tax havens who have spoken out against the consensus, sometimes at great personal risk.

Index

penguin.co.uk/vintage